The Ultimate VB .NET and ASP.NET Code Book

KARL MOORE

The Ultimate VB .NET and ASP.NET Code Book
Copyright ©2003 by Karl Moore

ISBN (pbk): 1-59059-106-2

Printed and bound in the United States of America 9 8 7 6 5 4 3 2

Trademarked names may appear in this book. Rather than use a trademark symbol with every occurrence of a trademarked name, we use the names only in an editorial fashion and to the benefit of the trademark owner, with no intention of infringement of the trademark.

Technical Reviewer: Franky Wong, Stjepan Pejic
Editorial Board: Steve Anglin, Dan Appleman, Ewan Buckingham, Gary Cornell, Tony Davis, Jason Gilmore, Chris Mills, Steve Rycroft, Dominic Shakeshaft, Jim Sumser
Project Manager: Nate McFadden
Copy Edit Manager: Nicole LeClerc
Copy Editor: Tom Gillen of Gillen Editorial, Inc.
Production Manager: Kari Brooks
Proofreader: Lori Bring
Compositor: Diana Van Winkle, vwdesign.com
Indexer: Valerie Perry
Cover Designer: Kurt Krames
Manufacturing Manager: Tom Debolski

Distributed to the book trade in the United States by Springer-Verlag New York, LLC, 233 Spring Street, 6th Floor, New York, NY 10013 and outside the United States by Springer-Verlag GmbH & Co. KG, Tiergartenstr. 17, 69112 Heidelberg, Germany.

In the United States: phone 1-800-SPRINGER, email orders@springer-ny.com, or visit http://www.springer-ny.com. Outside the United States: fax +49 6221 345229, email orders@springer.de, or visit http://www.springer.de.

For information on translations, please contact Apress directly at 2560 Ninth Street, Suite 219, Berkeley, CA 94710. Phone 510-549-5930, fax 510-549-5939, email info@apress.com, or visit http://www.apress.com.

The source code for this book is available to readers at http://www.apress.com in the Downloads section. You will need to answer questions pertaining to this book in order to successfully download the code.

Dedicated to the cream in my coffee.

Contents at a Glance

About the Author..*xv*

Acknowledgments ....*xvii*

Introduction ....*xix*

How To Use This Book...*xx*

Chapter 1   Moving from VB6 ....*1*

Chapter 2   Creating Great Windows Applications *21*

Chapter 3   Web Sites in Seconds! *63*

Chapter 4   Working with Data *125*

Chapter 5   The Lowdown on Web Services *177*

Chapter 6   From Microwaves to Pocket PCs:
             Special Project Types *201*

Chapter 7   More .NET Secrets *221*

Chapter 8   Unveiled: The Hidden .NET Language *309*

Chapter 9   The Quick C# Translation Guide *335*

Appendix *355*

Index *369*

Contents

About the Author...*xv*

Acknowledgments ....*xvii*

Introduction ....*xix*

How To Use This Book ....*xx*

Chapter 1 Moving from VB6 ....*1*

What Is .NET? *1*

Exploring Visual Studio .NET *3*

Creating a Web Application *9*

How Your Code Changes *13*

    Understanding the Framework *13*

    Integer Upgrades *14*

    Strings *14*

    Variant and Currency *15*

    Array Alterations *15*

    New Operators *15*

    Declaring Properties *16*

    User-Defined Types *17*

    Change the Scope *17*

    ByVal Is Default *17*

    Set Has Disappeared *18*

    Error Handling Changes *18*

    The Class Keyword *19*

Conclusion *20*

Chapter 2 Creating Great Windows Applications *21*

The Essentials *22*

Developer Secrets *26*

    Making Your Form Transparent *27*

    Who Stole the ToolTips? *27*

    Tricks of the Trade: Resizing Made Easy! *28*

    Five Steps to Split Panels, Explorer-Style *28*

    Highlighting Errors with the ErrorProvider *29*

    Learning the LinkLabel Control *30*

    Customizing the MonthCalendar Control *31*

Creating Your Own Number-Only Text Box 32

Displaying Animated GIFs Without the Browser Control 32

The Two Methods of Changing Tab Order 33

Secrets of Working with the System Tray 33

Save User Time: Add Autocomplete to Combo Boxes 34

The Power of Command-Line Parameters 37

How to Reset a Form 37

How to Snap the Cursor to a Button 39

Capturing the Screen, Quick and Easy 40

Stunning Navigation Bars with a Little-Known Freebie 41

Seven Steps to Taking Advantage of Windows XP Themes 42

The .NET Way of Checking for Previous Instances 44

Converting RTF to HTML 45

Drag and Drop from Windows Explorer 48

Dialog Boxes: What Did the User Click? 50

Text Printing Class... That Works! 51

The Secret Rebirth of .PrintForm 54

The Facts on Visual Inheritance 56

Looking at Windows, Performance Counters, and More 57

Protecting Your Code with Obfuscation 59

Best of All Worlds: Creating an Ultra-Thin Client 60

The Easy Way to Download Full Application Updates 62

Chapter 3 Web Sites in Seconds! 63

The Essentials 64

Developer Secrets 69

User Interface 69

Code Techniques 69

Optimization, Errors, and Other Tips 70

User Interface 71

Five-Step Checklist for the Validation Controls 71

Displaying Web Warning Messages: Technique 1 73

Displaying Web Warning Messages: Technique 2 75

Unveiled: How to Create a Default Enter Button 77

Wonders of the Little-Known SmartNavigation Property 78

The Secret Behind User Controls 78

Why the Panel Control Is Super Useful 79

Moving List Items Up and Down, Easily 81

Resizing in Web Applications 82

Stopping Your User from Right-Clicking 82

Creating Scrollable Micro Windows 83

Why You Should Learn CSS 84

Code Techniques *85*
Three Steps to Changing Your Page Title in Code *85*
How to Automatically Fill Out Email Fields *85*
Sending Mail in ASP.NET *87*
The Trick to Creating User-Friendly URLs *88*
Adding Real-Time HTML to Your Page *89*
The Secret to Uploading Files with Ease *90*
Storing Uploaded Files in Your Database *92*
Working with Uploaded Images *95*
Creating Images Dynamically *96*
Code for Generating Thumbnails on the Fly *98*
Five Steps to ASP.NET Authentication *100*
Forms Authentication, Without Web.config *102*
Authenticating Just Part of Your Site *103*
The Best Place to Store Your Settings *104*
Steal Fantastic Forum Code from Microsoft and Save Yourself Hours *105*
Integrating with PayPal's Instant Payment Notification *106*
Optimization, Errors, and Other Tips *106*
Subfolders in Web Applications: Confused? *106*
Choosing a Directory Other Than c:\inetpub\wwwroot\ *107*
Create Super-Fast ASP.NET Applications, with Caching *108*
Nine Steps to Successful Debugging *109*
Hiding Error Code from Your Clients *111*
Forget 404: Customizing Your "Page Not Found" *112*
Server.Transfer vs. Response.Redirect *113*
Using .IsClientConnected for Long Processes *114*
Preventing Client Caching, with Meta Tags *115*
Uploading Files Larger Than 4MB *115*
What to Do When Session_End Doesn't Work *116*
Spying on Your Web Host: Checking Uptime in .NET *117*
Can It Cope? Stress Testing Your Web Apps *119*
The Two Methods of Moving Web Servers *121*
Where to Put Your Files with an ASP.NET Host *122*
Uh-oh: Installing IIS After Visual Studio .NET *123*

Chapter 4   Working with Data *125*

The Essentials *126*
Developer Secrets *130*
Generating GUIDs in a Flash *131*
Making Your Own Connection String Creator *132*
Finding the Last Identity Number Added *133*
Cheating with SQL *134*

Returning Multiple Tables into a DataSet *136*

Checking Whether SQL Server Is Available *137*

Seven Steps to a Quick, Editable Windows Grid *138*

Nine Steps to a Quick, Editable Web Grid *141*

How to Use HTML in a Web Grid *147*

Using Hyperlinks in Your Web Grid *148*

Dates, Currency, Percentages: Formatting Your Web Grid Data *149*

Looking Good: Color-Coding Your Web Grid *151*

Little-Known Technique for Confirming Web Deletes *153*

Selecting Multiple Web Form Grid Items, Hotmail-Style *154*

Click Anywhere and Select, with a Web Grid *156*

The Lowdown on Using Dropdown Boxes in a Web Grid *158*

Speedy, Personalized Web Data Binding *167*

Quick and Easy Data Paging, with Your Web Grid *168*

Sorting in Seconds, with Your Web Grid *169*

Amazingly Simple Method for Exporting Your Web Grid to Excel *171*

Returning a DataSet from an Excel Spreadsheet *173*

Get Microsoft to Write Your Code:
Amazing Undocumented SQL Server Tool! *175*

Chapter 5   The Lowdown on Web Services *177*

The Essentials *178*

Developer Secrets *180*

Exposing Database Information, the Quick and Easy Way *181*

Five Things You Need to Do Before Publicizing Your Web Service *184*

Improving Performance with Easy Caching *185*

Online Translations: Get Your Programs Speaking Spanish in Seconds! *185*

Adding Google Search to Your Programs *187*

Querying the Amazon.com Web Service *190*

View the Real World in Your Application, with TerraServer *193*

Asynchronous Access: Secrets of Calling a Web Service
in the Background *197*

Web Services, Proxies, Connection Closed—Oh My! *198*

Change a Web Service URL, Without Recompiling *199*

Where to Find the Best Web Services Around *199*

Chapter 6   From Microwaves to Pocket PCs:
Special Project Types *201*

Plug into Windows: Creating Your Own Windows Service *202*

Installing Your Service *203*

Get the DOS Feel: Creating a Basic Console Application *206*

From Mobiles to Microwaves: Creating Applications with the MIT *208*

Creating Your Mobile Web Application *210*

Writing Mobile-Aware Code *212*

Testing Your Mobile Web Application *214*

Portable Computing: Creating Apps for Your PDA! *215*

Building for the Compact Framework *216*

Deploying Your Applications *218*

Going On from Here *220*

Chapter 7 More .NET Secrets *221*

Developer Secrets *221*
Working with the Internet *225*

Creating Your Own Web Browser *225*

How to Snatch the HTML of a Web Page *227*

How to Snatch HTML, with a Timeout *227*

Tricks of Parsing a Web Page for Links and Images *229*

Converting HTML to Text, Easily *231*

Real Code for Posting Data to the Web *232*

Adding a Web Shortcut to the Favorites *234*

Retrieving Your IP Address—And Why You May Want To *235*

Is an Internet Connection Available? *236*

Manipulating Files and Folders *237*

Two Easy-to-Use Functions for Reading and Writing Files *237*

Files: Moving, Deleting, Attributes, and More! *238*

Checking Whether Two Files Are Identical *239*

The Trick to Temporary Files *241*

Doing Directories *242*

"Watching" a Directory for Changes *243*

How Big Is That File—in English? *244*

Retrieving Special Folder Paths *245*

Which Program Handles That File Extension? *246*

Retrieving a Drive Serial Number *247*

The .NET Replacement for App.Path *248*

INI Files Will Never Die: How to in .NET *248*

Dates, Numbers, Strings *251*

Is That a Whole Number, or Not? *252*

Checking for a Date the Intelligent .NET Way *252*

1st, 2nd, 3rd: Using Ordinal Numbers in Your App *253*

Random Numbers… That Work! *255*

Finding the Number of Days in a Month *256*

Adding and Subtracting Days, Months, Years *257*

Calculating the Next Working Day *258*

Easy Check for a Leap Year *258*

Figuring Out Quarters *259*

Calculating the Years Between Two Dates *260*

Converting a String to "Proper Case" *261*

Storing Text Snippets on the Clipboard *262*

Generating Memorable Passwords, Automatically *263*

Encryption in Just Twelve Lines of Code! *265*

Implementing Powerful MD5 Encryption *266*

Converting a String into the Color Type *268*

Binding a Combo Box to Enumeration Values *269*

Graphics and Fonts *270*

Designing Your Own Arty Icons *270*

The Basics of Working with Fonts *271*

Crafty Conversion Between Graphic Formats *272*

Rotating and Flipping Is Easy! *273*

Drawing with Windows Forms *274*

Add an Exciting Gradient Backdrop, in Code! *277*

Starting Your Own Screensaver *278*

Using the Registry and Event Log *279*

How to Read and Write the Registry *280*

Putting Messages in the Event Log *281*

Distributed Computing *283*

The Cheat's Guide to XML *283*

Six Steps to Basic Transactions with COM+ *292*

Quick Guide to Using MSMQ *297*

Which to Choose: Web Services vs. Remoting *300*

Visual Studio Tips *302*

Writing a Developer TODO: List *302*

Storing Often-Used Code in the Toolbox *303*

Organizing Your Project with Folders *303*

Figuring out the Command Window *304*

Discovering Whether You're Running in the IDE *305*

Saving Time by Recording Macros *306*

Using the VS .NET Command Prompt *306*

The Old School: Upgrading, COM, and the API *307*

Chapter 8   Unveiled: The Hidden .NET Language *309*

How It Works *310*

Your Regex Library *311*

Exactly-One-Digit Checker *312*

Real Number Matcher *313*

Alphanumerical Matcher: No Spaces or Dots *313*

24-Hour Clock Time Check *314*

Identifying Valid Dates *314*

File Path and Extension Check *315*

Checking for Repeated Words *315*

Getting Capitalized Words *316*

Matching Numbers from a String *317*

Who Are You?—Name Checker *318*

Naughty-Word Filter Expression *319*

True Email Address Validation *319*

Validating a Web Site Address *320*

Internet URL Matcher: FTP, HTTP, HTTPS *320*

Checking for a Valid Domain *322*

IP Address Checker *322*

Extracting Links and Images from HTML *323*

Checking HTML Color Codes *323*

Credit Card Validation *324*

Password Format Enforcing Expression *324*

Defining Your Own HTML: Custom Tags, with Expressions *325*

ISBN Checker *328*

Is That a GUID? *328*

U.S. ZIP Code Checker *329*

U.S. Social Security Number Checker *329*

U.S. Phone Number Checker *330*

U.S. State Checker *330*

U.K. Postal Code Matcher *331*

U.K. National Insurance Number Check *331*

U.K. Telephone Number Validator *332*

Converting American and British Dates *332*

French, German, and Japanese Expressions *333*

The Simple Cure for "Loose" Expressions *333*

Chapter 9 The Quick C# Translation Guide *335*

Translating C# to VB .NET *336*

Translation Listing *337*

1. Comments: // welcome to C# *338*

2. Remove the End-of-Line Semicolon; *338*

3. Data Types: int, bool, float, DateTime *339*

4. Functions: public bool writeEventLog(string entry) *339*

5. Methods: public void activateAlarm() *340*

6. Variables: string strText; *340*

7. String Contents: \n and @ *341*

8. Objects: myObject = new myClass(); *341*

9. Scope: public, private, internal, static *342*

10. Arguments: ref and out keywords *342*

11. Arithmetic: x++; *343*

12. If-Then: if (x > y) { ... } else {...} *343*

13. Comparison: == and != and & and | *344*

14. Select Case: switch {x} {...} *344*

15. Loops: for (x=1; x<=10; x+=1) {...} *345*

16. Errors: try {...} catch {...} finally {...} *347*

17. The Mystery of this *348*

18. Events: obj.event += new class.delegate(handler); *348*

20. Classes: Constructors and Finalizers *350*

21. Class Interfaces: myInterface myObject2 = (myInterface)myObject1; ...*351*

22. Class Inheritance Keywords: base, virtual, abstract, sealed *352*

Cheating at the Conversion *353*

Where to Go from Here *353*

Appendix *355*

I: Installing VS.NET *355*

II: Default Project Files *358*

Windows Application *358*

Class Library *359*

Web Application *359*

Web Service *361*

III: Windows Form Controls *362*

IV: VB.NET Data Types *365*

V: VB.NET Naming Conventions *366*

Index *369*

About the Author

KARL MOORE lives in Yorkshire, England. He is author of *Karl Moore's Visual Basic .NET: The Tutorials*, and he runs his own international consultancy group, White Cliff Computing, Ltd. Karl is regularly featured at industry conferences and in leading development magazines, plus is a frequent voice on BBC radio.

You can visit his official Web site at www.karlmoore.com.

Acknowledgments

I HAD INTENDED to write this book without any external influence. It was just me, my laptop and the green fields of England, from where I merrily tapped out each new "secret" as and when it was discovered.

I was, of course, being entirely romantic. The process of writing a book may begin as a solitary endeavor but undoubtedly ends up a group effort to get only the best of the best into your hands. And it's that group to which this simple page is pledged.

As ever, the usual yet sincere thanks are extended to the Apress directors—Dan, Gary and Karen—for their continued support. Especially Dan, always ready to use a little midnight wit to simmer me down in moments of heat.

Big thanks are also extended to project manager Nate for his coordination skills, and for whom the phrase "It's pressure that turns stone into diamond" appears to have been coined. And what would a book of mine be without the mandatory appreciation of editor Tom Gillen (a.k.a., Mr. Tom), the only man to blatantly criticize my writing and get away with it. Almost.

Credit is also given to Franky and Stjepan, who both stepped in at short notice as technical reviewers. I have never had the pleasure of working with such thorough individuals. Franky, your cross-referencing skills are amazing.

Plus, the rest of the Apress gang: Kari and Grace, for their work in getting this book into production; Valerie, for having to go through the indexing process; Beth, for her marketing prowess.

Then, we have the people on my side of the Atlantic. Deep thanks go to my parents, David and Tricia, for being the eternal mountains of support they are. To my famous sister, Jo-Anne, for cheering me up when the road looked tough. To my friends—Mark, Katrina, Julie, Sinead, Jenny, and Alan—for showing me how to dance to Night Fever. And to everyone at White Cliff, who continued working, even when I wasn't.

You know, Gonzo says that strangers are just friends you haven't yet met. And so, it is to you, future friend, that I provide this final acknowledgement. Thank you for reading and making this group dream possible.

Introduction

"I am neither especially clever nor especially gifted. I am only very, very curious"

—*Albert Einstein*

HAVE YOU NOTICED that the majority of .NET books seem intent on hiding you from real-world code? You can buy a 1,500-page draft excluder, study it exclusively for a month, and still be none the wiser as to how you can put together even the most basic of programs.

Truth is, those authors don't have much of a clue.

I mean, they went to the conference. They figured out how it worked in theory. But when it comes to showdown at the Code Coral, guess who stole the mule and left for Kansas?

This book isn't like that. Okay, it's not quite "petite," but, then again, neither am I. It does, however, hold a vast amount of knowledge—reams of useful code snippets and .NET programming tips that I have personally discovered and developed over the past three years.

Let's clarify here. These aren't updated Visual Basic 6 code scraps: everything within these pages has been created and tested for VB .NET and ASP.NET. And it's all super useful: I don't even want to tell you just how many chunks of code I've written and scrapped during the production of this book.

Only the best survived. And you're holding them all.

Within these pages, you'll learn how to create exciting new XP-style interfaces. You'll figure out how to code ultra-thin Windows applications that automatically update via the Web. You'll learn dozens of hush-hush ASP.NET secrets, plus find out how you can steal Microsoft code and save hours of development time. You'll discover how to push your DataGrid to the max in Windows applications and on the Web. You'll figure out how to add powerful Google, Amazon, and TerraServer searches to your applications.

You'll uncover the truth behind creating fast programs that run on anything from PDAs to mobile phones to microwaves. You'll be exposed to a hidden .NET language. You'll be told why you need to know at least some C#, then given a cheat course on the basics.

Whether you're a hardened pro or a .NET newbie, this book is the bible you'll want to keep on your desk 24/7. And I am personally honored to have written it for you.

Thanks for learning with me.

How To Use This Book

THIS BOOK HAS two core uses. First, there's the Coke coaster mode. That's where you essentially use it as a reference book: a .NET bible, if you will. Just stick it next to your computer and use it to protect your shiny new desk from stains. It'll start looking tatty after a few months, but at least it's nearby should you ever wish to do anything semi-interesting with .NET.

Second, and rather more fun, you could just read it all, back to front. Or front to back, depending on your preferences. If you're new to .NET (especially if you're coming from Visual Basic 6), you'll want to start at the "Welcome to .NET!" chapter. This will give you an overview of what this whole .NET lark is about. It also walks you through creating a basic Windows application and simple ASP.NET Web site, plus looks at some of the core language changes.

If you've already used VB .NET or ASP.NET for a while, you're probably raring to get going with all the professional tips and techniques. Well, simply skip straight to the chapter you require, from "Creating Great Windows Applications" to "Unveiled: The Hidden .NET Language". The full contents list at the beginning of this book will really assist in locating the sections most useful to you.

Also, in case you don't relish the thought of retyping the many code snippets presented in this book, you can download the full source online from www.apress.com —alongside any fresh code snippets I added after we went to publication. Make sure you keep this book nearby however, as you'll be asked a couple of authentication questions first.

That's all: enjoy the book and happy VB'ing!

Karl Moore, July 2003
Yorkshire, England

CHAPTER 1

Moving from VB6

YOU'VE READ THE ARTICLES that promise it'll slash hours off your development time. You've seen the promotional videos showing what a glamorous Silicon Valley lifestyle you'll have as soon as you start using it. You've had one of those "Hate Linux, Love .NET" T-shirts thrust into your hands at the last PDC.

Yes, you've heard about .NET, and you get the idea that it's something to do with a fresh release of Visual Basic, too. But just what is it, and can you get up and running with the new system, *today?* It's possible. And, over the next twenty pages or so, I'll be showing you how.

We'll start our journey by looking at the big picture of .NET and just where Visual Basic fits in. Then we'll begin our whirlwind tour of the new .NET development environment, explaining how it differs from VB6 as we go about creating a simple application.

We'll also learn about the new project types and where you can find out more about them in this book. Finally, we'll spend quality time listing exactly how our actual code will alter. From core data type changes to new keywords, it's all here.

Ladies and gentlemen, this is your host, Karl Moore, requesting all passengers strap in tight. The plane to .NET is about to depart. And, at first, it may be one slightly turbulent ride....

What Is .NET?

Is it a single program? Is it a Web site? Is it an illiterate Cornishman's fishing implement?

Erm, no. So, what exactly is .NET?

Officially speaking, .NET "is the XML Web services platform, a way of working that allows you to create software as a service." It's a Microsoft vision based on *distributed computing*, the dream of sharing information over the Internet, no matter what operating system, device, or programming language you're using.

According to our favorite software giant, this .NET plan covers five core areas, not all of which have yet been fulfilled:

- development products

- server products (such as Windows 2000/2003 and SQL Server)

- foundation services (such as Passport and Alerts)

- devices (such as the Pocket PC)

- experiences (such as MSN and Office .NET)

The thing is, to developers, .NET *really* means that first item on the list—development products—and this part of their vision boils down to two key pieces of software: the .NET Framework and Visual Studio .NET.

The free .NET Framework is really the heart of the whole .NET idea, the whole distributed dream. It's a program that sits on top of your operating system and basically runs your .NET applications (whether regular Windows applications or Web sites). It handles program memory for you. It provides a store of functionality in its "base classes." It can talk to remote computers using XML. It does all the plumbing you really don't want to get involved in: it abstracts, it hides complexity, and it just works. Yet, behind it all, the truth is that *the .NET Framework is simply a clever Windows upgrade.*

> **TOP TIP** *You can imagine the .NET Framework as a smart runtime for your programs. And, if you don't have it installed, you can't run any .NET applications. The .NET Framework is distributed with Windows 2003 onward, and there's a great pressure on Microsoft to make any later revisions backward compatible (the current version is 1.1). Incidentally, you'll hear some people talk about companies creating versions of the .NET Framework that will run on other platforms. They're being slightly optimistic: right now it's available for Windows only.*

Next up, you have Visual Studio .NET, which is quite simply the next version of Visual Studio. Two versions of Visual Studio .NET have been released so far: version 2002, and version 2003 (codename "Everett"). Both of these play home to languages such as Visual C# .NET, Visual C++ .NET, and, of course, Visual Basic .NET (VB .NET).

Of these languages, C# is the real newbie. Rumored to be Bill Gates' .NET love child, the syntax looks very similar to that of VB .NET (more on that in Chapter 9). After that, we have C++ .NET, which is essentially the old C++ with extensions to tie it in with the .NET Framework. Everett users will also see J#, Microsoft's bid to port Java developers to the world of .NET. And finally we have VB .NET: the next version of Visual Basic, the product most important to us.

TOP TIP *Wondering where ASP.NET fits into it all? Well, ASP.NET isn't a language. It's simply a term that covers Internet projects and refers to a bunch of class libraries in the .NET Framework. You may utilize these classes in VB .NET, C#, or any other .NET language. We'll learn more about ASP.NET later.*

Now, before you can start using VB .NET, you need to get the .NET Framework and Visual Studio .NET installed onto your machine. If you haven't done that already, follow the guidelines in Appendix I. When you're ready, let's move on for our first glimpse of the new development environment.

Exploring Visual Studio .NET

If you haven't yet installed and configured Visual Studio .NET, head off to Appendix I and follow the instructions. When you're done, it's time to go exploring. Ready?

1. Launch Visual Studio .NET by selecting Start ➤ Programs ➤ Microsoft Visual Studio .NET ➤ Microsoft Visual Studio .NET.

You should be looking at a colorful start page, which replaces the rather bland New or Open pop-up of Visual Basic 6 fame. With its online links down the left-hand side, this page is intended to turn into something of a customizable developer portal.

2. Click on the New Project button.

This is more the sort of screen you're used to welcoming you in VB6. (See Figure 1-1). It allows you to select a new sort of project to create. However, the options here are most certainly different to those we'd find in the old school.

First off, you can create projects in any of the three or four default languages. Naturally, we're concerned with only Visual Basic here, but, even so, the available projects look confusing. Let's explain them now.

You've got the Windows Application, which is the equivalent of a standard EXE from the old school. Desktop applications will never die (more about these applications in Chapter 2). Next is the class library. Although COM has actually gone in .NET, this is your rough equivalent to an ActiveX DLL project. Moving on, and a Windows Control Library allows you to build your own controls, a sort of ActiveX control project.

Shortly after that, you have an ASP.NET Web application that mixes all the great Web capabilities of ASP with the Visual Basic ability to drag, drop, and code. It's a project that allows you to build fully functional Web sites in seconds. (Chapter 3 will reveal all.)

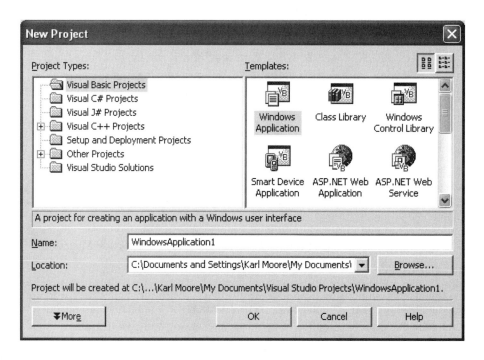

Figure 1-1. Creating our new Windows application project

An ASP.NET Web service is next on the list, a project that allows you to expose your code methods or functions over your network or the Internet. Other applications can then call these chunks of code and process the results. If you've ever dealt with sticky-sticky Simple Object Access Protocol (SOAP) in VB6, this is the native .NET implementation. (More on this in Chapter 5.)

Moving on, the Web control library allows you to build "controls" to use on Web pages. These are HTML based and have absolutely nothing to do with ActiveX. Next on the list is a console application that allows you to build a DOS-like console program, which was incredibly difficult in VB6 days (been there, wrote the article, still getting the complaints: full instructions in Chapter 6). Next, the Windows service project allows you to build your own service, which in the old days would require either the purchase of a third-party plug-in or a nightmarish amount of API code. (Find out how to do this in Chapter 6.)

Everett users, or those that have downloaded "extras" from the Visual Studio .NET site, may also find a couple of extra project types in their list. The Smart Device Application, for example, allows you to create programs to run on devices such as the Pocket PC. And the ASP.NET Mobile Web Application project type will enable you to create your own mini Web sites that are customized for less-powerful wireless devices, from mobile phones to microwaves. (More on both of these project types in Chapter 6.)

You can ignore any remaining project types as they're simply empty place-holders.

Let's begin this part of the book by creating a simple Windows application while looking at a couple of development environment changes.

3. Select the Windows Application icon.

4. Change the name to "Hello .NET".

5. Note the Location folder and click on OK.

You should now be staring at your new (and rather plain) Hello .NET project. Recognize anything?

In the middle window you should have your form, which is the screen your users will see when they run your final application. To the left, you have the toolbox, which holds controls ready to add to that form. (Click View ➤ Toolbox if you can't see it.) Check out the various tabs: you'll find a whole bundle here, many more than the intrinsic few you had with VB6.

These are part of the core .NET Framework, which means that all your users will automatically have them installed. So, if you do use something like the Open-FileDialog control in your application, you won't need to go bundling an extra DLL to ensure that it works on the client machine. It'll just *work*. Well, hurrah for that!

You'll find most of your old favorites here, too—with an occasional name change thrown in to warrant the purchase price, of course. The CommandButton became Button, for example. The Caption property of the Label turned into Text property. The Menu Editor turned into the MainMenu control. Still, nothing too serious.

Casting your eye over to the bottom right of your screen now, you'll find the trusty Properties window. No real difference here—some things never change. You'll find that your form has a few new interesting properties though, such as Opacity.

Moving upward slightly, you'll see the Solution Explorer, which is exactly the same as our old Project Explorer except that it can host multiple projects as part of your solution (like a Project Group). The extra tabs under the Properties and Solution Explorer windows allow you to use the help and explore classes in your application.

Let's move on.

6. Draw a button out onto your form.

7. Double-click on the button to open up the Code window under a new tab, as shown in Figure 1-2.

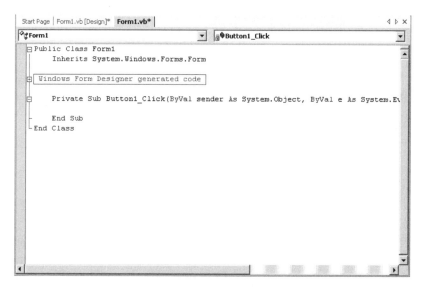

Figure 1-2. Our Code window

Wow! You don't remember writing that code? Hmm, me neither, actually. So where did it all just come from? Well, this is automatically generated code that describes your form. Let's explain it away, line by line.

First off, glance across to the Solution Explorer. Your form file is called Form1.vb—there's no .frm extension here. Most Visual Basic .NET code files end with a .VB extension. It's the content inside that describes what they are.

This explains why our form starts off with `Public Class Form1` and finishes with `End Class`. Yes, our form is really a class: in VB6, we could treat forms as though they were classes, but they weren't *really*. In VB .NET, they are. In fact, apart from "primitive data types" such as a Boolean or Integer, everything we use in VB .NET is based on a class—even strings and controls.

The next line, `Inherits System.Windows.Forms.Form`, tells VB .NET that this class "inherits" the functionality of a form, the functionality described in the `System.Windows.Forms.Form` part of the .NET Framework. (More on this later.)

The following line has a gray chunk displaying the words "`Windows Form Designer generated code`". This is a collapsed mound of code, which you can view in full by clicking the little + symbol to its left.

After you've done that, you'll probably wish you hadn't. This is your form in the nude. It includes descriptions of what controls you have on the form, along with their positioning and initial properties. Tsk, move over, *Playboy*.

> **TOP TIP** *You can automatically make regions of your code collapsible by adding* #Region *and* #End Region *keywords around the code.*

After this, we see our actual Button1_Click subroutine—finally, something you recognize. Or is it? First off, you have a couple of extra arguments here providing extra (and often useless) event information.

Also, in VB6, if you changed the name of the Button1_Click method, it would no longer run the code behind that method when you clicked on Button1. In VB .NET, this isn't the case: scroll to the end of the first line of Button1_Click here. See the Handles keyword? This is what determines which methods run when an event occurs.

Anyway, it's about time we added some code. And what simpler way to start than displaying the clichéd Hello World in a message box. Not difficult, right? Well, guess what? They changed that too. The new .NET way of displaying a message box is using the "shared" Show function of the MessageBox class.

8. Add the following code to respond to the click event of Button1:

```
MessageBox.Show("Hello World!")
```

Actually, I'm lying. You can still use MsgBox and all its related result constants, but MessageBox is the new and improved way of displaying messages within Windows forms like this.

> **TOP TIP** *Notice how your code is automatically formatted? Just write it, and VB .NET will position it for you. It'll also complete* If *statements and property declarations for you.*

> **ANOTHER TOP TIP** *If you make a coding error in VB .NET, it doesn't wait until you compile your application to point it out: it's immediately highlighted via a Word-style squiggly underline. Hovering your mouse cursor over the region displays a description of the problem.*

Let's run our application now.

9.   Press the F5 key or select Start from the Debug menu.

You'll see a bunch of information fly past an "output" window as your code is compiled. Ignore it; it just means that your final EXE file is being slapped together.

Within a few seconds, your program should pop up. Yes, it has a slightly different feel, and that Form icon definitely has to go. But, on the whole, it's not all that alien, and a click of your Button control should produce the results you expect. Right? Ace.

Well, that's our first glimpse of the Visual Studio .NET interface. A speedy exploration, yes, but it should've answered a few of the initial questions every VB6 developer has.

So, let's recap: what differences have we seen so far? A whole bundle of new and exciting project types are now available. We have a host of fresh intrinsic controls to play with. Most development files have a .VB extension. Form .VB files are really classes and include code that describes how the form is laid out. When your code compiles, a host of useless information spurts into the Output window.

Oh, and I forgot to mention: you have pretty pastel-colored menus, too. (See Figure 1-3.) Now you know where all those research and development dollars went.

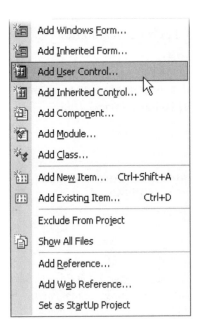

Figure 1-3. Pick a menu option, any menu option.

> **TOP TIP** *If you're wondering how to compile and distribute your .NET applications, we'll look at the topic in Chapters 2 and 3. We'll also figure out how to upgrade existing applications over in Chapter 7.*

So, we've briefly explored creating a simple Windows application in VB .NET. Yes, it's a shift from VB6, but mind blowing it ain't.

But that's not all. One of the most powerful areas of .NET is its ability to serve up highly interactive Web sites with just a few lines of code. We'll take a quick look at this important project type next.

Creating a Web Application

In the past, building interactive Web sites was about as easy to understand as the groupies behind PylonOfTheMonth.co.uk, and just as exciting.

However, with .NET comes ASP.NET, the next version of Active Server Pages (ASP). It's a technology that allows even old-hat Visual Basic developers to quickly put together their own intelligent Web sites.

> **TOP TIP** *Before getting started with any ASP.NET application, you need Internet Information Services 5.0 or above installed on your machine. If you don't have it, you can't play the game.*

Let's create a small sample site right now.

1. From the menu in Visual Studio .NET, select File ➤ New ➤ Project.

2. Select an ASP.NET Web Application project type, under the Visual Basic Projects folder.

3. Change the Location box to `http://localhost/hello`, then click OK. (See Figure 1-4.)

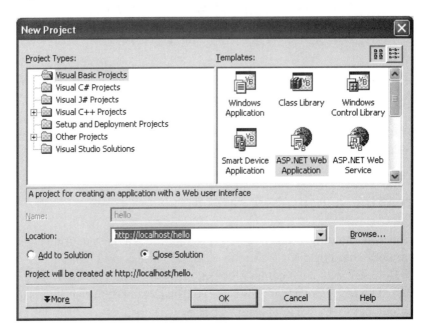

Figure 1-4. Creating a new ASP.NET Web application

TOP TIP *If you get a warning about Internet Explorer being offline or some such, launch Internet Explorer, cancel any attempts to dial up, then click on File and uncheck Work Offline. Tsk, computers, eh?*

You should now be looking at a pretty boring, dotted screen, christened WebForm1.aspx. This is the ASPX Web page your users will see.

Look at the left side of your screen. See the toolbox? These are controls you can use on your Web forms, similar to the way you have controls you can use with regular Windows forms. Let's try a couple now.

4. Drag and drop a Button and TextBox control anywhere on your Web form.

Next, cast your eyes over to the bottom right of your screen. Notice the Properties window? Again, just as you'd have with Windows forms, it's here you can change the properties and behavior of objects you're working with.

5.   Change the Text property of your button to "Say It To Me!" (See Figure 1-5.)

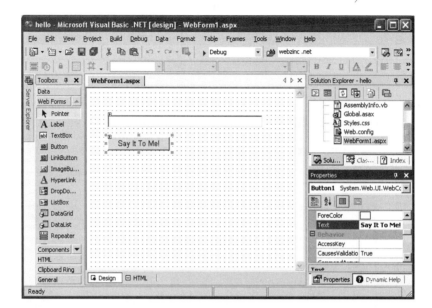

Figure 1-5. Painting our Web page

To complete our eye exercise regime, raise your blinkers ever so slightly so the Solution Explorer comes into view. These are all the extra files included to support your Web application. (A full listing of what these files do can be found in Appendix II.) For now, we're concerned with only the actual pages, those files ending with an .aspx extension.

Let's put our foot down now for the event you've all been waiting for. We're getting juicy: *we're adding code.*

6.   Double-click on your button.

You should be taken to the Code window. This is actually WebForm1.aspx.vb, the code behind your WebForm1.aspx page. Although the code content here may be different from that behind a Windows form, you'll notice that the structure is still pretty much the same.

Here, we have a public class called WebForm1. You can see that it inherits some of its functionality from the System.Web.UI.Page part of the .NET Framework, and that your Button1 and TextBox1 controls have been declared.

Before the End Class here, we also have the Load event listed, ready for you to insert code into—plus, of course, our button Click event. Let's add code to that now.

7. Add the following code to respond to your button Click event:

```
TextBox1.Text = TextBox1.Text + " Hi Worldies!"
```

So, let's recap. Now, when somebody visits our site and clicks on the button, we want to take the Text property of our TextBox control and add " Hi Worldies!" to the end of it. How will that work in real life? There's only one way to find out.

8. Press the F5 key to test your application.

9. Click on your "Say It To Me" button a few times. (See Figure 1-6.)

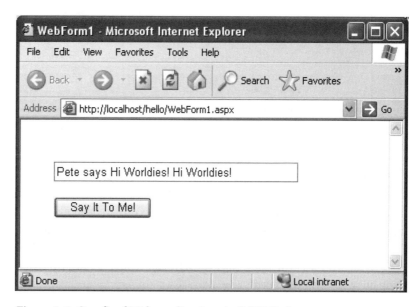

Figure 1-6. Our final Web application, in full IE6 glory

What happens? Try removing the text and clicking again. What if you type something in yourself and then click? Does it remember what you entered?

Also notice how, each time you click, the Web form is being "posted back" to the server (Internet Information Services, to be precise), your code runs, and fresh HTML results are returned? Where is that code running? Do you understand the concept here? If you have time, try adding a Calendar control to your page, then run your application and try clicking a few dates. Impressed?

We'll be revisiting the grand world of Web site projects in Chapter 3, plus take a smart look at Web services (part of ASP.NET) in Chapter 5.

How Your Code Changes

In just a few pages, we've looked at exactly what .NET is and figured out how we can quickly create both a Windows application and semi-interactive Web site. But these aren't the only areas to see change. The Visual Basic language itself has shifted, and this section provides an overview of the main differences.

Understanding the Framework

The big change for most developers is figuring out that thing called the .NET Framework. Well, you can imagine it as a very clever, very big runtime for your applications. It holds a mass of classes that allow you to do everything from plugging into databases to drawing graphics on the screen. An easy-to-use Windows API, if you will.

All those classes in the .NET Framework are available to any .NET language, meaning that, no matter whether you're a C# or VB .NET programmer, it's a level playing field.

Because there are literally thousands of these classes, they're split into "namespaces" to help organize everything. The master .NET namespace is called System. Filed under this System namespace is, for example, the Math class, which includes a shared function called Round. I can write code to access this function as so:

```
Dim dblResult As Double
dblResult = System.Math.Round(3.142, 1)
```

So, just by typing the namespace location, I've tapped into the .NET Framework to round my number for me.

> **TOP TIP** Shared *is a new keyword in VB .NET. It refers to a procedure in a class that doesn't require a new instance of that class to run it.*

If you're a die-hard fan of Visual Basic 6, you'll find equivalents for all the old VB functions in the Microsoft.VisualBasic namespace. But, where possible, you're best going with the new .NET Framework way of doing things. If you don't, well, it's just not cricket.

It's not just *your* code that needs the .NET Framework to run: your actual *applications* do, too. If you remember, earlier in this chapter we saw our Windows form tapping into the .NET Framework, by "inheriting" from `System.Windows.Forms.Form`, the `Form` class in the `System.Windows.Forms` namespace. And later, our Web application inherited from `System.Web.UI.Page`.

> **TOP TIP** *To save yourself having to type out full namespaces every time, you can use the* `Imports` *keyword to add a default "reference" to that particular namespace. You can also do this through the Project Properties dialog box.*

Integer Upgrades

Visual Basic has changed the way in which it stores integers to bring it in line with other languages. Thankfully, they've all been upgraded, meaning they now hold greater-ranging values, so you can still get away with doing it the old way. However, just in case you're conscious of wasting those extra bytes of memory, Table 1-1 shows how it's altered.

Table 1-1. Integer Changes

VISUAL BASIC 6	VB .NET	TYPE
Byte	Byte	8-bit integer
Integer	Short	16-bit integer
Long	Integer	32-bit integer
n/a	Long	64-bit integer

Also, if you're accustomed to converting your numeric data types to use the Windows API, *stop!* VB .NET is now on par, and you don't need any conversion. You can find a full list of VB .NET data types and what they can hold in Appendix IV.

Strings

Talking about the API, if you're a heavy user, you'll be used to passing about fixed-length strings. Well, you don't have those in VB .NET. Previously, you would have declared a string like so:

```
Dim MyString As String * 100
```

But, in the VB .NET world, you'll need to add a special attribute to accommodate these, like so:

```
<VBFixedString(100)> Dim MyString As String
```

The information in <angle brackets> is an attribute. We'll discuss these more later.

Variant and Currency

Variant and Currency? You *are* the weakest link, goodbye! Both of these aging data types have been thrown out the window. In VB .NET, the Object type can hold absolutely anything, so it's a good replacement for Variant. And the Decimal data type is a decent replacement for Currency, too.

Again, a full list of VB .NET data types and what they hold can be found in Appendix IV.

Array Alterations

Think you know arrays? Think again. In VB .NET, they've changed.

The big alteration is that arrays are now *always* zero based. That means you can't define the lower boundary yourself: it's always zero. A typical declaration will now look something like

```
Dim MyArray(9) As String
```

Here, we have a string array containing ten elements—from zero to nine. This also means that the VB6 LBound function is now pretty useless as it always returns 0.

The .NET Framework also contains new classes to help you handle "collections", such as the popular ArrayList. Some of these work like the VB6 Collection, while others work like simple lists or "queues". You can find out more about these by looking up "collections, .NET Framework" in the help index.

New Operators

Here's one cool change you'll soon get used to. Bringing VB .NET in line with other languages such as C++, you have new operators to shorten the way you write code. The most useful is +=, which can be used as so:

```
intNum += 1
```

This takes the value of intNum and adds 1 to it. It's the equivalent of the old

```
intNum = intNum + 1
```

You can also use other operators, as follows:

```
intNum -= 4  ' intNum = intNum - 4
intNum *= 2  ' intNum = intNum * 2
intNum /= 6  ' intNum = intNum / 6
```

The add operator works with strings also (and can be used interchangeably with the ampersand):

```
strText += " - appended text"
```

Declaring Properties

In the golden olden days, we'd create properties as separate Get, Set, and Let blocks. In VB .NET, they've been combined into one chunk, with a Get block to retrieve the property and a Set block to store it.

Here's an example property in VB .NET:

```
Dim mstrUsername As String

Public Property Username() As String
    Get
        Return mstrUsername
    End Get
    Set(ByVal Value As String)
        mstrUsername = Value
    End Set
End Property
```

This property also demonstrates the Return keyword, which passes back a value in your property or function, then immediately exits.

User-Defined Types

If you've worked with the API, you'll know it tends to call our user-defined types "structures." Well, get used to it: the Type keyword has been replaced with Structure. Here's an example user-defined type in VB .NET:

```
Public Structure MyStructure
    Dim Username As String
    Dim LogonCount As Integer
End Structure
```

The more complex structures can also include their own creation parameters ("constructors") and include methods, practically turning them into mini-classes.

Change the Scope

VB .NET now supports block-level scoping. If you typically declare all your variables at the top of your routine, you shouldn't run into any problems with this new feature.

But imagine this scenario: you declare a variable inside a loop and refer to it later outside the loop. In VB6, it's no problem. In VB .NET, however, it's outside the scope of the loop and therefore isn't available. It's something that's worth keeping in mind.

ByVal Is Default

By default, all parameters in VB .NET are passed ByVal (by value). In VB6, the default was ByRef (by reference). If you know what these keywords mean, you'll know how it might affect you, so make sure you change the ByVal keyword where required.

Set Has Disappeared

Virtually everything you use in VB .NET is an object. And, if you continued using VB6 syntax in VB .NET, that would mean having to use the Set statement to do something as simple as changing the value of a String variable. Not very sensible, I'm sure you'll agree.

Therefore, they decided to scrap the Set statement altogether. After all, if everything is an object, the Set keyword serves only to annoy. You can still try using it, but VB .NET will automatically remove and attempt to spank you silly.

Also, most default properties have disappeared in VB .NET. You can no longer do something like:

```
Dim MyString As String
MyString = TextBox1
```

Why not? Have a think about it. If you don't have the Set statement, you can't have defaults. It's not an obvious connection, but imagine changing "String" here to "Object". Now, exactly what are you trying to retrieve, a reference to the TextBox or the Text property? Have a ponder.

It's worth noting, however, that there is a way to create your own special default properties, such as an Item-style collection; however, as usual, certain rules apply. For more info, look up "default properties for class" in the help index.

Error Handling Changes

You can still use those favorite "On Error Goto" statements in VB .NET. However, there's also a new, more advanced way of dealing with errors, and it should be familiar to C++ and Java programmers. It's called *exception handling*, and it works by implementing a Try-Catch-Finally block.

Here's a skeletal example.

```
Try
    ' potentially problematic code goes here
Catch
    ' errors are caught here
Finally
    ' optional, runs at the end,
    ' whether an error occurred or not
End Try
```

Here, we add our code under the Try block. Should any errors occur while running it, the code inside the Catch block kicks in. At the end, whether an error occurred or not, the code within the Finally block executes.

You can also add a little code to analyze the "caught" error, include multiple Catch blocks to handle specific error types, or—by using the When keyword—run error code only when certain conditions apply. We'll demonstrate some of these techniques in the Essentials section of Chapters 2 and elsewhere within this book. Look up "catching exceptions" in the help index for more information.

You can also raise and pass back an error in your code, by "throwing an exception," like so:

```
Throw New System.Exception("An error has occured!")
```

The Class *Keyword*

Classes and their names are now defined according to the Class keyword. For example, here we're defining a class called Class1. We'd put all our code somewhere in the middle:

```
Public Class Class1

End Class
```

This format also allows you to put multiple classes inside one file, which is useful if you're dealing with particularly small, data-holding or related classes. This format also applies for modules, which use the Module keyword as opposed to Class.

One more point: classes now have "constructors" and "finalizers," as opposed to Class_Initialize and Class_Terminate. Also, as VB .NET is now a fully object-oriented language, you will find many enhanced object features, such as inheritance. We will be covering some of these techniques in this book. Alternatively, check out the MSDN help, or read the object discussions in my book, *Karl Moore's Visual Basic .NET: The Tutorials* (ISBN 1-59059-021-X) for more information.

Conclusion

Congratulations on reaching the end of this introduction to .NET!

We began with a look at what .NET means to Microsoft, then found out what it means to the people that matter: developers. We uncovered the .NET Framework and learned how it supports applications you can create in Visual Studio .NET.

After that, we got all hands-on, with a look at creating a couple of common applications in VB .NET: first off, a regular Windows program, and then a quick Web project. Finally, we explored some of the core language differences that developers moving from VB6 need to know.

Yes, it's changed. Yes, it's a pretty big change. But you don't have to scrap everything you know. Rather, build on it. Explore, embrace, be excited. It's new, it's exciting, it has possibilities.

When you're ready, start to move forward in this book. Pick up the basics with the *Essentials* sections, then learn to fly with the super-advanced tips that follow. If you'd prefer to be guided through some of the topics first, pick up *Karl Moore's Visual Basic .NET: The Tutorials* first. It'll guide you step by step to ensure that you get a solid grounding from the outset.

But, whatever you do, don't give up. It's that sole ability that marks every great programmer.

This is Karl Moore, welcoming you to .NET!

CHAPTER 2

Creating Great Windows Applications

DESPITE MORE AND MORE DEVELOPERS moving toward creating Web applications as the solution for many of today's business problems, the true power of Windows programs remains ever present.

Windows programs should be considered for several reasons. They're more reactive than Web sites. They allow you more control over what's happening on a computer. And they're better looking. At least, some of them are.

No, the fat client will never die. And, thankfully, the world of VB .NET relies on this, with the Windows application still being the default project type in Visual Studio.

So, just what is a Windows application to Visual Studio .NET? Well, it's a program that runs in Windows and typically consists of one or more forms (called "Windows Forms" in .NET).

The process of creating a Windows application is pretty simple: create a project, slap a few controls onto a form, change a bundle of properties, respond to events, and add code to glue the whole thing together.

This then compiles down to what we VB6 folk would call an *executable*. In the world of .NET, this is an "assembly," a unit of deployment for the .NET Framework. The term *assembly* can also be used to refer to DLLs too. (Basically, at least to regular VB .NET projects, your assembly is the main file that's created when you compile your application.)

After you've compiled, you simply need to distribute your assembly, perhaps alongside any other assemblies referenced in your application. No runtimes required. All you need to ensure is that the other machine has the .NET Framework installed— and, hey presto!

Okay, so that's *how*. Now, *what*.

In this chapter, we'll start by exploring the essentials of creating great Windows applications. Just to clarify, this isn't intended as any sort of tutorial. Rather, it simply recaps the basic points you'll need to know to create regular Windows form-based programs. Although you may find such basic pointers a little nauseating at this stage—especially if you've been using VB .NET for a while—when it comes to the likes of data access, you'll be glad of its reference value.

After the *Essentials* briefing, we'll move onto the *Developer Secrets*. These are all those crafty tips and code snippets I've personally created while programming for .NET over the past three years.

I'm not talking about "common code" here. I'm not going to tell you how to fill a TreeView control. That's the job of the help file and MSDN. Rather, these are the real and little-known tricks.

For instance, you'll learn how to check for a previous instance of your application—especially useful, as the PrevInstance property decided to take a hike. You'll figure how to create an ultra-thin, automatically updating fat client. You'll be given just the code to convert the contents of a RichTextBox control into HTML, then learn how to set up your application to work with Windows Explorer.

Sound interesting? Ready to indulge? Then let's get busy.

The Essentials

This section provides a brief overview of how you can start creating great Windows applications. It isn't intended as a tutorial, but rather a brief guide to the essentials—just enough to get you started, refresh your memory, or straighten out any particularly confusing points.

- You can create many different types of projects in Visual Studio. The most common is a Windows application, which is a standard Windows desktop program.

- To create a new Windows application project in Visual Studio .NET, click File ➤ New ➤ Project, select the Visual Basic Projects project type and choose the Windows Application template. Enter a name and location, then click on OK. This creates one "Solution" (similar to a VB6 Project Group), containing one "Project."

- To put together a regular Windows application project, you typically draw controls onto your form(s), change control properties using the Properties window, and add code to stick it all together. A description of all the inherent toolbox controls can be found in Section III of the appendix.

- To add a menu, drag and drop the MainMenu control onto your form. Next, simply click and type to create your menus. To create a hot key, use an ampersand before the desired character (that is, using &File will create an entry called File, which can be activated by pressing the Alt key and F). To change the properties of any individual menu item, select it and then edit its details through the Properties window. For example, to add a keyboard shortcut to a menu item, click the menu item, and select a new value for the Shortcut property through the Properties window.

- You can add a new file to your project, such as another form or module, by using the Project menu.

- If you want to display one form from another in your application, simply create a new instance of that form class and run the `.Show` method, as shown here:

```
Dim frmCalc As New Calculator()
frmCalc.Show()
```

- To display a form modally, run the `.ShowDialog` method instead of `.Show`. The form will be shown on top of all others in your application until either your code, or the user, closes it.

- To create an MDI application, set the `IsMdiContainer` property of your "master" form to `True`. Then, to display a child form within your master form, run code similar to the following, setting the `MdiParent` property to your master form:

```
' Code behind Form1, our master Form
Dim MyForm As New Form2()
MyForm.MdiParent = Me
MyForm.Show()
```

- To get a direct reference to the currently active MDI child form, reference the `ActiveForm` property of your master form object, as so:

```
' Code behind Form1, our master Form
Dim MyForm As Form
MyForm = Me.ActiveForm
MessageBox.Show(MyForm.Text)
```

- You can arrange your child windows by using the `LayoutMdi` method of your master form. You can set this to cascade your child windows, tile them horizontally or vertically, or arrange them as icons. Here's an example:

```
' Code behind Form1, our master Form
Me.LayoutMdi(MdiLayout.TileHorizontal)
```

- To maximize your form on startup, change its `WindowState` property to `Maximized`. To alter its default startup position to, say, center screen, change the `StartPosition` property.

- Errors in .NET can be handled in two ways. Firstly, using an "On Error" statement, such as "On Error Resume Next" (which is second nature to many Visual Basic 6 aficionados). However, the new .NET method of handling errors is more structured and consists of Try-Catch-Finally blocks. Here's an example:

```
Try
    Process.Start("c:\badfile.txt")
        Catch ex As Exception
            MessageBox.Show("Error occured - " & ex.Message)
Finally
    MessageBox.Show("The Finally block is optional. " & _
        "It always runs after everything else - " & _
        "whether an error occurred or not.")
End Try
```

- To run your application in debug mode, select Debug ➤ Start or press F5. To stop on a line in debug mode, move to the line and hit F9. Step through the code using F8, or the menu options in the Debug menu. To remove debugging from a line, move to it and press F9 once again.

- To change the startup object for your application—to, say, another form or Sub Main—right-click on your project in the Solution Explorer and select Properties. Choose the General menu under Common Properties, and select a startup object from the dropdown list.

- If you have purchased or downloaded third-party controls, you can use them by right-clicking on your toolbox, selecting Customize Toolbox, clicking on .NET Framework Components, and then browsing for your control. If you have created a Class Library assembly (akin to an ActiveX DLL) or downloaded a third-party .NET DLL assembly, you can reference and use its functionality by clicking on Project ➤ Add Reference, and then browsing for the component. You can also add existing class library projects directly to your solution. Look up "referencing objects" in the help index for more information.

- You can change the application name and copyright and versioning information by editing information in the AssemblyInfo.vb XML-structured file.

- To change the final name of your assembly, right-click on your project in the Solution Explorer, select Properties, and alter the Assembly Name value. The Root Namespace value refers the "namespace" under which your application sits. (In a Windows application, this isn't too important, but in a class library this will affect how users declare a class, that is, Dim MyObject As New MyNamespace.MyClass.)

- Compiling your application consists of selecting Build from the Build menu. This generates an executable file (with the .exe extension) in your project's Bin folder. This is a unit of deployment for the .NET Framework and is known as your assembly. It will run on any machine containing the .NET Framework.

- Compiled executable files produced by Visual Studio actually contain raw MSIL (Microsoft Intermediate Language) and metadata (descriptive information about your code). When code inside your EXE file is run for the first time on a machine, this MSIL code is optimized for the computer, fully compiled, and then locally cached.

- Having the MSIL and metadata helps the .NET Framework analyze your application, automatically handling memory and providing all the plumbing options it does. However, this is all automatic, and so it isn't something you must know about before building .NET applications.

- The default "configuration" for any solution is Debug mode. This creates "debug files" when you compile your application. Before releasing your final version, change the configuration, through the drop-down list on the "standard" toolbar, from Debug to Release. This removes all the debug symbols, stops VS .NET producing the PDB debug file in your Bin folder, and further optimizes your code.

- Third-party assemblies (such as controls and DLLs) used in your application are typically placed in the Bin folder when you compile. The exception to this are "strong-named" assemblies, which are accessible by all applications and registered in a global Windows assembly registry called the *global assembly cache* (GAC). For example, all of the .NET Framework base classes are strong named and registered in the GAC. If you use third-party strong named assemblies, create a setup project to distribute your application (this should automatically distribute and register the assembly in the user's GAC for you), but, if you don't, simply copy the files from your Bin folder to get your application running on another machine.

- All of the Toolbox controls and other base Framework classes are included by default in every installation of the .NET Framework. You don't need to distribute any extra DLLs to use them in your application.

- For information on creating a setup project and installing the .NET Framework on client machines, check out the Microsoft guide at `http://msdn.microsoft.com/library/en-us/dnnetdep/html/dotnetframedepguid.asp`.

- To change the default application icon, right-click on your project in the Solution Explorer and select Properties. Choose the Build menu under Common Properties, and then choose an icon. This will be the icon shown when your executable is viewed through the Windows Explorer.

Developer Secrets

So, you want to get your hands on all the juicy secrets, huh? Then step this way, as we prepare to unveil the following gems for creating great Windows forms applications:

- Making Your Form Transparent

- Who Stole the ToolTips?

- Tricks of the Trade: Resizing Made Easy

- Five Steps to Split Panels, Explorer Style

- Highlighting Errors with the ErrorProvider

- Learning the LinkLabel Control

- Customizing the MonthCalendar Control

- Creating Your Own Number-Only Textbox

- Displaying Animated GIFs Without the Browser Control

- The Two Methods of Changing Tab Order

- Secrets of Working with the System Tray

- Save User Time: Add Autocomplete to Combo Boxes

- The Power of Command-Line Parameters

- How to "Reset" a Form

- How to Snap the Cursor to a Button

- Capturing the Screen, Quick and Easy

- Stunning Navigation Bars with a Little-Known Freebie

- Seven Steps to Taking Advantage of Windows XP Themes

- The .NET Way of Checking for Previous Instances

- Converting RTF to HTML

- Drag and Drop from Windows Explorer

- Dialog Boxes: What Did the User Click?

- Text Printing Class… That Works!

- The Secret Rebirth of `.PrintForm`

- The Facts on Visual Inheritance

- Looking at Windows, Performance Counters, and More

- Protecting Your Code with Obfuscation

- Best of All Worlds: Creating an Ultra-Thin Client

And that's just the beginning. Later in this book, after we've covered other project types such as ASP.NET Web sites, we'll move onto database secrets, a hidden .NET language, special file manipulation code, and much more—all of which you can easily use straight away in your Visual Basic applications.

Making Your Form Transparent

You can give your Windows form a great transparent look by altering its `Opacity` property. Set this anywhere between 0% (completely transparent) and 100% (regular opaque) to see the windows underneath your application.

Who Stole the ToolTips?

If you haven't already noticed, someone stole the `ToolTip` property in .NET. If you want little popup messages to appear when you hover your mouse over a button or whatever, you'll need to figure out the ToolTip control.

Here's how it works. Firstly, you add an instance of the ToolTip control to your form. This is an invisible component that actually displays the message. You can alter its properties through the Property window, such as the popup delay or whether it is `Active`.

Next, you need to add the actual ToolTip messages. Click on any of your controls and scroll down to the `Misc` section (presuming you order your property list by category). You'll see a property called something like `ToolTip on ToolTip1`: This is a fresh property that your ToolTip instance gave every control on your form.

Simply set this property to your ToolTip message—and that's a wrap!

Tricks of the Trade: Resizing Made Easy!

When the user resizes your Windows form at runtime, all of your controls will stay in place by default. They will not automatically resize with the form. You can change this behavior by editing the Anchor property of a control.

The Anchor property determines which sides of a form a control will stretch with. After the default, the most common setting for this property is "Top, Bottom, Left, Right"—meaning the control will stretch with all sides of your form, behaving like the majority of resizable Windows applications.

The Dock property of a control is also useful when positioning and resizing controls. It allows you to dock a control to a particular side of a form and stick with that side, regardless of how the form is resized. To set this, simply select a new region via the Dock property drop-down menu.

Five Steps to Split Panels, Explorer-Style

 Download supporting files at www.apress.com.
The files for this tip are in the "Ch2–Split Panels" folder.

If you're looking to create the split-panel look seen in many modern applications, you'll be happy to learn that a new .NET Splitter control can help you achieve exactly that.

Here are the simple steps to creating the split-panel look in your own programs:

1. Add the control you want to appear down the left of your screen to your form. This could be a TreeView control, if you're going for the Explorer effect, or a Panel control if you want to add numerous controls (such as a list of icons for a menu, in the style of Outlook).

2. Set the Dock property of this control to Left.

3. Add a Splitter control to your form. It should automatically set its Dock property to Left. This is the widget your users will "grab" to resize the panels.

4. Add your final control to your form. If you're continuing that elusive Explorer look, this will probably be the ListView control.

5. Set the Dock property of this control to Fill. (Click on the box in the center.)

And that's it. Try running your application. Your users will be able to "drag" the Splitter and your two controls/panels will automatically resize. (See Figure 2-1.)

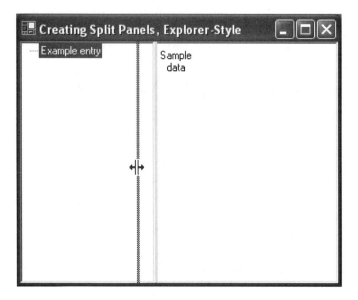

Figure 2-1. Our Splitter control in action

Highlighting Errors with the ErrorProvider

The ErrorProvider control provides a great way of providing visual user feedback. If a problem occurs—say, your user entered an incorrect customer number into a text box—you can use the ErrorProvider to add a flashing error icon next to the control, along with a ToolTip describing the error.

The following code demonstrates use of the ErrorProvider in its simplest form. The code assumes that you have a Windows form containing an instance of the ErrorProvider control called ErrorProvider1, and a TextBox control called TextBox1:

```
' Set an error on a control
ErrorProvider1.SetError(TextBox1, "Invalid Phone Number - Try Again")
' Remove the error
ErrorProvider1.SetError(TextBox1, "")
```

The first line here sets the error. This results in a blinking error icon to the right of the control, which displays the error as its ToolTip. (See Figure 2-2.) By default, the blinking stops as soon as you view the error message. The second line here removes the error flag.

It's worth noting that each of these settings—icon, blink style, and rate—is completely customizable. Simply edit the ErrorProvider control via the Properties window. Also, the ErrorProvider does a particularly good job working with data bound forms. Check out "ErrorProvider component, overview" in the help index for more information on this feature.

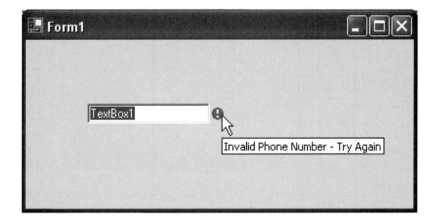

Figure 2-2. Neat visual error handling with the ErrorProvider component

Learning the LinkLabel Control

The LinkLabel control is a great addition to your programming toolbox. It looks and acts like a Web page hyperlink, however has all the functionality of a regular Button.

By default, the link appears in blue, and changes to red when clicked on. These defaults can be altered by changing the LinkColor and ActiveLinkColor properties. The LinkLabel control has a Click event, to which you can add code to respond to a click. If you want the link to change to its default VisitedLinkColor, set the LinkVisited property to True either in code, or through the Properties window.

If you want your LinkLabel to open a Web site, use code similar to the following behind its Click event:

```
System.Diagnostics.Process.Start("http://www.karlmoore.com/")
LinkLabel1.LinkVisited = True
```

Customizing the MonthCalendar Control

Your control toolbox includes an incredibly useful control called the MonthCalendar control. (See Figure 2-3.) However, few programmers really appreciate quite how customizable this widget really is. You can change virtually any aspect of how it works.

As you'd expect, you can alter colors and fonts. The ForeColor, TitleBackColor, TitleForeColor, TrailingForeColor, and Font properties will help you out there. You can also alter the minimum and maximum dates that can be selected, either through the Properties window or in code, with the MinDate and MaxDate properties.

The ScrollChange property determines the number of months the control moves when its scroll buttons are clicked. ShowToday and ShowTodayCircle dictate whether today's date is highlighted and circled.

And there's still more. For example, ShowWeekNumbers displays the week numbers, which is highly useful to true business applications. You can change the FirstDayOfWeek property to another day, too, if necessary. The AnnuallyBoldedDates, BoldedDates, and MonthlyBoldedDates properties allow you to add dates, in code or through the Properties window, that are highlighted perhaps on a monthly or annual basis.

But best of all is probably CalendarDimensions. Use the Properties window to alter the Width and Height values to view multiple months at once, perhaps creating a six-month or full-year view in your desktop application at once. Highly useful!

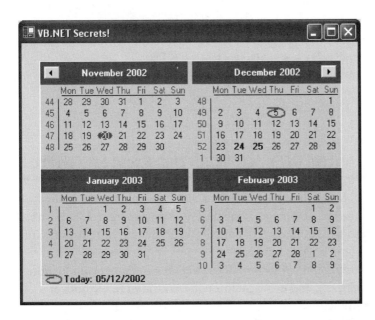

Figure 2-3. The MonthCalendar control. Is there anything it can't *do?*

Creating Your Own Number-Only Text Box

Download supporting files at www.apress.com.
The files for this tip are in the "Ch2—Number-Only Text Box" folder.

In some instances, you'll want to restrict the user to entering only a numeric value in a TextBox control on your Windows form.

To do this, you need to write code to check every key press in that textbox. You need to verify that the ASCII key value of each typed character is not less than 48 (the number 0 key) and not greater than 57 (the 9 key). If it's outside these ranges, you simply tell the TextBox control that you have "handled" that character and it doesn't get added to the box.

Here is a chunk of sample code you could add underneath a TextBox KeyPress event to do this:

```
If Asc(e.KeyChar) < 48 Or Asc(e.KeyChar) > 57 Then
    ' Cancel non-numeric characters
    e.Handled = True
End If
```

Another way to do this would be to create a list of allowable characters. Here, for example, we're allowing numbers, spaces, colons, and dashes:

```
Dim strAllowableChars As String
strAllowableChars = "0123456789-: "
' If the character they have entered isn't in our list...
If InStr(strAllowableChars, e.KeyChar.ToString) = 0 Then
    ' Cancel the character
    e.Handled = True
End If
```

Displaying Animated GIFs Without the Browser Control

When it comes to displayed animated images in a Windows application, many developers instantly head off and incorporate the Web browser control. This isn't only going a little overboard for the sort of benefits an animation will provide your application—but it's completely unnecessary.

You see, the PictureBox control automatically handles animated GIFs for you. Simply set the Image property, and it'll cycle through frame after frame both at design time and at runtime.

Want to create your own animated GIFs? Try checking out Paint Shop Pro and Animation Shop from Jasc Software at www.jasc.com.

The Two Methods of Changing Tab Order

In Windows forms, the tab order determines which controls receive the focus and in what order as your user presses the Tab key.

To stop a control from receiving the focus when your user presses the tab key, set its TabStop property to False. To change its tab order, alter the TabIndex property to a value starting at 0, where 0 is the first control to receive the focus.

However, a simpler way is to select View ➤ Tab Order from the menu, and then select your controls in the proposed tab order. The TabIndex property will be automatically set for you. (See Figure 2-4.)

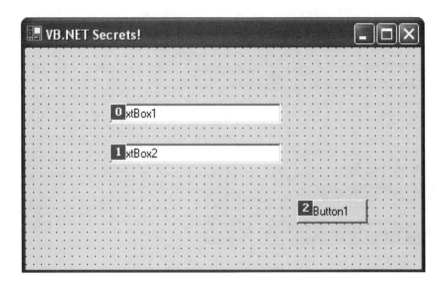

Figure 2-4. Visually setting our tab order

Secrets of Working with the System Tray

Working with the Windows system tray was never the easiest of tasks. Officially called the *status notification area*, it always involved a bundle of API calls and a little too much effort than it actually deserved. In .NET however, it's all about knowing which controls to use.

The heart of the whole process is the NotifyIcon component. Found in the toolbox, you'll need to drag and drop this little beast straight onto your form or component. Then you need to get editing those properties: change the Icon property to the icon you wish to display in the system tray and Text to the name you wish to appear as a ToolTip.

Try running your form or component as it stands so far: exactly zero lines of code later and your application can already display an icon in the system tray. But I'm guessing you want to do just a little more than that.

Most applications display a menu when the user selects the icon. For this, you need to add another toolbox component: the ContextMenu. If you've dropped this straight onto a form, you'll be able to edit it just like a regular menu: add separators, write code to respond to the Click events of the individual menu items, and so on. Then change the ContextMenu property of the NotifyIcon component to point to your new menu. Next, run your application and click on your icon in the system tray—result achieved!

If, on the other hand, you simply want to run a little code or display a form when your icon is clicked, then check out the useful events supplied by the NotifyIcon property. You have Click, DoubleClick, MouseDown, MouseMove, and MouseUp. Simply use the code window to select one of these, and start writing your code.

And that's it. Two controls, a couple of properties, and a handful of events are all you need to know to master the system tray. (See Figure 2-5.)

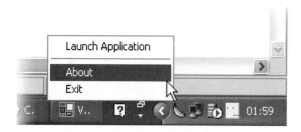

Figure 2-5. Is that a banana in my system tray?

Save User Time: Add Autocomplete to Combo Boxes

 Download supporting files at www.apress.com.
The files for this tip are in the "Ch2–AutoComplete" folder.

Develop an application in a program such as Microsoft Access and all your combo boxes will by default incorporate autocomplete, that ability to be able to tap a few characters in a drop-down list and have the nearest matching selection picked out for you.

In Visual Basic, however, there's no such intrinsic support. If you want autocomplete, you've got to do it yourself. And this tip shows you how.

Simply add the following methods to your form. The first is called
AutoCompleteKeyUp and accepts a combo box and KeyEventArgs objects as
arguments. You need to call this in the KeyUp event of your combo box: it looks at
what the user has typed and selects the most appropriate match. The second is
called AutoCompleteLeave and should be called when the Leave event of your combo
box is fired. This one simply takes whatever you've finally chosen and cases it
properly, as per the matching selection in the combo box.

Let's look at those functions now:

```
Public Sub AutoCompleteKeyUp(ByVal Combo As ComboBox, _
    ByVal e As KeyEventArgs)
    Dim strTyped As String
    Dim intFoundIndex As Integer
    Dim objFoundItem As Object
    Dim strFoundText As String
    Dim strAppendText As String
    ' Ignore basic selection keys
    Select Case e.KeyCode
        Case Keys.Back, Keys.Left, Keys.Right, Keys.Up, _
            Keys.Delete, Keys.Down, Keys.CapsLock
            Return
    End Select
    ' Find what user has typed in list
    strTyped = Combo.Text
    intFoundIndex = Combo.FindString(strTyped)
    ' If found...
    If intFoundIndex >= 0 Then
        ' Get list item (actual type depends on whether data bound)
        objFoundItem = Combo.Items(intFoundIndex)
        ' Use control to resolve text - in case data bound
        strFoundText = Combo.GetItemText(objFoundItem)
        ' Append the typed text to rest of the found string
        ' (text is set twice due to a combo box quirk:
        '  on certain platforms, setting just once ignores casing!)
        strAppendText = strFoundText.Substring(strTyped.Length)
        Combo.Text = strTyped & strAppendText
        Combo.Text = strTyped & strAppendText
        ' Select the appended text
        Combo.SelectionStart = strTyped.Length
        Combo.SelectionLength = strAppendText.Length
    End If
End Sub
```

```
Public Sub AutoCompleteLeave(ByVal Combo As ComboBox)
    ' Correct casing when leaving combo
    Dim intFoundIndex As Integer
    intFoundIndex = Combo.FindStringExact(Combo.Text)
    Combo.SelectedIndex = -1
    Combo.SelectedIndex = intFoundIndex
End Sub
```

And here's how you may call these functions from your combo box:

```
Private Sub ComboBox1_KeyUp(ByVal sender As Object, _
    ByVal e As System.Windows.Forms.KeyEventArgs) Handles ComboBox1.KeyUp
    AutoCompleteKeyUp(ComboBox1, e)
End Sub
Private Sub ComboBox1_Leave(ByVal sender As Object, _
    ByVal e As System.EventArgs) Handles ComboBox1.Leave
    AutoCompleteLeave(ComboBox1)
End Sub
```

That's all you need to create your own autocomplete combo boxes. (See Figure 2-6.) And if you're feeling really adventurous, you might even want to wrap all of this up into a neat little user control. But we'll leave that for another tip.

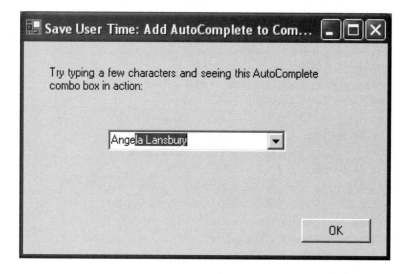

Figure 2-6. Our autocomplete combo box strutting its stuff

The Power of Command-Line Parameters

Command-line parameters can be incredibly useful because they allow users or other applications to pass startup information to your program. For example, if your program was called myapp.exe, they might run the following:

```
myapp.exe /nodialogs
```

Here, we have one command-line parameter, "/nodialogs". In VB6, we could read this using the Command property. In VB .NET, this has been replaced with the System.Environment.GetCommandLineArgs function, which returns an array of any passed startup parameters.

And here's a chunk of code to show you just how to read them:

```
Dim MyStartupArguments() As String, intCount As Integer
MyStartupArguments = System.Environment.GetCommandLineArgs

For intCount = 0 To UBound(MyStartupArguments)
    MessageBox.Show(MyStartupArguments(intCount).ToString)
Next
```

How to Reset a Form

 Download supporting files at www.apress.com.
The files for this tip are in the "Ch2–Reset Form" folder.

If you've created a data entry–style Windows form that needs "resetting" with each addition, all the necessary code to clear the TextBox controls, uncheck the CheckBox controls, deselect combo boxes, *ad infinitum,* can all get a little repetitive—particularly if you have to write it for multiple forms.

This is where the following method could prove useful. Simply pass in a form as a parameter, and it'll reset the main data entry controls: TextBox, CheckBox, and ComboBox, even those hidden away inside Tab Pages and other container controls. You might want to extend this routine to cater for RadioButton, ListBox, CheckedListBox, DomainUpDown, NumericUpDown, MonthCalendar, and DateTimePicker controls, too, depending on your requirements: simply edit the ClearControl method. To ensure flexibility, this subroutine automatically bypasses all controls with "skip" somewhere in the Tag property.

Here's the code:

```
Public Sub ResetForm(ByVal FormToReset As Form)
    ' Resets the main data entry controls on the passed FormToReset
    Dim objControl As Control
    ' Loop around every control on the form and run the reset method
    For Each objControl In FormToReset.Controls
        ResetControl(objControl)
    Next
End Sub

Public Sub ResetControl(ByVal ControlToReset As Control)
    ' Resets the core control, then loops and
    ' resets any sub controls, such as Tab pages
    Dim intCount As Integer
    ClearControl(ControlToReset)
    If ControlToReset.Controls.Count > 0 Then
        For intCount = 1 To ControlToReset.Controls.Count
            ResetControl(ControlToReset.Controls(intCount - 1))
        Next
    End If
End Sub

Public Sub ClearControl(ByVal ControlToClear As Control)
    ' Clears the value of a particular control -
    ' you may wish to extend this to suit your exact needs
    If InStr(ControlToClear.Tag, "skip", CompareMethod.Text) = 0 Then
        If TypeOf (ControlToClear) Is System.Windows.Forms.TextBox Then
            ControlToClear.Text = ""  ' Clear TextBox
        ElseIf TypeOf (ControlToClear) Is System.Windows.Forms.CheckBox Then
            Dim objCheckBox As System.Windows.Forms.CheckBox = ControlToClear
            objCheckBox.Checked = False ' Uncheck CheckBox
        ElseIf TypeOf (ControlToClear) Is System.Windows.Forms.ComboBox Then
            Dim objComboBox As System.Windows.Forms.ComboBox = ControlToClear
            objComboBox.SelectedIndex = -1 ' Deselect any ComboBox entry
        ' If
```

s function behind your form, as so:

How to Snap the Cursor to a Button

 Download supporting files at www.apress.com.
The files for this tip are in the "Ch2–Snap to Control" folder.

If you're attempting to create that foolproof Windows application, one great technique to use is that of snapping the cursor to a particular control, thus anticipating the user's next click.

The following neat little function does exactly that. Simply pass in a control to get it started: it'll calculate the exact bottom middle location of the control and then snap the cursor to that position. (See Figure 2-7.) Here's the code:

```
Public Sub SnapToControl(ByVal Control As Control)
    ' Snaps the cursor to the bottom middle of the passed control
    Dim objPoint As Point = Control.PointToScreen(New Point(0, 0))
    objPoint.X += (Control.Width / 2)
    objPoint.Y += ((Control.Height / 4) * 3)
    Cursor.Position = objPoint
End Sub
```

And here's how you might use this to snap to, say, a Button control:

```
SnapToControl(Button1)
```

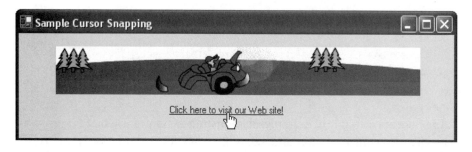

Figure 2-7. A simple little application, this time snapping to a LinkLabel control

Capturing the Screen, Quick and Easy

Download supporting files at www.apress.com.
The files for this tip are in the "Ch2–Screen Capture" folder.

When it comes to showing people how to capture the screen, most VB .NET authors I've seen tend to revert to the old school method of working: using the API. There is, however, a better way.

The following function is called GetScreenCapture and returns an Image object. It captures the screen by running a series of "Print Screen" key presses, which puts a screen grab on the clipboard, ready for my nifty little function to devour and return. (See Figure 2-8.) My function accepts a FullScreen argument, too: pass True to capture the whole screen, and False to capture just the active window.

Here's the code:

```
Public Function GetScreenCapture( _
    Optional ByVal FullScreen As Boolean = False) As Image
    ' Captures the current screen and returns as an Image object
    Dim objSK As SendKeys
    Dim imgCapture As Image
    If FullScreen = True Then
        ' Print Screen pressed twice here as some systems
        ' grab active window "accidentally" on first run
        objSK.SendWait("{PRTSC 2}")
    Else
        objSK.SendWait("%{PRTSC}")
    End If
    Dim objData As IDataObject = Clipboard.GetDataObject()
    Return objData.GetData(DataFormats.Bitmap)
End Function
```

And here are a couple of examples demonstrating how to use that Image object—firstly, saving it as a file, and, secondly, using it to set the Image property of a PictureBox control:

```
GetScreenCapture(True).Save("c:\screengrab.bmp", _
    System.Drawing.Imaging.ImageFormat.Bmp))
PictureBox1.Image = GetScreenCapture()
```

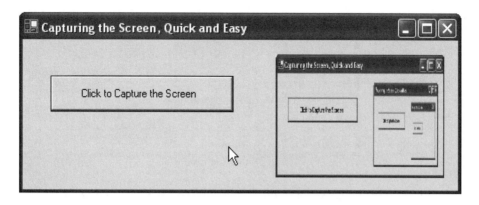

Figure 2-8. My sample application, capturing the active window (again and again)

Stunning Navigation Bars with a Little-Known Freebie

Download supporting files at www.apress.com.
The files for this tip are in the "Ch2–XtraNavBar" folder.

If you've ever used Office, Windows XP, or Visual Studio .NET (which I'm hoping you have), you may have admired the user interface and wondered how you could implement something like that yourself.

Well, unless you're willing to invest weeks into creating your own superior user interface components, you'd typically have to shell out a thousand bucks on some fancy third-party solution. Unless, of course, you read on.

Software group Developer Express has developed a whole range of user interface components and, to promote its new .NET range, is giving away their $99 XtraNavBar Suite to anyone who knows the download address.

The component has been written from the ground up for .NET and allows you to add that "professional" Microsoft feel to any application within seconds, with support for taskbars, sidebars, XP themes, and more. (See Figure 2-9.) All for the grand price of zero.

To download and register your copy, simply head to www.devexpress.com/free. This "backdoor" will remain open indefinitely, but, just in case you miss the offer, I've arranged to bundle the installation with the downloadable source for this book at www.apress.com. Enjoy!

Figure 2-9. Sample navigation bars, all created with the free XtraNavBar Suite

Seven Steps to Taking Advantage of Windows XP Themes

A lot has been written about how to integrate your application with Windows XP themes, and most of it is complete hogwash. I've personally wasted hours trying to figure out how to get it working.

All the online tutorials I've encountered, including MSDN, are critically flawed in their "how to" description. This top tip, however, hopefully isn't.

So, what are Windows XP themes? Themes are a sort of limited, user-selected "skin" for the operating system, a "make it look nice" feature introduced in XP and to be continued and expanded upon in future versions of Windows.

Providing theme support in your application gives it that integrated Windows feel (for example, the default Windows XP theme gives all buttons an orange outline glow as the user hovers over—something your own applications can inherit) and sets it up for greater customization in later versions of the operating system.

But how? Firstly, we design our application as normal, occasionally setting a button style to System. Then we create a manifest file from a template I'll provide and add it as a resource to our final executable. The contents of this manifest file tell the application to bind itself to ComCtl6, the Windows Common Controls component that will then draw the controls for your application and apply the themes as relevant.

And here are the seven easy steps to get it all up and running:

1. Design your application as normal. Where possible, set the FlatStyle property of your controls to System. This is very important.

2. When you're ready to roll out the final version of your application, compile your program. Open the Bin folder through Windows Explorer, right-click and select the Version tab. Make a note of the file version *exactly* as it is displayed here.

3. Create a new file on your machine and call it "MyManifest.manifest".
    Using Notepad, or a similar text editor, add the following text to this file:

```
<?xml version="1.0" encoding="UTF-8" standalone="yes"?>
<assembly xmlns="urn:schemas-microsoft-com:asm.v1"
    manifestVersion="1.0">
<assemblyIdentity
    version="Insert Your Exact Version Number Here"
    processorArchitecture="X86"
    name="Name of Application"
    type="win32"
/>
<description>Description of Application</description>
<dependency>
    <dependentAssembly>
        <assemblyIdentity
            type="win32"
            name="Microsoft.Windows.Common-Controls"
            version="6.0.0.0"
            processorArchitecture="X86"
            publicKeyToken="6595b64144ccf1df"
            language="*"
        />
    </dependentAssembly>
</dependency>
</assembly>
```

4. Back in Visual Studio .NET, open your actual assembly, which is typically
    the executable file you just compiled. Click on File ➤ Open ➤ File, and
    then select your assembly.

5. Right-click anywhere on the new window and select Add Resource.
    Choose Import and select your MANIFEST file. You will be asked for a
    resource type. Type "RT_MANIFEST" and click on OK.

6. In the Properties window, change the ID of the strange screen that has
    appeared from 101 to 1. Click on File ➤ Close to close this window, and
    accept any changes. Do the same with the next window, displaying details
    about your executable file, again ensuring that you save changes.

7. Go back to Windows Explorer and give your application a test run, then
    uncork the champagne! (See Figure 2-10.) If you get an error message, it's
    likely you either typed out the MANIFEST file incorrectly, or used the
    wrong version number—in which case go back and try again.

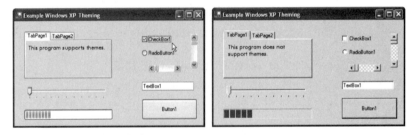

Figure 2-10. Two applications: one supporting the default XP theme, the other "theme-less"

The .NET Way of Checking for Previous Instances

Download supporting files at www.apress.com.
The files for this tip are in the "Ch2–Previous Instances" folder.

It's often useful to check whether another instance of your application is already running. The prime use for this is to ensure that only one instance of your program is active at any one time by checking during startup, and, if one is already running, providing that instance with the focus, then quitting.

In Visual Basic 6, you had the App.PrevInstance property to check. In VB .NET, we need to check whether the current process name is already running. That's what our code does here, encapsulated in the PrevInstance function. It returns a True if your application is already running on the same machine:

```
Public Function PrevInstance() As Boolean
    If Diagnostics.Process.GetProcessesByName _
        (Diagnostics.Process.GetCurrentProcess.ProcessName).Length > 1 Then
        Return True
    Else
        Return False
    End If
End Function
```

You might use this code as so:

```
If PrevInstance() = True Then
    ' Get all previous instances
    Dim Processes() As Process
    Processes = Diagnostics.Process.GetProcessesByName( _
        Diagnostics.Process.GetCurrentProcess.ProcessName)
```

```
       ' Activate the first instance
      AppActivate(Processes(0).Id)
       ' Exit the current instance
      Application.Exit()
   End If
```

> **TOP TIP** *There's a little bug you may run into when using this code that turns the hair of most developers a funny shade of gray. If your application name is greater than fifteen characters, and running on either Windows NT or 2000, your code won't be able to tell whether a previous instance is running. It's weird, but true. The solution is to upgrade to XP or higher, or change your application name (Project ➤ Properties).*

Converting RTF to HTML

```
Download supporting files at www.apress.com.
The files for this tip are in the "Ch2–RTF to HTML" folder.
```

One amazingly common developer request is a method of converting the contents of a RichTextBox control to HTML. But, unless you're willing to spend hundreds on a third-party text editing control, you're out of luck. Even in VB .NET, Microsoft has chosen to remain ignorant to this much-desired feature.

So, you need to do it yourself, and the following chunk of code I've put together should get you started. Just pass it a RichTextBox control as a parameter, and it'll return a string of HTML, ready for you to perhaps save to a file. (See Figure 2-11.)

It doesn't handle more-complicated features, such as images or tables, but it will easily cope with fonts, sizes, colors, bold, italic, and paragraphs. Of course, you're more than welcome to expand it to exactly suit your needs.

You can call this code, as so:

```
strHTML = ConvertToHtml(RichTextBox1)
```

And here's the actual ConvertToHTML function:

```
Public Function ConvertToHTML(ByVal Box As RichTextBox) As String
    ' Takes a RichTextBox control and returns a
    ' simple HTML-formatted version of its contents
    Dim strHTML As String
    Dim strColour As String
```

```vb
Dim blnBold As Boolean
Dim blnItalic As Boolean
Dim strFont As String
Dim shtSize As Short
Dim lngOriginalStart As Long
Dim lngOriginalLength As Long
Dim intCount As Integer
' If nothing in the box, exit
If Box.Text.Length = 0 Then Exit Function
' Store original selections, then select first character
lngOriginalStart = 0
lngOriginalLength = Box.TextLength
Box.Select(0, 1)
' Add HTML header
strHTML = "<html>"
' Setup initial parameters
strColour = Box.SelectionColor.ToKnownColor.ToString
blnBold = Box.SelectionFont.Bold
blnItalic = Box.SelectionFont.Italic
strFont = Box.SelectionFont.FontFamily.Name
shtSize = Box.SelectionFont.Size
' Include first 'style' parameters in the HTML
strHTML += "<span style=""font-family: " & strFont & _
  "; font-size: " & shtSize & "pt; color: " & strColour & """>"
' Include bold tag, if required
If blnBold = True Then
    strHTML += "<b>"
End If
' Include italic tag, if required
If blnItalic = True Then
    strHTML += "<i>"
End If
' Finally, add our first character
strHTML += Box.Text.Substring(0, 1)
' Loop around all remaining characters
For intCount = 2 To Box.Text.Length
    ' Select current character
    Box.Select(intCount - 1, 1)
    ' If this is a line break, add HTML tag
    If Box.Text.Substring(intCount - 1, 1) = Convert.ToChar(10) Then
        strHTML += "<br>"
    End If
    ' Check/implement any changes in style
    If Box.SelectionColor.ToKnownColor.ToString <> strColour _
```

```
                Or Box.SelectionFont.FontFamily.Name <> strFont Or _
                Box.SelectionFont.Size <> shtSize Then
                strHTML += "</span><span style=""font-family: " _
                  & Box.SelectionFont.FontFamily.Name & _
                  "; font-size: " & Box.SelectionFont.Size & _
                  "pt; color: " & _
                  Box.SelectionColor.ToKnownColor.ToString & """>"
            End If
            ' Check for bold changes
            If Box.SelectionFont.Bold <> blnBold Then
                If Box.SelectionFont.Bold = False Then
                    strHTML += "</b>"
                Else
                    strHTML += "<b>"
                End If
            End If
            ' Check for italic changes
            If Box.SelectionFont.Italic <> blnItalic Then
                If Box.SelectionFont.Italic = False Then
                    strHTML += "</i>"
                Else
                    strHTML += "<i>"
                End If
            End If
            ' Add the actual character
            strHTML += Mid(Box.Text, intCount, 1)
            ' Update variables with current style
            strColour = Box.SelectionColor.ToKnownColor.ToString
            blnBold = Box.SelectionFont.Bold
            blnItalic = Box.SelectionFont.Italic
            strFont = Box.SelectionFont.FontFamily.Name
            shtSize = Box.SelectionFont.Size
        Next
        ' Close off any open bold/italic tags
        If blnBold = True Then strHTML += "</b>"
        If blnItalic = True Then strHTML += "</i>"
        ' Terminate outstanding HTML tags
        strHTML += "</span></html>"
        ' Restore original RichTextBox selection
        Box.Select(lngOriginalStart, lngOriginalLength)
        ' Return HTML
        Return strHTML
    End Function
```

> **TOP TIP** *Looking to turn HTML back into text? Check out my "Converting HTML to Text, Easily" tip in the "Working with the Internet" section, within Chapter 7.*

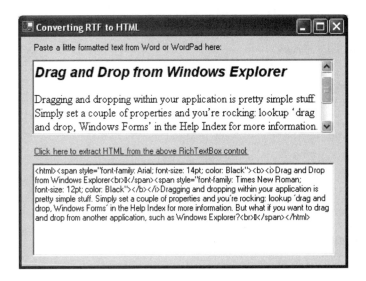

Figure 2-11. Our code doing its stuff: translating RTF into HTML

Drag and Drop from Windows Explorer

Download supporting files at www.apress.com.
The files for this tip are in the *"Ch2–Drag and Drop Explorer"* folder.

Dragging and dropping within your application is pretty simple stuff. Simply set a couple of properties and you're rocking: look up "drag and drop, Windows Forms" in the help index for more information. But what if you want to drag and drop from another application, such as Windows Explorer?

One of the most commonly requested, yet infrequently answered Windows form questions is "How can I let my users drag and drop files and folders directly into my applications?" It's simple; just follow these three easy steps:

1. Change the AllowDrop property of the control you want users to drop the files onto to True. This could be a ListBox control, a Panel control, or even your form itself.

2. Add code to the DragOver event of the control, so the typical "copy" icon is displayed when files are dragged over.

```
' As dragged over, check data is file drop
If e.Data.GetDataPresent(DataFormats.FileDrop) Then
    ' Display the copy (or other) icon
    e.Effect = DragDropEffects.Copy
End If
```

3. Finally, add code to the DragDrop event of the control, to receive and process information about the dropped files.

```
' Check this is a file drop
If (e.Data.GetDataPresent(DataFormats.FileDrop)) Then
    ' Retrieve list of files and loop through string array
    Dim strFiles() As String = e.Data.GetData(DataFormats.FileDrop)
    Dim intCount As Integer
    For intCount = 0 To strFiles.Length
        MessageBox.Show(strFiles(intCount))
    Next
End If
```

And that's it! In three simple steps, your application is ready to interoperate with Windows Explorer or any other application that supports the standard Windows file drag-and-drop routines. (See Figure 2-12.)

Of course, we're simply displaying the dropped files or folders in a message box. However, you could be doing something much more exciting: generating an MP3 play list, processing special work files, loading documents into your own mini word processor, and so forth. The possibilities are endless.

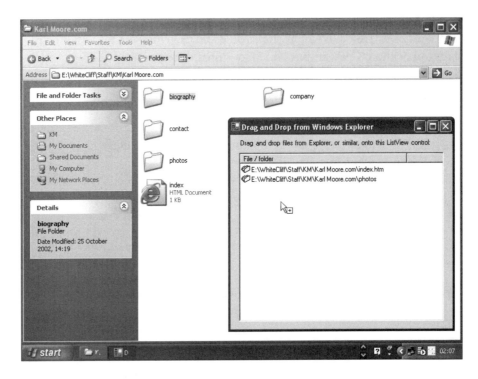

Figure 2-12. Dragging and dropping from Windows Explorer

Dialog Boxes: What Did the User Click?

If you work a lot with your own popup dialog boxes rather than simply using the MessageBox class, you might be interested to learn about the new way in which Microsoft has made it easy to pass a response back to the code that displayed the dialog box.

In older versions of Visual Basic, you'd typically display the form, setup properties and enumerations to set and retrieve the user response—and more. Now, it's much easier, with the DialogResult property.

Here's how it works: you create your dialog box as usual. You might be asking the user a simple question, or getting him or her to confirm or cancel an action. For each response, add a button to the dialog box and change its DialogResult property to the result you wish that button to return.

Next, from your calling form, create an instance of your dialog form in code and run .ShowDialog. This opens the form modally and keeps it there until your user clicks on one of the response buttons. As soon as they do, the form closes and the result is passed back as the result of the .ShowDialog function, as so:

```
Dim objForm As New Form2()
' If you need set any properties on
' the form, do it here!
If objForm.ShowDialog = DialogResult.Yes Then
    MessageBox.Show("You clicked Yes!")
Else
    MessageBox.Show("You did not click Yes!")
End If
```

It's pure simplicity!

Text Printing Class… That Works!

Download supporting files at www.apress.com.
The files for this tip are in the "Ch2–Printing" folder.

You can print from your program in a number of ways. One option, for example, is to automate Microsoft Word, edit a document in code, and then programmatically print it out.

However, if you're looking to print directly from your application, the .NET Framework provides a number of components to help you in the System.Drawing.Printing namespace.

The core component here is PrintDocument. At its simplest, printing involves instantiating a PrintDocument object, setting its properties, and calling the Print method. With each page to be printed, PrintDocument raises a PrintPage event, to which you need to add your own printing logic. Other key classes in the same Printing namespace include PrinterSettings, PageSettings, and PrintPreviewControl.

As you can imagine, this is a large area and can get relatively complex. The following class attempts to simplify one of the most common uses: the simple printing of text. Simply add the following class code to your project and use as directed.

It's worth noting that this class actually works, as opposed to the less-functional TextFilePrintDocument class bundled by Microsoft in the Windows Forms Quick-Start tutorials, which only reads from text files plus cuts out as soon as a blank line is encountered. This class is also neatly encapsulated and allows you to change its font through a simple property, unlike Microsoft's second attempt with its highly publicized 101 VB .NET Samples.

Here's the code:

```vb
Public Class TextPrint
    ' Inherits all the functionality of a PrintDocument
    Inherits Printing.PrintDocument
    ' Private variables to hold default font and text
    Private fntPrintFont As Font
    Private strText As String
    Public Sub New(ByVal Text As String)
        ' Sets the file stream
        MyBase.New()
        strText = Text
    End Sub
    Public Property Text() As String
        Get
            Return strText
        End Get
        Set(ByVal Value As String)
            strText = Value
        End Set
    End Property
    Protected Overrides Sub OnBeginPrint(ByVal ev As Printing.PrintEventArgs)
        ' Run base code
        MyBase.OnBeginPrint(ev)
        ' Sets the default font
        If fntPrintFont Is Nothing Then
            fntPrintFont = New Font("Times New Roman", 12)
        End If
    End Sub
    Public Property Font() As Font
        ' Allows the user to override the default font
        Get
            Return fntPrintFont
        End Get
        Set(ByVal Value As Font)
            fntPrintFont = Value
        End Set
    End Property
    Protected Overrides Sub OnPrintPage(ByVal ev _
        As Printing.PrintPageEventArgs)
        ' Provides the print logic for our document

        ' Run base code
```

```
MyBase.OnPrintPage(ev)
' Variables
Static intCurrentChar As Integer
Dim intPrintAreaHeight, intPrintAreaWidth, _
    intMarginLeft, intMarginTop As Integer
' Set printing area boundaries and margin coordinates
With MyBase.DefaultPageSettings
    intPrintAreaHeight = .PaperSize.Height - .Margins.Top - .Margins.Bottom
    intPrintAreaWidth = .PaperSize.Width - .Margins.Left - .Margins.Right
    intMarginLeft = .Margins.Left 'X
    intMarginTop = .Margins.Top   'Y
End With
' If Landscape set, swap printing height/width
If MyBase.DefaultPageSettings.Landscape Then
    Dim intTemp As Integer
    intTemp = intPrintAreaHeight
    intPrintAreaHeight = intPrintAreaWidth
    intPrintAreaWidth = intTemp
End If
' Calculate total number of lines
Dim intLineCount As Int32 = CInt(intPrintAreaHeight / Font.Height)
' Initialize rectangle printing area
Dim rectPrintingArea As New RectangleF(intMarginLeft, intMarginTop, _
    intPrintAreaWidth, intPrintAreaHeight)
' Initialise StringFormat class, for text layout
Dim objSF As New StringFormat(StringFormatFlags.LineLimit)
' Figure out how many lines will fit into rectangle
Dim intLinesFilled, intCharsFitted As Int32
ev.Graphics.MeasureString(Mid(strText, _
            UpgradeZeros(intCurrentChar)), Font, _
            New SizeF(intPrintAreaWidth, intPrintAreaHeight), objSF, _
            intCharsFitted, intLinesFilled)
' Print the text to the page
ev.Graphics.DrawString(Mid(strText, _
    UpgradeZeros(intCurrentChar)), Font, _
    Brushes.Black, rectPrintingArea, objSF)
' Increase current char count
intCurrentChar += intCharsFitted
' Check whether we need to print more
If intCurrentChar < strText.Length Then
    ev.HasMorePages = True
Else
    ev.HasMorePages = False
```

```
            intCurrentChar = 0
        End If
    End Sub
    Public Function UpgradeZeros(ByVal Input As Integer) As Integer
        ' Upgrades all zeros to ones
        ' - used as opposed to defunct IIF or messy If statements
        If Input = 0 Then
            Return 1
        Else
            Return Input
        End If
    End Function
End Class
```

We could use this class as follows:

```
' Create object, passing in text
Dim MyPrintObject As New TextPrint(TextBox1.Text)
' Set font, if required
MyPrintObject.Font = New Font("Tahoma", 8)
' Issue print command
MyPrintObject.Print()
```

The Secret Rebirth of `.PrintForm`

Download supporting files at www.apress.com.
The files for this tip are in the "Ch2–Print Form" folder.

If you've managed to print anything in .NET, you'll know it's no mean task. What, you may ask, happened to the old `.PrintForm` method of VB6 fame? Unfortunately, like a number of older features, it got sold out in the name of "standardization."

But don't fret: with just a few lines of extra code, we can bring it back from the dead. How? Simply follow these four easy steps:

1. Design your form as usual, adding all the required controls you wish to be printed.

2. From your toolbox, add one PictureBox, PrintDocument, and PrintDialog controls to your form. Your code will use these to support the printing of your form. For this code sample, I've named my controls MyPictureBox, MyPrintDocument, and MyPrintDialog, respectively. The PictureBox is the only "visible" control, which you can make invisible if you wish.

3. Add the following code behind your form. These routines perform the basic function of taking a screenshot and sending the results to the printer. The main method is PrintForm:

```
Public Sub PrintForm()
    ' Takes a screenshot, then initiates the print
    GrabScreen()
    MyPrintDialog.Document = MyPrintDocument
    If MyPrintDialog.ShowDialog = DialogResult.OK Then
        MyPrintDocument.Print()
    End If
End Sub


' API call to help generate final screenshot
Private Declare Auto Function BitBlt Lib "gdi32.dll" _
    (ByVal hdcDest As IntPtr, ByVal nXDest As Integer, _
    ByVal nYDest As Integer, ByVal nWidth As Integer, _
    ByVal nHeight As Integer, ByVal hdcSrc As IntPtr, _
    ByVal nXSrc As Integer, ByVal nYSrc As Integer, _
    ByVal dwRop As System.Int32) As Boolean


' Variable to store screenshot
Private bmpScreenshot As Bitmap


Private Sub GrabScreen()
    ' Performs a screenshot, saving results to bmpScreenshot
    Dim objGraphics As Graphics = Me.CreateGraphics
    Dim objSize As Size = Me.Size
    Const SRCCOPY As Integer = &HCC0020

    bmpScreenshot = New Bitmap(objSize.Width, _
        objSize.Height, objGraphics)
    Dim objGraphics2 As Graphics = objGraphics.FromImage _
        (bmpScreenshot)
    Dim deviceContext1 As IntPtr = objGraphics.GetHdc
    Dim deviceContext2 As IntPtr = objGraphics2.GetHdc

    BitBlt(deviceContext2, 0, 0, Me.ClientRectangle.Width, _
        Me.ClientRectangle.Height, deviceContext1, 0, 0, SRCCOPY)
    objGraphics.ReleaseHdc(deviceContext1)
    objGraphics2.ReleaseHdc(deviceContext2)
End Sub
```

```
Private Sub MyPrintDocument_PrintPage(ByVal _
    sender As System.Object, ByVal e As _
    System.Drawing.Printing.PrintPageEventArgs) _
    Handles MyPrintDocument.PrintPage
    ' Method that handles the printing
    Dim objImageToPrint As Graphics = e.Graphics
    objImageToPrint.DrawImage(bmpScreenshot, 0, 0)
    bmpScreenshot.Dispose()
    objImageToPrint.Dispose()
    e.HasMorePages = False
End Sub
```

4. Add a Print button to your control, add code to run the PrintForm method, and then simply wait and let our code run its magic. Don't forget, you may wish to make certain controls (such as the Print button itself) invisible before running the PrintForm method, then making it visible again afterward.

And that's quite simply all you need to print your form. Admittedly, it's not as easy as .PrintForm, but when the code is already written and ready to roll, who's complaining?

The Facts on Visual Inheritance

Visual inheritance allows you to create one "master" form, and then have other Windows forms inherit its layout and code. For example, you might create one master form for your program's wizard, and then add further wizard forms that automatically inherit its appearance and functionality, customizing each as appropriate.

To use visual inheritance, first design and code your master form, then build your application (Ctrl+Shift+B). Next, select Project ➤ Add Inherited Form from the menu. Enter a name, click on Open, and choose the form you wish to inherit from. Then, further customize this form to meet your needs.

It's worth noting that any changes you make here will not alter your original form; rather, they will just override the original settings inherited from your master form.

Looking at Windows, Performance Counters, and More

Building great applications isn't all about amazing code snippets that can make your programs look great and run like the wind. It's also about being intelligent—and one big part of that is the ability for your program to look at the world around it (Windows) and figure out exactly what's happening.

Well, as you can imagine, this is one obviously huge area, so I'll be brief and provide just a few core code tips that'll give you a great starting point when trying to find out just what you want.

First off, to find out about your current environment—such as command-line arguments, the user domain name, tick count, and so on—simply explore the System.Environment class. There's no need for any sticky API calls. Here's a System.Environment example that retrieves the name of the current version of Windows:

```
x = System.Environment.OSVersion.ToString
```

To discover more about the actual system itself—such as the computer name, number of monitors attached, whether visual aids should be used rather than audio, the default icon size, and so on—check out the System.Windows.Forms.SystemInformation class. Here's an example that checks whether the computer booted normally (that is, didn't use safe mode):

```
If System.Windows.Forms.SystemInformation.BootMode = _
    BootMode.Normal Then
        ' Computer booted in normal mode
End If
```

Finally, performance counters are an excellent way of tapping into exactly what the system is up to. This is one huge subject on its own, and a mound of books has already been written on the subject. However, in brief, performance counters report on the status of the system and its applications. They're predefined and return a number, which you can look at in a variety of formats (an instantaneous figure, an average, percentage, et cetera).

Examples include the amount of system memory available, a processor's busy time, the number of ASP.NET applications running, or even how many SQL Server connections you have open. (See Figure 2-13.)

You can browse the existing performance monitors by using the Server Explorer (View ➤ Server Explorer), expanding upon your server and exploring the Performance Counters node. If you see an item you think you'll want to use in your code, you can drag it onto your form and manipulate the newly created PerformanceCounter object in code, or just do it all in code. The following snippet demonstrates the latter, displaying the amount of available memory in a message box:

```
Dim perfFreeMemory As New PerformanceCounter("Memory", _
    "Available MBytes")
MessageBox.Show("There are " & perfFreeMemory.NextValue & _
    "MB of memory available on your system. This program requires more.")
```

A bundle of .NET-specific performance counters are available, too—and good system administrators will be more than familiar with these figures, which you can analyze through the PerfMon.exe tool. The .NET revolution also allows you to set up your own custom performance counters with ease, recording data such as the number of sales per second. You can learn more about all of this by looking up "performance counters" in the help index, and then browsing the subcategories.

> **TOP TIP** *If you're attempting to use performance monitors in ASP.NET applications, you may initially find yourself experiencing a bundle of "Access denied" error messages. That's because .NET is picky about exactly who can and can't see this system information. You can resolve this by following the security guidelines at* http://aspnet.4guysfromrolla.com/articles/041002-1.aspx, *or if you're simply wanting to retrieve data such as how long your Web server has been up, check out my tips in the next chapter.*

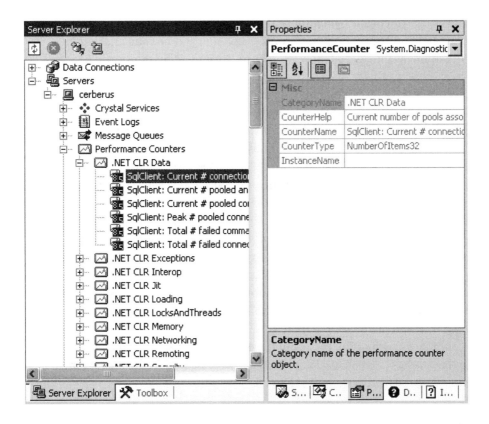

Figure 2-13. Viewing the available performance counters through the Server Explorer

Protecting Your Code with Obfuscation

Just how safe is your source code? It's a topic few developers consider until it's too late, but it's most certainly worth considering, especially when working with vulnerable Windows applications.

When you build your assembly, your project is compiled down to Microsoft Intermediate Language (MSIL) code. You can view this code and extra "metadata" information by using a tool such as ILDASM.exe (found within the depths of the VS .NET directory) to open a regular assembly.

True, it isn't especially easy to read nor follow, but it also isn't that difficult to get the gist of what's happening in your program. You'll also note that important strings, such as database passwords, are easily exposed for the world to see.

And that's not all: a new wave of .NET decompilers has swept onto the market that can take an assembly and turn it back into the original source code within seconds.

How can you protect your application? The only real route is to use an "obfuscator," an application that "jumbles up" your source code, making the logic extremely difficult to follow. More sophisticated obfuscators also encrypt strings, lay "decompiler" tricks, create difficult-to-follow program flows, and remove excess data, thereby reducing the size of the final assembly.

One such obfuscator is the cheesy-named Dotfuscator, available in both Community and Professional editions. Users of Visual Studio .NET 2003 ("Everett") will find they already have the Community edition installed on their machine in Programs ➤ Microsoft Visual Studio .NET 2003 ➤ Visual Studio .NET Tools ➤ Dotfuscator Community Edition, whereas VS .NET 2002 users can download this free version from `www.preemptive.com/dotfuscator/dotcomdld.html`.

Produced by the software group PreEmptive, this "lite" version performs basic obfuscation on any assembly. It ships with only a noncommercial license, however, which means that you'll need to upgrade if you're using it professionally.

How do you use it? Unfortunately, like the interface, you'll find the help file relatively unhelpful. However, for basic obfuscation, simply launch the application, create a new project, add your file via the Trigger tab, select the destination directory via the Build tab, and then select File ➤ Build.

For more information, check out the official FAQ at `www.preemptive.com/dotfuscator/DotfuscatorFAQ.html` or look up "Dotfuscator" in the help index (ensure that the filter is set to "No Filter").

Best of All Worlds: Creating an Ultra-Thin Client

Chat with any modern developer about a new system you require and they'll instantly start talking about Web-based applications. Why? There's a very simple reason: because "fat" Windows programs are just too difficult to maintain.

Who has which version? How can you ensure that all your employees start using the new system at the same time? There are workarounds… but why bother, when you can simply create a Web application?

The problem is that "thin" Web applications are inflexible. They don't give you full control. Your typical Web page can't send something to the user's printer, nor save files to a special area on the hard drive. They're also often slow or unavailable.

In brief, Windows programs are much better in terms of control, but worse in terms of maintainability. Web applications are great in terms of maintainability, but terrible in terms of control.

But what if you could solve this problem, by automatically updating your Windows applications? You can, with just a few lines of extra code. And, over the next couple of pages, I'm going to share my two favorite techniques for doing just that.

Downloading Code "Live" from a Web Server

This first technique works best for smaller applications, or programs that have portions of them that update frequently. It's based on something called *reflection*, a new .NET method of allowing your code to "see" other code, a sort of more-advanced late binding.

Here's how it works: you begin by creating the portion of your application that requires updating. (It may even be an entire program in its own right.) Then you make your assembly available on a Web server, typically via your intranet.

Next, you create your nonupdating application: this could simply be a small "loader" application, or a regular program with a link to the updating portion that you created earlier. This application loads your assembly from the intranet and perhaps displays a form from inside that assembly, or creates an instance of a class and runs a function (this is the .NET *reflection* feature coming into play).

It may sound complicated, but there are really just a couple of lines of code you'll need to use. And here they are.

```
' Load assembly
Dim MyAssembly As System.Reflection.Assembly = _
    System.Reflection.Assembly.LoadFrom("http://address/app.exe")
' Create instance of the form and show it
Dim MyForm As Form = _
   MyAssembly.CreateInstance("YourAssemblyNamespace.Form1")
MyForm.Show()
```

Here, the code loads the assembly from a Web address, creates a new instance of the Form1 class within the assembly, and then shows that form. You could add this sort of code to the Sub Main method of your "loader" application, or behind one of your menu items—and, hey presto, you've got a *live* application. When you need to update, simply replace your assembly on the Web server.

Also, .NET is pretty clever. If the assembly you've "loaded" references another assembly, it will go back to your Web server to check for it. That means, http://address/ to check for it. That means, if you're feeling exceptionally smart, you might just want to split your "live" application out into multiple parts. For example, in this newly downloaded assembly, you may include a regular reference to another assembly and display a form from within that too. When the local machine spots this code, .NET will go back to the Web server, attempt to load that assembly, and then continue with your code. This way, you can split your application up into portions and access *on demand*. The method also stops any large delays in downloading assemblies, as the application is now split into many smaller "parts," all of which can work together without problem.

But, as ever, there's something you need to watch out for. It's security. By default, the .NET Framework only partially trusts applications downloaded from the Internet and hence restricts exactly what they can do on your machine.

To sort this situation, from the control panel, choose Administrative Tools ➤ Microsoft .NET Framework Wizards. Double-click on the Trust an Assembly option, specify your assembly Internet address and grant it full permissions. (On larger networks, a system administrator should be able to automate this for you.) Other workarounds include adding the site your assembly is hosted on to the list of Internet Explorer trusted sites, and then using the Adjust .NET Security wizard to grant all trusted sites with full permissions—but that's all for another day. Look up "code access security" in the help index for more information.

The Easy Way to Download Full Application Updates

Download supporting files at www.apress.com.
The files for this tip are in the "Ch2–Updater Component" folder.

However, it's more than possible that first solution won't suit you. Perhaps you've created a commercial application that won't be used inside a corporation with a speedy intranet. Rather than downloading a fresh assembly every time a portion of your program is accessed, you simply want it to check for updates over the Web and download the latest version of the whole program, if available.

That's absolutely possible, but slightly more complicated.

But why do more work than you have to? Microsoft has already written its own free .NET application updater component, which has just been released online at www.gotdotnet.com/team/windowsforms/appupdater.aspx. (You'll also find a copy with the downloadable source code for this book.)

The component comes with full source, samples, and a walkthrough. It can easily check for an update, prompt your user to download the upgrade, replace your core assembly, and it even has support for on-demand installation. And hundreds of lines of code to handle all this processing have already been written for you. It's one of my personal favorites and definitely worth checking out.

Well, that's how to automatically update your Windows programs and have the best of both worlds: complete control and no maintenance worries.

Enter stage left: return of the fat client. Hurrah and hujjah!

CHAPTER 3

Web Sites in Seconds!

A COUPLE OF YEARS AGO, the computing world saw a great divide. Developers found themselves in one of two categories: those who created programs for the desktop, such as Visual Basic wizards, and those who specialized in writing applications for the Web, such as ASP developers.

With .NET, this digital divide no longer exists. Microsoft has revamped its old Active Server Pages (ASP) technology, renaming it ASP.NET and bundling it as part of the .NET Framework.

And because Visual Basic .NET is built on top of the .NET Framework, VB developers can now create amazingly interactive Web sites in the same amount of time it takes to knock together a regular "Hello World" Windows app.

That's right: for VB .NET developers, there's no new language to learn. There are a couple of fresh concepts, perhaps, but nothing drastic. ASP developers will experience a slight learning curve, but it's still relatively painless. The divide has been stitched up.

So, how can you create your own Web apps using your favorite programming language? Simply launch Visual Studio .NET and create a new ASP.NET Web application. This is created directly on your Web server, exposed through Internet Information Services (IIS).

After you create your project, you'll be presented with a Web form, along with a bundle of toolbox widgets. Similar to the way in which you create a Windows application, you just drag and drop controls onto your form. When you're ready, open the code window and respond to a Click event, or some such, writing a few lines to perhaps change the page or display a couple of search results.

That's it—nothing too drastic, nothing too different from what you already know. It's an *evolution*.

In this chapter, we're going to start by briefly reviewing the essentials of Web applications: what you need to get up and running, how to handle "postbacks," working with sessions... that sort of stuff.

Then we'll dive straight into the real gold: all those nifty ASP.NET secrets. I'll show you how to create a default Enter button (using a technique few ASP.NET developers know exist), I'll share blocks of ready-to-run code for dealing with uploaded files, I'll demonstrate the secrets of generating images on the fly, and I'll even reveal how you can save hours of development time by stealing Microsoft's own code.

Just read on....

The Essentials

Before we get started, let's go back to the basics and review all the essentials you need to know for developing your own ASP.NET application. You probably know most of this already, but it'll serve as a great refresher and an excellent desk reference. You'll find a couple of nicely wrapped functions for working with cookies and the Session object here, too.

- ASP.NET is part of the .NET Framework. Its predecessor was ASP. You need a minimum of Windows 2000/XP (or greater) with Internet Information Services 5.0 to run the ASP.NET portion of the .NET Framework.

- Using Visual Studio .NET, you can create ASP.NET Web applications. Each Web application typically consists of one or more Web forms, which each represent interactive ASPX pages on your site.

- To create a new Web application project in Visual Studio .NET, click File ➤ New ➤ Project, select the Visual Basic Projects project type, and choose the ASP.NET Web application template. Specify a Web address as the project location, and click on OK.

- By default, a Web page opens in GridLayout, which positions controls "absolutely" on a page. To change this, select DOCUMENT in the Properties window and change the pageLayout property to FlowLayout.

- To create a Web application using VB .NET, paint your Toolbox controls onto a Web form, set properties as appropriate, and add Visual Basic code to glue it all together.

- The toolbox contains two types of controls for use on ASP.NET Web pages: ASP.NET server controls and HTML controls. The ASP.NET Web Form controls are the most powerful, rendering on the server and allowing full programmatic control. The HTML controls are simply regular browser objects, such as a Submit button; this is the sort of control you could add through the likes of Microsoft FrontPage.

- Controls on ASP.NET Web pages don't have Name properties, as Windows applications do. Rather, they have an ID, which is exactly the same thing. It's the name you use to refer to the control in code.

- ASP.NET (part of the .NET Framework) intercepts every ASPX page request or postback made to your server. ASP.NET takes the information given, processes it, runs any relevant code, and then returns its HTML results to the client. Typically, all code is run on the server side.

- ASP.NET and its classes *think* before sending results back to the client. For example, if the client browser supports only HTML 3.2, it will attempt to send only pure HTML 3.2 back. If, however, the target client supports some of the more-advanced features you may have used in your pages, these are sent down the line.

- A postback occurs when your user makes a request to your Web page (by, say, clicking on an ASP.NET Button control on the page) and the browser resubmits its data to the Web server (to, say, run your VB .NET code behind the button). However, the code in your page Load event runs regardless of whether this is the first time a page has loaded or whether this is a postback. You can ensure that code in your page Load event runs only once by using code similar to the following:

```
If Page.IsPostBack = False Then
    ' This code runs only once
End If
```

- If you've used ASP in the past, you'll be happy to know the Application, Response, Request, Server, Session, and User objects are all still available to you. They may work slightly differently, but their core responsibilities remain the same.

- In Web forms, the "state" of your controls is maintained automatically, unlike with regular ASP. This is done using a hidden __VIEWSTATE field. For example, the __VIEWSTATE may store the Text property of a Label control, ensuring that that property remains consistent as the user posts back a form, and so on.

- The Session object allows you to store information about an individual's "session" with your application. For example, you may store a visitor's name, the last product they looked at, or the items in their online shopping basket. Following are common functions for storing and retrieving items from the Session object (for the "Page" argument, pass in your current page—which you can refer to by using the Me keyword—as a parameter):

```
Public Sub AddItemToSession(ByVal ItemName As String, _
    ByVal Item As Object, ByVal Page As System.Web.UI.Page)
        ' Adds an item to the current session
        ' Sample usage from within an ASP.NET page:
        ' - AddItemToSession( "Username", "John", Me)
    If IsItemInSession(Page, ItemName) Then
        Page.Session.Item(ItemName) = Item
    Else
        Page.Session.Add(ItemName, Item)
```

```
        End If
    End Sub

    Public Function GetItemFromSession(ByVal ItemName As String, _
        ByVal Page As System.Web.UI.Page) As Object
        ' Returns an item from the current session
        If IsItemInSession(Page, ItemName) Then _
            Return Page.Session.Item(ItemName)
    End Function

    Public Function IsItemInSession(ByVal ItemName As String, _
        ByVal Page As System.Web.UI.Page) As Boolean
        ' Returns a true if item with ItemName is in session
        If Not Page.Session.Item(ItemName) Is Nothing Then Return True
    End Function

    Public Sub ClearSession(ByVal Page As System.Web.UI.Page)
        ' Clears the session
        Page.Session.Clear()
    End Sub
```

- The Application object *works* in exactly the same way as the Session object. However, the difference is that, whereas the Session object can hold information for every unique visitor, the Application object holds one set of data for the whole application. So, use the Session object when you want to store and retrieve information for the current user, and use the Application object when you want to store and retrieve something for all users, such as a commonly accessed data set.

- Information stored in the Session object expires after a default time period of twenty minutes. This period can be changed by editing the Web.config file. Data in the Application object stays alive while your actual ASP.NET Web application is running (that is, while your site actually has live visitors that haven't "expired").

- You can add code to run when your ASP.NET Web application starts or ends or when a Session starts or ends through the Global.asax file in your application. You can also add controls to the Design mode of this file: adding a timer, for example, will enable you to run code at set intervals whenever your application is running. The Global.asax file is sometimes referred to as the *ASP.NET application file*, and you can see why.

- Cookies allow you to store information more permanently, through your users' machines. The following functions allow you to easily set and retrieve cookie values. This is a simple "one-value cookie" implementation, but more sample code can be found by looking up "Cookies1 sample" and "Cookies2 sample" in the help index.

```
Public Sub SetCookie(ByVal Item As String, _
   ByVal Value As String, ByVal Page As System.Web.UI.Page)
   ' Sends a cookie down to the user
   ' Sample usage from within an ASP.NET page:
   '  SetCookie("Username", "John", Me)

   Dim objCookie As New System.Web.HttpCookie(Item, Value)
      objCookie.Expires = DateTime.MaxValue
   Page.Response.AppendCookie(objCookie)
End Sub


Public Function GetCookie(ByVal Item As String, _
   ByVal Page As System.Web.UI.Page) As String
   ' Retrieves a value from a cookie
   ' Sample usage from within an ASP.NET page:
   '  x = GetCookie("Username", Me)
   Dim objCookies As System.Web.HttpCookieCollection
      objCookies = Page.Request.Cookies
   If Not objCookies Is Nothing Then
      If Not (objCookies.Item(Item) Is Nothing) Then
         Return objCookies.Item(Item).Value
      End If
   End If
End Function
```

- Query strings allow you to pass values in the URL of a Web page request. For example, a search at Google.com for "Visual Basic" will take you to http://www.google.com/search?q=Visual+Basic, where the query string is everything after the question mark. You can see here that we have one parameter called "q" that has a value of "Visual Basic". (The + is an encoded space, which is sometimes referred to as a "GET" request.) You can use the Page.Request.QueryString object to examine the value of a parameter. The following function attempts to simplify the process:

```
Public Function GetQueryString(ByVal ItemName As String, _
   ByVal Page As System.Web.UI.Page) As String
   ' Returns a string from the query string parameter or
   ' nothing if unavailable (allowing you to check for Nothing)
```

```
' Sample usage from within an ASP.NET page:
' - GetQueryString("q", Me)
If Not Page.Request.QueryString.Item(ItemName) Is Nothing Then
    Return Page.Request.QueryString.Item(ItemName).ToString
End If
End Function
```

- To encode a string for use in a query string, use the `Server.UrlEncode` function. To decode a query string parameter, use the `Server.UrlDecode` function.

- To find out the server path of your Web application for, say, saving an uploaded file to a directory or reading a file on the server, use the `Server.MapPath` function. You'll also need to ensure that you have appropriate read/write permissions. To find out your server name, use the `Server.MachineName` property.

- Debugging your Web application is as simple as debugging a regular Windows application. To mark a line for debugging, move to the line and press F9. To run your application, select Debug ➤ Start (or press F5) and interact through your Web browser. When your marked line of code is encountered, the application will pause and allow you to step through each line by selecting Debug ➤ Step Into (or pressing F8).

- Compiling your application consists of selecting Build from the Build menu. This generates a DLL file in your project's Bin folder, which contains your code and powers your ASPX pages.

- The default configuration for any solution is Debug, which creates "debug files" when you compile your application. Before releasing your final version, change the configuration (visible on the Standard toolbar or by selecting the menu item Build ➤ Configuration Manager) from Debug to Release, which removes all the debug symbols and optimizes your code further. It also stops unsightly code being displayed in your error messages.

- ASP and ASP.NET Web pages can work alongside each other without problem. This means that porting a larger Web site can be easily broken down into stages, upgrading just the pages you have redeveloped.

Developer Secrets

Being a relatively new area, few developers have yet had the chance to really dive into the nitty gritty of ASP.NET. Thankfully, I have, and in this chapter I'm going to share more developer secrets with you than anywhere else in this book. Let's look at the list.

User Interface

- Five-Step Checklist for the Validation Controls

- Displaying Web Warning Messages: Technique 1

- Displaying Web Warning Messages: Technique 2

- Unveiled: How to Create a Default Enter Button

- Wonders of the Little-Known SmartNavigation Property

- The Secret Behind User Controls

- Why the Panel Control Is Super Useful

- Moving List Items Up and Down, Easily

- Resizing in Web Applications

- Stopping Your User from Right-Clicking

- Creating Scrollable Micro Windows

- Why You Should Learn CSS

Code Techniques

- Three Steps to Changing your Page Title in Code

- How to Automatically Fill Out Email Fields

- Sending Mail in ASP.NET

- The Trick to Creating User-Friendly URLs

- Adding Real-Time HTML to Your Page

- The Secret to Uploading Files with Ease

- Storing Uploaded Files in Your Database

- Working with Uploaded Images

- Creating Images Dynamically

- Code for Generating Thumbnails on the Fly

- Five Steps to ASP.NET Authentication

- Forms Authentication, Without Web.config

- Authenticating Just Part of Your Site

- The Best Place to Store Your Settings

- Steal Fantastic Forum Code from Microsoft and Save Yourself Hours

- Integrating with PayPal's Instant Payment Notification

Optimization, Errors, and Other Tips

- Subfolders in Web Applications: Confused?

- Choosing a Directory Other Than c:\inetpub\wwwroot\

- Creating Super-Fast ASP.NET Applications, with Caching

- Nine Steps to Successful Debugging

- Hiding Error Code from your Clients

- Forget 404: Customizing Your "Page Not Found"

- `Server.Transfer` vs. `Response.Redirect`

- Using `.IsClientConnected` for Long Processes

- Preventing Client Caching, with Meta Tags

- Uploading Files Larger Than 4MB

- What to Do When `Session_End` Doesn't Work

- Spying on Your Web Host: Checking Uptime in .NET

- Can It Cope?—Stress Testing Your Web Apps

- The Two Methods of Moving Web Servers

- Where to Put Your Files with an ASP.NET Host

- Uh-oh: Installing IIS After Visual Studio .NET

Raring to go? Get ready to delve into the wonderful world of ASP.NET....

User Interface

From adding your own default Enter button to the real secret behind user controls, this section deals in all the ASP.NET tips and techniques concerning things your surfer actually sees: the user interface. And we open with the...

Five-Step Checklist for the Validation Controls

In the olden days of ASP, one big developer nightmare was trying to validate information coming from the users. What if they entered the word "sixty-three" instead of the numeral "63" in the age field? You can hardly put that into a numeric SQL Server field. What if they entered "not@home" as their email address? Don't think so, user.

So, developers had to figure out validation, and it was a long and arduous battle.

Thankfully, ASP.NET includes a whole bundle of server controls specially designed to handle this task and save a mound of time in the process. The controls are as follows:

- RequiredFieldValidator: Use this when you have a field that needs a value entered, such as a password box on a login screen.

- CompareValidator: Use this to compare two items, such as ensuring that the values of two boxes contain the same information (that is, for a double email check) or that a box contains a number above a defined value.

- RangeValidator: Use this to check that an item is within a particular range, such as a box containing an income value between $20,000 and $30,000.

- RegularExpressionValidator: Use this to check an item against a regular expression, such as checking a box containing an email address against the regular expression "\w+([-+.]\w+)*@\w+([-.]\w+)*\.\w+([-.]\w+)*" (which describes a valid email address. I know: it's confusing).

- CustomValidator: Use this when you want to run your own custom client-side JavaScript or VBScript functions.

How do you use these controls? Well, they're all actually incredibly simple. Here's my five-step checklist to using any of these controls on your Web page.

1. Drag the validation control that most suits your function onto your Web page, perhaps next to the control you wish to validate.

2. Change the `Display` property of your control to `Dynamic`. By default, the Web page leaves room for the error message, even before it's displayed, and having an invisible block of white on your page doesn't always look very good. Changing this property to `Dynamic` means the space is allocated as and when required.

3. Change the `ControlToValidate` property, using the dropdown list to select a control on your Web Form. This is the input control you wish to check ("validate"), such as a TextBox or ListBox.

4. Change the `ErrorMessage` property to something a little more English than its current value (for example, "Please enter an email address!").

5. That's it, if you're using the RequiredFieldValidator. However, for all other validation controls:

    a) CompareValidator: If you're wanting to compare the value of two controls, change the `ControlToCompare`, `Operator`, and `Type` properties as appropriate. If you're wanting to compare the control to a value, change the `ValueToCompare`, `Operator`, and `Type` properties.

    b) RangeValidator: Select the minimum and maximum values in the `MinimumValue` and `MaximumValue` properties, respectively. You may also need to change the `Type` property to `Currency`, or `Integer`, for example.

    c) RegularExpression: Select a fresh regular expression from the list, through the `ValidationExpression` property, such as Internet URL or U.S. ZIP Code. Alternatively, you can specify your own: Chapter 8 "Unveiled: The Hidden .NET Language" discusses nothing but regular expressions. Oh, the laughs.

    d) CustomValidator: This is a little trickier. Firstly, you need to write a function behind your Web page in either JavaScript or VBScript, which passes back a value, depending on whether your own custom data check has passed or not. Secondly, you need to set the `ClientValidationFunction` to the name of your function. If you want to try this, your best bet is to click on the `ClientValidationFunction` property and press F1: the help displays a highly useful sample you'll be able to adopt for your own use.

And that's it. Every time your user tries to click on a button on your Web page that has its `CausesValidation` property set to `True`, the validation routines kick in. These run on the client side in JavaScript, validating information and displaying error messages as appropriate. If validation isn't successful, the form isn't "allowed" to be submitted.

But what happens if the users' browser does not support JavaScript, or JavaScript is disabled? As a double-check, validation also occurs on the server. But let's imagine your user has clicked an important button to add information to your database. Although the validation may have run on the server, your button code still runs—and could potentially add a load of "bad" information to your database. As such, all code that relies on "good" data needs to check that validation has passed, like this:

```
If Page.IsValid = True Then
    ' No problems, continue
End If
```

This checks to see whether the page `IsValid` property equals `True`. This means that validation has passed and there were no problems, so you can merrily continue, rather than processing all that potentially dodgy data.

One last point: the ValidationSummary control provides an overview of errors raised on your page. Simply add it at a convenient location on your page, and it'll summarize any errors on your behalf. It can also display the errors in a message box to ensure that your user gets the idea. Key properties to change here are `HeaderText`, `DisplayMode`, `ShowMessageBox`, and `ShowSummary`.

Displaying Web Warning Messages: Technique 1

Download supporting files at www.apress.com.
The files for this tip are in the "Ch3—Warning 1" folder.

One of the problems in trying to dish out warnings on a Web page is that it's all very passive. Not awfully in-your-face. You can't always force a reaction, as you can with a Windows application.

That's why I like this little tip. It's a simple five-step method of raising a JavaScript alert warning (a message box on a Web page) that you can call with just one line of code from anywhere on your ASP.NET Web page. Here's how to set it up.

1. Switch to the HTML view of your Web form and add the following immediately after the close of the <body> tag:

```
<script>
<asp:Literal id="ltlAlert" runat="server"
    EnableViewState="False">
 </asp:Literal>
</script>
```

2. Switch back to Design view and save your Web form. This has set up your Literal server control manually. You couldn't have done this visually, due to the <script> tags we needed to add.

3. Enter the code window behind your Web form and add the following line beneath the Public Class and Inherits lines, which allows us to manipulate this control in code:

```
Protected WithEvents ltlAlert As System.Web.UI.WebControls.Literal
```

4. Add the following code snippet behind your Web form. This takes a string and incorporates it into a JavaScript "alert" command, which is then placed on the Web page as pure HTML:

```
Private Sub Say(ByVal Message As String)
    ' Format string properly
    Message = Message.Replace("'", "\'")
    Message = Message.Replace(Convert.ToChar(10), "\n")
    Message = Message.Replace(Convert.ToChar(13), "")
    ' Display as JavaScript alert
    ltlAlert.Text = "alert('" & Message & "')"
End Sub
```

5. Whenever you want to display an in-your-face message, simply call this Say function in your code, as the following snippet demonstrates (see Figure 3-1 to see it in action.):

```
Say("Sorry, your password is invalid! " & _
    Microsoft.VisualBasic.vbNewLine & _
    "Please try again, or click Signup to register now.")
```

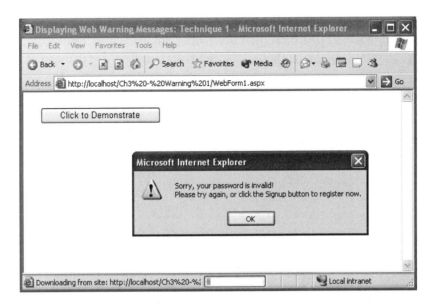

Figure 3-1. An in-your-face Web error messages with just one line of code!

Displaying Web Warning Messages: Technique 2

Download supporting files at www.apress.com.
The files for this tip are in the "Ch3—Warning 2" folder.

At times you may want to draw attention to an important message but without being overly loud. Sometimes, all you want to say is "Thank you! Your information has been stored" or "Finished: All your outstanding reviews have been completed."

In these situations, a message box is a little bit of overkill. Slightly more placid is the technique of displaying a whole Web page with just your core message at its center. I also prefer to add automatic redirects on such pages, so that, after a few seconds, the user gets taken back to the previous page, or through to the next.

You can achieve this goal in two different ways. The first is to create a separate page that perhaps accepts a message in the query string, displays that message, and then redirects your user to the new page.

Alternatively, you can do it *wholly* in code, which is just what we're going to do here. I've created a small method holding the HTML for a simple Web page (although you could perhaps load the text from a file). Inside that page, you'll find numerous "variables" (such as "%message-title%') that get replaced by the method. When ready, we push the modified HTML down the wire as a response to our client.

The HTML also contains a HTTP Refresh command, which by default takes the user back to the previous page. So, in brief, when you call the function, it displays your message for a number of seconds and then returns to the issuing page. (See Figure 3-2.)

Here's the function you'll need:

```
Public Sub DisplayMessage(ByVal MessageTitle As String, _
    ByVal MessageDetails As String, _
    Optional ByVal PageTitle As String = "Attention!", _
    Optional ByVal DelayInSeconds As Integer = 2)
    ' Core HTML, with refresh
    Dim strResponse As String = "<html><head><title>" & _
        "%page-title%</title><META HTTP-EQUIV=""Refresh"" " & _
        "CONTENT=""%delay%; url=javascript:history.back();"">" & _
        "</head><body><div align=""center""><center>" & _
        "<table border=""0"" cellpadding=""0"" cellspacing=""0"" " & _
        "width=""100%"" height=""100%""><tr><td width=""100%"">" & _
        "<p align=""center""><b><font face=""Arial"" size=""6"">" & _
        "%message-title%</font></b></p><p align=""center"">" & _
        "<font face=""Arial"" size=""3""><b>%message-details%</b>" & _
        "</font></td></tr></table></center></div></body></html>"
    ' Replace defaults
    strResponse = strResponse.Replace("%page-title%", PageTitle)
    strResponse = strResponse.Replace("%message-title%", MessageTitle)
    strResponse = strResponse.Replace("%message-details%", _
        MessageDetails)
    strResponse = strResponse.Replace("%delay%", _
        DelayInSeconds.ToString)
    ' Display response
    Response.Clear()
    Response.Write(strResponse)
    Response.End()
End Sub
```

Go try it out. It's neat, it's simple, and it's suitable for the majority of regular user messages.

Don't forget: this is the raw version. You can very easily modify it to take your user to another page, just by adding an extra parameter. Maybe you want to make the whole error page template driven. Either way, this snippet is at least a good step in the right direction.

Figure 3-2. Another way to display messages, albeit somewhat "quieter" than the last

Unveiled: How to Create a Default Enter Button

This is one of those little code snippets you can pull your hair out trying to find. And no help file nor book I've come across actually makes a reference to it. So, surely it can't be that important?

Imagine you've created an ASP.NET Web page with a search button. The user taps a phrase into a textbox and presses Enter. On most regular Web pages (think Google), the form would be submitted and the results returned. In other words, the search button is automatically "clicked" for you.

However, on an ASP.NET Web page, pressing the Enter key resubmits the form to the server, but doesn't actually do anything... which is pretty useless, really.

So, how do you set a default button to be clicked when the user presses Enter? Simply add the following line to your page Load event, replacing "btnSearch" with the name of your button:

```
Page.RegisterHiddenField("__EVENTTARGET", "btnSearch")
```

This line of code uses a hidden Page method called RegisterHiddenField, which adds a hidden field to your form associating __EVENTTARGET with the name of your button. When you press Enter on a control, such as a TextBox, the browser recognizes this standard hidden field and "clicks" on the button for you.

Wonders of the Little-Known SmartNavigation *Property*

Smart navigation is a little-known Internet Explorer feature that enables the individual controls on your Web forms to maintain focus between postbacks, as well as allows you to suppress that flicker that occurs as you load the new page.

To turn on this little-known feature, simply set the smartNavigation property of your ASPX page to True. You can also apply the property to all project pages, by adding the <pages> tag to the following location within your Web.config file:

```
<configuration>
<system.web>
<pages smartNavigation="true"/>
</system.web>
</configuration>
```

Note that smart navigation works on only Internet Explorer 5 and above; however, ASP.NET will automatically detect this and serve up the "smart" code only if the target browser supports it.

Also, I'd personally advise that you test it against any third-party menu controls or scripts you may have running: it is prone to falling over on particularly advanced pages.

The Secret Behind User Controls

User controls are an often misunderstood arrow in your ASP.NET quiver. They're not difficult, and they're not exclusively reserved for large Web sites, but they could save you hours in development time.

So, what exactly *are* they? Well, if you've used ASP before, a Web user control is essentially an include file with frills. For everyone else, they're a method of creating a piece of a page once, and then including it on numerous other Web pages.

For example, you may have a green menu with pretty icons, each linking to a different part of your site. You really don't want to go designing that manually for every single page. Rather, create the menu once as a user control, then go slot it onto your other pages where necessary. You could do the same with a "Subscribe to our newsletter" box. Or the header logo on your site. Or the copyright notice.

Here's how you can get started with user controls in four easy steps.

1. In your Web application project, select Project ➤ Add Web User Control from the menu. Choose a name and click on Open.

2. Start designing your user control. Don't forget: this shouldn't be a complete Web page but rather a small subset, such as a login box or copyright notice. Add code just as you would with a regular ASP.NET Web form.

3. When finished, close and save your user control.

4. On the page you want to use or test your user control, drag and drop the ASCX file from the Solution Explorer onto your page. You may drop it directly onto a raw page or position it within a table cell.

That's it! Admittedly, the gray glyph may look a little drab now, but, as soon as you run your application, it'll be replaced with whatever functionality you've built into your user control. And you can use this same user control again and again, on as many pages as you wish. When you need to make changes, however, you have to edit only one file.

What a perfect way to save time and duplication of efforts!

Don't forget the real secret here: you can't overuse user controls. They're useful *everywhere*. If you think something is going to occur more than two or three times on your site, turn it into a user control.

> **TOP TIP** *Many developers are discouraged from getting to grips with user controls due to the way they're shown in VS .NET at design time: as that small gray glyph. You can't change this, but you can make the situation easier by setting aside areas in which to "put" controls. For example, you may create a table and place your header control inside a specifically sized cell at the top of the page. Or you may draw out a Panel control and put the user control inside that. Using these techniques, you can at least "reserve" areas of the page for your controls to fill. For more clever ways of utilizing Web user controls, including through "template" pages, download the book source code from www.apress.com and check out ReadMe.txt.*

Why the Panel Control Is Super Useful

The Panel control is often overlooked as being one of those features that ASP.NET threw into the pack for completeness, despite the fact that no one would ever *really* use it. Incorrect!

One really amazing use for the Panel control is partitioning bits of HTML off from the rest. As an example, you may have a page that displays information about an employee. The page may have different sections depending on what information it has about the individual: background, education, references, photograph, and so on.

The problem is that not all of that information may be available, and displaying a whole section when no data is present seems pretty pointless. This is an instance where we'd be able to use the Panel control to hold the individual sections on your page, then choose to make the appropriate sections visible or invisible in code, as appropriate.

You could do something similar with a logon panel: one panel could display a username and password box while the other provides links for those who have already had their credentials validated. You could then make either one or the other invisible, depending on the logon status.

How can you do all this? It's simple. Just add the Panel control to your form, perhaps setting its Width property to 100% if you wish to spread it across the available width. Next, start designing and coding within the panel, adding server controls, text, images, and anything you want. Do this for each "section" you want to create.

Then, to make the HTML behind a panel visible or invisible to the client, simply set its Visible property in code. No problem! (See Figure 3-3.)

One quick tip: if you have already designed your page in a designer such as FrontPage and want to create these panel "regions" yourself, simply move the <asp:Panel> opening and closing tags, placing them around the HTML you want to appear or disappear, then get manipulating in code.

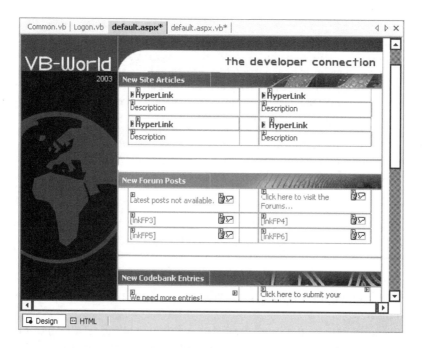

Figure 3-3. It's difficult to see, but the New Forum Posts section is contained inside a Panel control. If there are no posts or there's a problem connecting to the server, it isn't displayed. Another excellent use.

Moving List Items Up and Down, Easily

 Download supporting files at www.apress.com.
The files for this tip are in the "Ch3—Move List Items" folder.

It's common practice to have a bundle of items in a list and have the user sort them, using Up and Down buttons. However, the code for such a simple-sounding operation is, alas, a little more difficult.

Your best bet is to encapsulate such logic into a neatly wrapped function to save time and help debugging. Or, even better, just copy my own ready-to-run snippets, functions to easily move entries up and down for you:

```
Public Sub MoveSelectedItemUp(ByVal List As _
   System.Web.UI.WebControls.ListControl)
      ' Move the selected item in the passed ListBox
      ' up one, if possible. Sample usage:
      ' - MoveSelectedItemUp(ListBox1)
      If Not List.SelectedItem Is Nothing Then
          Dim objListItem As System.Web.UI.WebControls.ListItem, _
            intPosition As Integer
          objListItem = List.SelectedItem
          intPosition = List.Items.IndexOf(objListItem)
          List.Items.Remove(objListItem)
          List.Items.Insert(IIf(intPosition = 0, 0, _
            intPosition - 1), objListItem)
      End If
End Sub

Public Sub MoveSelectedItemDown(ByVal List As _
   System.Web.UI.WebControls.ListControl)
      ' Move the selected item in the passed ListBox
      ' down one, if possible
      If Not List.SelectedItem Is Nothing Then
          Dim objListItem As System.Web.UI.WebControls.ListItem, _
            intPosition As Integer
          objListItem = List.SelectedItem
          intPosition = List.Items.IndexOf(objListItem)
          If intPosition = List.Items.Count - 1 Then Exit Sub
          List.Items.Remove(objListItem)
          List.Items.Insert(intPosition + 1, objListItem)
      End If
End Sub
```

Simply call either `MoveSelectedItemUp` or `MoveSelectedItemDown` as relevant, passing in your list control, like so:

```
MoveSelectedItemDown(ListBox1)
```

A lot of code for a simple operation, yes—but at least you didn't have to write it!

Resizing in Web Applications

Windows applications now have amazingly powerful methods for automatically resizing the controls on your forms. Web applications, however, have no official method to control sizing.

So the trick is to learn how to use percentages. For example, imagine that you have a TextBox server control inside a table. If you want that textbox to take up the entire table width, no matter how the page or table is resized, change its `Width` property to `100%`.

Strangely, this is a little-known ASP.NET developer technique. Most tend to know that you can use percentages when it comes to tables and frames, but few know that controls can be sized this way also.

So, where possible, use percentages. They'll allow your entire application to look smart at any size.

Stopping Your User from Right-Clicking

Want to prevent your user from performing any of the other commands available by right-clicking on a Web page in Internet Explorer? It's not foolproof, but this neat little HTML edit usually does the trick.

Just alter the opening `<body>` tag of your HTML to the following:

```
<BODY oncontextmenu="return false">
```

When the menu is requested, the `oncontextmenu` event runs, and we instantly cancel it using JavaScript. This is especially potent as a method for stopping the user from viewing your source, when used in conjunction with a menu-less browser window.

Great stuff!

Creating Scrollable Micro Windows

Imagine that you're displaying a large table of results on your page. Wouldn't it be nice to show the table inside a neat scrollable micro window, rather than serving up one big messy page?

It's completely possible, and it requires only the smallest of changes.

Here's a quick sample that demonstrates the technique. It uses a div tag and relevant sizing and overflow attributes to define the micro window. Nested between the opening and closing <div> tags is the content we want to encapsulate (in this case, the HTML from our data grid).

```
<div style="width:100%; height:200; overflow:auto;">
  <asp:datagrid id=MyDataGrid runat=server />
</div>
```

To add this effect, open your project in Visual Studio .NET and enter HTML view in the ASPX page that you want to change. Make your alterations, using this sample as a template, then switch back to Design view. You'll notice the designer automatically recognizes the tags and displays your DataGrid (or other controls) inside a micro window of the size you specified. It's perfect! (See Figure 3-4.)

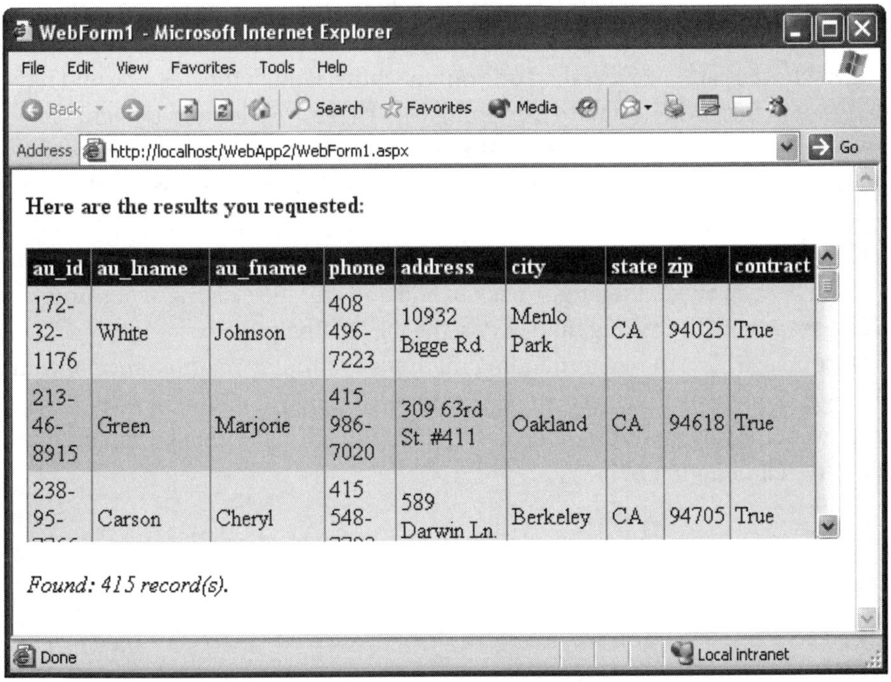

Figure 3-4. An example of the easy "micro window" in play

Why You Should Learn CSS

This book was not written as a "learn this, learn that" guide. It was designed to unveil quick, fast, and furiously fantastic tricks and techniques to rocket your programming skills. This tip however is a little different: it merely *recommends*.

I'd like to suggest that you spend a few minutes of your day learning cascading style sheets (CSS).

What are they? Cascading style sheets, typically abbreviated to just "style sheets", are a method of designing a set of "styles" that affect how a page looks. You may, for example, create a style that tells all table cells to have a blue background with bold, ten-point Arial text and links that turn purple as you hover over them. Or you could have a style that tells the body of the page to display a particular background image and change the color of the scrollbar.

Why use style sheets? Well, they can offer you the ability to do things that you can't using regular HTML (changing that scrollbar color, for example). However, more importantly, they offer you a method of centrally controlling the visual style of your site.

For example, you could put all your styles into a CSS file (indeed, by default, all Web application projects contain the Styles.css template) and then "link" the file to your pages, so that they all inherit the styles in your one file. It allows for *maintainability*.

Both Visual Studio .NET and FrontPage include excellent CSS editors, but before you get started, you'll need to learn a little more.

If you have FrontPage installed on your machine, launch the help file and navigate through the contents tab to Designing Web Pages ➤ Styles and Designing Web Pages ➤ Cascading Style Sheets. Alternatively, follow the CSS tutorials online at www.htmlgoodies.com. Both sources provide an excellent introduction to the topic.

If you want to use Visual Studio .NET to add style sheets, select Project ➤ Add New Item ➤ Style Sheet, then right-click to add and edit the existing styles. You can also read more by looking up "CSS" in the VS .NET help index.

Of course, while I'm recommending methods to simplify maintenance of your Web pages, I might also suggest you look into separating your content layer from your presentation layer, through the use of XML and XSLT. But that's a separate topic and all for another book!

Code Techniques

Looking to generate thumbnails on the fly? Or wondering where you can steal Microsoft code to build your own online forums, in minutes? This section has all the answers—and a whole bundle of other neat ASP.NET code techniques.

Three Steps to Changing Your Page Title in Code

If I asked you to change the title of your Web form in code, you'd be forgiven for looking for a "title" or "text" property somewhere. The problem is, that mysterious property doesn't exist: Microsoft forgot to put it in. If you want to change your page title programmatically, you have to do it yourself. Here's how.

Firstly, switch to the HTML view on your Web form. Near the top of your page, you'll see the title tag, looking something like `<title>WebForm1</title>`. Replace this with `<title runat="server" id="PageTitle"></title>`. Here, you're creating a title tag that runs on the server and has an ID, meaning you can manipulate it in code.

Next, switch back to Design mode and open up the code window behind your form. At the top of your page, under the `Inherits` line, add the following line of code to declare the server title tag you've just added:

```
Protected PageTitle As System.Web.UI.HtmlControls.HtmlGenericControl
```

Our third and final step involves changing the page text. Behind the `Load` event of your page, or in response to some similar event, set the `InnerText` property of the `PageTitle` tag to your new page title. Here's my sample code:

```
PageTitle.InnerText = "Welcome! - Last Updated 20/05/2004"
```

And that's it: one line of code and your page title has changed. Hey presto!

How to Automatically Fill Out Email Fields

Most ASP.NET developers know—or can guess—that the Hyperlink control allows you to link through to other Web sites just by changing the `NavigateUrl` property. Many will also be aware that, changing the `NavigateUrl` property to something like "mailto:karl@karlmoore.com", you'll open the default mail client, ready to send a message to karl@karlmoore.com.

However, you can add a number of tags to this "mailto:" command to insert default values into email fields. For instance, adding a "subject" query string parameter so the `NavigateUrl` property looks like "mailto:karl@karlmoore.com?subject=Thanks" will open the mail client when clicked on, with a message to karl@karlmoore.com and a subject of "Thanks".

Other tags you can use include `body` for inserting text in the body of a message, `cc` for specifying courtesy copy recipients, and `bcc` for blind courtesy copies.

So, one example of a clever "mailto:" tag could be as follows:

```
mailto:karl@karlmoore.com?subject=Thanks&body=I learned a lot about
hyperlinks&cc=karl.moore@whitecliff.net; mark.williams@whitecliff.net
```

This should be all on one line and will open the default mail client, ready for sending a mail message to karl@karlmoore.com. The default subject will be "Thanks", the body will be "I learned a lot about hyperlinks", and both karl.moore@whitecliff.net and mark.williams@whitecliff.net will be CC'ed. (See Figure 3-5.)

Note that this trick isn't specific to the Hyperlink control nor ASP.NET: it will work with any hyperlink or similar feature. Nevertheless, it's an interesting snippet of knowledge that's worthy of shelving somewhere in your developer's library.

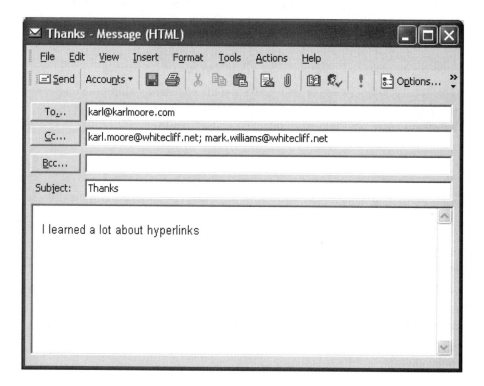

Figure 3-5. The result of our specially formatted `mailto:` *link*

Sending Mail in ASP.NET

 Download supporting files at www.apress.com.
The files for this tip are in the "Ch3–Send Mail" folder.

Sending mail from a Web page is perhaps one of the most commonly requested code snippets. And, to make your life easier, here's a function that encapsulates all the functionality for you. Simply call it, passing in the appropriate arguments, and you're sorted:

```
Public Function SendMail(ByVal [To] As String, _
    ByVal From As String, ByVal Subject As String, _
    ByVal Body As String, ByVal IsHTML As Boolean, _
    Optional ByVal SmtpServer As String = "domain.com") As Boolean
    ' Sends a mail message using the specified details
    ' - returns a False if delivery fails
    Try
        Dim objMsg As New System.Web.Mail.MailMessage()
        SendMail = True
        With objMsg
            .To = [To]
            .From = From
            .Subject = Subject
            .Body = Body
            ' .BodyFormat specifies whether the Body is
            ' in plain text or HTML format
            .BodyFormat = IIf(IsHTML = True, _
                System.Web.Mail.MailFormat.Html, _
                System.Web.Mail.MailFormat.Text)
        End With
        System.Web.Mail.SmtpMail.SmtpServer = SmtpServer
        System.Web.Mail.SmtpMail.Send(objMsg)
    Catch
        SendMail = False
    End Try
End Function
```

Our code here simply composes a new MailMessage object and attempts to send it through the specified server, returning a True if successful. We're using a default SMTP server of domain.com, which should be altered to your own local mail server.

And here's how you might call this function:

```
blnMailSent = SendMail("karl@karlmoore.com", "talk2us@whitecliff.net", _
    "This is my subject", "This is my body", False, "whitecliff.net")
```

Of course this doesn't handle more-complicated mail situations, such as checking email, sending through nonlocal authenticated mail servers, or administering POP3 accounts. For such functionality, you'll want to check out a third-party control such as devMail.net from `www.devmail.net`.

The Trick to Creating User-Friendly URLs

If you've spent time surfing some of the new ASP.NET sites, you may have noticed the more advanced ones have started incorporating *user-friendly URLs*.

For example, rather than providing `http://www.yoursite.com/profile.aspx?username=john` to link to a personal profile page (where the "id" is in the query string), some sites are providing URLs such as `http://www.yoursite.com/john.aspx`. These work in exactly the same way as the URL with an embedded query string, yet look *much* nicer.

But how is this possible? Well, it all works via a little nifty use of the `Application_BeginRequest` method, inside your Global.asax file, which fires off whenever any request is made to your Web application. Inside this method, we look at the path requested by the user, then figure out the page our surfer *really* wants (typically, the page actually incorporating a query string). We then transparently feed this *real* page back down to the user.

For example, imagine a request comes through to view `webservices.aspx`. Our code behind the `Application_BeginRequest` event kicks in and extracts any relevant information from the path, such as the `webservices` portion. Then our code figures out what page the user really wants to see—perhaps "viewarticle.aspx?title=webservices"—and rewrites the path to deliver *that* page back to the user. Note that your visitor is still on the `webservices.aspx` page; to them, the URL does *not* change. It remains user-friendly.

You could implement this method of creating aesthetically-pleasing URLs in a number of different ways; however, this extraction of the main part of the path (i.e., `webservices`) to use in a query string (i.e., `viewarticle.aspx?title=webservices`) is the most common.

Here's a little template code to add to the Application_BeginRequest method of your Global.asax file:

```
' Get paths and data positions
Dim strPath As String = Request.FilePath
Dim intStart As Integer = strPath.LastIndexOf("/") + 1
Dim intEnd As Integer = strPath.LastIndexOf(".aspx")
Dim intLength As Integer = intEnd - intStart
' Extract main part of filename (ie, bit between "/" and ".aspx"
Dim strPageName As String = strPath.Substring(intStart, intLength)
' Rewrite path to send data back from other page
Context.RewritePath("viewarticle.aspx?title=" & strPageName)
```

Be warned that this code does not make any exceptions. *All* pages for this application will have their paths rewritten. You may wish to add a little code to parse the path and check the user is in the /articles/ folder or some such before "redirecting".

Implemented correctly, this is one fantastic little trick. Good luck!

Adding Real-Time HTML to Your Page

Have you ever visited a Web site that displays a message such as "Attempting to connect to host...", then a few seconds later displays a confirmation such as "Done"—all on the same page? It almost "streams" the information down to your page, *live*. Wonder how that's done?

It works like this: the page begins sending its text down to the client, then pauses before the "result" HTML (that is, "Done") is sent to the user. Your code runs and does its processing, perhaps doing a little database work. When ready, the "result" is sent down to the user. It's real-time HTML processing, and it works using a property called BufferOutput.

The most common method of using this is when writing code directly behind the ASPX page, where the code is inserted in <% code marks %>, rather than using the more typical Visual Basic "code behind" techniques taught in this book.

In this ASPX page situation, simply set the Response.BufferOutput property to False as your page loads, then, just before the portion where you want to return your result, write code to do your work, then spurt out the response with a Response.Write. It's nothing special, but it'll send all the HTML down to your user until your code is encountered. It'll then run your code and display any results you output.

The BufferOutput property being set to False is the real trick here. This tells the page that it doesn't have to wait for the contents of the entire page to be generated before sending to the client—rather, it can "go with the flow" and send it as it becomes available.

When it comes to the regular "code behind" pages more familiar with VB .NET developers, it's all a little more complicated. However, here's a simple sample that'll demonstrate the technique. Just create a new application and add the following code to your page Load event, then run it and see what happens:

```
Response.BufferOutput = False
Response.Write("Processing your query...")
Dim x As Integer
For x = 1 To 100000000
    ' Waste time! - your genuine code would replace this loop
Next
Response.Write(" FINISHED!")
```

Here's a little tip: when running this for the first time, the ASP.NET on-demand compiler kicks in, and you probably won't notice what happened. Simply hit refresh and watch again.

The Secret to Uploading Files with Ease

Download supporting files at www.apress.com.
The files for this tip are in the "Ch3—Uploading Files" folder.

In the golden olden days of ASP, managing a file upload was pretty difficult. Most developers reverted to digging deep in their wallets to purchase a third-party add-on to help them achieve the desired result. No longer.

Thanks to the new ASP.NET features, you can now upload files with practically a few lines of code. And the following four easy-to-follow steps show you exactly how to do it.

1. Add a File Field control to your form. You'll find this under the HTML tab on the toolbox. You'll have seen this control when uploading attachments through Hotmail, or when sending files to a Web site.

2. Right-click on the File Field control and check the Run as Server Control option. This allows you to manipulate the control in code, sort of like a less-functional ASP.NET server control.

3. Change the ID of your File Field control to something more understandable, such as "fileUpload".

4. Enter the HTML view of your Web form and find the opening `<form>` tag. You'll need to edit this to add the parameter `encType="multipart/form-data"`. Your `<form>` tag may look something like this when you're finished:

```
<form id="Form1" method="post" encType="multipart/form-data"
    runat="server">
```

And that's it. (See Figure 3-6.) You've set up your form to receive file uploads. But after the user has selected a file and submitted your form, how do you manipulate the sent file? The easiest technique is to run a simple line of code, like this:

```
NameOfFileFieldElement.PostedFile.SaveAs(Server.MapPath("uploadedfile.txt"))
```

Pretty simple, really. You might also want to check that the user has uploaded a valid file first, before saving (unless you're really into errors). The following function does this for you, checking for null uploads and zero byte files:

```
Public Function FileFieldSelected(ByVal FileField As _
    System.Web.UI.HtmlControls.HtmlInputFile) As Boolean
        ' Returns a True if the passed
        ' FileField has had a user post a file
        If FileField.PostedFile Is Nothing Then Return False
        If FileField.PostedFile.ContentLength = 0 Then Return False
        Return True
End Function
```

TOP TIP *If you get an "access denied" error when trying to save files directly to your Web application folder, go check your permissions. Ensure that your virtual directory in IIS has read and write permissions. (Change this through IIS.) You may also want to ensure that your ASP.NET, guest, or impersonated accounts have appropriate permissions, both for computer access and for the actual folder itself. (To change this, right-click on the folder, select Sharing and Security, and then select the Security tab.)*

The problem is that both you and I know that 95% of people reading this don't really want to go ahead and store files directly on the server file system. Rather, you want to save information into your database, into that SQL Server "image" field.

Every publication I've seen so far manages to conveniently skip this topic. But not this one....

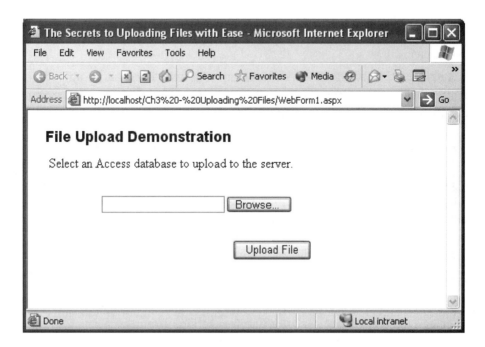

Figure 3-6. Click on the button and pick a file!

Storing Uploaded Files in Your Database

 Download supporting files at www.apress.com.
The files for this tip are in the "Ch3–Storing Files in Database" folder.

First, a few tips on storing files inside your SQL Server database.

For convenience, you'll really need to store at least three bits of information about your file to get it out in the same shape as you put it in. I'd suggest "data" (a field that will hold your actual file as a byte array, data type "image"), "type" (a field to hold details of the type of file it is, data type "varchar"), and "length" (a field to hold the length in bytes of your file, data type "int").

I'd also recommend "downloadName", a field to hold the name that the file had when it was uploaded, data type "varchar". This helps suggest a name should the file be downloaded again via the Web.

The problem you have is translating the information from the File Field control into an acceptable format for your database. For a start, you need to get your file into a byte array to store it in an image field. You also need to extract the file type, length, and the download name. Once you have this, set your fields to these values using regular ADO.NET code.

So, how do you get this information? It's simple: just use the following ready-to-run code snippets, passing in your File Field control as an argument. Each function will return just the information you want to feed straight into your database, from a byte array for the image field to a string for the file type.

```
Public Function GetByteArrayFromFileField( _
    ByVal FileField As System.Web.UI.HtmlControls.HtmlInputFile) _
    As Byte()
    ' Returns a byte array from the passed
    ' file field controls file
    Dim intFileLength As Integer, bytData() As Byte
    Dim objStream As System.IO.Stream
    If FileFieldSelected(FileField) Then
        intFileLength = FileField.PostedFile.ContentLength
        ReDim bytData(intFileLength)
        objStream = FileField.PostedFile.InputStream
        objStream.Read(bytData, 0, intFileLength)
        Return bytData
    End If
End Function


Public Function FileFieldType(ByVal FileField As _
    System.Web.UI.HtmlControls.HtmlInputFile) As String
    ' Returns the type of the posted file
    If Not FileField.PostedFile Is Nothing Then _
        Return FileField.PostedFile.ContentType
End Function


Public Function FileFieldLength(ByVal FileField As _
    System.Web.UI.HtmlControls.HtmlInputFile) As Integer
    ' Returns the length of the posted file
    If Not FileField.PostedFile Is Nothing Then _
        Return FileField.PostedFile.ContentLength
End Function
```

```
Public Function FileFieldFilename(ByVal FileField As _
   System.Web.UI.HtmlControls.HtmlInputFile) As String
      ' Returns the core filename of the posted file
      If Not FileField.PostedFile Is Nothing Then _
         Return Replace(FileField.PostedFile.FileName, _
         StrReverse(Mid(StrReverse(FileField.PostedFile.FileName), _
         InStr(1, StrReverse(FileField.PostedFile.FileName), "\"))), "")
   End Function
```

Sorted! One question remains, however. Once you've got a file inside a database, how do you serve it back up to a user? First, get the data back out of SQL Server using regular ADO.NET code. After that? Well, here's a handy function that'll do all the hard work for you. Simply pass the data from your table fields and hey presto:

```
Public Sub DeliverFile(ByVal Page As System.Web.UI.Page, _
   ByVal Data() As Byte, ByVal Type As String, _
   ByVal Length As Integer, _
   Optional ByVal DownloadFileName As String = "")
      ' Delivers a file, such as an image or PDF file,
      ' back through the Response object
      ' Sample usage from within an ASP.NET page:
      ' - DeliverFile(Me, bytFile(), strType, intLength, "MyImage.bmp")
      With Page.Response
         .Clear()
         .ContentType = Type
         If DownloadFileName <> "" Then
            Page.Response.AddHeader("content-disposition", _
               "filename=" & DownloadFileName)
         End If
         .OutputStream.Write(Data, 0, Length)
         .End()
      End With
   End Sub
```

Simply pass your byte array, file type, and length, and it'll send it straight down to your surfer. If it's an image, it'll be displayed in the browser window. If it's a regular file, you'll be prompted for download.

If it's made available for download, this function also allows you to specify a suggested download file name, a technique that many ASP.NET developers spend weeks trying to figure out. Easy!

Working with Uploaded Images

 Download supporting files at www.apress.com.
The files for this tip are in the "Ch3—Working with Images" folder.

Whether you're building the simplest of photo album Web sites or a fully fledged content management system, the ability to work with uploaded images is a vital one, and with ASP.NET, it's a real doddle.

The following code snippet shows you how, by example. It takes a data stream from the File Field control and converts it into an image object, adding simple error handling should the uploaded file not actually be an image. The code then uses this image object to extract a few core details about the file, from its dimensions to file type:

```
' Get data into image format
Dim objStream As System.IO.Stream = _
  MyFileField.PostedFile.InputStream
Dim objImage As System.Drawing.Image
Try
    ' Get the image stream
    objImage = System.Drawing.Image.FromStream(objStream)
Catch
    ' This is not an image, exit the method (presuming code is in one!)
    Exit Sub
End Try
' Filename
Dim strOriginalFilename As String = MyFileField.PostedFile.FileName
' Type of image
Dim strImageType
If objImage.RawFormat.Equals(objImage.RawFormat.Gif) Then
    strImageType = "This is a GIF image"
ElseIf objImage.RawFormat.Equals(objImage.RawFormat.Bmp) Then
    strImageType = "This is a Bitmap image"
ElseIf objImage.RawFormat.Equals(objImage.RawFormat.Jpeg) Then
    strImageType = "This is a JPEG image"
ElseIf objImage.RawFormat.Equals(objImage.RawFormat.Icon) Then
    strImageType = "This is an icon file"
ElseIf objImage.RawFormat.Equals(objImage.RawFormat.Tiff) Then
    strImageType = "This is a TIFF file"
Else
    strImageType = "Other"
```

```
End If
' Dimensions
Dim strDimensions As String
strDimensions = "Width in pixels: " & objImage.Width & _
   ", Height in pixels: " & objImage.Height
' Send raw output to browser
Response.Clear()
Response.Write(strOriginalFilename & "<p>" & strImageType & _
   "<p>" & strDimensions)
Response.End()
```

Creating Images Dynamically

 Download supporting files at www.apress.com.
The files for this tip are in the "Ch3–Dynamically Create Images" folder.

Ask any ASP developer who has ever tried to dynamically create his own images and he'll tell you it's a nightmare. In fact, it's more than a nightmare. It's practically hell. The only true solution? Reverting to an expensive, dodgy, third-party control to do the work for you.

With ASP.NET, however, you can develop your own dynamic images with ease. Simply create an image object and use the new GDI+ features to add objects to that image, such as text, rectangles, and ellipses. After that, you can simply stream straight back down to the client.

But covering the graphics features in depth would require at least another two books, and, unfortunately, we don't have that much room. So, I'm going to share a sample that demonstrates creating a small "Empty Karl's Basket" button, alongside a little blue-and-yellow bullet point. (See Figure 3-7.) It's the sort of personalized graphic you'll find on sites such as Amazon.com.

Just add the following code to the page Load event of a Web form. That Web form will then feed back this image as its output. In other words, your Web browser will recognize the page as a graphic. This means that, if you wanted to reference the image in an Image control, say, you'd specify the source (the ImageUrl) as being YourWebFormName.aspx.

Here's the code:

```
' Create image - you could even load an image
' from a file and edit it in code
Dim objBitmap As Bitmap = New Bitmap(120, 30)
```

```
Dim objGraphics As Graphics = Graphics.FromImage(objBitmap)
' Fill background
objGraphics.FillRectangle(New SolidBrush(Color.LightBlue), _
   0, 0, 120, 30)
' Create blue-yellow bullet point
objGraphics.FillEllipse(New SolidBrush(Color.Blue), 3, 9, 10, 10)
objGraphics.FillEllipse(New SolidBrush(Color.Yellow), 4, 10, 8, 8)
' Draw text next to bullet point
objGraphics.DrawString("Empty Karl's Basket", _
    New Font("Tahoma", 8), New SolidBrush(Color.Green), 16, 8)
' Send down to client
Response.Clear
Response.ContentType = "image/jpeg"
objBitmap.Save(Response.OutputStream, _
   System.Drawing.Imaging.ImageFormat.Jpeg)
' Tidy up
objGraphics.Dispose()
objBitmap.Dispose()
```

At its very least, this code demonstrates passing images back down to the browser via a Web page. Now all you need to do is brush up on your GDI+ skills, and the world of dynamic image generation is your oyster. For more information and a series of tutorials, use the help index to look up "images, GDI+"—or check out some of the graphic methods you can utilize in the "Drawing with Windows Forms" tip in Chapter 7.

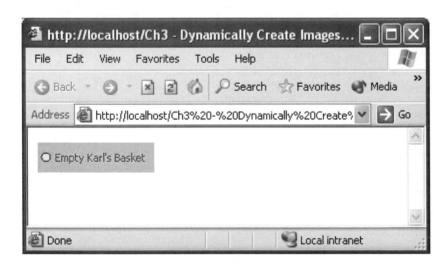

Figure 3-7. The result of our code: hey, it's my shopping basket. Apparently.

Code for Generating Thumbnails on the Fly

 Download supporting files at www.apress.com.
The files for this tip are in the "Ch3—Thumbnails" folder.

If you've ever attempted to create image thumbnails for your site, you'll know it's a tiresome task. You either do it manually, or use an inflexible system such as the FrontPage thumbnail feature.

However, as you've seen in previous tips, ASP.NET gives us tremendous control over how our images work. As such, we should be able to generate thumbnails on the fly... and this snippet will enable you to do just that.

Create a new Web form (thumbnail.aspx) and add the following code behind the page Load event:

```
' Initialize objects
Dim objImage, objThumbnail As System.Drawing.Image
Dim strServerPath, strFilename As String
Dim shtWidth, shtHeight As Short
' Get image folder path on server - use "\" string if root
strServerPath = Server.MapPath("WebAppImageFolder\")
' Retrieve name of file to resize from query string
strFilename = strServerPath & Request.QueryString("filename")
' Retrieve file, or error.gif if not available
Try
    objImage = objImage.FromFile(strFilename)
Catch
    objImage = objImage.FromFile(strServerPath & "error.gif")
End Try
' Retrieve width from query string
If Request.QueryString("width") = Nothing Then
    shtWidth = objImage.Width
ElseIf Request.QueryString("width") < 1 Then
    shtWidth = 100
Else
    shtWidth = Request.QueryString("width")
End If
' Work out a proportionate height from width
shtHeight = objImage.Height / (objImage.Width / shtWidth)
' Create thumbnail
objThumbnail = objImage.GetThumbnailImage(shtWidth, _
  shtHeight, Nothing, System.IntPtr.Zero)
```

```
' Send down to client
Response.ContentType = "image/jpeg"
objThumbnail.Save(Response.OutputStream, Imaging.ImageFormat.Jpeg)
' Tidy up
objImage.Dispose()
objThumbnail.Dispose()
```

If you follow this code through, you should see what happens. The filename is retrieved from the query string and the image loaded into memory. The new width is then taken and a proportionate height calculated (an important usability feat that few demonstration code snippets take into account). Then, a newly sized thumbnail is generated and sent straight back down to the client.

After compiling, you'd call this page by typing something like the following URL into your browser: `http://localhost/WebAppFolderName/thumbnail.aspx?filename=myfile.gif&width=100`. (See Figure 3-8.) You'd use this URL as the image source for, say, an Image control.

Don't forget: after you've generated the thumbnail, you can still dynamically edit your image. Using the last tip, for example, you could add a little copyright notice next to each thumbnail. Powerful stuff, this imaging lark.

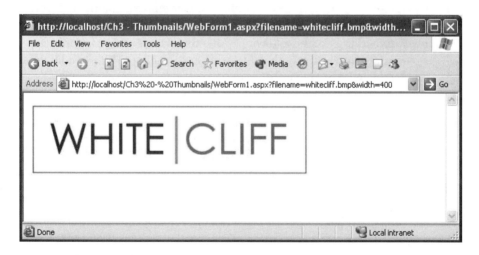

Figure 3-8. The White Cliff logo, resized to perfection

Five Steps to ASP.NET Authentication

 Download supporting files at www.apress.com.
The files for this tip are in the "Ch3–Authentication" folder.

If you've created a Web application in Visual Studio .NET, you should be aware that—by default—anyone can access your pages. However, there is a way to keep nosy, unwanted types out. It's called *authentication.*

ASP.NET includes support for three core types of authentication: Windows, which allows only certain Windows accounts to access a page; Passport, which uses the Microsoft Passport universal login system to verify a user (a pay service); and Forms, the most popular method of authentication, which we'll be covering here.

When a user attempts to access a page that uses Forms authentication, they get redirected to a login screen. From here, your surfer can provide a username and password. You then validate the credentials and grant or deny access to your pages accordingly.

Want to set up ASP.NET Forms authentication? Just follow my five quick and easy steps.

1. Open the Web.config file in your Solution. This stores a number of settings for your Web application. Edit the `<authentication>` elements so that it reads something like the following. (Alter usernames and passwords as appropriate, and watch both your casing and spacing.) This provides your application with a list of valid users.

   ```
   <authentication mode="Forms">
       <forms>
           <credentials passwordFormat="Clear">
               <user name="test1" password="password" />
               <user name="test2" password="password" />
           </credentials>
       </forms>
   </authentication>
   ```

2. Still in the Web.config file, remove the `<allow users="*" />` line from within the `<authorization>` element. This line grants access to anyone, and we've just erased it.

3. Still within the `<authorization>` element, add the following line to deny access to all unknown users (that is, those not authenticated):

   ```
   <deny users="?" />
   ```

4. Create a page called login.aspx. By default, all unauthenticated users will be redirected to this page. Add TextBox controls (txtUsername and txtPassword) for your browser to supply credentials. Also, add a CheckBox control (chkPersist) to be used if the user wants his or her machine to automatically log them in next time.

5. Behind a login button on your login.aspx page, add code similar to the following to authenticate your user:

```
If System.Web.Security.FormsAuthentication.Authenticate( _
    txtUsername.Text, txtPassword.Text) = True Then
    System.Web.Security.FormsAuthentication.RedirectFromLoginPage( _
        txtUsername.Text, chkPersist.Checked)
Else
    Response.Write("Invalid credentials - go back and try again!")
End If
```

And that's it! Now, whenever a user visits a page in your application—and they're unauthenticated—they'll be redirected to login.aspx. From there, they'll be able to provide credentials. The .Authenticate method attempts to match these with a valid username and password combination in Web.config. If the credentials are invalid, a generic error message is displayed. If everything is fine, the .RedirectFromLoginPage method runs, taking the username and whether the login "persists" (that is, is remembered by the computer between sessions) as arguments, then sends the user back to the initially requested page. (See Figure 3-9.)

After this, whenever you need to refer back to the username, simply check out the User.Identity.Name property. And, when the user requests to explicitly log out, run code similar to the following:

```
System.Web.Security.FormsAuthentication.SignOut()
Response.Redirect("login.aspx")
```

TOP TIP *If you don't want to use login.aspx as your login form, you can change the page by adding a* loginUrl *attribute to the* <forms> *element of your Web.config file. For example, the following tag makes myloginpage.aspx the default login page:* <forms loginUrl="myloginpage.aspx" />

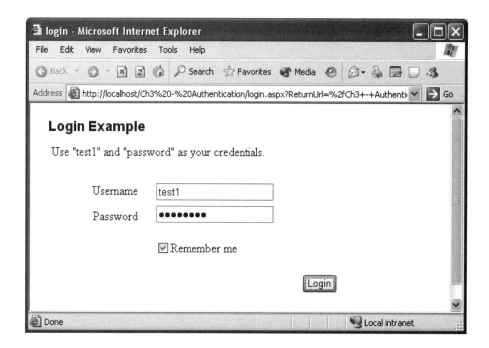

Figure 3-9. Authentication kicking in, as I try to access a restricted page

Forms Authentication, Without Web.config

The sort of Forms authentication discussed in the last tip is, however, relatively limited. Unless you have just a few core user groups, which can be easily stored in Web.config, it's not awfully useful. And the passwords are stored in plain text XML, which means that anyone in your development team could retrieve them (unless you encrypt to MD5 format and change the `passwordFormat` attribute).

So, how can you authenticate users using information from a database, say?

It's easy: simply omit the `.Authentication` method in the procedure. In its place, add your own code, perhaps querying a table using ADO.NET code and validate the provided information. If it's acceptable, run the `.RedirectFromLoginPage` method. Everything else will work as normal.

Note that, if you want to remove the sample users from your Web.config file, replace the whole `<authentication><form>...</authentication>` section with just `<authentication mode="Forms" />`.

Authenticating Just Part of Your Site

Sometimes you don't want to authenticate all of your Web application. In some situations, you may just want to keep a couple of pages, such as a basket checkout form, available to only those authorized users.

Yes, you could try doing it manually by remembering some sort of session variable and/or by using cookies. But a much neater solution is to use a little-known trick that allows you to still use ASP.NET Forms authentication, but only with an exclusive number of pages on your site.

Here's how:

1. Alter your Web.config file so it uses Forms authentication. You can do this by following the first step in the "Five Steps to ASP.NET Authentication" tip, if you'll be using Web.config to store the users. Or simply change the <authentication> element to <authentication mode="Forms" />, if you're going to authenticate using your own database, et cetera. In this tip however, we're not going to deny regular, unauthenticated visitors.

2. Still in your Web.config file, just underneath the <configuration> element, add the following code, replacing "checkout.aspx" with the page you want to protect. This will ensure that ASP.NET denies access to any unauthenticated users attempting to view this page. You can add as many <location> blocks as you wish and can include filenames and folders in the path.

```
<location path="checkout.aspx">
  <system.web>
    <authorization>
      <deny users="?" />
    </authorization>
  </system.web>
</location>
```

3. Go ahead and create your login.aspx page as you did in the last tip.

And that's it! You've created a Web application that uses Forms authentication but grants access to all users by default. You've then added a clause in Web.config that states all those users who are attempting to view checkout.aspx must be authorized first—and are therefore redirected to login.aspx when they access the page.

Note that these changes to the Web.config file are the only real difference to the authentication process. The other methods of logging out, retrieving the username, and so on all work in exactly the same way as with full authentication.

The Best Place to Store Your Settings

 Download supporting files at www.apress.com.
The files for this tip are in the "Ch3–Settings" folder.

Many Web developers end up storing important pieces of data—database connection strings, passwords, default settings—as troublesome constants. The problem with this is that they're difficult to edit: the slightest of changes means a complete recompile.

However, with ASP.NET, there is an easier way. It's likely you're well aware of the Web.config file, which stores settings for your applications, such as the session state timeout and authentication mode. It can also hold your *own* settings.

How? It's easy. Simply add your own personal settings to the Web.config file, like this:

```
<configuration>
...
<appSettings>
    <add key="serverName" value="diomedes" />
</appSettings>
...
<system.web>
...
</system.web>
</configuration>
```

Here, I've added a key called "serverName" containing a value of diomedes. You can list as many values here as you like: just keep adding <add> elements. And how do you read the value in your code? Simply reference the AppSettings collection of the System.Configuration.ConfigurationSettings class, as so:

```
x = System.Configuration.ConfigurationSettings.AppSettings("serverName")
```

And don't forget: Web.config is just an XML file and easily editable without a recompile. You could even use a third-party control, such as the Web.config editor from Hunterstone to simplify all your administration (get your free copy of v1.3 from www.hunterstone.com/downloads.aspx). Easy!

Steal Fantastic Forum Code from Microsoft and Save Yourself Hours

I've always found bulletin boards to be the easiest method of generating visitor loyalty at a site. The trouble is, the very best ones always take an absolute age to build. But who mentioned doing it yourself?

Back in July 2001, ASP author Scott Mitchell decided to create his own bulletin board as a pet .NET project. Within months, Microsoft had stepped onto the scene and adopted it as its very own online ASP.NET forum, which you can find online at www.asp.net. (See Figure 3-10.)

Well, after months of new features and major tweaking, our favorite software giant has quietly unveiled the full source code for download at www.asp.net/Forums/Download—and for free, too!

At the time of writing, the code release was still in a very well-developed beta mode, but there are big plans to release the absolute final version over the coming months.

It's only a quick tip, but it could save you hours.

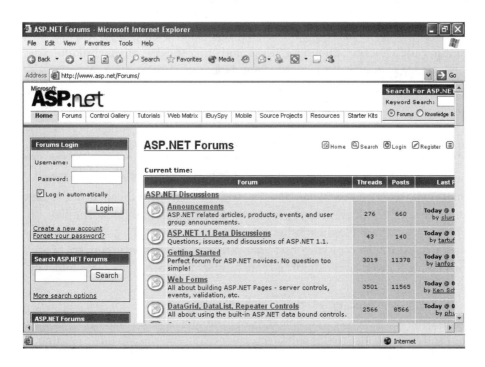

Figure 3-10. Have all this forum functionality, in seconds!

Integrating with PayPal's Instant Payment Notification

 Download supporting files at www.apress.com.
The files for this tip are in the "Ch3–PayPal" folder.

As the PayPal payment service continues to grow in popularity, so does the number of developers wanting to integrate it into their sites. Thankfully, it's relatively simple, merely involving a number of cross-server calls to ensure that the payment has completed successfully.

To help get you up and running, however, BlueVisionSoftware.com has produced a handy little instant payment notification (IPN) tutorial available online at www.bluevisionsoftware.com/WebSite/TipsAndTricksDetails.aspx?Name=PayPal.

It's written in C#, but it's easily understandable. (If you're confused, see Chapter 9!) We've also included the tutorial in the download that comes with this book, and it's available at www.apress.com. Check it out!

Optimization, Errors, and Other Tips

Want to give your site the truly professional edge? Then refine it with this selection of optimization tips, error handling tricks, and other sneaky code techniques. From creating your own 404 Page Not Found messages to creating a super-fast page with a couple of caching keywords, it's all here. Starting with...

Subfolders in Web Applications: Confused?

One of the big first questions that all those developing ASP.NET applications in Visual Studio .NET have is "what's the deal with subfolders?" I mean, if you've used FrontPage or ASP to develop sites previously, creating a site subfolder simply involved putting your files in another directory.

But Visual Studio .NET still bases your Web application on the concept of a project. And, for Web applications, all core "project files" are in the same folder by default.

It's easily overcome, however. Just right-click on your project in the Solution Explorer and select Add ➤ New Folder. Give the folder a name, then right-click again and add new files to this subdirectory—or drag and drop to move existing files to this folder.

It seems so simple when written like this, but the whole concept of dealing with subfolders trips up many of those new to Web applications. They *don't* all need to be in the same folder. And now you know!

Choosing a Directory Other Than `c:\inetpub\wwwroot\`

By default, when you create a Web application, your files get stored in the IIS root Web site folder—typically, `c:\inetpub\wwwroot\`. But if you're like me, you won't like storing everything in that one folder. Rather, you have separate folders on separate drives housing separate projects.

How, then, can you get Visual Studio .NET to create and run a Web project from another directory?

Firstly, create the folder you wish to house your project. Next, we need to set this up as a "virtual folder," a directory that looks as though it's running from the IIS root Web site folder yet is actually pointing elsewhere.

To do this, right-click on your folder in Windows Explorer and click on Properties. Select the Web Sharing tab and choose the Share this folder option. Enter an alias (see Figure 3-11), then click on OK to the dialog box, and OK again on the Properties page.

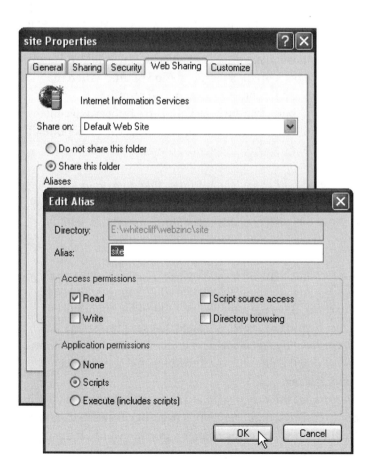

Figure 3-11. Specifying a virtual folder alias for our new location

Your directory is now accessible via http://localhost/youralias/ (or you can replace localhost with your machine name). In other words, if you put an index.htm file in your newly created directory, it would be displayed when you type the above address into your browser.

Thirdly and finally, create a new Web application in Visual Studio .NET, specifying your new http://localhost/youralias/ address as the location. It'll get created in the folder you want. Not too difficult when you know how!

Create Super-Fast ASP.NET Applications, with Caching

Download supporting files at www.apress.com.
The files for this tip are in the "Ch3–Caching" folder.

Some pages on your Web site will be awfully "expensive" to generate. By this, I mean that they take time for your server to put together: perhaps your page grabs the latest stock figures from an external site, perhaps it performs a long company calculation, perhaps it simply delves into your database and retrieves a news story.

Either way, it all takes expensive processor time, and it would be seriously useful if you could just cache those pages once they've been generated and automatically serve that same page back up for a certain period of time. When the period is up, the page can then run its code once again and refresh.

This sounds like a great method of optimizing your site—but perhaps not completely easy to implement. Well, actually, it is. In fact, to set the most popular form of ASP.NET caching into action, you'll need only one line of code. Here's how....

If you want to cache your page for, say, ten minutes, first open your ASPX page in Design mode. Next, click on the HTML button (or, from the menu, select View ➤ HTML Source). Just above the <%@ Page Language="vb" … > directive, add the following line of code:

```
<%@ OutputCache Duration="600" VaryByParam="None" %>
```

This tells ASP.NET to cache the page after its first request for ten minutes (600 seconds). You can test caching by creating a page that simply displays the time as it loads, while incorporating an OutputCache directive with a short Duration attribute. Then, keep refreshing the page in your browser. Only after the set Duration will the time update itself.

You may be wondering what the VaryByParam attribute is all about. Well, it tells ASP.NET whether it should cache all requests for this page, or cache separate versions depending on whether the query string changes (in other words, if the "parameters" to the page change).

For example, if you want two versions of a page cached when someone requests "article.aspx?id=10" and "article.aspx?id=11", then you'll want to change your OutputCache directive to

```
<%@ OutputCache Duration="600" VaryByParam="id" %>
```

Alternatively, if you want a version of the page cached whenever any parameter alters, simply use a wildcard, as so:

```
<%@ OutputCache Duration="600" VaryByParam="*" %>
```

Here, no matter whether you request "article.aspx?id=12" or "article.aspx?tag=loveshack", a different version of the page will be cached and reserved whenever requested again within the specified duration.

If you're interested in caching just portions of your page, it's interesting to note you can also use this technique in user controls. (See the "The Secret Behind User Controls" tip earlier in this chapter.) This could perhaps allow you to have certain parts of the page updated with every request, whereas other, more common elements simply refresh every hour or so.

A quick word of warning: be careful not to overuse caching. Used wisely, caching can greatly increase the performance of your Web applications. Used in a crazed, insane fashion—say, on a free text search page—it'll bring your server to a grinding halt.

You can learn more about ASP.NET caching by looking up "ASP.NET caching" in the help index. Surprising, that.

Nine Steps to Successful Debugging

It's terrible when it happens—but, rest assured, it will happen. You see, debugging Windows programs is a pretty simple process and one not prone to failure. But debugging Web applications is much more fallible.

So, what should you do if you attempt to start debugging a Web application and get the dreaded "Unable to start debugging on the Web Server" error? Here's your one-stop checklist:

1. Are you working offline in Internet Explorer? Launch Internet Explorer and look in the File menu. If "Work Offline" is checked, click on it to deselect the option, restart Visual Studio .NET, and try again.

2. Does Web.config have any syntax errors? If it does, you won't be able to start debugging. To check this, click on Debug ➤ Start Without Debugging and see if your browser reports an error. If it does, fix it and try again.

3. Are you sure you're running Windows 2000, Windows 2003, or Windows XP? If so, continue to the next step. If you're debugging a remote ASP.NET application under Windows NT4, you'll need to launch the application without debugging, then manually attach to it. Look up "debugging ASP.NET Web applications, system requirements" in the help index for more information. A word of advice: *upgrade.*

4. Are you a member of the Debuggers Users group? You may be logged on as Administrator, but it's still worth checking. If you're not in the group, you may be denied your debugging rights.

5. Does your Web.config file have its Debug attribute set to True? If not, you're going nowhere. You might also want to check that the Configuration Manager lists your project as Debug and not Release. (Use the dropdown box on the standard menu to alter, or choose Build ➤ Configuration Manager.)

6. When you created the project, did you specify an IP address rather than a machine name? If so, launch Internet Explorer, choose Internet Options, select the Security tab, and add the IP address to the list of trusted sites. Then try again.

7. Did you install IIS after Visual Studio .NET? If so, you'll need to do a little fixing. Use the help index to look up "installing Internet Information Server". Midway through the software requirements, you'll find instructions telling you how to install IIS. It also provides advice on configuring and repairing IIS after installing Visual Studio .NET. Follow the guidelines.

8. Are the IIS security settings set up properly? You can check this by launching the Internet Services Manager in Windows 2000/2003, or Internet Information Services in Windows XP (found under the Administrative Tools option on the Programs menu). Navigate to your Web server, locate the Default Web Site node, right-click and select Properties, choose the Directory Security tab, and select Edit. Ensure that Anonymous Access and Integrated Windows Authentication are checked, then click on OK in all open dialog boxes.

9. And finally, is the Web application virtual folder set up correctly? You can check this by launching the Internet Services Manager in Windows 2000/2003, or Internet Information Services in Windows XP. Navigate to your Web server, expand the Default Web Site node, and find your application folder in the list. If it looks like regular Windows Explorer, it hasn't been set up correctly. To fix this, right-click on the folder, select Properties, click on the Create button, and then click on OK to save.

Hiding Error Code from Your Clients

One of the most beautiful features of ASP.NET is its rich error reporting. When something goes wrong, it highlights the exact lines of offending code, provides an explanation of the problem, and, if it's feeling merry, even suggests a solution from time to time.

The problem is that you really don't want your visitors viewing code behind your applications. For a start, it may breach your site security. For seconds, it's just not *pretty*. So, how do you stop it from happening?

First off, stop telling VS .NET to create the debug file containing a copy of your code. You can do this by altering the application mode from Debug to Release. Use either the dropdown box on the standard VS .NET menu for this, or select Build ➤ Configuration Manager and edit through the dialog box. Next, turn off debugging by editing the Web.config file so the `<compilation>` element reads `<compilation debug="false" />`.

Well, that may stop your code from appearing, but it won't get rid of those awful generic error pages. You can, however, replace them with your own, slightly more elegant apologies. Simply alter the `<customErrors>` element in Web.config to something like `<customErrors mode="On" defaultRedirect="genericerror.aspx" />`. (See Figure 3-12.) No problem!

> **TOP TIP** *With a defaultRedirect, ASP.NET automatically passes the filename of the page that generated the error in the query string, as a parameter called "aspxerrorpath". You may wish to use this in your error page, perhaps to suggest an alternative page or log the request to an errors file.*

Figure 3-12. Our edited Web.config file

Forget 404: Customizing Your "Page Not Found"

 Download supporting files at www.apress.com.
The files for this tip are in the "Ch3–Page Not Found" folder.

In the last tip, we discovered how to stop your code being displayed when an error occurs. We also found out how to redirect the user to a certain page when such problems arise. Well, this also kicks in with such irritations as the dreaded "404, Page Not Found".

In those situations where a requested page is not found on the Web server, you might want to display your own custom message rather than a generic error message. You can do that easily, just by expanding the <customErrors> element of your Web.config file.

The following snippet shows part of an edited Web.config file that redirects to genericerror.aspx when regular errors occur, or 404.html when a file not found occurs (see Figure 3-13), or 403.html when a permission-denied server error occurs.

```
<configuration>
  <system.web>
  ...
    <customErrors mode="On"
        defaultRedirect="genericerror.aspx">
      <error statusCode="404"
        redirect="404.html" />
      <error statusCode="403"
        redirect="403.html" />
    </customErrors>
  ...
  </system.web>
</configuration>
```

Figure 3-13. Error 404 redirection kicking in, when I access a nonexistent page

Server.Transfer vs. Response.Redirect

If you read a lot of industry magazines and ASP.NET code samples, you may find that, although the majority uses Response.Redirect to send the user to another page, some seem to prefer the rather mysterious-sounding Server.Transfer. So, what's the difference?

Well, Response.Redirect simply sends a message down to the browser telling it to move to another page. So, you may run code like
Response.Redirect("WebForm2.aspx") or
Response.Redirect("http://www.karlmoore.com/") to send the user to another page.

Server.Transfer is similar in that it sends the user to another page with a statement such as Server.Transfer("WebForm2.aspx"). However, the statement has a number of distinct advantages and disadvantages.

Firstly, transferring to another page using Server.Transfer conserves server resources. Instead of telling the browser to redirect, it simply changes the "focus" on the Web server and transfers the request. This means you don't get quite as many HTTP requests coming through, which therefore eases the pressure on your Web server and makes your applications run faster.

But watch out: because the "transfer" process can work on only those sites running on the server, you can't use Server.Transfer to send the user to an external site. Only Response.Redirect can do that.

Secondly, Server.Transfer maintains the original URL in the browser. This can really help streamline data entry techniques, although it may make for confusion when debugging.

That's not all: the Server.Transfer method also has a second parameter— "preserveForm". If you set this to True, using a statement such as Server.Transfer("WebForm2.aspx", True), the existing query string and any form variables will still be available to the page you are transferring to.

For example, if your WebForm1.aspx has a TextBox control called TextBox1 and you transferred to WebForm2.aspx with the preserveForm parameter set to True, you'd be able to retrieve the value of the original page TextBox control by referencing Request.Form("TextBox1").

This technique is great for wizard-style input forms split over multiple pages. But there's another thing you'll want to watch out for when using the preserveForm parameter. ASP.NET has a bug whereby, in certain situations, an error will occur when attempting to transfer the form and query string values. You'll find this documented at http://support.microsoft.com/default.aspx?id=kb;en-us;Q316920.

The unofficial solution is to set the enableViewStateMac property to True on the page you'll be transferring to, then set it back to False. This records that you want a definitive False value for this property and resolves the bug.

So, in brief: Response.Redirect simply tells the browser to visit another page. Server.Transfer helps reduce server requests, keeps the URL the same and, with a little bug-bashing, allows you to transfer the query string and form variables.

> **TOP TIP** *Don't confuse* Server.Transfer *with* Server.Execute, *which executes the page and returns the results. It was useful in the past, but, with ASP.NET, it's been replaced with fresher methods of development. Ignore it.*

Using .IsClientConnected *for Long Processes*

If you're performing a long process or calculation behind a Web page, it's a good idea to periodically check whether your client is still connected. You may want to do this at set intervals in your code, or just before sending your results down to the browser.

You can do this through the innovatively titled property, `Response.IsClientConnected`. It'll return a `True` if the client is still connected to the server. If it isn't, you'll want to run a `Response.End` and exit your code.

Preventing Client Caching, with Meta Tags

If you're dealing with time-sensitive information in your ASP.NET Web pages, you probably don't want browsers caching your pages away somewhere. You want the content to expire immediately, so the only way users can view the information again is to revisit and obtain the latest data from your site.

You can control caching in the client browser through the use of meta tags. They have nothing to do with ASP.NET and are handled purely on the client side, but I've included this tip as this exact question is regularly raised at even the most high profile .NET development groups.

So, here's how you do it. Just add the following meta tag to your HTML, within the <head> tags, to expire your content immediately:

```
<META HTTP-EQUIV="Expires" CONTENT="0">
```

You can also attempt to tell the browser to not bother caching this page at all, with the following meta tag:

```
<meta http-equiv="pragma" content="no-cache">
```

Either works: just tap them out and you're finished.

Uploading Files Larger Than 4MB

By default, the size limit for ASP.NET uploads is set at 4MB. Although this is large enough for most sites, if you're dealing in particularly hefty uploads, there's a little-known technique for upping the cap.

Simply open machine.config in the <Windows>\Microsoft.NET\Framework\ <currentversion>\Config folder and locate the following setting:

```
<httpRuntime maxRequestLength=4096>
```

Now, simply alter the `maxRequestLength` value to a figure of your choice. To allow uploads of up to 8MB, for example, change the value from 4096 to 8192.

What to Do When Session_End Doesn't Work

It's one of the most common complaints on the newsgroups: "Hey! My Session End event doesn't fire. The code I want to run when the Session finishes just never runs." And then you get the whiz kid that replies with "It's a bug. You can't rely on it on that End event. Use another method."

Important note: the whiz kid is wrong.

If the code you've entered in your Global.asax file to run when the Session End event fires doesn't appear to be kicking in, one of the following three things could be at fault:

1. You're not using InProc. The mode attribute of the <sessionState> element in your application Web.config file must be set to "InProc". If it isn't, the End event simply cannot fire.

2. You're not using the Session. The Session End event can't fire if there's no Session to End. Are you sure your application is storing information through the Session object?

3. Your code is flawed. There's an error somewhere in the code that responds to the End event. Try running your application in debug mode, with a short <sessionState> timeout attribute. Visit the page and then wait. Does the End event kick in? Does an error occur in your code?

There is quite seriously *no* other excuse for your code not running. There's no mysterious bug. There are no weird setup issues or reasons for not trusting the Session End event. It works, no excuses.

> **TOP TIP** *Another common developer complaint is Global.asax events being fired off multiple times (i.e., the code behind a Timer event runs multiple times, even though the event should've only fired once). When multiple versions of an event fire off asynchronously, the code running may "overlap" with itself and cause problems. One highly underused trick that stops this occuring is to temporarily "freeze" your Web application when you begin such code, which ensures nothing else happens while your event code is running, then "unfreeze" at the end. You can do this by running* Application.Lock *at the beginning of your code and* Application.UnLock *at the close. Simple, but a true lifesaver.*

Spying on Your Web Host: Checking Uptime in .NET

Download supporting files at www.apress.com.
The files for this tip are in the "Ch3–Spy on Web Host" folder.

Okay, so your host promises 99.999% uptime, but are they really delivering? Unless you're either checking every couple of seconds or dishing out for some monitoring service, you really don't have much of an idea.

That is, until now.

ASP.NET Web pages served up through IIS are delivered through an ASP.NET "worker process" (aspnet_wp.exe). This file executes your code and puts all the ASP.NET pieces together. If we could access this worker process, we may be able to look at how long it had been running, its current state, and perhaps even a history, showing previous instantiations of the worker process.

Well, you can. And the following snippet of code shows you exactly how:

```
Dim strReport As String
Dim objInfo As ProcessInfo = ProcessModelInfo.GetCurrentProcessInfo
' Get time information
strReport = "ASP.NET was started at " & _
    objInfo.StartTime.ToString & ". " & _
    "It has been running for " & _
    objInfo.Age.Days & " days, " & _
    objInfo.Age.Hours & " hours and " & _
    objInfo.Age.Minutes & " minutes. "
Response.Write(strReport)
' Get other info
strReport = "The process ID is " & _
    objInfo.ProcessID & ". " & _
    "Current status is " & _
    objInfo.Status.ToString & ". " & _
    "Peak memory used was " & _
    objInfo.PeakMemoryUsed & ". " & _
    "Request count is currently " & _
    objInfo.RequestCount & "."
Response.Write(strReport)
```

It may look a little weird, but all we're doing here is retrieving a `ProcessInfo` object that contains information about the current worker process. This is then formulated into a string using key properties and spurted out to the user, through `Response.Write`. Try it out: you'll be given an instant server status report.

The `ProcessModelInfo` class also has a `GetHistory` method, which allows you to retrieve information about previous instances of the `aspnet_wp.exe` process. It returns an array of `ProcessInfo` objects. Either use a `For...Next` loop to retrieve this information or bind direct to a DataGrid.

There's also a technique for retrieving the amount of time that your actual server has been running (not just the ASP.NET worker process). Simply nab the `TickCount` from the `Environment` class, which lists the number of milliseconds the machine has been running. After that, either perform a few simple calculations— or, slightly easier, convert it into a period of time (a `TimeSpan` object), and then retrieve the appropriate properties. (See Figure 3-14.) Here's my snippet of code that does exactly that:

```
Dim tsAge As TimeSpan = _
    TimeSpan.FromMilliseconds(Environment.TickCount)
Dim intDaysUp As Integer = tsAge.Days
Dim intHoursUp As Integer = tsAge.Hours
Dim intMinsUp As Integer = tsAge.Minutes
Response.Write("The server has been up " & _
    intDaysUp & " days, " & intHoursUp & _
    " hours and " & intMinsUp & " minutes.")
```

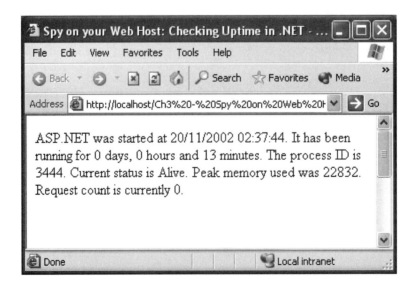

Figure 3-14. ASP.NET only been running for 13 minutes? Sounds dodgy. Change your host.

Can It Cope? Stress Testing Your Web Apps

It's the new face of that old, often troublesome Web Application Stress package. It's a tool designed to see whether your site can stand up against heavy traffic. It's distributed with the Enterprise and Architect editions of Visual Studio .NET. It's the curiously christened... Application Center Test (ACT).

Here's how it works. You launch ACT and record a browser session, simulating a regular user. You may explore the site, do a little searching, upload a couple of files, or do whatever users typically do at your site. Then you tell ACT to rerun that test over and over again, perhaps simultaneously and with great speed. When finished, you check out the results to see how both your server and ASP/ASP.NET applications stood up to being thrashed.

Start by launching ACT: click on Programs ➤ Microsoft Visual Studio .NET ➤ Microsoft Visual Studio .NET Enterprise Features ➤ Microsoft Application Center Test. You'll see a bundle of existing samples. To record your own, right-click on the Tests node and choose New Test. Skipping through the wizard, select Record a New Test, then click on the button to start recording. An empty Internet Explorer browser window will appear.

> **TOP TIP** *Using a dial-up networking connection? It's poorly documented, but ACT won't record test sessions through a regular dial-up. In fact, even if you're recording on the* `http://localhost/` *server while a dial-up connection is active in the background, it'll refuse to record. Yes, it's annoyingly picky: try disconnecting and attempting once more.*

Ensure that you are not working offline (if so, uncheck this mode using the File menu), then start acting like a user: browse, login, search. Play around for a minute or three. When you're done, stop using the browser window and return to ACT, clicking on Stop Recording. Provide your test with a name, then finish the wizard.

Your test should now appear under the list of tests. Select it and view the VBScript code that's generated for you. If you need to remove any unnecessary requests, simply comment out the `call SendRequest#` line in the `Sub Main` method at the bottom of your test script.

So, you have your test recorded. Now, let's look at its settings: right-click on your test and select Properties. This is where you choose how far to push your application, selecting parameters such as how many simultaneous browser connections you want to simulate or how long you wish to run the test. You can also use the Counters tab to monitor certain parts of your system as the site is being accessed, potentially enabling you to track down bottlenecks. The Users tab also lets you specify a list of test users to log in to your site (although this requires a little custom programming and a surf through the help files). Click OK when finished.

When you're ready to begin, add any notes for this test in the top panel, then right-click on your test and select Start Test. You'll be shown a summary as the whole thing churns away. If you're curious, you can also click Show Details for an instant graphical view of how it's all going.

After the test has finished, you'll probably want to see, detailed report as to how it went. Click on Close, then select the Results node and highlight your test run. You should be presented with a graphical report showing how well your site handled the situation—or not, as the case may be. Here, you'll be able to see how many application requests per second the Web server was able to handle, how long it took the server to respond and how much bandwidth you used per second. (See Figure 3-15.)

If you chose to record performance counters, you should also be able to view data about how your machine handled itself, too. If you wish, you can check multiple tests and compare results. More information about analyzing the content in these reports can be found in the ACT help file under "Analyzing the Test Results."

If your site didn't hold up as well as you thought it should—reacting slowly and producing connection errors—you might want to start looking at how you can optimize your application a little more. For example, you may implement caching, rewrite inefficient code, distribute your application over multiple machines (a "Web farm"), or simply upgrade your server.

No matter what the outcome, it's always good practice to stress test your application in preparation for the real world. Because you never know when that next flood of visitors will be checking in.

> **TOP TIP** *If you have the urge, you can even use ACT directly from within Visual Studio .NET. When creating a new project, select Other Projects ➤ Application Center Test Projects ➤ ACT Project. From here, you can record a test and then run it within VS .NET. You don't get the fancy user interface nor the handy samples, plus all the results are reported there and then in the text-only Output window, but it's a potentially useful integration.*

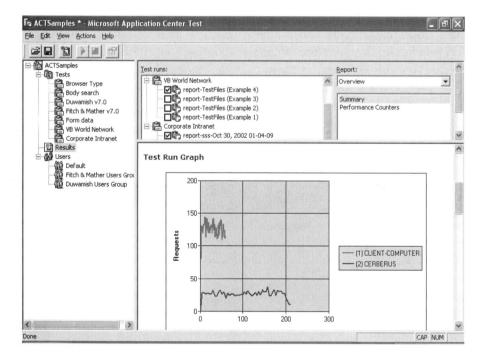

Figure 3-15. A little test I ran earlier with a bottle-necking application

The Two Methods of Moving Web Servers

So, your Web application has become a real company success, but, despite all your fine-tuning, it's starting to slow down. Why? The server just isn't powerful enough. It's time to move, but how?

You can choose between two methods. The first is the absolute easiest: simply open your project and click on Project ➤ Copy Project. Alter the destination project folder to refer to your new server, select exactly what you want to copy, and click OK. (See Figure 3-16.) No problem.

However, everyone knows—more often than not—there are special "configuration issues" and "setup requirements" administrators require that hinder such an easy deployment.

In these situations, you'll require a manual move. To do this, first enter your actual application folder (something like c:\inetpub\wwwroot\YourAppName\). Next, copy all the required files and folders across to a desired directory on the remote server. If you're moving your source code as well, edit the YourAppName.vbproj.webinfo XML-based file so it points to your application on the new server.

Next, you'll have to set up this directory as a virtual folder in IIS. To do this, on the remote machine, click on Start ➤ Programs ➤ Administrative Tools, then select Internet Services Manager (Windows 2000/2003) or Internet Information Services (Windows XP). Expand on your machine name, right-click Default Web Site, and select New ➤ Virtual Directory. Follow the wizard, providing an alias, specifying the directory containing the new files, and setting up permissions.

And that's it for the manual move. You'll now be able to access your application at `http://newserver/alias/`. Simple!

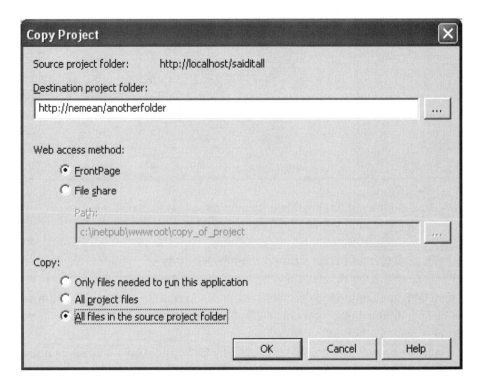

Figure 3-16. Pick yer choices and copy yer files!

Where to Put Your Files with an ASP.NET Host

If you're developing your ASP.NET Web application on the server you intend to run it on, you'll find deployment a real doddle: just hand out the address. Don't worry about the security of your source code: IIS will automatically prevent anyone from downloading it. And when it comes to administration? Simply open the project straight from the Web server and start changing. Supercool!

However, if you're exposing your ASP.NET Web application through a host account, it's most likely that you'll be given just one "virtual folder," a single application within IIS. That's great if you're just uploading one core application—you merely have to access your folder via FTP, transfer all your application files, access through your URL, and, hey presto!

More likely, however, is that a developer will have multiple ASP.NET Web applications to upload—a root application, for example, and a separate project he wants to place in an "admin" subdirectory. If you do a direct upload from here, the separate admin project will simply not work: its assembly (the DLL file in the Bin folder) is in the wrong location. Try it and you'll see. There are other considerations, too, such as the location of Global.asax.

So, if you're uploading multiple ASP.NET Web applications, follow this three-point checklist for trouble-free deployment:

1. Create a Bin directory via FTP in your root application folder. Go through every Web application you plan to upload and move its contents (typically your assembly DLL, any referenced components, and a possible debug file) into this one directory.

2. You're allowed only one Web.config and Global.asax file per IIS application. Choose the files you want to use and upload them directly into your root folder. Make sure you do not upload a Web.config file into any other directory: it'll cause an error in that directory, whereas excess Global.asax files simply get ignored.

3. Finally, upload the rest of your files (typically just ASPX pages) into the relevant locations and subdirectories, and then attempt to access via your URL. They'll all automatically find their supporting assemblies in the root Bin folder, plus use the Web.config and Global.asax files you uploaded.

It's always confusing at first, but follow these three steps to take real advantage of your hosting account and save yourself a good few bucks. Good luck!

Uh-oh: Installing IIS After Visual Studio .NET

If you install IIS after Visual Studio .NET, you'll need to do a little reconfiguring before you can successfully create your own ASP.NET applications. Thankfully, it's relatively simple: just look up "installing Internet Information Server" in the help index. Halfway through the page, you'll find full instructions on how to install IIS, optionally reconfigure FrontPage extensions, and, finally, repair the .NET Framework. Enjoy!

CHAPTER 4

Working with Data

DATABASES ARE VITAL to the world of programming. In my early days, I shivered at the *D* word, but now practically every application needs somewhere to store information about employees, customers, orders, whoever, whatever.

In the past, we've had DAO, RDO, and ADO, an alphabet soup of acronyms representing technologies that allow us to access databases in code. With the launch of the .NET Framework, we're introduced to ADO.NET, the all-new method of plugging into all our favorite database formats—and there's not a Recordset in sight.

How does it work? You have a bundle of objects in the `System.Data` namespace: one set for accessing OLE databases such as Oracle or Access, and another fine-tuned for accessing SQL Server (*plug plug*).

The concept of the aging ADO Recordset is replaced with the ADO.NET DataSet, which is essentially a bundle of tables in one object, with possible relationships between them. You also have a `Command` object specific to both SQL Server and OLE databases, allowing you to get close to your data and execute SQL statements directly. These `Command` objects can work with `DataReader` objects, which are like forward-only, read-only Recordsets.

Confused? You will be.

In fact, if you haven't touched ADO.NET before, I'm willing to bet that you'll find the *Essentials* portion of this chapter scarier than *Developer Secrets*. The trick is, however, not to be overwhelmed... simply curious.

What will we learn in this chapter? As ever, we begin with the basics to either refresh your knowledge or get you up and running as quickly as possible. Then, we're going to dive straight into those amazing secrets.

We'll discover how to send our data straight to the user as an Excel spread-sheet with just a couple of lines of code (Excel not required!). You'll find out how to quickly create editable feature-full data grids for both Windows and the Web. We'll even get the lowdown on all those little-known developer tricks, such as paging, sorting, confirming deletes, color coding, and much, much more.

Ready to rumble? Read on!

The Essentials

The world of databases is a big one, and in .NET there's much to learn. Many books have been written on this topic alone. Here, however, we're just dedicating a few core bullet points to ensure that everyone gets the feel of how ADO.NET works, whether you're moving from the VB6 school or are a seasoned professional who's already well accustomed to its trials and tribulations.

If you're brand new to the world of databases, you'll probably feel this is all a bit too much, too soon. In that case, I'd recommend you check out a more gradual introduction, such as the whole database walkthrough in *Karl Moore's Visual Basic .NET: The Tutorials* (ISBN 1-59059-021-X).

Once again, before we begin this section, let me remind you: don't worry if you can't understand every single point. The *Developer Secrets* are completely self-contained and don't rely on your knowledge of what follows. But, of course, it helps.

- Databases are just a storage place for information.

- You can edit databases—create tables, add data, set up stored procedures, design relationships, and so on—through the Visual Studio .NET Server Explorer. Click on View ➤ Server Explorer to access, right-click on the Data Connections node and select Add Connection to connect into a database, then expand and click to perform edits or make additions. The Servers node also has inherent support for SQL Server databases.

- To quickly bind information from a table to a grid (the DataGrid control) in either Windows forms or Web forms, simply drag and drop your table from the Server Explorer, add a DataGrid control and set its `DataSource` property, then fill and bind in code. These techniques are demonstrated in the tips, "Seven Steps to a Quick, Editable Windows Grid" (follow the instructions up to Step 6 and "Nine Steps to a Quick, Editable Web Grid" (follow the instructions to Step 5).

- To bind data to controls on a Windows form, drag and drop your table from the Server Explorer onto your Windows form. Right-click on the `DataAdapter` object that is added, select Generate DataSet, change the suggested DataSet name if required, and then click OK. Add controls to your form to display information from the table, then for each, click on the dropdown menu for the `Text` property, underneath the (DataBindings) section. In the dropdown menu, drill down to your DataSet, then table, finally selecting the field you want to bind to. The form is now set up for data binding. Here is a bunch of sample code snippets for making it all work together:

```
' Fill DataSet with info from DB
DataAdapter1.Fill(DataSet11)
' Move forward one record, updating bound fields
BindingContext(DataSet11, "TableName").Position += 1
' Move backward
BindingContext(DataSet11, "TableName").Position -= 1
' Add new record
BindingContext(DataSet11, "TableName").AddNew()
' Delete record
Dim intIndex As Integer
intIndex = BindingContext(DataSet11, "TableName").Position
BindingContext(DataSet11, "TableName").RemoveAt(intIndex)
' Update DB with any DataSet changes
DataAdapter1.Update(DataSet11)
```

- Most databases talk in a version of Structured Query Language (SQL). Here are samples of common SQL statements, for easy reference:

```
SELECT * FROM customers
INSERT INTO customers (id, name, address)
    VALUES(123, 'Joshua Kadison', '101 Bime Street, Texas')
UPDATE customers
    SET balance = 899.12
    WHERE id = 123
DELETE FROM customers
    WHERE id = 123
```

- Part of the .NET Framework is ADO.NET, the new non-COM version of ADO (ActiveX Data Objects). ADO.NET contains classes that allow you to interact with databases in code. You may, for example, create a new table or retrieve information about a customer with a SQL statement.

- All the ADO.NET classes are stored under the System.Data namespace. This namespace is further split into two main namespaces: SqlClient, which contains classes designed and optimized to work with SQL Server, and OleDb, which contains classes for working with OLE databases such as Access and Oracle.

- The only real difference between classes in the SqlClient and OleDb classes is the prefix (Sql or OleDb in front of the classes) and the way you declare the connection string. (SQL Server doesn't require you to insert a provider: it knows it's SQL Server, whereas, with OLE DB, you need to specify which database driver to use.) Most times, you can simply edit these two items and you'll be able to convert code snippets between the two formats.

- If you don't have SQL Server on your machine, you can always download and distribute the free "poor man's" version, Microsoft Desktop Engine (MSDE). To do this, run InstMSDE.exe from your Microsoft Visual Studio .NET 2003\SDK\v1.1\Samples\Setup\msde folder (if running VS .NET 2003, "Everett") or Microsoft Visual Studio .NET\FrameworkSDK\Samples\Setup\MSDE (if running VS .NET 2002). This tool lacks the visual editors, and it tends to bottleneck at a certain level of performance.

- In ADO.NET, you can choose between two main methods of working with databases in code. The first involves creating a Command object, which holds a SQL statement, and executing it directly against the database. You may also retrieve results into a VB6-style open, forward-only, read-only Recordset called a DataReader. This is typically used for quick, lightweight operations. The second method involves creating a DataAdapter, then using the SQL statement behind this to fill a DataSet, which is like a VB6 Recordset that has the ability to store multiple, possibly related tables (think shaped Recordsets). You can then update information in the DataSet and pass it back to the DataAdapter to update the appropriate records. This is more useful for relational data that could require more complicated editing.

- Here is a code template using the Command method of executing a SQL statement, written for SQL Server (the period in the connection string is a method of referring to your *local* database server):

```
Dim MyConnection As New SqlClient.SqlConnection _
    ("server=.;database=MySample;trusted_connection=true")
Dim MyCommand As New SqlClient.SqlCommand( _
 "INSERT INTO MyTable(val1, val2) VALUES('My', 'Sample')", MyConnection)
MyConnection.Open()
MyCommand.ExecuteNonQuery()
MyConnection.Close()
```

- Here is a code template using the Command method of retrieving information into a DataReader, written for SQL Server:

```
Dim MyCommand As New SqlClient.SqlCommand( _
    "SELECT * FROM MyTable", MyConnection)
Dim MyReader As SqlClient.SqlDataReader
MyReader.Open()
MyReader = MyCommand.ExecuteReader
Do While MyReader.Read = True
    MessageBox.Show(MyReader.Item("MyColumnName"))
Loop
MyReader.Close()
MyConnection.Close()
```

- Here we find a selection of typical template code using the more feature-rich, yet memory-expensive DataAdapter method of manipulating data—this time using an Access database:

```
' General object declarations
Dim objConnection As New OleDb.OleDbConnection( _
    "Provider=Microsoft.Jet.OLEDB.4.0;Data Source=c:\mydb.mdb")
Dim objDataAdapter As New OleDb.OleDbDataAdapter( _
    "Select * from MyTable", objConnection)
Dim objCommandBuilder As New OleDb.OleDbCommandBuilder( _
    objDataAdapter)
Dim objDataSet As New DataSet(), objRow As DataRow
' Fill your DataSet with schema information
objDataAdapter.FillSchema(objDataSet, SchemaType.Source, "MyTable")
' Fill your DataSet with the result of your SQL statement
objDataAdapter.Fill(objDataSet, "MyTable")
' Add a record
objRow = objDataSet.Tables("MyTable").NewRow
objRow.Item("ColumnName") = "Value"
objDataSet.Tables("MyTable").Rows.Add(objRow)
' Find and edit a row
objRow = objDataSet.Tables("MyTable").Rows.Find("PrimaryKeyValue")
objRow.Item("ColumnName") = "Value"
' Delete a row
objRow.Delete()
' Update the backend database
objDataAdapter.Update(objDataSet)
```

- The DataAdapter method of working allows you to fill your DataSet with multiple tables, then create relationships among them. Here is a code template showing how you may work with that relationship in code:

```
' Setup relationship
objDataSet.Relations.Add("RelationshipName", _
    objDataSet.Tables("ParentTableName").Columns("PrimaryKeyName"), _
    objDataSet.Tables("ChildTableName").Columns("ForeignKeyName")
' Get access to first row
objParentRow = objDataSet.Tables("ParentTableName").Rows(0)
' Loop through each child record for this parent row
For Each objChildRow In objParentRow.GetChildRows("RelationshipName")
    MessageBox.Show(objChildRow.Item("AnyColumnName"))
Next
```

- To summarize the main objects used in the previous code snippets: the Connection object provides the link to the database; the DataAdapter object provides the communications link between the database and DataSet; the DataSet object is generic (not specific to any particular type of database) and holds multiple tables of editable in-memory database information, allowing you to set up relationships among the tables; the DataReader object is a one-table, forward-only, read-only version of a DataSet; and a Command object holds a SQL statement that you can execute directly against a database.

- A *transaction* refers to a bunch of statements that must be completed as a whole or not at all. These are used in the database world to ensure the integrity of your data. Here is a code template for implementing transactions, using the SQL Server classes:

```
Dim MyTransaction As SqlClient.SqlTransaction
MyTransaction = MyConnection.BeginTransaction
Try
    ' Perform processing here, perhaps adding or
    ' deleting data via Command objects.
    ' Be sure to set the Transaction property of your
    ' Command object(s) equal to the MyTransaction object
    MyTransaction.Commit()
Catch
    ' Errors occured, so rollback any changes made
    MyTransaction.Rollback()
End Try
```

- You can also use parameters and call stored procedures using the Command object. See the help index for more information.

- Full instruction on using all the ADO.NET objects listed here is given in *Karl Moore's Visual Basic .NET: The Tutorials*, which is also available from Apress at www.apress.com.

Developer Secrets

Tired of the bare bones? Want to get stuck into the real meat behind databases in .NET? Then check out the following supercool developer secrets:

- Generating GUIDs in a Flash

- Making Your Own Connection String Creator

- Finding the Last Identity Number Added

- Cheating with SQL

- Returning Multiple Tables into a DataSet

- Checking Whether SQL Server Is Available

- Seven Steps to a Quick, Editable Windows Grid

- Nine Steps to a Quick, Editable Web Grid

- How to Use HTML in a Web Grid

- Using Hyperlinks in Your Web Grid

- Dates, Currency, Percentages: Formatting your Web Grid Data

- Looking Good: Color-Coding Your Web Grid

- Little-Known Technique for Confirming Web Deletes

- Selecting Multiple Web Form Grid Items, Hotmail-Style

- Click Anywhere and Select, with a Web Grid

- The Lowdown on Using Dropdown Boxes in a Web Grid

- Speedy, Personalized Web Data Binding

- Quick and Easy Data Paging, with Your Web Grid

- Sorting in Seconds, with Your Web Grid

- Amazingly Simple Method for Exporting Your Web Grid to Excel

- Returning a DataSet from an Excel Spreadsheet

- Get Microsoft to Write Your Code—Amazing Undocumented SQL Server Tool!

Raring to get started? On your marks, get set....

Generating GUIDs in a Flash

 Download supporting files at www.apress.com.
The files for this tip are in the "Ch4–GUIDs" folder.

GUIDs (globally unique identifiers) are 128-bit integers that are automatically generated based on approximately two zillion frequently varying factors. In brief, they're useful when you need a value that you can be assured will not match any other anywhere else. Probably.

The SQL Server data type "uniqueidentifier" stores a GUID. You can either generate this value within SQL Server, using the NEWID() function (perhaps specifying the function as the default value for all new rows), or you can generate the GUID outside of SQL Server and insert it manually.

If you're doing the latter, this tip can help out. Here's a function for instantly generating your own GUID in VB .NET:

```
Public Function GetGUID() As String
    ' Returns a new GUID
    Return System.Guid.NewGuid.ToString
End Function
```

Here, our code simply uses the NewGuid function of the System.Guid namespace to return a value. If you've ever done this in VB6, you'll appreciate how very compact this simple code block really is. Finally, here's how you may use this function:

```
Dim MyGUID As String
MyGUID = GetGUID()
```

Making Your Own Connection String Creator

Download supporting files at www.apress.com.
The files for this tip are in the "Ch4–OLE DB Conn String" folder.

You're often required to generate OLE DB connection strings for use in your code; however, it's never an easy task. You can either rummage through the documentation and attempt to piece together your own, or use the VS .NET Server Explorer to make a connection and then inspect its properties.

One handy alternative, however, is to type the following code into Notepad, saving the file with a .vbs extension. Whenever you need a connection string in the future, simply launch the file. It'll run your VBScript, visually prompt you for the database details, and then offer the final connection string for you to copy from an InputBox:

```
Dim objDataLinks, strRetVal
Set objDataLinks = CreateObject("DataLinks")
On Error Resume Next ' ignore cancel
strRetVal = objDataLinks.PromptNew
On Error Goto 0
If Not IsEmpty(strRetVal) Then
InputBox "Your Connection String is listed below.", _
```

```
        "OLE DB Connection String", strRetVal
End If
Set objDataLinks = Nothing
```

You can also use this method to generate a SQL Server connection string: simply select the Microsoft OLE DB Provider for SQL Server driver and enter your details as normal. (See Figure 4-1.) When you get the returned connection string, simply remove the "Provider" portion. Easy!

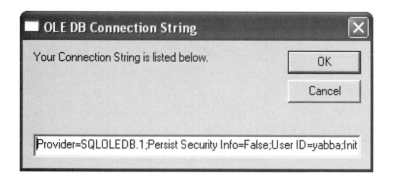

Figure 4-1. Fill out your databases details, then copy the OLE DB connection string.

Finding the Last Identity Number Added

 Download supporting files at www.apress.com.
The files for this tip are in the "Ch4–Select @@Identity" folder.

Everyone has this problem: you've just added a record to your SQL Server database and need to figure out what the automatically generated identity number was, so you can use the value as a foreign key in some child table.

It took me a good while before I figured this one out. You simply need to issue the "select @@identity" command to SQL Server, and it'll return a one-field response that contains the last identity number added during your connection.

Let's look at a commented example:

```
' Variable to hold the identity value of our record
Dim MyIdentityValue As Integer
' Setup sample connection and command
Dim objConnection As New SqlClient.SqlConnection( _
```

```
            "server=NEMEAN;database=MYDATABASE;" & _
            "user ID=USERID;password=PWD")
    Dim objCommand As New SqlClient.SqlCommand( _
        "INSERT INTO author (authorname) " & _
        "VALUES('Karl Moore')")
    ' Open connection and execute INSERT command
    objConnection.Open()
    objCommand.Connection = objConnection
    ' Execute and check minimum of one record affected...
    If objCommand.ExecuteNonQuery > 0 = True Then
        ' Setup separate command to retrieve identity value
        Dim objIdentifier As New _
            SqlClient.SqlCommand("Select @@Identity", objConnection)
        Try
            ' Return value of field
            MyIdentityValue = objIdentifier.ExecuteScalar
        Catch
            MyIdentityValue = 0
        End Try
    End If
    ' Close connection
    objConnection.Close()
```

Cheating with SQL

So, you're developing all those SQL Server applications—and keep forgetting the difference between an inner join and an outer join? Unsure whether you should Order By, Sort By, or Group By? Then maybe it's about time you started to cheat.

You see, there's an easy way to write SQL—visually! Simply use the Server Explorer to open up your SQL Server, then right-click on the Views node. Select New View, add the tables you wish to use in your query—then begin designing, specifying any sorting or criteria. Right-click on a blank area of the table view and select Property Pages to specify further options.

The designer is also particularly useful when dealing with date and time fields, as it automatically incorporates any required SQL Server functions for you. Just design the query as you would in, say, Microsoft Access.

> **TOP TIP** *The designer may be cool—but don't trust the relationships it auto-matically adds for you. Hover your mouse over a relationship to view its details. If it's incorrect, select with your mouse and press Delete. To create a relationship, drag and drop one field onto the other. Right-click and select Property Pages to alter its details.*

When you've finished, click on Query ➤ Run to test that it produces your required results. When you're happy, simply take text from the SQL pane and remove all instances of the useless *dbo* term (SQL Server adds this for the view and it will ruin your statement when used in data access code)—and that's it! (See Figure 4-2.)

You can now put your SQL statement to work, and you've saved an hour in writing and debugging in the process. Not a bad two minutes' work.

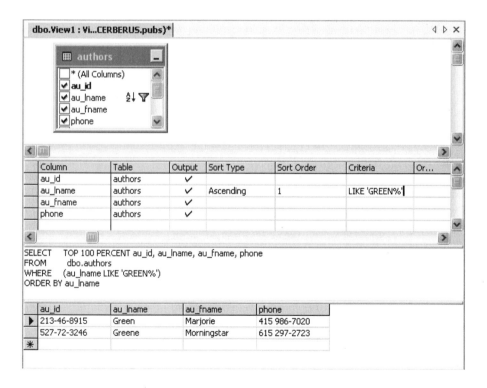

Figure 4-2. Putting together our SQL statement the easy way

Returning Multiple Tables into a DataSet

 Download supporting files at www.apress.com.
The files for this tip are in the "Ch4–Multiple Tables in DataSet" folder.

One of the big new features of the DataSet over the old Recordset is its ability to hold multiple tables of data at a time. But how many developers take advantage of this feature? How many still use multiple DataSet objects to hold multiple tables?

Don't answer that one.

If you find yourself victim, then you might want to add the following code snippet to your basket. It accepts a connection string and string array of table names. It returns a DataSet containing all the tables requested (not, of course, accounting for errors)—ready for you to add relationships, apply rules, schemas, and all the other whizzy techniques you may wish to embrace.

Here's the code you'll need:

```vb
Public Function GetDataSet(ByVal ConnectionString As String, _
    ByRef Tables() As String) As System.Data.DataSet

    ' Create connection, command object and empty DataSet
    Dim objConn As New System.Data.SqlClient.SqlConnection(ConnectionString)
    Dim objCmd As New System.Data.SqlClient.SqlCommand()
    objCmd.Connection = objConn
    objCmd.CommandType = System.Data.CommandType.Text
    Dim objDS As New System.Data.DataSet()

    Try
        ' Create new DataAdapter
        Dim objDA As New System.Data.SqlClient.SqlDataAdapter(objCmd)
        objDA.SelectCommand = objCmd
        ' Open connection
        objConn.Open()
        ' Populate the DataSet with specified tables
        Dim intCount As Integer
        For intCount = 0 To Tables.GetUpperBound(0)
            objCmd.CommandText = "SELECT * FROM " & Tables(intCount)
            objDA.Fill(objDS, Tables(intCount))
        Next

    Catch e As Exception
        ' Calling code must check for thrown errors
```

```
        Throw e
    Finally
        ' Clean up
        objConn.Close()
    End Try
    Return objDS
End Function
```

And here's how you might call this function:

```
Dim MyDataSet As New DataSet()
Dim Tables(2) As String
Tables(0) = "authors" : Tables(1) = "sales" : Tables(2) = "titles"
MyDataSet = GetDataSet("data source=localhost;initial catalog=pubs;" & _
    "persist security info=False;user id=sa;pwd= ", Tables)
```

Checking Whether SQL Server Is Available

 Download supporting files at www.apress.com.
The files for this tip are in the "Ch4–SQL Server Online Check" folder.

When you're designing applications that work with databases over the Internet, perhaps the largest problem you face is ensuring that everything can actually connect to everything else. You need to ensure that your users have a valid connection to the Net, and you need to ensure that your database server is up and running.

It's not a typically easy process—and it's a topic that attracts an unusually large amount of error handling code.

However, why not take the simple route and avoid potential big errors later on by checking whether your SQL Server is available to the user before starting your database code?

The following function does just that for you. Simply call IsSQLServerAvailable, passing in your server or IP address. It attempts a connection and returns a True if everything seems fine. Here's the code:

```
Public Function IsSQLServerAvailable(ByVal ServerAddress As String) As Boolean
    ' Tests an SQL Server connection by name or IP address
    Try
        ' Attempt to get server address
        Dim objIPHost As New System.Net.IPHostEntry()
```

```
            objIPHost = System.Net.Dns.Resolve(ServerAddress)
            Dim objAddress As System.Net.IPAddress
            objAddress = objIPHost.AddressList(0)
            ' Connect to port 1433, most common SQL Server
            ' port. If your target is different, change here
            Dim objTCP As System.Net.Sockets.TcpClient = _
                New System.Net.Sockets.TcpClient()
            objTCP.Connect(objAddress, 1433)
            ' No problems (hurrah!)
            ' Close and cleanup
            objTCP.Close()
            objTCP = Nothing
            objAddress = Nothing
            objIPHost = Nothing
            ' Return success
            Return True

        Catch ex As Exception
            ' Server unavailable, return fail value
            Return False
        End Try
    End Function
```

And here's how you might call this function:

```
Dim blnCanConnect As Boolean
blnCanConnect = IsSQLServerOnline("maxsql001.maximumasp.com")
```

Seven Steps to a Quick, Editable Windows Grid

One of the most common requests when dealing with databases is the ability to display a grid that "binds" to a table or view, displaying information and allowing you to quickly edit data. The good news is that it's a relatively simple process in .NET—and the following seven steps will guide you through the exact process.

Ready to rumble?

1. Open the Server Explorer (View ➤ Server Explorer). If you're connecting into a SQL Server database, expand the Servers node, locate your target machine (if not available, click on the Connect to Server icon and specify the machine name), and then drill down to your database. If you're connecting into another type of database, right-click on the Data Connections node, select Add Connection, and connect into your database.

2. Expand the list of tables (or views) and drag the one you want to bind to your grid onto your Windows form. Two components will be created: a Connection object, which connects into the database, and a DataAdapter object, which acts as the "phone line" between your Connection object and your actual set of data (your DataSet).

3. Right-click on the DataAdapter and choose Generate DataSet. A dialog box will appear, about to create the template upon which your DataSet will be based. (A DataSet based on a template like this is called a *typed DataSet*, whereas the template itself is a customizable *XML schema*, sometimes referred to as an *XSD* file [XML Schema Definition].) Ensure that New is selected and replace the suggested name with something more sensible, such as "Customer". Ensure that the "Add this DataSet to the designer" option is checked. Click on OK when finished. Two things will happen: a Customer.xsd (or similar) template will be added to your Solution, and a DataSet component will be added to your form, based on the template. Rename your new DataSet to, say, "dsCustomer".

4. Drag and drop a DataGrid control from the toolbox onto your form. Resize as appropriate, then right-click and select Auto Format. Choose a new style, such as "Professional 3" or "Colorful 3".

5. Change the DataSource property of your DataGrid control, selecting your DataSet table from the dropdown list.

6. Add the following line of code to respond to your form Load event or place it behind a button. It tells your DataAdapter to talk through the connection, retrieve data, then pass it into your DataSet (which is feeding the DataGrid):

```
MyDataAdapter.Fill(MyDataSet)
```

7. Add the following code to respond to your form Closing event, or place it behind a button. It tells your DataAdapter to talk through the connection, updating the source database with any changes made to the DataSet (which may have been through editing the DataGrid):

```
MyDataAdapter.Update(MyDataSet)
```

And that's it: now all you have to do is run and test! (See Figure 4-3.)

If you've already created your data objects in code, simply set the `DataSource` property of your DataGrid to your DataSet table in code, then continue from Step 6.

> **TOP TIP** *Don't want a certain column displayed in your Windows form DataGrid? Simply configure your DataAdapter so it pulls back only the information you want. (Right-click on the DataAdapter and select Configure Data Adapter.) Be careful when excluding primary keys, however, as this can cause problems when editing and updating. Alternatively, use views or customize the more flexible ASP.NET DataGrid. (See the "Nine Steps to a Quick, Editable Web Grid" tip next.) The official Microsoft workaround for "hiding" columns is more complex, as no properties for the columns are exposed directly. However if you're interested, check out* `http://support.microsoft.com/default.aspx?scid=KB;EN-US;q317951`.

> **ANOTHER TOP TIP** *Although the Web has plenty of .NET resources, few have spent time collating real Windows DataGrid newsgroup questions quite as well as George Shepherd. Check out his FAQ for answers to common puzzlers at* `www.syncfusion.com/FAQ/WinForms/FAQ_c44c.asp`. *It's C# based, but still highly understandable. (See Chapter 9 if you feel confused!)*

au_id	au_lname	au_fname	phone	address	city	state	zip	contract
172-32-1176	White	Johnson	408 496-7223	10932 Bigge	Menlo Park	CA	94025	☑
213-46-8915	Green	Marjorie	415 986-7020	309 63rd St.	Oakland	CA	94618	☑
238-95-7766	Carson	Cheryl	415 548-7723	589 Darwin Ln	Berkeley	CA	94705	☑
267-41-2394	O'Leary	Michael	408 286-2428	22 Cleveland	San Jose	CA	95128	☑
274-80-9391	Straight	Dean	415 834-2919	5420 College	Oakland	CA	94609	☑
341-22-1782	Smith	Meander	913 843-0462	10 Mississippi	Lawrence	KS	66044	☐
409-56-7008	Bennet	Abraham	415 658-9932	6223 Bateman	Berkeley	CA	94705	☑
427-17-2319	Dull	Ann	415 836-7128	3410 Blonde S	Palo Alto	CA	94301	☑
472-27-2349	Gringlesby	Burt	707 938-6445	PO Box 792	Covelo	CA	95428	☑
486-29-1786	Locksley	Charlene	415 585-4620	18 Broadway	San Francisco	CA	94130	☑
527-72-3246	Greene	Morningstar	615 297-2723	22 Graybar H	Nashville	TN	37215	☐
648-92-1872	Blotchet-Halls	Reginald	503 745-6402	55 Hillsdale Bl	Corvallis	OR	97330	☑
672-71-3249	Yokomoto	Akiko	415 935-4228	3 Silver Ct.	Walnut Creek	CA	94595	☑
712-45-1867	del Castillo	Innes	615 996-8275	2286 Cram Pl.	Ann Arbor	MI	48105	☑
722-51-5454	DeFrance	Michel	219 547-9982	3 Balding Pl.	Gary	IN	46403	☑
724-08-9931	Stringer	Dirk	415 843-2991	5420 Telegrap	Oakland	CA	94609	☐
724-80-9391	MacFeather	Stearns	415 354-7128	44 Upland Hts	Oakland	CA	94612	☑
756-30-7391	Karsen	Livia	415 534-9219	5720 McAuley	Oakland	CA	94609	☑
807-91-6654	Panteley	Sylvia	301 946-8853	1956 Arlingto	Rockville	MD	20853	☑
846-92-7186	Hunter	Sheryl	415 836-7128	3410 Blonde S	Palo Alto	CA	94301	☑
893-72-1158	McBadden	Heather	707 448-4982	301 Putnam	Vacaville	CA	95688	☐
899-46-2035	Ringer	Anne	801 826-0752	67 Seventh Av	Salt Lake City	UT	84152	☑
998-72-3567	Ringer	Albert	801 826-0752	67 Seventh Av	Salt Lake City	UT	84152	☑

Figure 4-3. My example DataGrid. It's quite big.

Nine Steps to a Quick, Editable Web Grid

Download supporting files at www.apress.com.
The files for this tip are in the "Ch4–Web Grid" folder.

Setting up your own editable Windows DataGrid may be an absolute doddle, but creating the equivalent grid for the Web is a little more complicated. Most books simply show you how to display data—and conveniently manage to skip the editing, deleting, adding, and updating stages. But not this one.

Here, we're going to create a template page that will allow you to display data from a table. You'll be able to add new records. Delete records. Edit existing records. Update the backend database. It'll handle most of your simple table operations. I've written all the code for you—and if there's any piece of functionality you don't want, just don't add it.

Let's get started.

1. Open the Server Explorer (View ➤ Server Explorer). If you're connecting into a SQL Server database, expand the Servers node, locate your target machine (if not available, click on the Connect to Server icon and specify the machine name), then drill down to your database. If you're connecting into another type of database, right-click on the Data Connections node, select Add Connection, and connect into your database.

2. Drag the table you want the grid to be based upon onto your Web form. Two components will be added—a `Connection` object, which connects into the database, and a `DataAdapter` object, which acts as the "phone line" between your `Connection` object and your actual set of data (your DataSet).

> **TOP TIP** *To preview the data coming back from your DataAdapter, right-click on your DataAdapter object and select Preview Data. To change what is returned (for example, to remove certain columns or add calculated fields), right-click and select Configure Data Adapter, and then use the designer to prepare a customized SQL statement. Do not remove primary keys: instead, make them invisible. (See the next Top Tip.)*

3. Right-click on the DataAdapter and choose Generate DataSet. A dialog box will appear, about to create the template upon which your DataSet will be based. (A DataSet based on a template like this is called a *typed DataSet*, whereas the template itself is a customizable *XML schema*, sometimes referred to as an *XSD* file.) Ensure New is selected and replace the suggested name with something more sensible, such as "Customer".

Ensure that the "Add this DataSet to the designer" option is checked. Click on OK when finished. Two things will happen: a Customer.xsd (or similar) template will be added to your Solution, and an invisible DataSet object will be added to your form, based on the template. Rename the DataSet template to, say, "dsCustomer".

4. Drag and drop a DataGrid control from the toolbox onto your form. Resize as appropriate, then right-click on and select Auto Format. Choose a new style, such as "Professional 3" or "Colorful 3".

5. Add the following code template to respond to the page Load event. This retrieves your table data from the database and binds it to your DataGrid. Be sure to replace MyDataAdapter and MyDataGrid with names of your own DataAdapter and DataGrid objects:

```
If Not IsPostBack Then
    MyDataAdapter.Fill(MyDataSet)
    MyDataGrid.DataSource = MyDataSet
    MyDataGrid.DataBind()
    DataSave(MyDataSet)
    ' The DataSave function will be added later.
    ' Remove this line and stop here if you want
    ' a read-only DataGrid
End If
```

6. Right-click on your DataGrid and select Property Builder. Select the Columns property sheet and ensure that "Create columns automatically at run time" is checked. This means that the columns are dynamically created from your table. Next, we're going to add one button to allow you to select a record, perhaps for editing or deleting. Under the "Available columns" list, expand Button Column, highlight Select, and use the ">" button to move it across to the "Selected columns". The properties of this new column button will appear below. Change its Text property to a square bracket and its Button type to a PushButton. Click on OK when finished. You should be able to see the new record select button in your grid.

> **TOP TIP** *If you want to display only certain columns in the DataGrid, you can selectively choose those required through the Property Builder. Firstly, in the General property sheet, select your data by choosing your DataSet and table for the* DataSource *and* DataMember *properties. Next, in the Columns property sheet, uncheck "Create columns automatically at run time", and then move individual fields from the list of available columns (under "Data Fields") over to the selected columns list. Click on OK when finished and continue the instructions.*

7. Add the following code to respond when the `SelectedIndexChanged` event of your DataGrid occurs. This event fires when a record is selected. This code simply highlights the row, making your selection more obvious:

```
Dim intCount As Integer
For intCount = 1 To MyDataGrid.Items.Count
    MyDataGrid.Items(intCount - 1).BorderStyle = BorderStyle.Groove
Next
MyDataGrid.SelectedItem.BorderStyle = BorderStyle.Dashed
```

8. Add the following functions behind your Web form. They provide a clean and easy way of saving and retrieving the DataSet containing our table data. Here our application uses the page `ViewState` (encrypted HTML sent back and forth between posts), but you could easily change it to use the `Session` or `Application` object if you're dealing with large tables:

```
Public Sub DataSave(ByVal DataSet As DataSet)
    If DataExists() Then
        ViewState.Item("__Data") = DataSet
    Else
        ViewState.Add("__Data", DataSet)
    End If
End Sub
Public Function DataRetrieve() As DataSet
    Return CType(ViewState.Item("__Data"), DataSet)
End Function
Public Function DataExists() As Boolean
    If Not ViewState.Item("__Data") Is Nothing Then Return True
End Function
```

9. Add six buttons to your Web Form, above the grid: Add, Delete, Edit, OK, Cancel, and Update. These will be action buttons. You will click on Add to add a new record, Delete to remove a record, Edit to edit an existing record, OK to accept an edit, Cancel to cancel an edit, and Update to save all changes to the backend database. If you don't want to implement any one of these features, simply leave it out. Behind each of those buttons, add the relevant snippet of code (you may wish to incorporate your own error handling code, too):

```
' Code to respond to the Click event of the ADD button:
'Desc: Adds a new row to the DataSet, rebinds to the
'DataGrid, then makes the row editable
If DataExists() = False Then Exit Sub
MyDataSet = DataRetrieve()
```

```vbnet
Dim rowNew As System.Data.DataRow = MyDataSet.Tables(0).NewRow
' Enter sample values for non-null fields here
' ie, rowNew.Item("uniqueTag") = "sample"
' Alternatively, use separate text boxes for input
' and add field values in code, as above.
MyDataSet.Tables(0).Rows.Add(rowNew)
MyDataGrid.EditItemIndex = MyDataGrid.Items.Count
MyDataGrid.DataSource = MyDataSet
MyDataGrid.DataBind()
DataSave(MyDataSet)

' Code to respond to the Click event of the DELETE button:
' Desc: Deletes the selected row, updates the DataSet & rebinds
If DataExists() = False Then Exit Sub
If MyDataGrid.SelectedIndex = -1 Then Exit Sub
MyDataSet = DataRetrieve()
MyDataSet.Tables(0).Rows(MyDataGrid.SelectedIndex).Delete()
MyDataGrid.EditItemIndex = -1
MyDataGrid.SelectedIndex = -1
MyDataGrid.DataSource = MyDataSet
MyDataGrid.DataBind()
DataSave(MyDataSet)

' Code to respond to the Click event of the EDIT button:
' Desc: Makes the selected row editable, then rebinds
If DataExists() = False Then Exit Sub
If MyDataGrid.SelectedIndex = -1 Then Exit Sub
Dim MyDataSet As DataSet = DataRetrieve()
MyDataGrid.DataSource = MyDataSet
MyDataGrid.EditItemIndex = MyDataGrid.SelectedIndex
MyDataGrid.DataBind()

' Code to respond to the Click event of the OK button:
' Desc: Cycles through the TextBox controls used during a standard edit,
' puts the values back in the DataSet, then rebinds. Add error handling
' as appropriate.
' NOTE: This code relies on the first column being a selection (>)
' button (it starts counting the cells from position 1, not 0). If you
' remove that button, you may have to change this code.
If DataExists() = False Then Exit Sub
If MyDataGrid.EditItemIndex = -1 Then Exit Sub
Dim intCount As Integer
Dim MyDataSet As DataSet = DataRetrieve()
With MyDataGrid
```

```
        For intCount = 1 To .Items(.EditItemIndex).Cells.Count
            If intCount = .Items(.EditItemIndex).Cells.Count Then Exit For
            ' Check that a control exists in this position
            If .Items(.EditItemIndex).Cells(intCount).Controls.Count Then
                ' Check for a standard TextBox
                If TypeOf (.Items(.EditItemIndex).Cells(intCount). _
                    Controls(0)) Is TextBox Then
                    Dim strValue As String = CType(.Items(.EditItemIndex). _
                        Cells(intCount).Controls(0), TextBox).Text
                    If strValue <> "" Then
                        ' This isn't null, so store value
                        MyDataSet.Tables(0).Rows(.EditItemIndex).Item( _
                            intCount - 1) = strValue
                    Else
                        ' Treat empty value as null
                        MyDataSet.Tables(0).Rows(.EditItemIndex).Item( _
                            intCount - 1) = System.DBNull.Value
                    End If
                End If
            End If
        Next
        .SelectedIndex = -1
        .EditItemIndex = -1
        DataSave(MyDataSet)
        .DataSource = MyDataSet
        .DataBind()
End With


' Code to respond to the Click event of the CANCEL button:
' Desc: Used to cancel an edit. Deselects an selected rows and
' exists the edit mode, then rebinds.
If DataExists() = False Then Exit Sub
MyDataGrid.SelectedIndex = -1
MyDataGrid.EditItemIndex = -1
MyDataGrid.DataSource = DataRetrieve()
MyDataGrid.DataBind()


' Code to respond to the Click event of the UPDATE button:
' Desc: Updates the underlying database, then rebinds.
' Add error handling code as appropriate.
If DataExists() = False Then Exit Sub
MyDataAdapter.Update(DataRetrieve)
MyDataGrid.DataSource = DataRetrieve()
MyDataGrid.DataBind()
```

> **TOP TIP** *Receive a "Login failed" error when running this code? Your Web application is attempting to gain access to your database, but it doesn't have permission. You'll need to do one of two things: either change the* ConnectionString *property of your* Connection *object to use a valid SQL Server username and password, rather than "integrated security" (launch the Enterprise Manager to set up new users, then see the "Finding the Last Identity Number Added" tip code for an example username/password SQL Server connection string), or use the Computer Management tool to increase permissions of the ASPNET user account (not recommended for security purposes).*

From this code base, you can do practically anything using the Web DataGrid and a little imagination. You could create a form that allows you to add items through regular input boxes, then adds a new row to the editable DataGrid in code. You could modify it so the DataSet actually contains items in a user's shopping basket, with an update feature to change quantities. You could simply use it to create a power user system that allows a privileged few to access and edit data in key administration tables within your company database.

In short, you can display your data on the Web in many different ways—and everyone wants to do something slightly different. Here, I've provided a standard code framework that will allow you to perform the most commonly requested tasks: adding, deleting, editing, and updating records in a table. (See Figure 4-4.) It's now up to you to customize and take this base model to new heights.

> **TOP TIP** *Although you may be working with the DataGrid here, don't be afraid to access your data direct through the* DataSet *object. In the* Essentials *section, we looked at sample code to do this—and you can easily mix that code in with the preceding templates for a more personalized, powerful solution.*

The techniques that follow this tip will be particularly useful to those who have become acquainted with the Web DataGrid and how it works. They gradually get more advanced, assuming a working knowledge of the DataGrid and ADO.NET technologies. So stay curious and have fun; there's a lot to do with this beast.

I'd like to conclude this first look at the Web DataGrid with one important recommendation: although this tip and others throughout the chapter include code showing how to add rows and edit data in the Web DataGrid, it's troublesome and not always aesthetically pleasing. If you want the simpler life, take my advice: just use the DataGrid to display data, and use your own individual Web form controls to accept input and edit data.

Trust me. It'll cure 95% of your DataGrid headaches and user complaints.

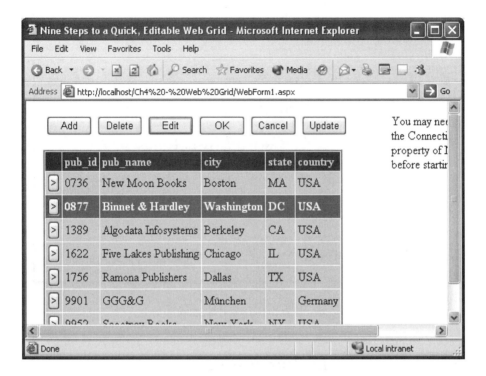

Figure 4-4. A selected record in my final, editable Web grid

How to Use HTML in a Web Grid

Often, it'd be useful to display HTML in a Web grid. Many content management systems, for example, store HTML-formatted text in key fields. Wouldn't it be useful to see bold text as actual bold text, rather than a bundle of <b> tags?

Well, it's simple. Just use it!

Because the Web grid output is fed straight to a browser, with none of your cell text being encoded, any tags in your fields will be rendered directly. This means that, if you've used a bold tag, it'll be rendered as bold text. If you've used a line break or image, it'll be rendered as a line break or image. (See Figure 4-5.)

Now *that's* the sort of quick and simple tip I like!

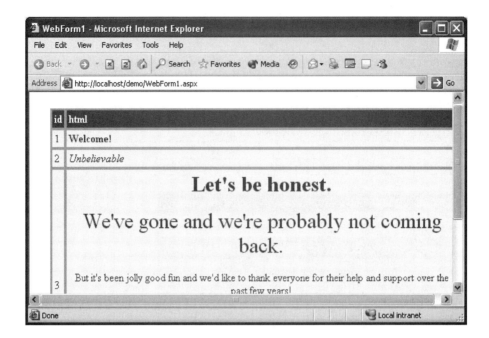

Figure 4-5. Demonstrating simple HTML in a Web grid

Using Hyperlinks in Your Web Grid

Hyperlinks form the backbone of the World Wide Web. They turn a five-minute checking-mail session into an all-night mega-surf. They're important, they connect the Web—and, as such, it makes sense that you may want to use them in your Web grid.

How? You need to set up a special HyperlinkColumn object to be displayed in your grid, specifying which field contains the text to display for the link, and which contains the actual link destination (that is, the hyperlink URL).

In this example, we're going to imagine that we've got a table of company details containing address and Web site information. We'll be designing our grid hyperlinks using the visual Property Builder.

So, you have a DataGrid on your Web form. Right-click and select Property Builder. Under the General property sheet, ensure that the DataSource and DataMember options are selected. This tells the DataGrid what data it is working with. Next, choose the Columns property sheet. Under the list of available columns, move the fields you want to display in your grid (under Data Fields) across to the list of selected columns.

Finally, set up our hyperlink column. Move down in the list of available columns, select HyperLink Column, and move it across to the list of selected columns. You will see a bunch of properties below. Firstly, choose the Text field—this will be displayed as the text to the hyperlink. Next, select the URL field—this should hold the ultimate destination of the link, a Web address. Note that the URL field will need to contain an "http://" prefix.

> **TOP TIP** *Does your database simply contain the Web address in* www.karlmoore.com *format rather than* http://www.karlmoore.com*? No fear. Just select your field, then, in the "URL format string" box, enter the text: http://{0}. This will insert "http://" before your field text.*

Next, choose a target from the dropdown box. If you don't specify this property, it'll use the page default. Other options include selecting "_blank" to open in a new window, or perhaps "_search" to open in the IE search bar. You may also want to set text for the "Header text" box, which will set the title for that particular column.

Click on OK when finished, and then bind as usual (follow "Nine Steps to a Quick, Editable Web Grid" through to Step 5 for quick, read-only binding). Sorted—a quick and easy data list, hyperlinks and all!

Dates, Currency, Percentages: Formatting Your Web Grid Data

Ask the DataGrid to show your information, and it'll display exactly what it found in your database. It doesn't give a thought to formatting and frankly couldn't care whether it's dealing with dates, money, or percentages. The good thing is, you can make it care.

How? Firstly, set up your DataGrid as normal. Then, right-click and click to open the Property Builder. Choose the Columns property sheet and uncheck the "Create columns automatically at run time" box, then individually move the fields you wish to view over to the selected columns list.

Next, for each column you wish to apply special formatting for, click and enter a new value in the "Data formatting expression" box. The following table lists the most requested expression types, ready to be customized to your exact requirements:

EXPRESSION	DESCRIPTION
{0:C}	Formats the data as a default currency item (that is, $39.95)
{0:D3}	Formats the data as a zero-padded, four-character-wide number (such as 0023)
{0:N2}%	Formats the data as a two decimal place number followed by a '%' symbol (that is, 59%)
{0:0.0}	Formats the data as a number, rounding to one decimal place (that is, 36.5)
{0:D}	Formats the data as a long date string (such as "Thursday, December 25, 2003"; see Figure 4-6)
{0:dd-MM-yy}	Formats the data as a dd-MM-yy date (that is, "20/05/04")

When you've finished entering formatting expressions, just click on OK to close the DataGrid Property Builder and run your application. Hey presto!

TOP TIP *While you're using the Property Builder, you may wish to further customize your DataGrid. For example, try changing the Header Text on the Columns sheet. Or you may wish to select your column on the Format sheet, and select a new column width or specify alignment of the cell contents.*

Note that a number of formatting attributes are derived from the default machine culture. For example, the en-us culture will display a $ as the currency symbol, whereas the en-gb culture will display the £ symbol. To change the culture, specify the culture attribute in the Page directive or in the Web.config file (add culture="xx-xx" to the default <globalization> section). You should be particularly aware of this if you are using an offshore Web host.

TOP TIP *Looking to format data in your Windows application DataGrid? It's not as easy as you'd imagine. Read the MSDN article at* http://msdn.microsoft.com/library/en-us/dv_vstechart/html/ vbtchformattingwindowsformsdatagridvisualbasicprimer.asp *to learn more.*

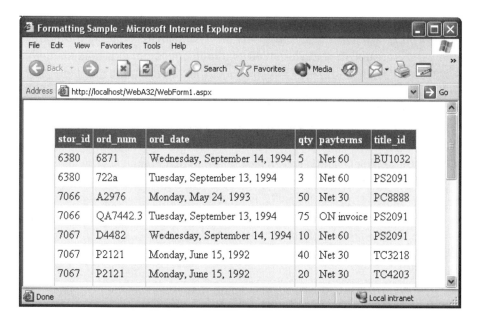

stor_id	ord_num	ord_date	qty	payterms	title_id
6380	6871	Wednesday, September 14, 1994	5	Net 60	BU1032
6380	722a	Tuesday, September 13, 1994	3	Net 60	PS2091
7066	A2976	Monday, May 24, 1993	50	Net 30	PC8888
7066	QA7442.3	Tuesday, September 13, 1994	75	ON invoice	PS2091
7067	D4482	Wednesday, September 14, 1994	10	Net 60	PS2091
7067	P2121	Monday, June 15, 1992	40	Net 30	TC3218
7067	P2121	Monday, June 15, 1992	20	Net 30	TC4203

Figure 4-6. A sample grid, with the order date field using the {0:D} *formatting expression*

Looking Good: Color-Coding Your Web Grid

Download supporting files at www.apress.com.
The files for this tip are in the "Ch4–Color Coding Grids" folder.

Grids on Web pages are great—but, among the mass of information you're displaying, it's sometimes difficult to spot important data such as overdue orders, special offer products, large expense accounts.

One technique for dealing with this is to color-code your Web grid. For example, you might want to check if a particular field value is greater than 100. If it is, you may want to change the background color or alter the style of the text.

You do this by responding to the ItemDataBound event of the DataGrid, which fires once for each "item" being put onto the grid during a binding operation. We then check that the "item" is a proper data row (and not a header row, for example), analyze the value of a particular field, and then change it as appropriate.

Here's an example that checks the second cell for a number value greater than 50 (the second cell being index number one, following the zero-based numbering system). If it is greater, the individual cell containing the number is bolded, the fore color set to white and the back color to a purple variant. If the number is 50 or less, the back color for the whole row is set to a light gray ("white smoke") and the border style changed to dotted. Simply add the following code behind the ItemDataBound event of the DataGrid (see Figure 4-7):

```
If e.Item.ItemType = ListItemType.Item Or _
    e.Item.ItemType = ListItemType.AlternatingItem Then
    If CType(e.Item.Cells(1).Text, Integer) > 50 Then
        e.Item.Cells(1).BackColor = Color.Plum
        e.Item.Cells(1).ForeColor = Color.White
        e.Item.Cells(1).Font.Bold = True
    Else
        e.Item.BackColor = Color.WhiteSmoke
        e.Item.BorderStyle = BorderStyle.Dotted
    End If
End If
```

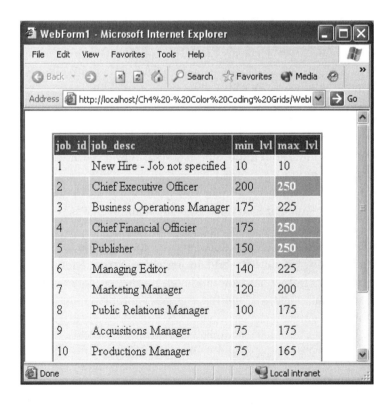

Figure 4-7. My sample color-coded Web grid

Little-Known Technique for Confirming Web Deletes

 Download supporting files at www.apress.com.
The files for this tip are in the "Ch4–Confirming Deletes" folder.

This next code technique is a real gem—one of those tips you rarely find printed, but, when you figure out how it works, you won't be able to get enough of it. This tip shows you how to run a snippet of JavaScript to confirm an action, such as the deletion of a record, all on the client side. Best of all, it takes just one line of code.

Simply add the following code behind your delete button:

```
MyDeleteButton.Attributes("onclick") = _
    "return confirm('Are you sure you wish to delete this record?');"
```

This adds a small piece of JavaScript to run when the client-side "onclick" event occurs for the rendered HTML button. The "Are you sure?" prompt then appears, and, if the user confirms, a True is returned and the click is processed. Otherwise, it simply cancels itself out.

However, this doesn't accommodate those developers using actual Delete buttons in DataGrid columns. In such a situation, you need to catch the individual Delete buttons as the data bind occurs and add this "onclick" attribute.

The following snippet of code assumes that you have a Web DataGrid with Delete buttons in the first column (index zero). Note that it currently explicitly checks for a Button control, not a PushButton. (Ensure that the "Button type" is set correctly in the Property Builder, or alter the code.) Simply add the following to respond to the ItemDataBound event of the DataGrid control, ready to fire when any data bind occurs (see Figure 4-8):

```
If e.Item.ItemType = ListItemType.Item Or _
    e.Item.ItemType = ListItemType.AlternatingItem Then
    If e.Item.Cells(0).Controls.Count > 0 Then
        If TypeOf (e.Item.Cells(0).Controls(0)) Is Button Then
            Dim btnDelete As Button = CType(e.Item.Cells(0).Controls(0), Button)
            btnDelete.Attributes("onclick") = _
                "return confirm('Are you sure you wish to delete this record?');"
        End If
    End If
End If
```

And that's it: simple, effective, and pretty hush-hush.

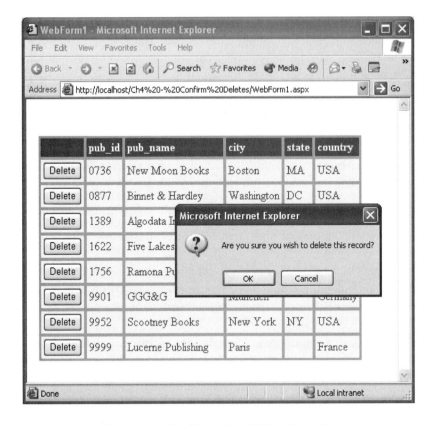

Figure 4-8. Confirm your Web deletes in a Web grid, easily!

Selecting Multiple Web Form Grid Items, Hotmail-Style

 Download supporting files at www.apress.com.
The files for this tip are in the "Ch4—Select Multiple" folder.

Selecting and, say, deleting items one by one can be a real pain. Email services such as Hotmail and Yahoo! Mail recognize that and allow you to select multiple messages through a little checkbox, then zap them all at once. Well, anything Hotmail can do, we can do... and quicker.

To create a selection checkbox, first set up your Web DataGrid as normal—displaying anything from order information to mail messages. Next, right-click the DataGrid and select Property Builder. Choose the Columns property sheet and add a "Template Column" to the list of selected columns, moving it to the top of the list (the first column). Set the "Header text" value if you wish. Click OK when finished.

Back on your Web page, right-click on your DataGrid again, this time choosing Edit Template, then selecting your new Template Column. This is your template for this particular field. Drag and drop a CheckBox control into the ItemTemplate portion, changing its ID property to chkSelect. When finished, right-click on the DataGrid again and select End Template Editing. You should be able to see the difference on your DataGrid.

Next, add a button to your Web form. This will be the button your user clicks after selecting records to delete (or perform some other action upon). Add code behind the button Click event similar to the following:

```
Dim objItem As DataGridItem
For Each objItem In MyDataGrid.Items
    ' Ignore invalid items
    If objItem.ItemType <> ListItemType.Header And _
        objItem.ItemType <> ListItemType.Footer And _
    objItem.ItemType <> ListItemType.Pager Then
        ' Retrieve the value of the check box
        Dim blnDelete As Boolean
        blnDelete = CType(objItem.Cells(0).FindControl("chkSelect"), _
            CheckBox).Checked
        If blnDelete = True Then
            ' Delete this row from the underlying DataSet, ie.
            ' LocalDS.Tables(0).Rows(MyDataGrid.SelectedIndex).Delete
            ' You can also retrieve the value of a field on the row, ie.
            ' MyVariable = objItem.Cells(5).Text
            ' ... then rebind.
        End If
    End If
Next
```

Here, our code walks through each valid item in the DataGrid, searching for our control in the first cell (zero index) and analyzing whether it's checked. If it is, that's where your code can step in to take action—probably deleting the record in the underlying DataSet, then rebinding, as per example code in the "Nine Steps to a Quick, Editable Web Grid" tip.

And that's it. (See Figure 4-9.) You should now be able to select multiple cells and perform an operation en masse, such as a delete, in seconds! You may even want to merge this tip with the next for even more power over your data.

Figure 4-9. Selecting multiple items in our Web grid, Hotmail-style

Click Anywhere and Select, with a Web Grid

Download supporting files at www.apress.com.
The files for this tip are in the "Ch4–Click Anywhere" folder.

Web applications are not like Windows applications. We know that. But, by using tricks such as the SmartNavigation property we covered in the last chapter, you can give your sites more intelligence, allowing them to be much more responsive and to work better.

This next tip adds to that repertoire. Using the following code, you can click anywhere in a DataGrid and have the record you were over selected (or, rather, have your code behind the SelectedIndexChanged event run). This is especially useful for those with a speedy Internet connection, or using an intranet site, where postbacks are hardly noticed.

Anyway, here's the code. It assumes the very first column contains a Select button of the PushButton variety. (You need to add this and any related code yourself, but you can make the actual button invisible through the Property

Builder, if you wish to do so.) Our code finds this Select button and, through the highly hush-hush `GetPostBackClientHyperlink` function, returns the name of the script that runs when that button is clicked. This script is then set to run whenever the `onclick` event of your row runs. In other words, when the user clicks anywhere on your row, the Select button script kicks into play. (See Figure 4-10.)

Ready to go? Just add the following code to respond to the `ItemDataBound` event of the DataGrid control:

```
If e.Item.ItemType = ListItemType.Header Or _
    e.Item.ItemType = ListItemType.Footer Or _
    e.Item.ItemType = ListItemType.Pager Then Exit Sub
If e.Item.Cells(0).Controls.Count > 0 Then
    If TypeOf (e.Item.Cells(0).Controls(0)) Is Button Then
        Dim btnSelect As Button = CType(e.Item.Cells(0).Controls(0), _
            Button)
        e.Item.Attributes("onclick") = _
            Page.GetPostBackClientHyperlink(btnSelect, "")
    End If
End If
```

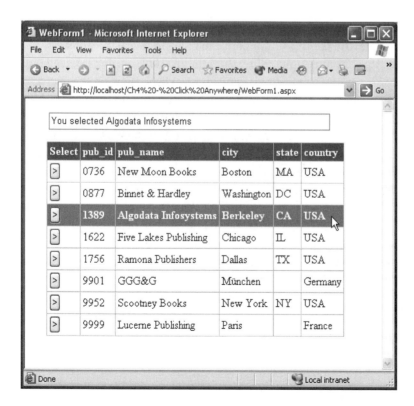

Figure 4-10. Click anywhere and select, with this crafty code

The Lowdown on Using Dropdown Boxes in a Web Grid

 Download supporting files at www.apress.com.
The files for this tip are in the "Ch4–Drop Down in Web Grid" folder.

Want to add a dropdown box to your Web page, populated with values from your table? You're in for a sweet surprise—it's easy!

Just add the DropDownList control to your Web form and set the DataSource, DataMember, DataTextField, and possibly the DataValueField properties. As soon as you fill the DataSource, the bound DropDownList will automatically populate itself with a list of fields and values. You can then find out what the user selects through its SelectedItem property.

If you want to add dropdown boxes inside your Web grid, however, you're in for a shocker. It's pretty darn difficult.

Practically every public sample demonstrating the use of dropdown boxes in Web grids is unfeasible: the samples are based on pure text fields (not foreign keys), the old selected dropdown values aren't preserved when you enter the Edit mode, and the update code is always buggy as hell. But there are so many different ways of implementing a dropdown box solution, so it's hardly surprising so much confusion abounds.

I spent the best part of one whole week figuring out how dropdown boxes worked with the DataGrid control—and, here, I'm going to reveal the quickest, most stable technique I found for handling the situation. My solution is based on what I deem to be the most common use for dropdown lists: allowing the user to select an "English" value for a foreign key field. For example, you may have a news article table containing a "reporterid" field. Your actual list of reporter names, however, will most likely be in another table altogether. Your task is to make the fact that your main table uses a foreign key totally transparent: the user just wants to be able to select a reporter, period. That's what this tip shows you.

To begin with, let's get access to our core data. Locate your "parent" and "child" tables via a data connection in the Server Explorer (View ➤ Server Explorer), then drag and drop onto your Web form. When you've finished, you'll be left with one Connection object and two DataAdapter objects. (As usual, you may wish to alter the ConnectionString property of the Connection object to specify a user id and password value.) Right-click on one of the DataAdapter objects and select Generate Dataset. In the list of tables, check both your tables. Leave the rest of the defaults and click on OK. An XSD template will be created and a typed DataSet added to your form, which we'll use to feed our DataGrid. So far, this is all pretty standard stuff. (See Figure 4-11.)

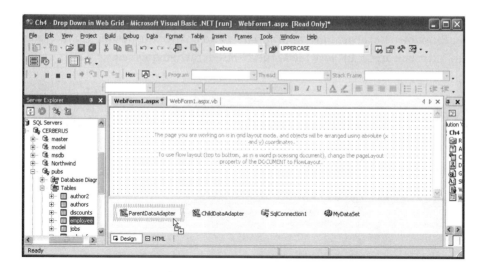

Figure 4-11. My Web form so far, hosting one Connection, *two* DataAdapters, *and a typed DataSet*

TOP TIP *Don't be too afraid of graphically dragging and dropping tables. Back in the Visual Basic 6 days, visually designing database applications like this was deemed bad practice. With VB .NET however, it's exactly the same as instantiating objects and using them in code—just a little easier.*

Add a DataGrid to your Web form and design it as necessary. When ready, open the Property Builder and, on the General property sheet, specify the DataSource, DataMember, and, optionally, the Data key field. These values should all point to the parent "news article" table in your DataSet. Next, switch to the Columns property sheet, uncheck "Create columns automatically at run time" and add an "Edit, Update, Cancel" button to the selected columns list. This button will be used to begin editing of a row.

Next, manually add all the data fields you wish to view in your grid to the selected columns list, ensuring that you include both the primary key and foreign key fields, making both invisible by unchecking the Visible checkbox. Spend a few minutes setting any column properties required, such as "Header text".

Then, cycle through each of those data columns and choose a sort expression from the dropdown box. Make sure you choose the name of the field supplying data for that column. (See Figure 4-12.) Although this sort expression value is typically used for sorting columns of data (see the "Sorting in Seconds, with Your Web Grid" tip), we'll be using it as a record of which columns bind to which database fields. You'll see why later.

Finally, add a "Template Column" to the list. This is the column that will hold your dropdown box. Position it appropriately and change the header text if required. Click on OK to close the Property Builder when finished.

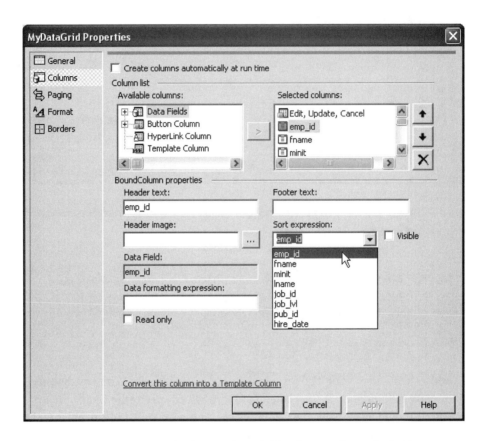

Figure 4-12. Setting properties for our DataGrid columns, through the Property Builder

Moving on, and it's time to set up this new template column. Right-click on your DataGrid, select Edit Template, and choose the column you just added. The middle two portions of this "template" are most important: the ItemTemplate section displays what will appear in the cell when you're viewing data, and the EditItemTemplate shows how that cell will look when you're editing data.

In the ItemTemplate section, drag and drop a DropDownList control. We want this to display a noneditable list of options, with one selected. Change the Enabled property of the control to False and provide it with a name through the ID property. I'm calling mine "ddl1".

In the EditItemTemplate section, drag and drop another DropDownList control. (See Figure 4-13.) This is what the user will see when they enter Edit mode. Keep its Enabled property set to True this time, so they can change the selection, then change the ID property. I'm setting mine to "ddl2".

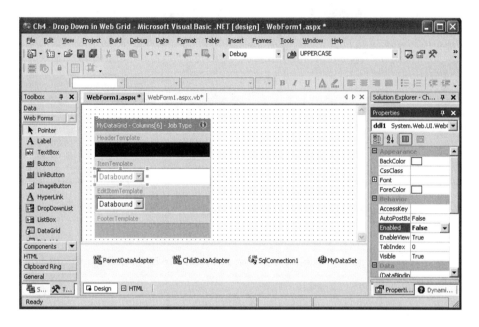

Figure 4-13. Designing how our template cell will look, in View and Edit mode

Next, we need to think about getting our actual list of options into our dropdown boxes. Change the DataSource property of both boxes to point to our main DataSet and the DataMember to point to the child "reporter" table. Next, you need to choose the DataTextField (the field that contains the text options you want the dropdown to display) and the DataValueField (the field containing the key value for this option, such as an "id" field). As soon as we populate the DataSet, these dropdown boxes will automatically fill with values from our table.

When finished, right-click on the DataGrid and choose End Editing. Notice how your DataGrid appears now? (See Figure 4-14.)

Next, let's think about adding code. Much of this will be relatively standard; however, we'll also need to do a little special processing. For example, we'll need to write code to initially select the correct value from our dropdown field—taking the foreign key value and choosing an appropriate option from the list. We'll also need to handle the update, by taking the value from our dropdown and putting it into the foreign key field, then cycling through the edited text boxes and updating the backend DataSet as you would usually. As you'll see, the DataGrid really does very little of this work for you.

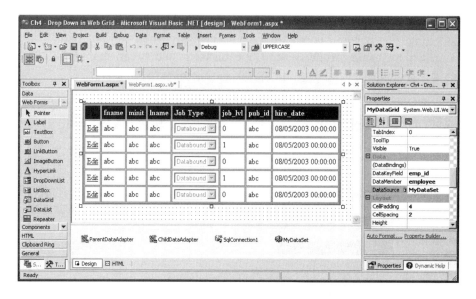

Figure 4-14. How the DataGrid looks so far, dropdown box and all

We'll begin with a simple chunk of standard code, to be added in response to the page Load event:

```
If Not IsPostBack Then
    ParentNewsArticleDataAdapter.Fill(MyDataSet)
    ChildReporterDataAdapter.Fill(MyDataSet)
    MyDataGrid.DataBind()
End If
```

Here, we're simply using our two DataAdapters to fill our DataSet with two chunks of information: the table containing our parent "news article" data, and the child table containing our "reporter" data. We've already set the DataGrid DataSource and DataMember properties, so we simply do a .DataBind to put it into action.

This is all standard stuff. Next, we're going to add a little special code to run after we've initiated the .DataBind. We'll add it to respond to the grid ItemDataBound event, which fires once for every row "item" being displayed in a data bound DataGrid. Here goes:

```
' If this is a valid item...
If e.Item.ItemType = ListItemType.AlternatingItem Or _
    e.Item.ItemType = ListItemType.Item Then
    ' Retrieve the foreign key value
```

```
    Dim intForeignKey As Integer = _
        e.Item.Cells(FOREIGN_KEY_COL_NUM).Text
    ' Find the dropdown containing our list of options
    Dim ddl As DropDownList = _
        CType(e.Item.FindControl("ddl1"), DropDownList)
    ' Select the correct entry in the dropdown
    ddl.SelectedIndex = _
        ddl.Items.IndexOf( _
        ddl.Items.FindByValue(intForeignKey))
End If
```

Here, we check that we're dealing with a valid item. We then begin by retrieving our foreign key value. (Replace FOREIGN_KEY_COL_NUM with the column number containing your foreign key value. You may wish to use the Property Builder to help find the column number, remembering to start counting at zero and include any hidden fields.) Next, we find our dropdown list on the row and select the relevant item depending on the foreign key value. Do you see how that works?

So, that's selected the DataGrid dropdown in regular View mode. Now how about editing?

You may remember the Edit-Update-Cancel button we added earlier. When the user clicks on Edit, the EditCommand of the DataGrid fires. And that's exactly the event this next block of code should run in response to:

```
' Select the current row for 'edit mode'
MyDataGrid.EditItemIndex = e.Item.ItemIndex
' Refill DataSets with information
ParentNewsArticleDataAdapter.Fill(MyDataSet)
ChildReporterDataAdapter.Fill(MyDataSet)
' Rebind data
MyDataGrid.DataBind()
' Select default dropdown option, as earlier
Dim ddl As DropDownList = _
    CType(MyDataGrid.Items(MyDataGrid.EditItemIndex). _
    FindControl("ddl2"), DropDownList)
ddl.SelectedIndex = _
    ddl.Items.IndexOf( _
    ddl.Items.FindByValue(e.Item.Cells(FOREIGN_KEY_COL_NUM).Text))
```

Much of the code here is typical of that you'd find responding to an edit event. We set the .EditItemIndex. We populate our DataSets again and rebind. Then we run special code to locate our second dropdown (the editable one) and preselect the correct default value. (Again, replace FOREIGN_KEY_COL_NUM with the column number containing your foreign key value.) Great stuff.

What's left to do? Well, we've handled displaying a default item in regular View mode and preselecting one in Edit mode. The user will then begin editing the grid, and, when finished, either click on Update, wishing to store the changes, or Cancel to forget about them. (See Figure 4-15.)

Figure 4-15. Visualizing the Update and Cancel options our user will have after clicking on Edit

When the user clicks on Update, the DataGrid `UpdateCommand` event runs—then it's over to you to take the alterations and update your database. That's just what this next chunk of slightly more confusing code does, to be run in response to the `UpdateCommand` event:

```
' Step one: Put dropdown list value into foreign key field
CType(e.Item.Cells(FOREIGN_KEY_COL_NUM).Controls(0), TextBox).Text = _
    CType(e.Item.FindControl("ddl2"), DropDownList).SelectedItem.Value()


' Step two: Fill DataSet and identify row to edit
ParentDataAdapter.Fill(MyDataSet)
ChildDataAdapter.Fill(MyDataSet)
Dim objEditedRow As DataRow = MyDataSet.Tables(0).Rows.Find( _
    CType(e.Item.Cells(ID_NUM).Controls(0), TextBox).Text)


' Step three: Cycle through valid "data" cells and put
'             information back in underlying DataSet
Dim intCount As Integer
For intCount = 0 To e.Item.Cells.Count - 1
    If e.Item.Cells(intCount).Controls.Count > 0 Then
        If TypeOf (e.Item.Cells(intCount).Controls(0)) Is TextBox Then
            ' This appears to be a TextBox-holding "data" cell
            Dim strValue As String = CType(e.Item.Cells(intCount). _
                Controls(0), TextBox).Text
```

```
                    ' Put value (or null if empty) back into relevant DataSet field
                    If strValue = "" Then
                        objEditedRow.Item(MyDataGrid.Columns(intCount). _
                            SortExpression) = System.DBNull.Value
                    Else
                        objEditedRow.Item(MyDataGrid.Columns(intCount). _
                            SortExpression) = strValue
                    End If
                End If
            End If
    Next

    ' Update backend data
    ParentNewsArticleDataAdapter.Update(MyDataSet)

    ' Deselect DataGrid items and rebind
    With MyDataGrid
        .SelectedIndex = -1
        .EditItemIndex = -1
        .DataSource = MyDataSet
        .DataBind()
    End With
```

This code consists of three core steps. In the first, we retrieve the value behind our dropdown and put it in the foreign key field. (Replace FOREIGN_KEY_COL_NUM with the column number containing your foreign key value.) In the second, we fill our DataSet as normal, then filter using the primary key value to locate the row our user has edited. (Replace ID_NUM with the column number of your primary key value.) The third and final step cycles through all the cell TextBox controls, figures out which field the data inside each box belongs to (using the column sort expression value), and updates the underlying DataSet. We then deselect any DataGrid items and rebind. It looks confusing, and the DataGrid does none of the work for us, but the underlying process is actually relatively simple.

Finally, we need to add code to respond just in case the user clicks on Cancel. This is relatively standard code and should be added to respond to the CancelCommand event. We simply reset the grid and rebind:

```
MyDataGrid.SelectedIndex = -1
MyDataGrid.EditItemIndex = -1
ParentNewsArticleDataAdapter.Fill(MyDataSet)
ChildReporterDataAdapter.Fill(MyDataSet)
MyDataGrid.DataBind()
```

And that's it! (See Figure 4-16.) Admittedly, it seems one heck of a long process for something so relatively simple, but, if you've seen some of the other demonstrations of this technique elsewhere, you'll appreciate the concise nature of this blighter. And, once you've done it a couple of times, well, let's just say it gets a little easier. *Phew.*

> **TOP TIP** *For simplicity and to ensure this tip can run "standalone," it uses the standard Edit-Update-Cancel button integrated into the DataGrid. If you're building on top of the "Nine Steps to a Quick, Editable Web Grid" tip, you may wish to edit certain parts of this code so it kicks in behind your own Edit-Update-Cancel buttons and possibly uses the* DataSave, DataRetrieve, *and* DataExists *routines. You may also want to add your own error handling or concurrency checks, too. Or you might just decide you've already pushed editing with the DataGrid too far and opt for a third-party solution. Your call.*

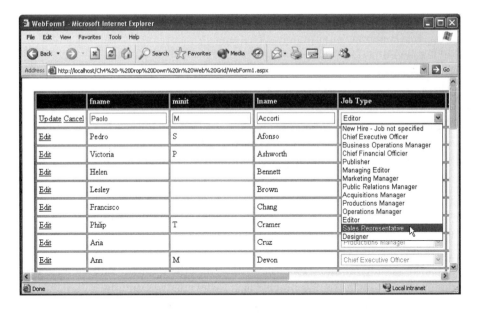

Figure 4-16. Give yourself a promotion: demonstrating an editable Web grid dropdown

Speedy, Personalized Web Data Binding

If you're simply viewing data using your Web grid and want to personalize the output a little more, then you'll be pleased to know that, despite the rumors, it's actually pretty simple and can be done without even delving into those special `<asp>` tags you find dotted in most books.

To personalize the DataGrid, first set it up as usual. In the General property sheet of the Property Builder, choose a DataSource, DataMember, and an optional Data key field. Under the Columns property sheet, uncheck "Create columns automatically at run time" and instead add the data fields you require to the list of selected columns.

Now, cycle through each of the columns in the selection column list and click on the "Convert this column into a Template Column" link at the bottom of the property sheet. This takes the standard DataGrid method of displaying information from a DataSource and changes it into a template, letting you edit how each column field looks. Click on OK to close the Property Builder.

Next, right-click on the DataGrid, select Edit Template, and look at the ItemTemplate section for one of your columns. You'll notice that it already contains one label, which links to a field in your table through the `DataBindings` property.

Begin your customization. You may, for example, add two Label controls and change the `DataBindings` property so that one points to, for example, Container ➤ DataItem ➤ FirstName, while the second binds to Container ➤ DataItem ➤ LastName. You could perhaps add a little text as a prefix to the field value, too.

There are more possibilities. You may add a HyperLink control and change DataBindings so that the `Text` and `NavigateUrl` are provided by fields from your table. You might use your data to supply the `ImageUrl` property of an ImageButton control: simply select the field containing your filename. (You may also wish to change the Format box to something such as `http://www.yoursite.com/images/{0}` if you wish to add a prefix to your filename. The {0} will get replaced with the data from your field.) You could even merge all of the above and create a single column listing of all your catalog products: pictures, descriptions, purchase links, and all.

> **TOP TIP** *Want to customize even further? Delve straight into the HTML. Right-click on your DataGrid and select View HTML Source.*

When finished, right-click on the grid and select End Template Editing. Then bind view your data as normal.

In brief, with the ItemTemplate (and related) sections, you can really push the way your DataGrid displays its simple bound data. Truthfully, in-grid editing is troublesome, but when you're just viewing... the power is yours!

> **TOP TIP** *In case you're wondering, the DataList control works in much the same way as the DataGrid when you get to this level of customization. It holds advantages and disadvantages over the DataGrid—for example, although you can't edit through the DataList, you can list rows horizontally or vertically. The brother Repeater control can also be bound, but it requires editing of the <asp> tags in HTML and is more limited in the way it works. Look up "DataList control, vs. other list controls" in the help index for more information.*

Quick and Easy Data Paging, with Your Web Grid

Download supporting files at www.apress.com.
The files for this tip are in the "Ch4–Paging" folder.

Most Web developers tend to shiver at the mere mention of the word *paging*. Even old-hat ASP.NET programmers are a little confused over its implementation. Many of the new .NET books devote a chapter or so to the subject—but it really isn't that complicated.

Paging is a method of splitting results in your DataGrid over multiple "pages." Google uses paging in its search results. Yahoo! uses paging if it can't fit all its matching sites onto one page. It's useful—and can be set up in seconds.

First off, set up your DataGrid as usual. Add all your regular binding code. When you're done, right-click on the grid and select Property Builder. Choose the Paging property sheet and check "Allow paging". Alter the page size so it represents the number of items you want to display on any one page. You may also want to change the navigation text just below. Click OK when finished.

Next, add code similar to the following to respond to the PageIndexChanged event of your DataGrid control:

```
MyDataGrid.CurrentPageIndex = e.NewPageIndex
' Bind your data again here. You could load DataSet
' from ViewState, database, etc. For example:
MyDataAdapter.Fill(MyDataSet)
MyDataGrid.DataBind()
```

And that's it—just fire off your DataGrid as normal and you've got instant paging! (See Figure 4-17.)

> **TOP TIP** *If you're going to use editing with paging, watch out when updating your DataSet. If you're doing it purely on position, remember that, after you move to a new page, your first item will not correlate with the first item in your DataSet. You'll have to code around this. You can find out the current page by looking up the* .CurrentPageIndex *property, and find out the number of items displayed per page with the* .PageSize *property.*

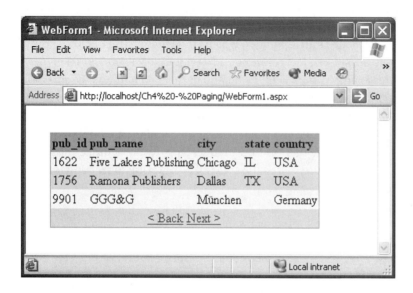

Figure 4-17. Simple paging in seconds!

Sorting in Seconds, with Your Web Grid

Download supporting files at www.apress.com.
The files for this tip are in the "Ch4–Sorting" folder.

When you're looking at a grid full of data, it's natural to want to order it somehow. You may want to view employees by salary amount, from the highest paid to the lowest. Or view a customized query showing an alphabetical list of sales staff and their respective telephone numbers.

That's all easy, with sorting—something the ASP.NET DataGrid provides excellent built-in support for. Here, I'm going to demonstrate the sorting technique in its simplest form, but you can greatly expand upon this to build a much more elegant solution.

First of all, set up your DataGrid as normal, adding all your regular binding code. When done, open up the Property Builder and, in the General property sheet, set the DataSource, DataMember, and optional Data key field for your table. Moving on to the Columns property sheet, uncheck "Create columns automatically at run time", and then move all the fields you want to view in this DataGrid across to the list of selected columns.

Next—and this is the important bit—specify a "sort expression" value for each of the columns you're going to allow your users to sort by. This will turn the column header into a hyperlink that, when clicked, will fire an event. This event will receive your sort expression value as an argument, which you can then use to reorder the data appropriately. So, select a few columns and a related sort expression. For the purpose of this example, stick with the default of the field name as the sort expression. (You'll see why it makes things easier next.) Click on OK when finished.

Next, we're ready to add code to handle this sorting ourselves. No, this process isn't automatic—we need to somehow reorder our data and then rebind to the DataGrid. I'm going to handle this by simply requerying my data source, although with an extra ORDER BY clause. Here's the code I'll be entering to respond to the SortCommand event of my DataGrid:

```
' Reset index, in case on a different page
MyDataGrid.CurrentPageIndex = 0
' Change SELECT statement, using the passed in 'sort expression'_
  value we specified earlier
MyDataAdapter.SelectCommand.CommandText = _
  "SELECT * FROM mytablename ORDER BY " & e.SortExpression
' Refresh data and rebind
MyDataAdapter.Fill(MyDataSet)
MyDataGrid.DataBind ()
```

Here, you can see that my code initially resets the index, in case we're on another "page" of the DataGrid somewhere. It then uses our DataAdapter to alter the underlying SELECT statement, ordering by the current sort expression (the field name we specified earlier). Note that there are other, more elegant ways of handling this, rather than directly rewriting the SELECT text, but, for simplicity and demonstration purposes, this technique's a winner. Finally, we refill the DataSet and bind it back to the DataGrid.

We're almost there now. To activate all your hard work, all you need to do is select your DataGrid and change its AllowSorting property to True.

And that's it! (See Figure 4-18.) Your grid will now allow you to click on the header text of any of your "sort-aware" columns and put them in correct, ascending order. With a little imagination, you can also expand on this code base to allow "reverse sorts" too. Have a play around!

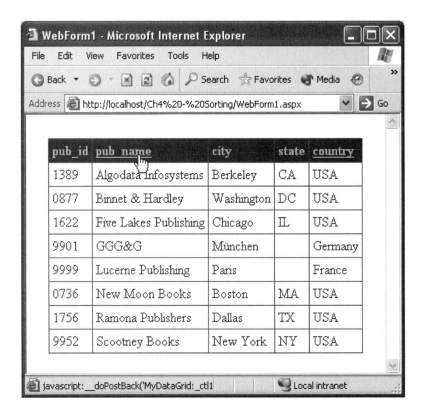

pub_id	pub_name	city	state	country
1389	Algodata Infosystems	Berkeley	CA	USA
0877	Binnet & Hardley	Washington	DC	USA
1622	Five Lakes Publishing	Chicago	IL	USA
9901	GGG&G	München		Germany
9999	Lucerne Publishing	Paris		France
0736	New Moon Books	Boston	MA	USA
1756	Ramona Publishers	Dallas	TX	USA
9952	Scootney Books	New York	NY	USA

Figure 4-18. Click and sort, in just a few lines of code

Amazingly Simple Method for Exporting Your Web Grid to Excel

 Download supporting files at www.apress.com.
The files for this tip are in the "Ch4–Export to Excel" folder.

There are some things that developers just won't tell you about... little secrets and hidden developer tricks that take weeks to find out about but just minutes to pass on. This book is all about exposing such golden nuggets, and this next baby is a prime example.

Over the next few paragraphs, I'll be demonstrating how to take a regular ASP.NET DataGrid and feed it back down to your user as though it were an actual Excel spreadsheet—and you don't even need Excel on your server. Best of all, it takes only just a few extra lines of code.

Firstly, work on getting information to your DataGrid as normal, but ensure that you don't incorporate any special features such as Select buttons or paging. However, you can apply as much color or text formatting as you wish: right-click, select Auto Format, go wild.

Next, add code similar to the following to respond to the page Load event:

```
' Put information into your DataGrid, for example:
MyDataAdapter.Fill(MyDataSet)
MyDataGrid.DataSource = MyDataSet.Tables(0)
MyDataGrid.DataBind()


' Tell browser this is 'Excel' information
' and prepare to send down info
Response.ContentType = "application/vnd.ms-excel"
Response.Charset = ""
Me.EnableViewState = False


' Get the DataGrid HTML from the control,
' then write straight to the browser
Dim objSW As New System.IO.StringWriter()
Dim objHTW As New System.Web.UI.HtmlTextWriter(objSW)
MyDataGrid.RenderControl(objHTW)
Response.Write(objSW.ToString())
Response.End()
```

Here, our code fills the DataGrid and then tells the browser it'll be sending down Excel information. The HTML for the DataGrid is then retrieved and pushed down. Excel then translates this into its own cells, and your user simply sees an Excel spreadsheet containing your data embedded in their browser. (See Figure 4-19.)

TOP TIP *A word of warning, folks. A bug in the release version of Office 2000 means that accessing an ASP or ASPX page (such as MyForm.aspx) with an embedded Excel resource like this results in a blank page. (See Knowledge Base article KB266263.) The workaround is that, when linking to your Excel page, add a placebo query string or just a simple question mark (MyForm.aspx?) at the end of the filename. Alternatively, don't stream the DataGrid direct to the browser: prompt the user to open or save (read on to find out how).*

What if you want to create an Excel page that will actually open in Excel—or prompt the user to save it as an actual file? Easy, just add the following line to the preceding code, around where you set the `.ContentType` property:

```
Response.AddHeader("content-disposition", "attachment;filename=myfile.xls")
```

This prompts the user to either open or save with a default name of myfile.xls. It also has the benefit of not suffering from the bug mentioned in the preceding tip.

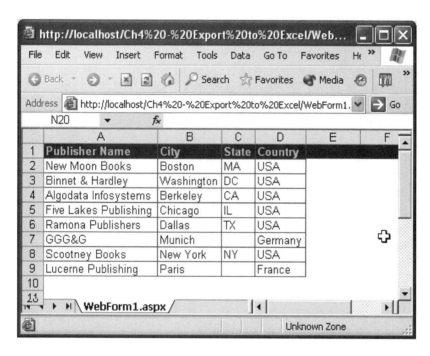

Figure 4-19. My Web grid, embedded as an Excel sheet within Internet Explorer

Returning a DataSet from an Excel Spreadsheet

 Download supporting files at www.apress.com.
The files for this tip are in the "Ch4–DataSet from Excel Worksheet" folder.

You won't find many developers proclaiming Excel to be the future of data storage. Even if you're storing only a small amount of data—perhaps settings or a selection list—it's still worthwhile going with the registry, XML files, or a simple Access database.

But some programmers swear by the effectiveness of Excel. Why? Because it's almost as common as Word, and the majority of users seem able to find their way about pretty easily. So they make simple user-definable values or selection lists available through a simple workbook.

The following code snippet uses OLE DB code to access a named range within an Excel workbook and return it as a DataSet object, ready for binding to a Windows DataGrid, for example.

How do you set up a named range? Just select a region on an Excel worksheet (whether that be one cell, a number of cells, a column, or even the whole sheet), and then click in the Name Box to the top-left of the screen. Type in a new name for the range, and press Enter. (Use the Insert ➤ Name menu to make further edits.) When finished, you're all set to run the code.

And here it is, comments and all:

```
Public Function GetDataFromExcel(ByVal FileName As String, _
  ByVal RangeName As String) As System.Data.DataSet
    ' Returns a DataSet containing information from
    ' a named range in the passed Excel worksheet
    Try
        Dim strConn As String = "Provider=Microsoft.Jet.OLEDB.4.0;" & _
            "Data Source=" & FileName & ";Extended Properties=Excel 8.0;"
        Dim objConn As New System.Data.OleDb.OleDbConnection(strConn)
        objConn.Open()
        ' Create objects ready to grab data
        Dim objCmd As New System.Data.OleDb.OleDbCommand( _
            "SELECT * FROM " & RangeName, objConn)
        Dim objDA As New System.Data.OleDb.OleDbDataAdapter()
        objDA.SelectCommand = objCmd
        ' Fill DataSet
        Dim objDS As New System.Data.DataSet()
        objDA.Fill(objDS)
        ' Cleanup and return DataSet
        objConn.Close()
        Return objDS
    Catch
        ' Possible errors include Excel file
        ' already open and locked, et al.
        Return Nothing
    End Try
End Function
```

As an example, here's how you might call the function, using a workbook called MyTestWorkbook.xls in the same directory as the executable, plus a named range called SampleNamedRange. It then takes the first table in the returned DataSet and binds it to our Windows DataGrid. (See Figure 4-20.) Not bad for one line of code:

```
DataGrid1.DataSource = GetDataFromExcel(Application.StartupPath & _
    "\MyTestWorkbook.xls", "SampleNamedRange").Tables(0)
```

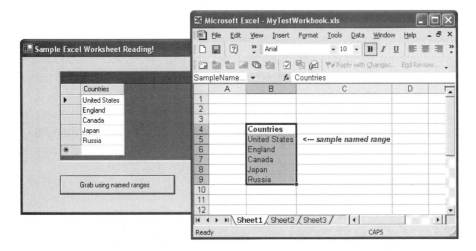

Figure 4-20. My sample application, grabbing data straight from an Excel workbook

Get Microsoft to Write Your Code: Amazing Undocumented SQL Server Tool!

Truth be known, a lot of development work is pretty repetitive stuff. You write a routine once, then need to write a similar routine for another table. So you copy and paste. Ten times. Then you find an error in the original routine and begin editing. Again.

I don't know about you, but I hold my hands up and confess that I've fallen afoul of this madness.

But there's one little solution that only a tiny bunch of French developers know about. It's a tool called SQL Server Centric .NET Code Generator, created by Senior Developer Evangelist at Microsoft France, Pascal Belaud. And it's a cure for the common code.

Bundled with 150 enterprise templates, it generates stored procedures, three-tier data access classes (including a basic user interface), and even documentation —in seconds.

And, with continuous debugging from Microsoft itself, you can be assured that you're working with the neatest code and adopting the latest practices around. And, to keep you up to date, Belaud and his team make constant improvements and post a fresh release every 60 days or so.

How come you've never heard about it? Because it's officially an "unsupported" software tool from Microsoft France. The truth of the matter, however, is that it's the main tool used by Microsoft Consulting Services, the division that implements Microsoft solutions for customers with more than 1,000 base users. Supposedly "normal" developers don't usually get to hear about such power tools.

How can you get your hands on a copy? Surf down to `www.Microsoft.fr/olymars/webupdate.xml` and begin playing with your own copy (see Figure 4-21) in minutes. And yes, to cap it all, it's absolutely free!

A word of warning: although amazingly detailed and highly powerful, this program is not always the most user friendly of developer tools. I'd definitely recommend you download the English tutorial and spend time becoming acquainted with how everything fits together before generating any real-life code.

It'll pay off, no doubt.

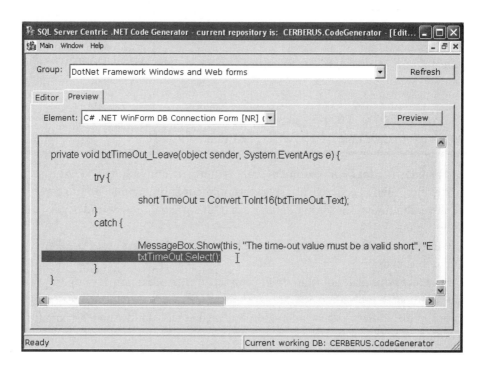

Figure 4-21. My free copy of SQL Server Centric .NET Code Generator in action

CHAPTER 5

The Lowdown
on Web Services

ASK MICROSOFT WHAT .NET actually *is*, and they'll tell you it's the software giant's "XML Web services platform." Ask them what the XML Web services platform is, and they'll say it's "a way of working that allows you to create software as a service."

Web services are a method of exposing your code functions to the world. You make certain functions available over HTTP. Other applications call these, and your application returns the results as XML. The receiving program then parses the response and continues processing.

With the .NET Framework, Microsoft provides ASP.NET for Web development. Included under this header is Microsoft's implementation of this new Web service industry communication standard. And, as we saw in the first paragraph, it's so important that Microsoft considers it to be the heart of .NET.

Why is it so important? In the future, Microsoft expects to see a world thriving on Web services, living on a dream of distributed computing. If your application needs to perform some complicated processing, it'll just tap into an external Web service to do the job, rather than requiring hours of extra development time.

Indeed, there are even unofficial plans for applications such as Microsoft Word to be supported by numerous Web services, maybe as a mechanism to allow users to access their documents from any machine in the world or perhaps as a way to actually supply and update the software, potentially cutting down on piracy and distributing updates in a more streamlined fashion. You could, in theory, end up merely "hiring" Word from Microsoft, or paying an annual subscription fee.

But, whatever the future holds, the truth is that Web services as they stand today are useful: they enable you to get computers talking together.

And you can create Web service applications in just a few lines of code. Yes, the Web services standard is built on XML and HTTP, but .NET is the first mainstream language to hide all this complexity from you. You simply need to write your functions, tell Visual Basic .NET which you want to "expose," and then write other applications to "consume" those functions.

If you're new to Web services, you'll want to get acquainted with the *Essentials* in this chapter. Many authors write whole books on the topic, but all the vital stuff is listed here, with a few short bulleted points.

Of course, all the real juice comes with the *Developer Secrets*. Here, you'll learn the five crucial things you need to do before publicizing your service, figure out how to spy on your neighbors by tapping into TerraServer, plus learn how caching can make your services run like lightning.

Raring to go? Let's get busy!

The Essentials

Getting up and running with Web services isn't really all that difficult. If you're new to the topic, you'll learn all you need to get going in this quick list of bulleted points. And, if you're an old hat, well, you might just enjoy a refresher. Either way, let's explore:

- Web services are at the heart of the .NET vision. They provide a standard method of allowing computers to communicate with each other.

- For a Web service to work, you need two parts: a server and a client. The server is a computer containing the actual service itself. It exposes what it can do to the world through its interface. The client can discover this interface and then make certain requests. When the requests are received, the server runs the code behind the service and returns a result as appropriate.

- Examples of real-life Web services include a search engine (send the service a term and it'll return a list of matching sites), a credit check service (pass the service details of an individual and it'll return a rating), a news and horoscope service (simply retrieve the latest headlines and readings), and a dictionary (the client passes a word, the server returns a definition).

- To provide an existing technology for comparison, you can think of Web services as being arguably similar to the old DCOM. However, this new way of working is based on open standards; plus it's loosely coupled, allowing for less-troublesome development. (*Remoting* is another DCOM-like technology. Read the "Which to Choose: Web Services vs. Remoting" in Chapter 7 for more information.)

- All Web service requests are done through HTTP (hypertext transfer protocol), the protocol used when browsing Web pages. This typically means that Web service requests can penetrate most firewalls.

- Data returned from a Web service is passed back as pure XML (eXtensible Markup Language). This is a method of storing data through a series of tags. XML is an industry standard for storing relational data in a flat text format. It's also platform independent, and it looks a bit like HTML. But it isn't.

- To create a new Web service application project in Visual Studio .NET, click on File ➤ New ➤ Project, select the Visual Basic Projects project type, and choose the ASP.NET Web service template. Specify a Web address as the project location, and then click on OK.

- A new project will contain one Web service called Service1.asmx. You can add new Web services to a project by selecting Project ➤ Add Web Service from the menu. To author the code behind your Web service, right-click on the service in the Solution Explorer and select View Code.

- By default, none of your methods, functions, or properties are exposed as part of your Web service. To expose a chunk of code, prefix it with the <WebMethod()> attribute, as shown here:

```
<WebMethod()> Public Function GetDate() As DateTime
    Return Now
End Function
```

- You can view your Web service in a browser by simply building the project, then visiting its dynamically generated ASMX page. Another technique is to simply press the F5 key while working on your Web service project (or selecting Debug ➤ Start from the menu).

- To "discover" a Web service for use in your Visual Studio .NET application, select Project ➤ Add Web Reference from the menu. Specify the address of your Web service, press the Enter key, and then select Add Reference. Alternatively, browse the Microsoft UDDI Directory at http://uddi.microsoft.com/visualstudio.

- To "consume" the functionality of a Web service in your application, simply treat it as you would any regular object. The XML is all parsed out and handled for you. For example, the following code demonstrates a discovered Web service in use:

```
Dim MyObject As New localhost.Service1()
MessageBox.Show(MyObject.GetDate)
```

- Your application doesn't care about the physical location of the Web service it is calling. The data could be coming from your local computer, across a network, or from the other side of the world via the Internet. So long as that connection is available, the Web service works.

- Once you've compiled your Web service, it's ready to be accessed on your machine and available to be discovered with its URL. To distribute your Web service to another server, select Project ➤ Copy Project from the menu. Alternatively, copy your ASMX, CONFIG, and VSDISCO project files across to your IIS application directory, then create a subdirectory called Bin, and copy your compiled Bin/ProjectName.DLL assembly into it.

- Web service members can accept and return more than just base data types. They can take in and pass back anything, including DataSets, data-holding classes, and user-defined types (structures).

- By default, when you discover a Web service, Visual Studio .NET creates a folder and namespace through which you refer to your service in code (such as "*localhost*.Service1" or "*com.google.api*.GoogleSearchService"). You can change this namespace by selecting your Web Reference in the Solution Explorer and changing the `Folder Name` property.

Developer Secrets

Want to start implementing a couple of impressive Web services to gain friends and influence people? Then read on, as the following developer secrets are unveiled:

- Exposing Database Information, the Quick and Easy Way

- Five Things You Need to Do Before Publicizing Your Web Service

- Improving Performance with Easy Caching

- Online Translations: Get Your Programs Speaking Spanish in Seconds!

- Adding Google Search to Your Programs

- Querying the Amazon.com Web Service

- View the Real World in Your Application, with TerraServer

- Asynchronous Access: Secrets of Calling a Web Service in the Background

- Web Services, Proxies, Connection Closed—Oh My!

- Change a Web Service URL, Without Recompiling

- Where to Find the Best Web Services Around

Let's get busy!

Exposing Database Information, the Quick and Easy Way

One of the problems that most Web service developers soon run into is... well, they can be a little limiting. A function may return a `True` or `False`, a number or a string. But that's not very much, really, is it?

The clever developers pass about *smart data*. By that, I mean, instead of a simple data type, they pass back something containing more than just one piece of information. A structure (user-defined type) is a prime example of this. You may create a `CustomerType` structure and pass a value of this type back. Visual Studio .NET will recognize that you're passing a structure and expose its details, so users of your service can properly interpret the response.

However, one of the most useful types of smart data is the DataSet—and here we'll be looking at how to expose the information in a database table through a Web service, allowing your users to view and update, in just a few lines of code. Here's how....

Create your Web service, remembering to note the location. Using the Server Explorer (View ➤ Server Explorer), connect to a database and drag and drop the table you'd like to expose through this Web service onto your Service1.asmx page. (You may rename your page, but, for simplicity in this example, we're sticking with the filename Service1.asmx and the class name Service1.)

You should see two objects—a `Connection` and `DataAdapter`—created for you. The `Connection` object connects into the database, whereas the `DataAdapter` talks to the database through the connection, sending and retrieving information. You can learn more about these objects in Chapter 4.

Right-click on your `DataAdapter` and select Generate Dataset. Here, you'll be creating a template `DataSet` class, which you can create instances from. Edit the new `DataSet` name if required, and make a note for future reference. (For this sample, I'm going to call mine MyDataSetTemplate.) Next, ensure that your table is selected in the list, check the "Add this dataset to the designer" box, and click OK when you're finished. (See Figure 5-1.)

You may not realize it, but two things have happened here. Firstly, a new `DataSet`-based class has been added to your project, behind the new XSD file, customized to your table and fields. Secondly, an instance of this new `DataSet` class has been added alongside your `Connection` and `DataAdapter` objects. (For this tip, I'm going to rename mine from the default MyDataSetTemplate1 to MyDataSet.) This is known as a *typed* `DataSet` due to its hard-coded "typed out" knowledge of your database table and fields.

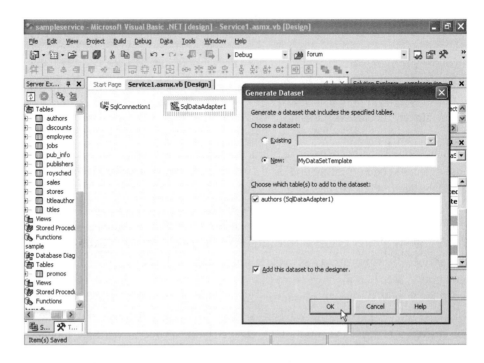

Figure 5-1. Setting up our initial data objects

Next, we need to add code to perform two simple actions: firstly, code to allow our client to retrieve data from the table; secondly, code to allow our client to pass back an edited DataSet for updating of the database. Press F7 to view the code window and add code similar to the following to your service:

```
<WebMethod()> Public Function GetData() As MyDataSetTemplate
    ' Passes populated typed DataSet back to client
    MyDataAdapter.Fill(MyDataSet)
    Return MyDataSet
End Function
<WebMethod()> Public Sub UpdateData(ByVal Data As MyDataSetTemplate)
    ' Updates the backend database where needed
    MyDataSet.Update(Data)
End Sub
```

When you're ready, click on Build ➤ Build Solution to compile your Web service. You can also press F5 (or click on Debug ➤ Start) to view the Web interface to your service, should you wish to do so. And that's it! You've built your server, and—with just a few lines of code—created a retrieval and update mechanism for your table data.

So, the server is complete. Now we need to work on our client, and this bit is even easier.

Create a new application of any type; a Windows application is easiest. From the menu, select Project ➤ Add Web Reference and type in the location of the Web service ASMX file you just edited, such as `http://localhost/mywebservicelocation/Service1.asmx`, and then press Return. When details of your service have finished loading, click on Add Reference. This will create a wrapper class for the Web service, allowing you to access its methods in your application.

Next, I'm going to add a little code to my application to access the data through my Web service. Yours may be similar, or completely different. The following snippet, however, should give you a decent idea of how the preceding, highly simple method of passing DataSets back and forth can work on the client side:

```
' Declare Service and DataSet class
Dim MyWebService As New localhost.Service1()
Dim MyDataSet As localhost.MyDataSetTemplate
' Grab data
MyDataSet = MyWebService.GetData
' Retrieve sample data - note the 'typed DataSet'
' Your table/fields will be different
Dim strText As String
strText = MyDataSet.Customers(0).Address
MessageBox.Show(strText)
' Update DataSet -
' again, your fields will be different
MyDataSet.Customers(0).Name = "Mr Bibbles"
' Send back to Web service
MyWebService.UpdateData(MyDataSet)
```

That's all you need to do on your client side. Try it out: you now have a fully working Web service that allows clients to connect, retrieve a complex `DataSet` full of information, update it locally, then pass back to the service for updating.

This template for working with Web services allows you to forget about handling all that sticky data access code in your applications: just connect to your service, retrieve, and get working. And imagine you move your supporting database to another machine: you need to update only your Web service. Your client applications continue to work as normal.

Don't forget: this isn't the end-all when it comes to working with `DataSet`s. You can do much more. You can add more tables. Incorporate security checks. Pass back `DataSet`s containing relationships between tables. Oh yes, much more. But, as I've demonstrated here, the backbone is incredibly simple; all it takes is a little imagination.

Five Things You Need to Do Before Publicizing Your Web Service

So, you've written the greatest Web service since SlicedBread.asmx, and now you want to tell the whole world about your creation? Well, before you do, ensure you follow this list of five quick changes that will give your service that professional touch:

1. Rename your class. Nobody likes dealing with a Web service called Service1, so, before you redistribute, make sure that you rename your class from something like `Public Class Service1` to something like `Public Class Customer`. Or something. Ahem.

2. Christen your ASMX file. You've renamed your Web service so it sounds all professional, but your clients are still accessing your service via the `http://localhost/Customer/Service1.asmx` file. Ugh. To combat this, simply rename your ASMX file by right-clicking on it in the Solution Explorer and selecting Rename.

3. Add a service description. What does your Web service do? Provide access to your customer database or allow you to send SMS messages? Well, you could just let your clients guess. However, a more user-friendly technique would be to add a description to the `<WebService>` attribute. So, before distributing, change your class as follows:

   ```
   <WebService(Description:="This class does amazing data tricks.")> _
   Public Class AmazingData
       ' ... etc ...
   End Class
   ```

   This description is used in the automatically generated Web interface, plus it's automatically absorbed by all clients using your service and utilized in the Visual Studio .NET programming environment.

4. Add method descriptions. Just as your service can include a description, so can your individual methods and functions. Again, this is used by the Web interface and Visual Studio .NET. And, again, it's simple to implement: just add a description to each `<WebMethod>` attribute, like so:

   ```
   <WebMethod(Description:="Returns current server date + time.")> _
   Public Function GetServerDate() As DateTime
       Return Now
   End Function
   ```

5. Change the namespace. You've already seen the .NET Framework organizing functionality into "namespaces." They're just unique identifiers for a certain set of functionality. That's all a namespace is here, too: a unique string that identifies this Web service. By default, VS .NET uses `http://www.tempuri.org/`, and you will need to change this to a unique value. The namespace you provide doesn't necessarily have to point to anything on the Web, but, if it does, I'd recommended that you at least own the domain you use (*ahem*). So, change the namespace to something unique before unveiling your service by altering the Namespace property of the <WebService> attribute, as so:

```
<WebService(Description:="Yadda", _
Namespace:="http://www.amazingdata.com/query/")> _
 Public Class AmazingData
  ' ... etc ...
 End Class
```

Improving Performance with Easy Caching

It's a little-known fact, but you can actually "cache" what a Web service gives out and automatically serve up the same response next time, seriously speeding up popular, processor-intensive services.

How? Simply specify a CacheDuration parameter in the WebMethod attribute, like this:

```
<WebMethod(CacheDuration:=60)> _
Public Function GetWeather() As String
    ' ... complicated code ...
End Function
```

Here, the Web server will cache and serve up the same results for GetWeather 60 seconds after the last query. You can see this cute tip in action by returning the time from a function. See what happens?

Online Translations: Get Your Programs Speaking Spanish in Seconds!

The Babel Fish is one of Douglas Adams's famed creations, an enormous green scaly amphibian that, when held to the ear, allows you to instantly understand any language. It's a concept that search engine AltaVista soon cottoned onto, with their online translation service at babelfish.altavista.com. It's pretty good, too: just tap in a site address or block of text, select a language, and off you go!

It's no longer limited to just the Web, however. Some bright spark at XMethods (www.xmethods.com) created a Web service interface to the site, meaning you can plug the translation feature straight into your Windows programs, mobile Web applications (see Chapter 6), or anywhere else. And the service is exceptionally easy to use, too.

To get started, fire up Visual Studio .NET and create a new project, such as a Windows application. Select Project ➤ Add Web Reference, and type in the URL of the Babel Fish WSDL (Web Service Definition Language) file—http://www.xmethods.net/sd/2001/BabelFishService.wsdl—then press Return. Click on Add Reference when the button becomes available.

Now, this service has only one simple function, BabelFish. It accepts two parameters: a translationmode and sourcedata. The sourcedata is quite simply the text you wish to translate, and the translationmode can be any of the following values, depending on the languages you wish to translate between:

TRANSLATION LANGUAGE	"TRANSLATIONMODE" VALUE
English to French	en_fr
English to German	en_de
English to Italian	en_it
English to Portugese	en_pt
English to Spanish	en_es
French to English	fr_en
German to English	de_en
Italian to English	it_en
Portugese to English	pt_en
Russian to English	ru_en
Spanish to English	es_en

Want to get started? Simply create a new instance of the BabelFishService stub class created for you and call the BabelFish function with these parameters, like this:

```
Dim objTranslate As New net.xmethods.www.BabelFishService()
Dim strText = objTranslate.BabelFish("fr_en", "comment traduire")
MessageBox.Show(strText)
```

And that's quite simply it. A small service, yes, but extremely powerful. To learn more about this service, including supported languages and character limitations, check out the link at the bottom of the XMethods site. Excellent!

Adding Google Search to Your Programs

Download supporting files at www.apress.com.
The files for this tip are in the "Ch5–Google" folder.

It started off as "that nerdy site with the funny name" and ended up as the world's #1 search engine. Yes, it's Google at www.google.com—an intelligent, easy-to-use searchable archive of more than two billion Web pages.

And thanks to the world of Web services, you can plug your application into this mass of knowledge, and with just a few lines of code.

How? First off, you'll need to checkout www.google.com/apis/ for information on the process. The main thing you'll want to do here is create a Google account. You'll be asked for your email address and other details, and, in return, you'll be provided with a license key. You need to use this when accessing the service.

Got your license key? Then fire up Visual Studio .NET and create a new project, such as a Windows application. Select Project ➤ Add Web Reference and type the URL of the Google WSDL file—http://api.google.com/GoogleSearch.wsdl as listed on the Google site—then press Return. Click on Add Reference when the button becomes available.

And now? Simply start using the service! To get you started, let's review a little sample code. Here's my own attempt at performing a simple search, returning a maximum of ten items for the term "Karl Moore" (I know, *narcissistic*):

```
' Create a new Google search object
Dim objSearch As New _
    com.google.api.GoogleSearchService()
' Invoke the search method
Dim objResults As _
    com.google.api.GoogleSearchResult = _
 objSearch.doGoogleSearch( _
"license-key-goes-here", _
"Karl Moore", 0, 10, False, "", False, _
"", "", "")
' Loop through result elements
Dim shtCount As Short
For shtCount = 0 To objResults.endIndex - 1
    MessageBox.Show(objResults.resultElements(shtCount).title & _
        " - " & objResults.resultElements(shtCount).URL)
Next
```

TOP TIP *The Google service will include <b> bold tags around text that you search for. This doesn't matter if you're developing for Web applications, where highlighting searched-for terms is actually quite user friendly. For Windows applications, however, which don't use HTML tags, you'll want to strip these out using a custom algorithm or regular expression. (See the tip "Converting HTML to Text, Easily" in the Internet section of Chapter 7.)*

So, that's a regular search. But there's more. Regular users of Google will know that when you accidentally mistype a search term, the engine will suggest a possible correct spelling. You can access that exact functionality through your Web service too, as so:

```
' Create a new Google search object
Dim objSearch As New _
    com.google.api.GoogleSearchService()
' Retrieve the suggest spelling, if any
Dim strSuggestion As String
strSuggestion = objSearch.doSpellingSuggestion( _
    "license-key-goes-here", _
    "Britnee Speyers")
MessageBox.Show(strSuggestion)
```

Thought that was it? You can also retrieve cached versions of a page (alongside the Google "this is a cached page, click here for the latest version", etc. HTML). Here's a little sample code:

```
' Create a new Google search object
Dim objSearch As New _
    com.google.api.GoogleSearchService()
' Retrieve cached version of a page
Dim bytPage() As Byte = _
 objSearch.doGetCachedPage( _
    "license-key-goes-here", _
    "www.karlmoore.com")
' Convert base 64 byte array to string
Dim strHTML As String = _
    System.Text.ASCIIEncoding.ASCII.GetString(bytPage)
MessageBox.Show(strHTML)
```

Here, I've simply demonstrated the three core features of the Web service. (See a snapshot of my sample application in Figure 5-2.) However this is just the surface: you can really delve into any of these areas, just download the Developer's Toolkit from `www.google.com/apis/`. By filling out a few of the extra `doGoogleSearch` parameters, for example, you can restrict results to a particular language, search within a particular topic, or alter the number of returned results. Be sure to check it out.

Also, it's worthwhile noting that, at the time of writing, the Google Web service was still in beta. It is, however, unlikely that Google will change the interface definitions (a prediction based on the way it has continued to keep certain redundant properties available, even though still in beta—a sure sign of a user-conscious organization, if not one lacking in a little foresight). In addition, be aware that (again at the time of writing) you are limited to 1,000 searches per day per license key, and that no commercial pay-per-search facility is yet available.

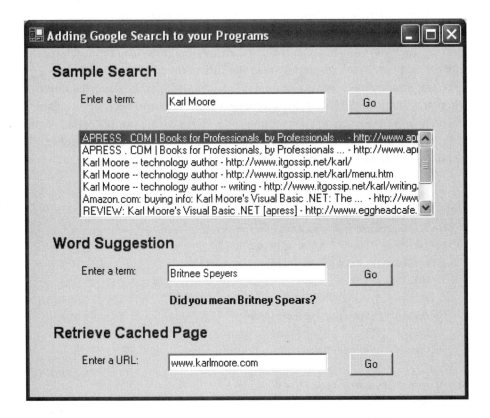

Figure 5-2. Plugging directly into the power that is Google, through Web services

Querying the Amazon.com Web Service

Download supporting files at www.apress.com.
The files for this tip are in the "Ch5–Amazon" folder.

Amazon.com calls itself the world's largest bookstore, and it's probably right. Stocking millions of titles from writers around the globe, it's a great source of information, and I openly admit to being a frequent customer.

Well, the floodgates have been opened. Amazon.com has made its mass database of information available to developers through Web services.

In a style similar to Google, the Amazon.com service starts by having you request a "token," which is essentially a developer ID you use in code to access the service. You can nab this by heading down to https://associates.amazon.com/ exec/panama/associates/join/developer/application.html. You can also download the official developer documentation at http://associates.amazon.com/exec/ panama/associates/join/developer/kit.html if you're feeling frisky.

Got your token? Then you're ready to begin developing. Open up the application in which you wish to consume this Web service. From the menu, select Project ➤ Add Web Reference and type in the URL of the Amazon .WSDL file— http://soap.amazon/com/schemas2/AmazonWebServices.wsdl per the documentation — then press Return. Click on Add Reference when the button becomes available.

And now? You're ready to start writing code. Here's a little sample code I've put together that takes a known ASIN (an Amazon standard identification number, which is the ISBN for book products) and returns a little information:

```vbnet
' Create new search service object
Dim objSearch As New _
            com.amazon.soap.AmazonSearchService()
' Define properties for a new ASIN request
Dim objASIN As New com.amazon.soap.AsinRequest()
With objASIN
    .asin = "159059021X"
    .devtag = "developer-key-goes-here"
    .type = "lite"
    .tag = "your-assoc-id"
End With
' Perform ASIN search request and
' return ProductInfo object
Dim objProductInfo As New com.amazon.soap.ProductInfo()
objProductInfo = objSearch.AsinSearchRequest(objASIN)
' Retrieve various details
Dim strNamePrice As String = _
```

```
            objProductInfo.Details(0).ProductName & _
            " costs " & objProductInfo.Details(0).OurPrice
    Dim strLink As String = objProductInfo.Details(0).Url
    Dim strImageURL As String = objProductInfo.Details(0).ImageUrlSmall
    ' Join together array of authors
    Dim strAuthors As String = Join( _
            objProductInfo.Details(0).Authors, ", ")
            MessageBox.Show(strAuthors)
```

Here, we set the properties of an `AsinRequest` object, specifying the ASIN, our token (the `.devtag` property), the type of search ("lite" or "heavy," depending on how much information you want returned), and the tag (replace this with your associate ID, if you have one—it'll place your ID into all links that you retrieve from the Web service to ensure you get your commission). Next, we use the `AmazonSearchService` object to execute our search and return a `ProductInfo` object. Here, we look at the first object (zero) in the `Details` property of the `ProductInfo` object and retrieve information about the product found during our search.

But, of course, we don't always know the ISBN before searching. Sometimes we want to search book titles. And that's my cue for another snippet of code, this time to search by keyword:

```
    ' Create new search service object
    Dim objSearch As New _
                com.amazon.soap.AmazonSearchService()
    ' Define properties for a new keyword request
    Dim objKeyword As New com.amazon.soap.KeywordRequest()
    With objKeyword
        .keyword = "Karl Moore"
        .devtag = "developer-key-goes-here"
        .mode = "books"
        .type = "heavy"
        .tag = "your-assoc-id"
        .page = "1"
    End With
    ' Perform keyword search request and
    ' return ProductInfo object
    Dim objProductInfo As New com.amazon.soap.ProductInfo()
    objProductInfo = objSearch.KeywordSearchRequest(objKeyword)
    ' Cycle through results
    Dim shtCount As Short
    For shtCount = 0 To objProductInfo.Details.Length - 1
        MessageBox.Show(objProductInfo.Details(shtCount).ProductName & _
            " - " & objProductInfo.Details(shtCount).Url)
    Next
```

Let's look at what's going on here. First, we fill out the properties of a `KeywordRequest` object. Special properties to note here include the keyword, the mode (here we have "books," but you could specify "classical" to search classical music—see Step 5 of the downloadable documentation for more information), and page (each page returns ten results, and we're retrieving the first page). Then we run the request, returning a list of matching `ProductInfo` items, and then we cycle through the bundle, displaying details of each in a message box. (Yes, this is a Windows application example! See Figure 5-3 for a screenshot of my own sample program, distributed with the source for this book.)

It's powerful stuff, but, as with most Web services, you learn much about how it works during development. And, following a week of working with this service, I also have a few top tips to share.

First off, it doesn't stop here. You can search Amazon.com by author, artist, category ("node"), product similarity, manufacturer, and more. The code is always similar to the stuff we have above: you create a `...Request` object, pass it to the `...SearchRequest` function of the `AmazonSearchService`, and then analyze the returned `ProductInfo` object.

Watch out, however: with many of those `...Request` objects, you have to fill out all of the properties. If you don't, you'll receive an error.

Also, despite its popularity, the Amazon.com Web service is still officially in beta, and, unlike the eternally stable Google, it shows. During the writing of this chapter, the service definition changed once, was often slow and regularly timed out. As you can see from some of my notes, the service isn't too user friendly, and the documentation completely lacks any sample .NET code.

Still, the service is immensely useful for developers creating everything from commission book links on their sites to those writing market research programs, and it *will* improve. To help you through, Amazon.com has a resources page at `http://associates.amazon.com/exec/panama/associates/join/developer/resources.html`. You'll also find a link for the support forums here, where you'll be able to obtain support from your .NET fellow gurus. Good luck!

> **TOP TIP** *ASP.NET developers will be pleased to hear that Dan Wahlin has encapsulated many of the Amazon.com Web service features into a neat user control, which includes more advanced features such as the ability to add items direct to the shopping basket. Find out more by visiting* `http://www.xmlforasp.net/codeSection.aspx?csID=76.`

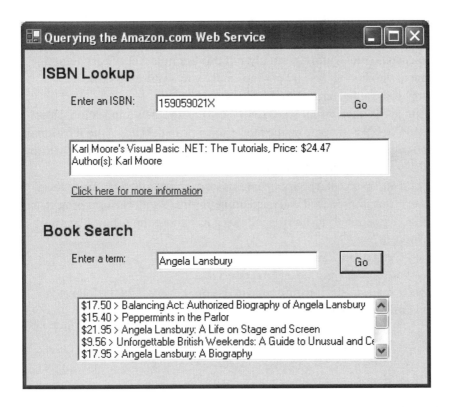

Figure 5-3. Our small application taps into Amazon.com, with a few lines of code

View the Real World in Your Application, with TerraServer

 Download supporting files at www.apress.com.
The files for this tip are in the "Ch5–TerraServer" folder.

The Statue of Liberty. Yankee Stadium. The Pentagon. Hoover Dam. Unrelated? I think not. You see, they're all listed in TerraServer, the mass Microsoft-supported Web service that allows you to view the world and all (or at least most/some) of its famous sites from the skies.

You can check out the Web version of this cool service at terraserver.microsoft.com, or you can use the power of Web services to plug straight into this functionality.

In this example, I'm going to show you how to connect into the service and then retrieve an image using its popular name, such as *White House* or *Statue of Liberty*. You can do much more, certainly, but this example will at least demonstrate some of the capabilities and perhaps make you aware as to how troublesome the graphic "crunching" code can get.

Ready to go? Launch Visual Studio .NET and create a new application. Select Project ➤ Add Web Reference from the menu and type in the URL of the TerraServer description page—http://terraservice.net/TerraService.asmx—then press Return. Click on the Add Reference button when available.

Next, add an Imports statement to save us from constantly referring to the net.terraservice namespace. If you're creating this in a Windows form project, you'll need to type something like the following just above the Public Class part of your form code:

```
Imports NameOfProject.net.terraservice
' ie, Imports WindowsApplication1.net.terraservice
```

Now we're ready to start writing code to use our service. Add the following commented method to your form (or class, or whatever):

```
Public Sub CreateBitmapFromPlaceName( _
    ByVal PlaceName As String, ByVal Filename As String)
    ' Size of image to create
    Const WIDTH As Integer = 600
    Const HEIGHT As Integer = 400
    ' Setup objects to use
    Dim objTheme As New Theme()
    Dim objScale As New Scale()
    Dim objTS As New TerraService()
    Dim objABB As AreaBoundingBox
    Dim imgImage As Image
    Dim objPF() As PlaceFacts
    Try
        ' Retrieve list of matching points
        objPF = objTS.GetPlaceList(PlaceName, 1, False)
        ' If no matches, exit
        If objPF.Length = 0 Then Exit Sub
        ' Settings - type of image and scale
        objTheme = Theme.Photo
        objScale = objScale.Scale2m
        ' Gets details of the final full image AreaBoundingBox
        objABB = objTS.GetAreaFromPt(objPF(0).Center, _
            objTheme, objScale, WIDTH, HEIGHT)
        ' Create objects to handle image in memory
        Dim objPFmt As System.Drawing.Imaging.PixelFormat = _
```

```
            System.Drawing.Imaging.PixelFormat.Format32bppRgb
        Dim imgTemp As Image = New Bitmap(WIDTH, HEIGHT, objPFmt)
        Dim objGraphics As Graphics = Graphics.FromImage(imgTemp)
        ' Create objects to store current locations
        Dim intStartX As Integer = objABB.NorthWest.TileMeta.Id.X
        Dim intStartY As Integer = objABB.NorthWest.TileMeta.Id.Y
        Dim x, y As Integer
        ' Cycle through the portions of our whole AreaBoundingBox,
        ' incrementally retrieving and stiching together our image
        For x = intStartX To objABB.NorthEast.TileMeta.Id.X
            For y = intStartY To objABB.SouthWest.TileMeta.Id.Y Step -1
                Dim objTID As TileId
                Dim imgTile As Image
                objTID = objABB.NorthWest.TileMeta.Id
                objTID.X = x
                objTID.Y = y
                imgTile = Image.FromStream(New System.IO.MemoryStream ( _
                    objTS.GetTile(objTID)))
                objGraphics.DrawImage(imgTile, _
                    (x - intStartX) * imgTile.Width - _
                    objABB.NorthWest.Offset.XOffset, _
                    (intStartY - y) * imgTile.Height - _
                    objABB.NorthWest.Offset.YOffset, _
                    imgTile.Width, imgTile.Height)
            Next
        Next
        ' Finally, save to the passed filename
        imgTemp.Save(Filename, System.Drawing.Imaging.ImageFormat.Bmp)
    Catch
        Return
    End Try
End Sub
```

Well, this is one pretty hefty piece of code. Let me walk you through it. We begin by defining the dimensions of the width and height of the image you want, then declare a few objects that we'll be using later on. Next, we retrieve a list of PlaceFacts objects, depending on the place name passed into the method, and exiting if we have no matches. After that, we initialize a couple of settings: the type of image and the scale. Moving on and the next line takes an area (WIDTH by HEIGHT) around the center of the first matching PlaceFacts object, creating a AreaBoundingBox object, which essentially defines the area for your image.

Continuing, our code then creates various objects to handle our image, then begins one big loop. Starting at the upper-left (northwest) point, it goes about chunk by chunk, retrieving an array of bytes from the Web service representing an image block (it has to move in this block format because the service returns images only to a maximum of 200 × 200 at any one time). As one loop moves across, collecting images, the second one moves down, and eventually the whole image is stitched together. Finally, our `Graphic` object is saved to the specified filename as a bitmap—ready to perhaps load into a control or stream down to a Web page.

We call this function a little like this (see Figure 5-4 to see my sample application in use):

```
CreateBitmapFromPlaceName("Statue of Liberty", "c:\myimage.bmp")
```

And that's it: one simple line of code, yes, but a disproportionate number of hours spent figuring how to make it work. However, that's still not all the TerraServer can do: this may be the most popular function, but there's always more to discover. Did you know you can retrieve the population of an area you've mapped, for example, or convert a longitude and latitude value to the nearest place name?

Check out `terraserver.microsoft.com` and click on the Web services link for documentation and examples. Good luck and enjoy the service!

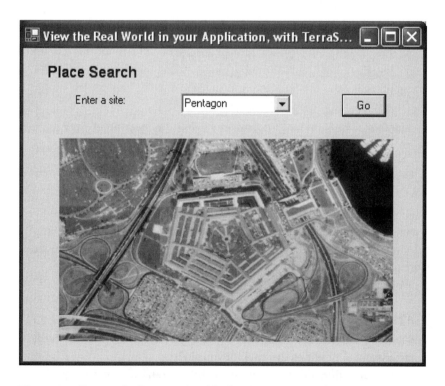

Figure 5-4. Spy on the Pentagon, with the Terraserver Web service.

Asynchronous Access: Secrets of Calling a Web Service in the Background

The problem with accessing Web services is that they can be a little time consuming. There's always a short delay when first opening any service connection. And, if the service is returning a lot of data or performing a lengthy operation, it can really bottleneck your application.

If the service is executing some critical process that your program absolutely requires in order to continue running, that's fine. But, if you're simply checking for new updates when your application starts up or retrieving news headlines to scroll in your program, you really want to quietly utilize your Web service in the background, rather than holding up your entire application as you access it.

Good news: you can do just that, by setting up a *callback* in your client application.

Here's how it works. Firstly, you create a callback method that will be called when the Web service has finished, then refer to this through something called a delegate. Next, you set up your Web service as normal and call the automatically generated Begin... version of the method you wish to run (for example, if you're calling a Web service function called GetCompanyName, you'd run BeginGetCompanyName), passing in the delegate you just set up.

The Begin method doesn't hang around: it initiates, then instantly allows your application to move onto the next line of code. In the background, your Web service is accessed... and, when the results are available, it runs your callback method, where you then get the results from the automatically generated End... version of the function you called (that is, EndGetCompanyName).

It sounds confusing, but it's actually relatively simple to code. Here's a commented Windows form sample to show how it would work, using a service on my local machine called SampleService, containing one function called GetCompanyName:

```
' Instantiating my sample Web service, containing one function - GetCompanyName
Dim objWS As New localhost.SampleService()

' Code to begin the asynchronous process
Private Sub Button1_Click(…) Handles Button1.Click
    objWS.BeginGetCompanyName(objCallback, 0)
    ' Last parameter here provides extra info about operation,
    ' we specify zero as we are sending no extra information
    MessageBox.Show("App code instantly continues running...")
End Sub

' My delegate, which refers to my callback function
Dim objCallback As New AsyncCallback(AddressOf MyCallbackFunction)
```

```
' Sample callback function
Sub MyCallbackFunction(ByVal Result As IAsyncResult)
    Dim strCompanyName As String
    strCompanyName = objWS.EndGetCompanyName(Result)
    MessageBox.Show(strCompanyName)
End Sub
```

Here's what happens when someone clicks on Button1 in this sample. The `Begin...` version of the code runs, and the Web service is accessed in the background. It's also passed a reference to `objCallback`, which simply points to our callback function. Then the code continues and the "App code..." message box is displayed.

When the service has returned a result, the system looks at `objCallback` and calls `MyCallbackFunction`, passing in a result. Here, we call the `End...` version of our Web service function, passing in the callback result parameter. This function returns the result of our Web service function, just as though we had called `GetCompanyName` synchronously. Finally, we simply display this returned value in a message box.

Looks confusing, sounds worse, but the technique is relatively simple once you've grasped the essentials. Try it out yourself on a sample service and see what it does for you. And who's betting you'll be the first to use it in your next project....

Web Services, Proxies, Connection Closed–Oh My!

Getting "connection closed" errors when attempting to access external Web services? Do you typically access the Internet through a proxy server? Well, a Web service works just like a regular HTTP request, and, as such, you need to tell your Web service about the proxy in code before you'll be allowed access.

Here's an example to demonstrate how:

```
Dim objMyService As New com.karlmoore.HomePage()
Dim objProxy As New System.Net.WebProxy("http://proxyserver/", 8080)
objMyService.Proxy = objProxy
' ... continue regular Web service code here ...
```

Here, you can see that we create a new `WebProxy` object and specify a few details. You can choose from a number of constructors, however here I've opted for the most common, specifying proxy server address and port. Then, we set the `Proxy` property of our service to point to this object and continue as usual. Problem solved.

Change a Web Service URL, Without Recompiling

Many developers are cautious of consuming Web services in their applications. They need to feel comfortable that a provider won't seriously alter their service definitions and stop their application from working. That's understandable... even advisable. There's a second major concern, too: what if the URL changes, or the service gets moved to a machine with a different name?

You could simply delete the Web service folder through the Solution Explorer, then add the Web reference again. Alternatively, you could just select your Web reference through the Solution Explorer, and change the `Web Reference URL` property. However, both of these solutions require a recompile to get everything working again.

There is another way, however: change the `URL Behavior` property to `Dynamic`. This will add an app.config file to your project containing the Web service URL. When you compile, a CONFIG file is generated alongside your EXE assembly.

You can now distribute your application as normal, with or without the CONFIG file. If the URL of your Web service changes, edit this file to incorporate the new address, then place it in the same directory as your assembly. It'll automatically "override" the default Web service URL. Sorted!

Where to Find the Best Web Services Around

Looking for the best Web services around? Then maybe you'd better check out the Yahoo! of Web services, XMethods at `www.xmethods.com`. (See Figure 5-5.)

At last check, the site listed hundreds of available services (some subscription based, many completely free), covering everything from a specially designated nationals database to international business headlines, airport code lookups to Biblical text retrieval, online SMS'ing to online horoscope readings, dictionaries to a FedEx package checker, atomic table information to an image format converter!

If you find an entry on the site you want to use, make note of its WSDL address (the URL ending in .wsdl or .asmx). In your Visual Studio .NET project, select Project ➤ Add Web Reference, type in the address, and press Return. Check the information that downloads and click on Add Reference, when available. Then use as you would a regular Web service.

It's all amazing stuff, and a site definitely worth bookmarking.

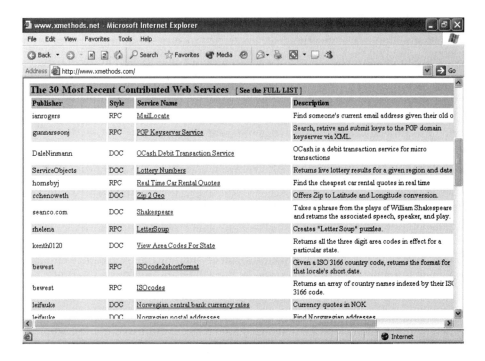

Figure 5-5. The latest Web service contributions, from the front page of XMethods

From Microwaves to Pocket PCs: Special Project Types

IF YOU'RE LIKE most Visual Studio .NET developers, as soon as you launched the program, you dashed off and created your own Windows application to see how the whole system had changed. After a while, you got bored and moved onto ASP.NET Web applications. Then, on the seventh day, you crowned yourself a guru and decided to rest.

However, like many programmers, it's just possible you may have missed some of the fresh new project types you can create in Visual Studio .NET—projects we've never been able to create before, or at least, without ten big headaches.

Creating a Windows service, for example, was previously a big-time problem: you either had to make seven zillion API calls and perform some low-level registering, or had to buy an expensive third-party component. Yet, no matter which option you chose, the process was still dodgy as hell, and most people who needed this functionality skipped across to C++. Not so in .NET: creating a service is pure simplicity.

Then there's the Console application, which gives you a DOS-style window for those times when a user interface isn't of prime importance. Yes, you could create these in Visual Basic 6... if you had the patience of two saints. Now, you just create a project, add a few function calls to the Sub Main procedure, and hit the Start button. Easy.

Then we have the Mobile Internet Toolkit (MIT). With this little baby, you can create Web applications to run on anything from mobile phones to microwaves, in almost the same way as you'd put together an ASP.NET Web site.

Finally, we have the ability to create applications for small portable devices, such as Pocket PCs, with the smart device application project type. The old days gave us eMbedded Visual Basic to do this, but programming inconsistencies and sticky development techniques made it a rough ride for developers. No more.

But still, each of these project types has its own little quirks and special requirements, and that's what this chapter is here for. It'll explain the core concepts, then show you how to get up and running with each of these three special project types in no time at all.

Sitting comfortably? Then I'll begin....

Plug into Windows: Creating Your Own Windows Service

A Windows service is one of those often-invisible programs that typically start with the operating system and hang about, silently running, until you shut down. Such services include virus checkers, disk-monitoring applications, and security programs.

If you wanted to create one of these programs just a couple of years ago, you'd either have to buy an expensive third-party VB add-on to assist in the process—or learn C++. In Visual Studio .NET, you can just do it directly in your fave programming language, in about five minutes flat.

How? Well, start off by creating your own Windows Service project in Visual Studio .NET. (See Figure 6-1.) You'll be shown a relatively blank design screen. What you do next is really up to you.

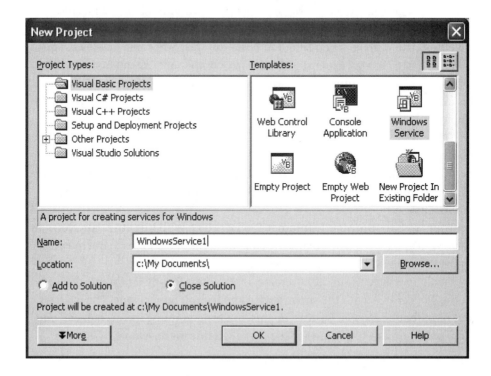

Figure 6-1. Creating a Windows Service project

One of the most common procedures in designing your Windows service is to add a Timer component and have it fire your service code every x seconds or minutes. How can you get this to work? While still in Design mode, open the Components tab of the toolbox and drag and drop a Timer component onto your service. Change its Interval property to the number of milliseconds between each time you want your code to run. (Remember, 1,000 milliseconds equal one second. If you want your code to run every ten minutes, for example, set this to 60000.) Next, add code to respond to the Elapsed event of your timer; this code may check for the availability of a Web site, process any outstanding database requests, remove redundant files, perform some form of calculation—anything really.

Another component that you may wish to use in your service is the FileSystemWatcher. This enables you to monitor a particular file or directory for changes. (See "Watching a Directory for Changes" in Chapter 7 for more information.) When these occur, events are raised. You can use this to dynamically monitor an area on your machine for alterations. As an example, you may be creating a system that keeps backups alongside an audit log, or records important system file changes in the event log.

A further possibility is to create a service as the server part of a remoting solution. (See "Which to Choose: Web Services vs. Remoting" in Chapter 7.) Your service simply sits in the background, waiting for clients to connect in and "talk".

You can also add code to respond to the overridden OnStart and OnEnd events. These are added by default to your service—just add code as necessary. For example, you may run a Timer1.Start during the OnStart event and a Timer1.Stop at the OnEnd event.

Your service also has the ability to override other events, such as OnPause, OnContinue, OnShutdown, and so on. You can respond to these by, in the Code window, selecting (Overrides) from the first dropdown box, and the event in the second. A skeletal overrides event will be created for you. Again, add code as you deem fit.

So, you finally decided how to design your own service and have just finished coding. Next, set its properties. To do this, open your service in Design mode and click on a blank region of the screen. In the Properties window, alter the Can... settings (such as CanPauseAndContinue and CanShutdown), typically depending on the events you have coded. You may also want to change the ServiceName.

Installing Your Service

Well, that's your service finished, but to install it we need to perform one last step. Right-click on your service in Design mode, and select Add Installer. This adds a new component to your project, containing a couple of objects that are used to provide details of your service during the installation. (See Figure 6-2.) If you don't add this installer component, the installation simply doesn't work.

> **TOP TIP** *If you want to add special code to run during installation, you can do this by responding to some of the events behind this installer. Find out more by looking up "Windows Service applications, adding installers to" in the help index.*

Peruse the properties of the two objects added: typically `ServiceProcessInstaller1` and `ServerInstaller1`. The most important properties here are the `DisplayName`, which is the friendly name given to a service; `StartType`, which determines whether the service starts `Manual` or `Automatic`; and `Account`, which determines the account your service logs on under. Edit if required.

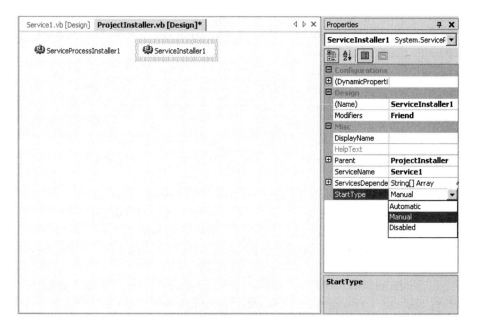

Figure 6-2. Setting up our installer component

And then? That's it! Just click on Build ➤ Build Solution to compile your application.

How do you actually get your service up and running? Well, include your project in a regular VS .NET setup and it'll do the job of installing it for you. Alternatively, you can go manual and use the `InstallUtil.exe` application to get it installed. Launch the Visual Studio .NET Command Prompt and type the following line:

```
InstallUtil.exe c:\YourProject\bin\YourApp.exe
```

Make sure you pay attention to the messages from this utility. If all is well, you've just completed your installation. Use the Server Explorer in Visual Studio .NET to check out the services running on your local machine (or others on your network). (See Figure 6-3.) After installing, yours should now be in the list; right-click and select Start to set it off. You can alter whether it starts by default by using the Services application (Program Files ➤ Administrative Tools ➤ Services), or setting the `StartType` property previously mentioned.

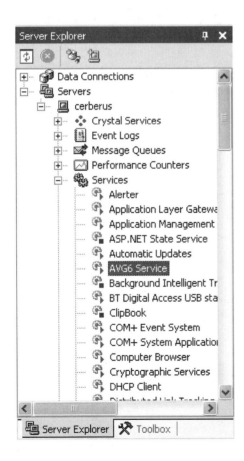

Figure 6-3. Viewing Services via the Server Explorer

But what good would be an install without an uninstall? Here's how to remove your Windows service using the InstallUtil.exe prompt once more:

```
InstallUtil.exe /u c:\YourProject\bin\YourApp.exe
```

And that's really all there is to know about creating your very own Windows service. Easy!

Get the DOS Feel: Creating a Basic Console Application

Very few developers ever attempted to create DOS-style console applications using previous versions of Visual Basic because it was just too darn difficult. Ever craving for a challenge, I went the whole hog—and even wrote an entire magazine feature showing exactly how it could be done. But, admittedly, it was bloomin' difficult.

Thankfully, with the release of Visual Studio .NET, Microsoft has realized console applications are back in fashion—and added built-in support for DOS-feel applications.

To get started, simply create a new project of the Console Application type. You'll be shown the simplest of Code windows—one module containing one method, Main. This Main method is the procedure that will run by default when your application fires. (See Figure 6-4.)

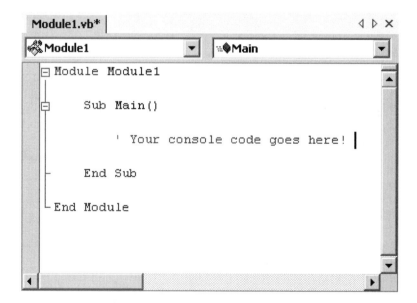

Figure 6-4. Say hello to the home of your console code!

What can you do from here? Well, console applications have really just a few core commands, all of which are available through the System.Console namespace, intrinsically available to your program. Let's cover the important ones now.

First, you need to know how to spurt something out at the user. The following code will print the specified line out to the console:

```
Console.WriteLine("Welcome to the Automatic Data Processor")
```

One way of just appending text to the current line is by using the Console.Write method. Here's an example:

```
Console.Write("Processing ...")
' start processing
Console.Write("...")
' more processing
Console.Write("... finished")
```

You'll also want to know how to receive input from the user. This can be done through the Console.ReadLine function, as so:

```
Dim strResponse As String
Console.WriteLine("Enter your age: ")
strResponse = Console.ReadLine
Console.WriteLine("You are " & strResponse & " years old")
```

How about adding blank lines? It's as simple as writing out an empty string:

```
Console.WriteLine("")
```

And what about incorporating a pause, for a "press return to continue" moment? Just do a Console.ReadLine without bothering to record the results:

```
Console.WriteLine("Press return to continue...")
Console.ReadLine()
```

After that, you can continue coding away as normal. Add functions, call Web services, read and write files. Your console application is no different to any other in the .NET range, except that it lacks any real user interface. And, if you're writing one of those applications that performs a bundle of data processing at 3:00 A.M. or executes a routine administrator task, that's absolutely perfect. Those sort of applications suit the formal, no-frills console application look wonderfully.

Well, that's all you really need to get going with your own console application. (See Figure 6-5.) Simply press F5 to run and test, or compile (select Build ➤ Build Solution from the menu), open up a command window, and run the executable in your Bin folder. Enjoy!

> **TOP TIP** *Console applications include built-in support for reading from text files (rather than pausing for user input) and outputting to text files (rather than sending text to the screen). To take advantage of this, use the* SetIn *and/or* SetOut *methods of the* Console *object, passing in new* TextReader *and/or* TextWriter *objects, respectively. For more information, look up "Console class, about Console class" in the help index.*

> **ANOTHER TOP TIP** *Want your console application to run at set times? Click on Programs ➤ Accessories ➤ System Tools ➤ Scheduled Tasks, then double-click on Add Scheduled Task and follow the wizard.*

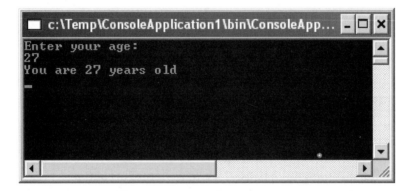

Figure 6-5. My sample console application in action

From Mobiles to Microwaves: Creating Applications with the MIT

For a long, long time, Microsoft has been touting this dream of information on any device, anywhere, anytime. But, at least when it comes to Visual Basic developers, the company hasn't done much to prove it. That is, until now.

Coinciding with the first release of Visual Studio .NET, Microsoft unveiled the Mobile Internet Toolkit, a neat Visual Studio .NET-integrated extension to the .NET Framework. MIT is a program that allows you to write your own Web applications that can be displayed on almost *anything*—from mobile phones to microwaves, Internet Explorer to handheld PDAs. Develop once and run anywhere.

How does it work? Well, after installing the MIT, you get to create a new type of project, a Mobile Web application. (See Figure 6-6.) Here you can design your minimalist application. It can do anything that your regular ASP.NET applications can, but, due to the limitations of some of the devices that may use your application, you're best keeping the actual graphical side to a minimum. Next, you make your application available as you would a regular ASP.NET Web app.

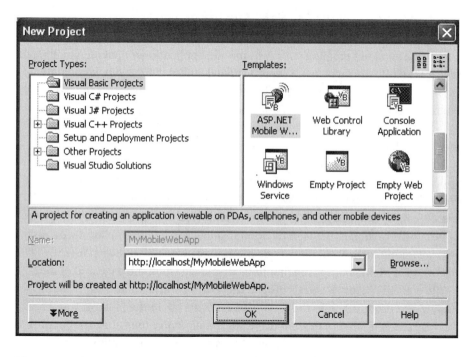

Figure 6-6. Creating a new ASP.NET Mobile Web application

When your application gets requested over the Net—through whatever device—the MIT steps in and figures out exactly what sort of machine is asking to view your pages. It then configures the output appropriately (that is, a certain dropdown box-style control will look like a regular dropdown on some devices, whereas on others it will render as a clickable list), and then sends your page down the wire in the language spoken by the device—HTML, cHTML (Compact HTML), or WML (Wireless Markup Language).

In short, the MIT allows you to create intelligent, mini "Web pages" that can be viewed on practically any device. You design once and let the MIT handle all that sticky "plumbing" you really don't want to get involved in.

> **TOP TIP** *Microsoft is slowly renaming the Mobile Internet Toolkit to* ASP.NET Mobile Controls. *It is, however, being awfully inconsistent about the process. Many parts of the Microsoft site use the terms interchangeably. Just keep in mind that the two terms refer to the same thing. During the rest of this section, I'm going to stick with* Mobile Internet Toolkit.

Creating Your Mobile Web Application

How do you go about creating your own mobile applications? First off, you'll need to access the MIT. If you're using Everett (Visual Studio .NET 2003), it's actually built into Visual Studio. If you aren't, however, or you want to access the latest device updates, you'll need to surf down to msdn.microsoft.com/vstudio/device/mitdefault.asp. The main MIT setup is a cool 4MB download. Just follow the simple installation wizard to get started.

Next, launch Visual Studio .NET and create a new ASP.NET Mobile Web Application project (or quite simply a Mobile Web application, if you aren't using Everett). You'll be shown MobileWebForm1.aspx. On the page, you have a small Form1 object. This represents a "page" on your device. Because most mobile pages will be relatively small, Microsoft decided to allow you to create a bundle on just one page (along with, naturally, a code method of switching between them). The first form on the page is the first to be displayed when the page is accessed.

You can either simply start typing in this Form control, or add controls, by dragging and dropping from the Mobile Web Forms tab in the toolbox. You'll be able to instantly figure out most of these from their icons: the Label, the TextBox (with its useful Numeric property for number-only input), the multiline TextView, the Command button, the Link, the SelectionList, the Image control, the excellently rendered Calendar control, and the validation controls. (See Figure 6-7.) You can add code to respond to most of these items just as you would a regular ASP.NET Web application.

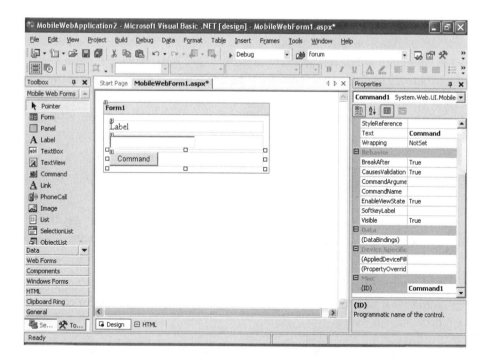

Figure 6-7. Designing our Mobile Web application

Other controls aren't quite so obvious however. The DeviceSpecific component allows you to target content at devices bearing particular properties, for example. One real favorite, however, is the PhoneCall control. Set its Text and PhoneNumber properties, and, on supporting phones, it'll turn into a link that allows your user to directly call that number. By default, if a device doesn't support dialing (Internet Explorer, for example), it'll display the Text and PhoneNumber properties alongside each other instead ("{0} {1}", the AlternateFormat default). Another way of handling this could be to put your own text in the AlternateFormat property and specify a link for the AlternateUrl.

So, you've added a few neat controls to your first form. Next, you begin coding in practically the same way as you would an ASP.NET Web application. Respond to Click events, change properties, and add code to respond to the form Activate event (the Web page Load equivalent).

Writing Mobile-Aware Code

Most of your code will be relatively standard and nothing special. But there are points where it's useful to write code that specifically finds out more about the device using your application. Enter stage left, the aptly named Device object. To demonstrate its use, I might run code similar to the following behind my form Activate event:

```
Dim blnMail As Boolean
blnMail = Device.CanSendMail
```

Here, I'm checking whether the device can respond to the "mailto:" tag. If it can, I might set a certain Link control to an email "mailto:" link. Otherwise, I might change it to point to a Web site. Here are the top dozen Device properties:

- Browser: Whether it's IE, Pocket IE, Microsoft Mobile Explorer, MyPalm, or some other beast, the Browser property gives you the name of your client browser.

- CanInitiateVoiceCall: Returns a True if the device can call someone.

- CanSendMail: Returns a True if the device supports the "mailto:" method of sending email, such as a Link control that has the NavigateUrl property set to mailto:karl@karlmoore.com.

- Cookies: Returns a True if the device supports cookies.

- HasBackButton: Can your user move back? This property returns a True if they can. This is great for deciding on whether to hide or implement your own Back button mechanism.

- IsColor: Returns a True if the device uses a color monitor.

- IsMobileDevice: Now, is that really a mobile, or are they just faking it with Internet Explorer? This property returns a True if they're using a recognized mobile device.

- PreferredImageMime: Returns the MIME type of the image content preferred by the device. You may wish to check this before setting the ImageUrl property of an Image control. If a GIF file is preferred, it'll return "image/gif", and, for a WBMP, it'll return "image/vnd.wap.wbmp" —otherwise, you're probably safe displaying a regular bitmap.

- `ScreenCharactersHeight`: Returns the approximate number of lines you can get onto a screen.

- `ScreenCharactersWidth`: Returns the approximate width of the display in characters.

- `ScreenPixelsHeight`/`ScreenPixelsWidth`: Returns the approximate height and width of the display in pixels.

- `SupportsBodyColor`: Returns a `True` if the device can display the backcolor of a form.

- `SupportsBold`/`SupportsItalic`/`SupportsFontName`/`SupportsFontColor`/ `SupportsFontSize`: Allows you to check whether certain text properties are available on the device.

- Plus all the regulars: When using the `Device` object, you get all the usual things you find when working with the `Request.Browser` property, such as the ability to retrieve the browser version, check the platform, and so on.

> **TOP TIP** *Instead of writing code to check the capabilities of a device and then changing its properties accordingly, you can configure your controls to "override" certain properties automatically depending on a "filter." This helps cut down on plumbing code. You can learn more about this by looking up "mobile controls, overriding properties" in the help index—or check out the "Going Mobile" chapters in another of my books:* Karl Moore's Visual Basic .NET: The Tutorials. *This title also demonstrates fresh techniques for handling images, without having to handle the aforementioned* `PreferredImageMime` *property.*

While writing your code, you might also want to watch out for a couple of state management differences between regular ASP.NET Web applications and your mobile sites. Firstly, most mobile devices do not support cookies. If you absolutely need to store something on the user's machine, insert it into the query string and get the user to bookmark the page. Secondly, any `ViewState` information is stored on the server (a history of `ViewState` is also maintained). As an alternative, use the `Session` object to store information for a user: it's more flexible than `ViewState`, you can access it from any page, and only one copy is stored at a time.

So, you've designed your first form, used a handful of nifty controls, and added a little mobile-aware code—now you're ready to move on and create the second. Well, to add another form, simply drag and drop a new Form control onto your page, set its ID and Title properties (optional), and begin adding controls and coding as before.

You'll also want to know how to move between two forms. You can do this in two different ways. Firstly, you can use a Link control and select your second form from the dropdown list of options in the NavigateUrl property. However, the most common method is to do it in code, by setting the ActiveForm property of your mobile page to your form control, like this:

```
ActiveForm = Form2
```

If you want to add a whole new mobile page to your project, select Project ➤ Add New Item, then select a new mobile Web form and click on Open. You can now continue designing as normal. But watch out: you can't redirect from one mobile Web page to another using a regular ASP.NET Response.Redirect. Instead, you have to use the following function of your mobile page (don't look at me!):

```
RedirectToMobilePage("mypage.aspx")
```

Testing Your Mobile Web Application

What next? Well, you've learned all you need to put a mobile Web application together, so finish off your project and get testing! Hit F5 to test your program in Internet Explorer. Better still, download the Microsoft Mobile Explorer emulator, which is available from the MIT download address given earlier. Other recommended test browsers include the Nokia Mobile Internet Toolkit from www.forum.nokia.com (see Figure 6-8) and the OpenWave Mobile Browser at developer.openwave.com/download/.

And, when you're ready to roll your site out to the world, what do you do? Simply treat it just like a regular ASP.NET Web application. (See the "Where to Put Your Files with an ASP.NET Host" tip in Chapter 3 for more information.)

That's all you need to know to develop applications that can run anywhere, any time, and on any device! Amazing stuff, and definitely something you can incorporate into that next big project, right?

Figure 6-8. My sample application in the Nokia simulator

Portable Computing: Creating Apps for Your PDA!

As devices such as the Pocket PC become almost as powerful as the machines sitting on our desks, it makes sense that more and more developers will want to start creating applications directly targeted at such platforms.

In the old days, however, this was pretty difficult. You had eMbedded Visual Basic, which allowed you to create Windows CE applications, but programming inconsistencies and sticky development techniques didn't make for an easy ride.

But, with the release of Everett (Visual Studio .NET 2003), Microsoft has introduced a new solution. It's a two-part fix that allows you to create applications to run on resource-constrained devices such as the Pocket PC and Windows CE handhelds, in almost the same way that you'd create a regular Windows application.

The first part to the solution is the .NET Compact Framework. This is a mini version of the .NET Framework, weighing in at almost 2MB (compared with 20MB+ for the full Windows version). The .NET Compact Framework runs on your device and includes a large selection of the core Framework classes, including a wide range of controls, plus even stretches to supporting Web services.

The second part to the solution is the ability to create a smart device application. This is like a tiny Windows application, with a typical Pocket PC form defaulting to 240×320 pixels. The program is built on top of the .NET Compact Framework (which can run on your development machine) and can be packaged into a CAB file and installed directly on your target device.

> **TOP TIP** *Are you using Visual Studio .NET 2002? Although the .NET Compact Framework betas allowed VS .NET 2002 users to create smart device applications, the final release ships only with Everett (Visual Studio .NET 2003), which means that you either upgrade or ship out.*

Building for the Compact Framework

How do you get started with developing for the .NET Compact Framework (CF)? Simply fire up Visual Studio .NET and create a new smart device application. You'll be presented with a wizard, asking what sort of application you'd like to create.

You'll need to choose the platform you wish to target and the type of application you'd like to create. As the industry moves more toward Pocket PC devices, the norm here would be to select a Windows application running on the Pocket PC.

> **TOP TIP** *Looking for a niche software market? Hundreds of developers create component libraries for the COM and .NET development worlds. But how many create class libraries for Pocket PC developers? Perhaps libraries that overcome the limitations imposed by the "trimming" of the .NET Compact Framework?*

After selecting your project type, you should be presented with your first form. From here, you can begin development just as with a regular Windows application, with a few obvious size restrictions. (See Figure 6-9.)

The big thing to remember here is that the framework supporting this type of project is not the .NET Framework. It's the .NET *Compact* Framework. This means that, although you can still develop your program as you would a regular Windows application, not everything will operate exactly as you expect.

For instance, controls will look different and may vary slightly in the way they operate, and certain classes may be unavailable or work in an altered fashion. But it's generally similar: you can add extra forms and open them using standard techniques; you can create smart device class libraries and reference them as you'd expect; and you can add Web references and interact with Web services as usual.

On the whole, it's a relatively easy shift.

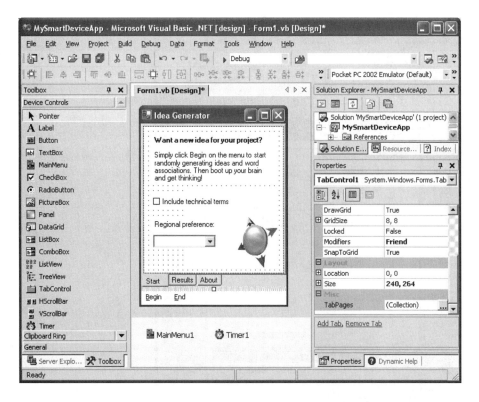

Figure 6-9. Visually designing my Pocket PC application in Visual Studio .NET

So, you've developed a neat Pocket PC project and want to give it a test run. But how? Simply follow the usual VS .NET debugging techniques: select Debug ➤ Start to begin. You should be asked which device you wish to deploy your application on.

For example, creating a Windows application for the Pocket PC will allow you the option of using the Pocket PC 2002 emulator (see Figure 6-10) or a live debug session with a connected Pocket PC. Choose your target and select Deploy.

If the .NET CF hasn't yet been installed on your device, VS .NET will install it for you and then run your application. This is where you step in: test your application, step through your code, and identify bugs. Just the same as with regular Windows applications.

> **TOP TIP** *The first time you run the Pocket PC 2002 emulator, you'll probably be asked to set up the device, "tapping" through the welcome screens. The emulator is actually a fully working version of the Pocket PC operating system and therefore reacts in the exact same manner. It's one of the best emulators I've seen.*

Figure 6-10. A sample application running in the Pocket PC 2002 Emulator

Deploying Your Applications

You've created that application and done the whole testing thing. Now you're ready to roll it out to .NET CF devices around the globe. What's to do?

First, as with regular Windows applications built for the full .NET Framework, a copy of the framework needs to be installed on the machine. This can be installed in RAM by downloading the setup from http://msdn.microsoft.com/ vstudio/device/golive.asp. This is absolutely required: attempting to run a smart device application without the .NET CF installed will raise an error.

> **TOP TIP** *Today, most devices will allow the .NET Compact Framework to be installed only into RAM. However, most future Pocket PCs and smart phone devices will come with the .NET Compact Framework already installed in the ROM.*

Second, you need to create your application setup. This is fully automated: simply select Build ➤ Build Cab File from within your smart device application project.

> **TOP TIP** *If you wish to distribute a bundle of files with your application (game images, for example), add them by right-clicking on your project and selecting Add ➤ Existing Item. You can also put files within subfolders. When installed on the device, the folders and files are extracted in the application root directory, ready for your application to utilize.*

Inside your project \Cab\<Configuration>\ folder, you'll find a variety of CAB files (alongside a mass of unimportant DAT files, which you may disregard). Each of these CAB files contains a version of your project specific to a particular processor for the platform you selected. For example, a Pocket PC application will generate versions for the ARM, X86, MIPS, and other processors.

However, as all Pocket PC devices are now standardizing on the ARM v4 processor, the most important CAB file in the list is MyProject_PPC.ARMV4.CAB. This is your project setup, created for the Pocket PC (PPC) ARM v4 processor.

When you're ready to deploy, you can deploy the relevant CAB to your device using ActiveSync (a PC-device synchronization feature that many PDA users will be aware of) or by setting up a file share on your machine, copying the CAB file onto your device, then single-clicking to automatically install.

You'd be forgiven for thinking the deployment portion of such smart device applications is currently a little immature. It was, apparently, something of an afterthought. You can expect improvements in the next revision (see msdn.microsoft.com/vstudio/device for the latest). Don't be surprised to find a bundle of third-party InstallShield-style solutions to hit the market shortly, too.

TOP TIP *Want to test CAB deployment on the Pocket PC 2002 emulator? You can simply set up a file share, then copy the CAB file across the emulator ROM, and run! Here's how: first, create a folder containing the CAB file, then set it up as a shared directory (typically, right-click, select Sharing and Security, select "Share this folder", and then click on OK). Next, in your Visual Studio .NET device project, select Tools ➤ Connect to Device. The emulator should appear in the background. On the emulator, select Start ➤ Programs ➤ File Explorer, then click on the network share icon at the bottom-middle of the screen. You should be prompted for the name of your machine (\\MyComputerName), followed by your user name, password, and domain (if required). Open the shared folder, and then click and hold on your CAB file as a series of dots draw themselves on the screen: eventually, a popup menu will appear. Select Copy. Next, switch back to browsing files on your device by clicking on the PDA-style icon at the bottom of the screen. Now select Edit ➤ Paste, and your CAB will be copied to the local machine. (This is required because networked files will not open over the network.) When copying has finished, single-click on the CAB to begin installation. If you receive a naming conflict error when connecting to your file share, it's because you're running on the same machine that you're connecting to. So, click on Start ➤ Settings, select the System tab, click on About, select the Device ID tab, change the Device name, and try again.*

Going On from Here

Although this brief introduction should give you enough fuel to get going with your own PDA applications, there's much more to learn.

For example, did you know that you can run the powerful SQL Server CE on your handheld? And you can write applications to create databases and access your data, perhaps even synchronizing live with a master SQL Server database? It's all true. (Check out the setup and help files in \Microsoft Visual Studio .NET 2003\CompactFrameworkSDK\v1.0.5000\Windows CE for more information.)

You can learn more about creating your own smart device applications by browsing the hidden samples distributed with Visual Studio .NET; they're in the \Microsoft Visual Studio .NET 2003\CompactFrameworkSDK\v1.0.5000\ Windows CE\Samples\VB\ folder or online at www.gotdotnet.com/team/netcf/ Samples.aspx. (Make sure you check out the MapPoint and Cave Man Hank samples!)

And, of course, Apress has their own plethora of books dedicated to the technology: try The Definitive Guide to the .NET Compact Framework by Dan Fergus and Larry Roof ($59.99, ISBN 1-59059-095-3) and SQL Server CE Database Development with the .NET Compact Framework by Rob Tiffany ($44.99, ISBN 1-59059-119-4).

But, for now, go and create. The shift is simple, and the results are pretty amazing.

CHAPTER 7

More .NET Secrets

I HAD TO OVERCOME two big obstacles in writing this book. The first was the three years I invested in discovering these secrets, then writing and debugging to ensure they worked on every platform and in every possible situation. The second was organizing them.

The .NET world is a huge one, and not everything can be easily categorized. We've already covered some of the biggies: Windows applications, Web sites, databases, and special project types. This chapter covers most of the other stuff.

Split into seven subsections, the following pages examine working with the Internet; manipulating files and folders; dates, numbers, and strings; graphics and fonts; using the registry and event log; distributed computing; and useful Visual Studio .NET tips.

It was, probably, one of most exciting chapters to write. It provides ready-to-run golden code snippets that show you how to give your application extra intelligence through the use of clever code. It shows you how to do things most .NET developers will never even be aware that the language is capable of.

I'll show you how to convert HTML to pure text, and in just a couple of lines of code. You'll be given a function to add a Web shortcut to the Favorites menu. I'll demonstrate how to transform bytes into an English file size, like 1.44Mb. You'll uncover the secrets of generating memorable user passwords, plus discover how to put together your own .NET screensaver and learn the tricks of encrypting data with just twelve simple lines of Visual Basic code. The advanced stuff is covered here too: XML, transactions with COM+, MSMQ, and more.

It's diverse, but it's fun. These are the code snippets you'll learn once and never forget.

Developer Secrets

Wanting to dive into all those beefy miscellaneous tips and techniques? Here's a rundown of what we're going to cover in this jam-packed chapter....

Working with the Internet

- Creating Your Own Web Browser

- How to Snatch the HTML of a Web Page

- How to Snatch HTML, with a Timeout

- Tricks of Parsing a Web Page for Links and Images

- Converting HTML to Text, Easily

- Real Code for Posting Data to the Web

- Adding a Web Shortcut to the Favorites

- Retrieving Your IP Address—And Why You May Want To

- Is an Internet Connection Available?

Manipulating Files and Folders

- Two Easy-to-Use Functions for Reading and Writing Files

- Files: Moving, Deleting, Attributes, and More!

- Checking Whether Two Files Are Identical

- The Trick to Temporary Files

- Doing Directories

- "Watching" a Directory for Changes

- How Big Is That File—in English?

- Retrieving Special Folder Paths

- Which Program Handles That File Extension?

- Retrieving a Drive Serial Number

- The .NET Replacement for App.Path

- INI Files Will Never Die: How to in .NET

Dates, Numbers, Strings

- Is That a Whole Number, or Not?

- Checking for a Date the Intelligent .NET Way

- 1st, 2nd, 3rd: Using Ordinal Numbers in Your App

- Random Numbers… That Work!

- Finding the Number of Days in a Month

- Adding and Subtracting Days, Months, Years

- Calculating the Next Working Day

- Easy Check for a Leap Year

- Figuring out Quarters

- Calculating the Years Between Two Dates

- Converting a String to "Proper Case"

- Storing Text Snippets on the Clipboard

- Generating Memorable Passwords, Automatically

- Encryption in Just Twelve Lines of Code

- Implementing Powerful MD5 Encryption

- Converting a String into the Color Type

- Binding a Combo Box to Enumeration Values

Graphics and Fonts

- Designing Your Own Arty Icons

- The Basics of Working with Fonts

- Crafty Conversion Between Graphic Formats

- Rotating and Flipping Is Easy!

- Drawing with Windows Forms

- Add an Exciting Gradient Backdrop, in Code!

- Starting Your Own Screensaver

Using the Registry and Event Log

- How to Read and Write the Registry

- Putting Messages in the Event Log

Distributed Computing

- The Cheat's Guide to XML

- Six Steps to Basic Transactions with COM+

- Quick Guide to Using MSMQ

- Which to Choose: Web Services vs. Remoting

Visual Studio Tips

- Writing a Developer TODO: List

- Storing Often-Used Code in the Toolbox

- Organizing Your Project with Folders

- Figuring out the Command Window

- Discovering Whether You're Running in the IDE

- Saving Time by Recording Macros

- Using the VS .NET Command Prompt

- The Old School: Upgrading, COM, and the API

Working with the Internet

From parsing a Web page for links to adding your shortcut to the Favorites, this section contains a whole bundle of techniques for utilizing the Internet with your favorite programming language.

Creating Your Own Web Browser

The WebBrowser control we became oh-so-familiar with in Visual Basic 6 has no .NET equivalent. To use it, we need to step back into the world of COM.

To add a WebBrowser control to a Windows form, right-click on the toolbox and select Customize Toolbox. Browse the list of available COM components and check the Microsoft Web Browser option, then click on OK. This will automatically create a "wrapper" for you, allowing you to use the COM component in .NET.

At the bottom of your toolbox control list, you'll now see an Explorer item. Draw an instance of this onto your form, and that's your browser window!

So, what can you do with it? Everything you could before. Let's review the most popular methods, most of which are self-explanatory:

```
AxWebBrowser1.Navigate ("http://www.vbworld.com/")
AxWebBrowser1.GoBack
AxWebBrowser1.GoForward
AxWebBrowser1.Stop
AxWebBrowser1.Refresh
AxWebBrowser1.GoHome      ' Visits the homepage
AxWebBrowser1.GoSearch    ' Visits the default search page
```

> **TOP TIP** *It may be a neat control, but the WebBrowser is prone to generating whopping great big error messages for any silly little matter. As such, don't feel bad for using those old "On Error Resume Next" statements liberally.*

We also have a number of particularly interesting properties:

```
strPageTitle = AxWebBrowser1.LocationName
strURL = AxWebBrowser1.LocationURL
AxWebBrowser1.Document...    ' Accessing page HTMLDocument object
```

You'll also find that the browser supports a bundle of cool events, including DocumentComplete (which fires when any Web page has finished loading), BeforeNavigate2 (which fires before a page is visited—set the Cancel property to True to cancel the request), and ProgressChange (which fires whenever the progress bar in Internet Explorer would change).

That's all you need to get your favorite Web control into .NET. (See Figure 7-1 for my sample application.) Good luck!

> **TOP TIP** *If you want to manipulate data inside a Web page, automatically filling out forms and extracting data, you'll need to do some heavy-duty work with the* WebBrowser.Document *object. Alternatively, check out the new WebZinc .NET component at* www.webzinc.net *for an easier solution.*

Figure 7-1. My Web browser application visiting some totally random Web site

How to Snatch the HTML of a Web Page

 Download supporting files at www.apress.com.
The files for this tip are in the "Ch7–Snatch HTML" folder.

Need to visit a competitor Web page and parse out the latest rival product prices? Looking to retrieve data from a company that hasn't yet figured out Web services? Whatever your motives, if you're looking to grab the HTML of a Web page, the following little function should be able to help.

Just call the following GetPageHTML function, passing in the URL of the page you want to retrieve. It'll return a string containing the HTML:

```
Public Function GetPageHTML(ByVal URL As String) As String
    ' Retrieves the HTML from the specified URL
    Dim objWC As New System.Net.WebClient()
    Return New System.Text.UTF8Encoding().GetString( _
        objWC.DownloadData(URL))
End Function
```

Here's an example of its usage:

```
strHTML = GetPageHTML("http://www.karlmoore.com/")
```

An extremely short function, but incredibly useful.

How to Snatch HTML, with a Timeout

 Download supporting files at www.apress.com.
The files for this tip are in the "Ch7–Snatch HTML with Timeout" folder.

The function I demonstrated in the last tip ("How to Snatch the HTML of a Web Page") is great for many applications. You pass it a URL, and it'll work on grabbing the page HTML. The problem is that it will keep trying until it eventually either times out or retrieves the page.

Sometimes, you don't have that luxury. Say you're running a Web site that needs to retrieve the HTML, parse it, and display results to a user. You can't wait two minutes for the server to respond, then download the page and feed it back to your visitor. You need a response within ten seconds—or not at all.

Unfortunately, despite numerous developer claims to the contrary, this cannot be done through the WebClient class. Rather, you need to use some of the more in-depth System.Net classes to handle the situation. Here's my offering, wrapped into a handy little function:

```
Public Function GetPageHTML(ByVal URL As String, _
        Optional ByVal TimeoutSeconds As Integer = 10) _
        As String
    ' Retrieves the HTML from the specified URL,
    ' using a default timeout of 10 seconds
    Dim objRequest As Net.WebRequest
    Dim objResponse As Net.WebResponse
    Dim objStreamReceive As System.IO.Stream
    Dim objEncoding As System.Text.Encoding
    Dim objStreamRead As System.IO.StreamReader

    Try
        ' Setup our Web request
        objRequest = Net.WebRequest.Create(URL)
        objRequest.Timeout = TimeoutSeconds * 1000
        ' Retrieve data from request
        objResponse = objRequest.GetResponse
        objStreamReceive = objResponse.GetResponseStream
        objEncoding = System.Text.Encoding.GetEncoding( _
            "utf-8")
        objStreamRead = New System.IO.StreamReader( _
            objStreamReceive, objEncoding)
        ' Set function return value
        GetPageHTML = objStreamRead.ReadToEnd()
        ' Check if available, then close response
        If Not objResponse Is Nothing Then
            objResponse.Close()
        End If
    Catch
        ' Error occured grabbing data, simply return nothing
        Return ""
    End Try
End Function
```

Here, our code creates objects to request the data from the Web, setting the absolute server timeout. If the machine responds within the given timeframe, the response is fed into a stream, converted into the UTF8 text format we all understand, and then passed back as the result of the function. You can use it a little like this:

```
strHTML = GetPageHTML("http://www.karlmoore.com/", 5)
```

Admittedly, this all seems like a lot of work just to add a timeout. But it does its job—and well. Enjoy!

> **TOP TIP** *Remember, the timeout we've added is for our request to be acknowledged by the server, rather than for the full HTML to have been received.*

Tricks of Parsing a Web Page for Links and Images

 Download supporting files at www.apress.com.
The files for this tip are in the "Ch7–Parse Links and Images" folder.

So, you've retrieved the HTML of that Web page and now need to parse out all the links to use in your research database. Or maybe you've visited the page and want to make a note of all the image links, so you can download at some later point.

Well, you have two options. You can write your own parsing algorithm, consisting of ten million InStr and Mid statements. They're often slow and frequently buggy, but they're a truly great challenge (always my favorite routines to write).

Alternatively, you can write a regular expression in VB .NET. This is where you provide an "expression" that describes how a link looks and what portion you want to retrieve (that is, the bit after *<a href="* but before the next *"* for a hyperlink). Then you run the expression and retrieve matches. The problem with these is that they're difficult to formulate. (See Chapter 8, "The Hidden .NET Language" for more information.)

So, why not cheat? Following you'll find two neat little functions I've already put together using regular expressions. Just pass in the HTML from your Web page, and it'll return an ArrayList object containing the link/image matches:

```
Public Function ParseLinks(ByVal HTML As String) As ArrayList
    ' Remember to add the following at top of class:
    ' - Imports System.Text.RegularExpressions
    Dim objRegEx As System.Text.RegularExpressions.Regex
```

```
                Dim objMatch As System.Text.RegularExpressions.Match
                Dim arrLinks As New System.Collections.ArrayList()
                ' Create regular expression
                objRegEx = New System.Text.RegularExpressions.Regex( _
                    "a.*href\s*=\s*(?:""(?<1>[^""]*)""|(?<1>\S+))", _
                    System.Text.RegularExpressions.RegexOptions.IgnoreCase Or _
                    System.Text.RegularExpressions.RegexOptions.Compiled)
                ' Match expression to HTML
                objMatch = objRegEx.Match(HTML)
                ' Loop through matches and add <1> to ArrayList
                While objMatch.Success
                    Dim strMatch As String
                    strMatch = objMatch.Groups(1).ToString
                    arrLinks.Add(strMatch)
                    objMatch = objMatch.NextMatch()
                End While
                ' Pass back results
                Return arrLinks
            End Function


        Public Function ParseImages(ByVal HTML As String) As ArrayList
                ' Remember to add the following at top of class:
                ' - Imports System.Text.RegularExpressions
                Dim objRegEx As System.Text.RegularExpressions.Regex
                Dim objMatch As System.Text.RegularExpressions.Match
                Dim arrLinks As New System.Collections.ArrayList()
                ' Create regular expression
                objRegEx = New System.Text.RegularExpressions.Regex( _
                    "img.*src\s*=\s*(?:""(?<1>[^""]*)""|(?<1>\S+))", _
                    System.Text.RegularExpressions.RegexOptions.IgnoreCase Or _
                    System.Text.RegularExpressions.RegexOptions.Compiled)
                ' Match expression to HTML
                objMatch = objRegEx.Match(HTML)
                ' Loop through matches and add <1> to ArrayList
                While objMatch.Success
                    Dim strMatch As String
                    strMatch = objMatch.Groups(1).ToString
                    arrLinks.Add(strMatch)
                    objMatch = objMatch.NextMatch()
                End While
                ' Pass back results
                Return arrLinks
            End Function
```

Here's a simplified example using the `ParseLinks` routine. The `ParseImages` routine works in exactly the same way:

```
Dim arrLinks As ArrayList = ParseLinks( _
    "<a href=""http://www.marksandler.com/"">" & _
    "Visit MarkSandler.com</a>")
' Loop through results
Dim shtCount As Integer
For shtCount = 0 To arrLinks.Count - 1
    MessageBox.Show(arrLinks(shtCount).ToString)
Next
```

One word of warning: many Web sites use relative links. In other words, an image may refer to /images/mypic.gif rather than `http://www.mysite.com/images/mypic.gif`. You may wish to check for this in code (perhaps look for the existence of "http")—if the prefix isn't there, add it programmatically.

And that's all you need to know to successfully strip links and images out of any HTML. Best wishes!

Converting HTML to Text, Easily

 Download supporting files at www.apress.com.
The files for this tip are in the "Ch7–HTML to Text" folder.

Whether you want to convert an HTML page into pure text so you can parse out that special piece of information, or you simply want to load a page from the Net into your own word processing package, this mini function could come in handy.

It's called `StripTags` and accepts an HTML string. Using a regular expression, it identifies all <tags>, removes them, and returns the modified string. Here's the code:

```
Public Function StripTags(ByVal HTML As String) As String
    ' Removes tags from passed HTML
    Dim objRegEx As _
        System.Text.RegularExpressions.Regex
    Return objRegEx.Replace(HTML, "<[^>]*>", "")
End Function
```

Here's a simple example demonstrating how you could use this function in code (see Figure 7-2 for my sample application):

```
strData = StripTags("<body><b>Welcome!</b></body>")
```

I admit, it doesn't look like much, but this little snippet can be a true lifesaver, especially if you've ever tried doing it yourself using `Instr` and `Mid` statements. Have fun!

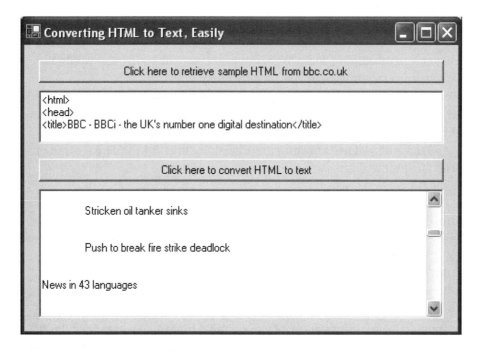

Figure 7-2. My sample application, retrieving HTML from www.bbc.co.uk, *then converting it to text*

Real Code for Posting Data to the Web

One of my early tasks when working with .NET was figuring out how to take a stream of data (in my case, an XML document) and post it to a CGI script, in code.

It wasn't easy. I ended up with two pages of code incorporating practically every Internet-related class in the .NET Framework. Months later now, and I've managed to refine this posting technique to just a few generic lines of code. And that's what I'd like to share with you in this tip.

The following chunk of code starts by creating a WebClient object and setting a number of headers (which you can change as appropriate). It then converts my string (MyData) into an array of bytes, and then uploads direct to the specified URL. The server response to this upload is then converted into a string, which you'll probably want to analyze for possible success or error messages.

```
' Setup WebClient object
Dim objWebClient As New System.Net.WebClient()
' Convert data to send into an array of bytes
Dim bytData As Byte() = System.Text.Encoding.ASCII.GetBytes(MyData)

' Add appropriate headers
With objWebClient.Headers
    .Add("Content-Type", "text/xml")
    .Add("Authorization", "Basic " & _
        Convert.ToBase64String( _
        System.Text.Encoding.ASCII.GetBytes( _
        "MyUsername:MyPassword")))
End With

' Upload data to page (CGI script, or whatever) and receive response
Dim objResponse As Byte() = objWebClient.UploadData( _
    "http://www.examplesite.com/clients/upload.cgi", _
    "POST", bytData)

' Convert response to a string
Dim strResponse As String = _
    System.Text.Encoding.ASCII.GetString(objResponse)

' Check response for data, errors, etc...
```

I initially used this code to submit details of new store locations automatically to mapping solution provider Multimap.com. It accessed the destination CGI script, providing all necessary credentials, streamed my own XML document across the wire, and then checked the XML response for any errors.

A few pointers here. Firstly, you can easily remove the "Authorization" header. This was included to demonstrate how you can upload to a protected source—which, although a common request, is not everyone's cup of tea. Secondly, the content type here is set to "text/xml". You can change this to whatever content type you deem fit—"text/html" for example, or perhaps "application/x-www-form-urlencoded" if you want to make the post look as though it were coming from a Web form. Finally, you don't always have to upload pure data like this;

you can also upload files with the `.UploadFile` function, or simulate a true form post, by submitting key pairs (such as text box names and related values) with the `.UploadValues` function.

Adding a Web Shortcut to the Favorites

 Download supporting files at www.apress.com.
The files for this tip are in the "Ch7–Adding Favorites" folder.

This is one of those cute little code snippets that you have a use for in practically every application. Applications that can do this look cool and intelligent—and it takes just a few simple lines of code. I'm talking about adding an Internet shortcut to the user's Favorites menu.

How do you do it? Well, the following function encompasses all the logic for you. It accepts a page title and a URL. Then it locates the current Favorites folder (which could vary greatly depending on the machine setup) and creates a URL file in that folder, based on the title you passed. Inside that file, it includes a little required text for an Internet shortcut, alongside your URL. And that's it—shortcut created!

Here's the code:

```
Public Sub CreateShortcut(ByVal Title As String, ByVal URL As String)
    ' Creates a shortcut in the users Favorites folder
    Dim strFavoriteFolder As String
    ' Retrieve the favorite folder
    strFavoriteFolder = System.Environment.GetFolderPath( _
        Environment.SpecialFolder.Favorites)
    ' Create shortcut file, based on Title
    Dim objWriter As System.IO.StreamWriter = _
        System.IO.File.CreateText(strFavoriteFolder & _
        "\" & Title & ".url")
    ' Write URL to file
    objWriter.WriteLine("[InternetShortcut]")
    objWriter.WriteLine("URL=" & URL)
    ' Close file
    objWriter.Close()
End Sub
```

To finish off this snippet, here are a couple of interesting calls to this procedure (see Figure 7-3 to see the created shortcuts in Internet Explorer):

```
CreateShortcut("Karl Moore.com", "http://www.karlmoore.com/")
CreateShortcut("Send mail to Karl Moore", "mailto:karl@karlmoore.com")
```

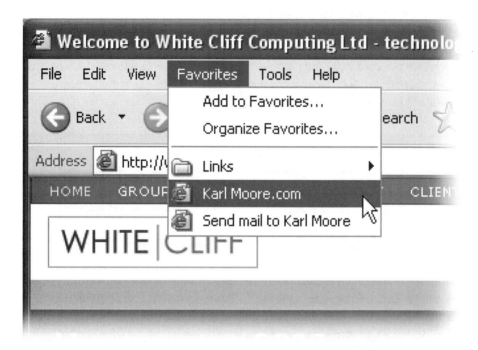

Figure 7-3. A couple of plug-plug Internet shortcuts added by my sample code

Retrieving Your IP Address—And Why You May Want To

Download supporting files at www.apress.com.
The files for this tip are in the "Ch7–IP" folder.

You may want to discover the IP address of your local machine for a number of reasons. You may, for example, be developing a messaging-style application using the .NET equivalent of the Winsock control—the Socket class (look up "Socket class" in the help index) and need to register the local IP in a central database somewhere.

So, how can you find out your IP address? The code is easy:

```
Dim objEntry As System.Net.IPHostEntry = _
    System.Net.Dns.GetHostByName( _
    System.Net.Dns.GetHostName)
Dim strIP As String = CType( _
    objEntry.AddressList.GetValue(0), _
    System.Net.IPAddress).ToString
```

Here, we pass our machine name to the GetHostByName function, which returns a valid IPHostEntry object. We then retrieve the first IP address from the entry AddressList array and convert it to a string. Simple!

Is an Internet Connection Available?

Download supporting files at www.apress.com.
The files for this tip are in the "Ch7–IsConnectionAvailable" folder.

Checking whether an Internet connection is available isn't always as easy as it sounds.

Admittedly, there is a Windows API call that can check whether a connection exists, but it's extremely fragile and returns incorrect results if the machine has never had Internet Explorer configured correctly. Oops.

The best method is to actually make a Web request and see whether it works. If it does, you've got your connection. The following neat code snippet does exactly that. Just call IsConnectionAvailable and check the return value:

```
Public Function IsConnectionAvailable() As Boolean
    ' Returns True if connection is available

    ' Replace www.yoursite.com with a site that
    ' is guaranteed to be online - perhaps your
    ' corporate site, or microsoft.com
    Dim objUrl As New System.Uri("http://www.yoursite.com/")
    ' Setup WebRequest
    Dim objWebReq As System.Net.WebRequest
    objWebReq = System.Net.WebRequest.Create(objUrl)
    Dim objResp As System.Net.WebResponse
    Try

        ' Attempt to get response and return True
```

```
        objResp = objWebReq.GetResponse
        objResp.Close()
        objWebReq = Nothing
        Return True
    Catch ex As Exception
        ' Error, exit and return False
        objResp.Close()
        objWebReq = Nothing
        Return False
    End Try
```

Here's how you might use this function in your application:

```
If IsConnectionAvailable() = True Then
    MessageBox.Show("You are online!")
End If
```

Manipulating Files and Folders

Wanting to "watch" a directory for file changes? Or find out the .NET replacement for App.Path? Or uncover how big that file is... in English? If you're looking for the best file and folder techniques for your VB .NET applications, simply read on.

Two Easy-to-Use Functions for Reading and Writing Files

 Download supporting files at www.apress.com.
The files for this tip are in the "Ch7–Read and Write Files" folder.

Reading and writing to simple text files is perhaps one of the most common tasks in the programming world. The old VB6 way of doing this is now defunct, and a new .NET method is here, involving objects within the System.IO namespace.

The following functions help simplify the process of reading and writing to files. The first is called ReadTextFromFile and accepts a filename as a parameter. It returns the text from the specified file:

```
Public Function ReadTextFromFile(ByVal Filename As String) As String
    ' Returns text from the specified file
    On Error Resume Next
    Dim strFileText As String
```

```
' Open the file and launch StreamReader object
Dim MyReader As System.IO.StreamReader = _
    System.IO.File.OpenText(Filename)
' Read all text through to the end
strFileText = MyReader.ReadToEnd
' Close the stream
MyReader.Close()
' Return data
Return strFileText
End Function
```

The second code snippet is a method called WriteTextToFile, and it accepts a filename and the text to write as parameters:

```
Public Sub WriteTextToFile(ByVal Filename As String, ByVal Text As String)
    ' Writes the passed Text into the specified file
    ' Create file and StreamWriter object
    Dim MyWriter As System.IO.StreamWriter = _
        System.IO.File.CreateText(Filename)
    ' Write text to the stream
    MyWriter.Write(Text)
    ' Close the stream
    MyWriter.Close()
End Sub
```

Here is an example of each of these code snippets in action:

```
WriteTextToFile("c:\myfile.txt", TextBox1.Text)
MessageBox.Show(ReadTextFromFile("c:\myfile.txt"))
```

Files: Moving, Deleting, Attributes, and More!

If you're looking to manipulate files using the .NET Framework base classes, you should be heading to the System.IO.File class, where you'll find functions to delete files, copy files, check file attributes, and much more.

Here is a commented example demonstrating the most common uses of the File class:

```
Dim objFile As System.IO.File
' Check for existence of a file
Dim blnExists As Boolean
blnExists = objFile.Exists("c:\unlikely.txt")
' Delete a file
objFile.Delete("c:\goodbye.txt")
' Copy a file
objFile.Copy("c:\source.txt", "e:\destination.txt")
' Move a file
objFile.Move("c:\oldlocation.txt", "e:\newlocation.txt")
' Check whether a file is read-only
Dim blnReadOnly As Boolean
blnReadOnly = CType(objFile.GetAttributes("c:\readonly.txt").ReadOnly, Boolean)
' Check whether a file is hidden
Dim blnHidden As Boolean
blnHidden = CType(objFile.GetAttributes("c:\hidden.txt").Hidden, Boolean)
' Check a file creation date
Dim datCreated As DateTime
datCreated = objFile.GetCreationTime("c:\created.txt")
```

It's worth noting that you don't have to create a new File object to use this functionality. The File class consists of what are known as *shared methods*, meaning that you can call them directly without having to instantiate a new object. This means you can delete a file with one direct line of code, like this:

```
System.IO.File.Delete("c:\goodbye.txt")
```

Checking Whether Two Files Are Identical

Download supporting files at www.apress.com.
The files for this tip are in the "Ch7—Check Files Are Identical" folder.

Checking whether the contents of two files are identical is a surprisingly common request in the programming world, but, beyond simply comparing file sizes, many developers are unsure about how to actually check this.

There's no need to worry. This excellent CompareFiles function does it all for you, initially comparing by size and then byte by byte. If the two file paths you pass in as arguments match, the function passes back a True; otherwise, it returns False.

Here's the code:

```
Public Function CompareFiles(ByVal File1 As String, _
    ByVal File2 As String) As Boolean
    ' Compares contents of two files, byte by byte
    ' and returns true if no differences
    Dim blnIdentical As Boolean = True
    Dim objFS1 As System.IO.FileStream = _
        New System.IO.FileStream(File1, System.IO.FileMode.Open)
    Dim objFS2 As System.IO.FileStream = _
        New System.IO.FileStream(File2, System.IO.FileMode.Open)
    ' Begin by checking length
    If (objFS1.Length <> objFS2.Length) Then
        blnIdentical = False
    Else
        ' Start looping through, comparing bytes
        Dim intByteF1 As Integer
        Dim intByteF2 As Integer
        Do
            intByteF1 = objFS1.ReadByte()
            intByteF2 = objFS2.ReadByte()
            If intByteF1 <> intByteF2 Then
                blnIdentical = False
                Exit Do
            End If
        Loop While (intByteF1 <> -1)
    End If
    ' Close files and set return value
    objFS1.Close()
    objFS2.Close()
    Return blnIdentical
End Function
```

Here's how you might call this function in your code:

```
If CompareFiles("c:\1.txt", "c:\2.doc") Then
    MessageBox.Show("Files are identical!")
Else
    MessageBox.Show("Files do not match!")
End If
```

The Trick to Temporary Files

 Download supporting files at www.apress.com.
The files for this tip are in the "Ch7–Writing to Temp File" folder.

Temporary files are incredibly useful. Most applications use them to store information while running some sort of processing. And you can too. When you're finished, either delete the temporary file or leave it for the next Windows "Disk Cleanup" operation to thwart.

But how do you go about working with temporary files? Well, firstly you need to get a temporary filename, and the System.IO.Path has a shared function called GetTempFileName to help you here. Then you simply write to the file as normal.

This handy little function wraps all this functionality up for you into one neat function. Simply call WriteToTempFile and pass in your data. It'll return your temporary file path:

```
Public Function WriteToTempFile(ByVal Data As String) As String
    ' Writes text to a temporary file and returns path
    Dim strFilename As String = System.IO.Path.GetTempFileName()
    Dim objFS As New System.IO.FileStream(strFilename, _
        System.IO.FileMode.Append, _
        System.IO.FileAccess.Write)
    ' Opens stream and begins writing
    Dim Writer As New System.IO.StreamWriter(objFS)
    Writer.BaseStream.Seek(0, System.IO.SeekOrigin.End)
    Writer.WriteLine(Data)
    Writer.Flush()
    ' Closes and returns temp path
    Writer.Close()
    Return strFilename
End Function
```

Here's how you might call this function in your code:

```
Dim strFilename As String = WriteToTempFile("My data for the temp file")
MessageBox.Show(strFilename)
```

Doing Directories

When it came to working with directories in Visual Basic 6, we had `MkDir`, `RmDir`, and `CurDir`. If you wanted anything more complicated, you either had to write your own API routines and sacrifice a few hours of development time, or reference the external FileSystemObject DLL and sacrifice the size of your final project, and, potentially, application speed.

In VB .NET, however, it's plain sailing... introducing the `System.IO.Directory` class!

Cram packed with shared methods, this class provides you with everything you need to create, move, delete, and check for the existence of directories. It also allows you to retrieve a list of files from a directory, plus obtain a list of the logical drives on your system.

Here's a chunk of sample code showing you how:

```
Dim objDir As System.IO.Directory

' Creates a directory
objDir.CreateDirectory("c:\mydata")
' Delete a directory, recursively
objDir.Delete("c:\temp", True)
' Get current directory
Dim strCurDir As String = objDir.GetCurrentDirectory
' Check whether a directory exists
Dim blnExists As Boolean = objDir.Exists("c:\mydata")
' Get string array of all directories in a path
Dim strDirectories() As String = objDir.GetDirectories("c:\Program Files\")
' Get files in a directory
Dim strFiles1() As String = objDir.GetFiles("c:\winnt")
' Get all *.DOC files in a directory
Dim strFiles2() As String = objDir.GetFiles("c:\my documents", "*.doc")
' Move a directory
objDir.Move("c:\backup", "c:\original")
' Retrieve array of drives
Dim strDrives() As String = objDir.GetLogicalDrives
```

As with the `System.IO.File` class, it's worth noting that you don't have to create a new `Directory` object to use this functionality. The `Directory` class consists of *shared methods*, meaning that you can call them directly without having to instantiate a new object. This means that you can create a directory with one direct line of code, like this:

```
System.IO.Directory.CreateDirectory("c:\mydata")
```

"Watching" a Directory for Changes

Directory "watching" is one of those really cool techniques that took quite a large lump of skill to implement successfully in Visual Basic 6. With this latest version of VB, however, you can get such functionality by utilizing the brand new FileSystemWatcher class.

The new System.IO.FileSystemWatcher class can be set up either in code or, rather easier, by dragging and dropping the FileSystemWatcher component from the toolbox Component tab onto your application.

Next, you need to start setting properties. First, there's the Path property, which you need to set to the path of the directory that you wish to monitor, such as "c:\" or "e:\whitecliff\". Next, there's the Filter property, where you specify which files you want to monitor. You can use "*.*" to keep an eye on everything in the directory, something like "*.doc" to check Word documents, or simply use an exact filename, such as "datalog.txt".

There's also the NotifyFilter property, which lists exactly what you want your FileSystemWatcher object to inform you about. The default is "FileName, DirectoryName, LastWrite," which means that you're informed when a filename or directory name is changed, or a file is written (that is, the LastWrite date and time changes). You can specify your own in code by typing the options from the dropdown list, separated by commas, or in code using the bitwise "Or" operator. Finally, there's the IncludeSubdirectories property. Change this to True if you want to monitor all subdirectories—or False otherwise.

And after you've set up your FileSystemWatcher object? Simply respond to its events (ensure that the EnableRaisingEvents property is set to True). You have the Changed, Created, Deleted, and Renamed events all at your disposal. Each will fire off whenever a related action occurs. For example, if you're monitoring "c:\mydata\", with a filter of "*.txt" and the default NotifyFilter property value, and your user or an application edits the contents of "c:\mydata\test.txt"—the Changed event will fire.

From within the event, you can use the "e" argument (the System.IO.FileSystemEventArgs object) to find out more about the altered file. You may use the e.FullPath property to find out the filename, for example—or analyze the ChangeType or Path.

> **TOP TIP** *There's an* Error *event associated with the* FileSystemWatcher *component, too. It only ever comes into play when far too many changes are being made at once (typically a result of badly chosen properties, or mass file alterations by the user) and the system just cannot cope. If it ever occurs, you'll know the events raised may not cover all items. Not always good to experience, but certainly a great event to be aware of.*

And that, quite simply, is how you can easily plug directly into the file system and directly monitor its contents. Doddle!

> **TOP TIP** *Certain users of the FileSystemWatcher component complain they receive multiple (sometimes delayed) events firing in their application, for even the simplest of operations. You may receive two or three notifications for a simple file copy in Windows Explorer, for example. The official explanation is that each operation consists of a number of simpler actions, which each raise their own events (see the note in 'FileSystemWatcher class,' about FileSystemWatcher class' in the help index). Unofficially, Microsoft has identified this as an issue and is working to resolve it. If this problem affects you, you need to create your own workaround—such as maintaining your own unique list of alterations and then running your code a few seconds after the last event has fired.*

How Big Is That File—in English?

 Download supporting files at www.apress.com.
The files for this tip are in the "Ch7–English File Size" folder.

Humans and computers sometimes just don't get along. Take file sizes, for example. What a human being would call one gigabyte, a computer would call 1073741824 bytes. How do you translate one into the other? Pull up a chair.

The following handy function takes a number of bytes and translates it into a readable "human" string. Here's the code:

```
Public Function ConvertBytes(ByVal Bytes As Long) As String
    ' Converts bytes into a readable "1.44 MB", etc. string
    If Bytes >= 1073741824 Then
        Return Format(Bytes / 1024 / 1024 / 1024, "#0.00") _
            & " GB"
    ElseIf Bytes >= 1048576 Then
        Return Format(Bytes / 1024 / 1024, "#0.00") & " MB"
    ElseIf Bytes >= 1024 Then
        Return Format(Bytes / 1024, "#0.00") & " KB"
    ElseIf Bytes > 0 And Bytes < 1024 Then
        Return Fix(Bytes) & " Bytes"
    Else
        Return "0 Bytes"
    End If
End Function
```

Here's an example of the function in use. Here, the length of my file is 3027676 bytes—and the `ConvertBytes` function returns "2.89MB". (See Figure 7-4.) Perfect:

```
Dim objInfo As New System.IO.FileInfo("c:\myfile.bmp")
MessageBox.Show("File is " & ConvertBytes(objInfo.Length))
```

Figure 7-4. My file size in English—all thanks to this nifty little function!

Retrieving Special Folder Paths

It's often useful to know the location of a particular folder. For example, you might want to know where the Favorites folder is, so you can add a link to your company Web site. Or you may need to know where the Desktop directory is, so you can save a file directly to it.

For this, the .NET Framework provides the `System.Environment.GetFolderPath` function. Simply call this, passing in a `SpecialFolder` enumeration. This will then return a string containing the appropriate path.

For example:

```
Dim MyFolderPath As String
MyFolderPath = System.Environment.GetFolderPath( _
            Environment.SpecialFolder.Favorites)
MessageBox.Show(MyFolderPath)
```

Which Program Handles That File Extension?

Download supporting files at www.apress.com.
The files for this tip are in the "Ch7–File Associations" folder.

Looking to open a program in its default application? Simply use the Start class and let Windows do the rest of the work for you, like this:

```
System.Diagnostics.Process.Start("c:\myfile.doc")
```

But sometimes you want a little more. Sometimes you want to retrieve the exact path to the default program associated with that file type.

With a little rummaging around in the registry, that's exactly what this next code snippet manages to achieve. Simply pass it the file extension, and it'll return the path of the associated application. Passing in the .doc extension on a machine running Office XP, for example, will return the exact path to the Microsoft Word executable.

It's worth noting that this function automatically handles system defined variables, plus removes a number of the excess parameters included in some registry entries. In other words, it *works*—and well, too, unlike many samples of this technique currently floating around the Internet.

Here's the function:

```
Public Function GetAssociatedProgram(ByVal FileExtension As String) As String
    ' Returns the application associated with the specified FileExtension
    ' ie, path\denenv.exe for "VB" files
    Dim objExtReg As Microsoft.Win32.RegistryKey = _
        Microsoft.Win32.Registry.ClassesRoot
    Dim objAppReg As Microsoft.Win32.RegistryKey = _
        Microsoft.Win32.Registry.ClassesRoot
    Dim strExtValue As String
    Try
        ' Add trailing period if doesn't exist
        If FileExtension.Substring(0, 1) <> "." Then _
            FileExtension = "." & FileExtension
        ' Open registry areas containing launching app details
        objExtReg = objExtReg.OpenSubKey(FileExtension.Trim)
        strExtValue = objExtReg.GetValue("")
        objAppReg = objAppReg.OpenSubKey(strExtValue & "\shell\open\command")
        ' Parse out, tidy up and return result
        Dim SplitArray() As String
        SplitArray = Split(objAppReg.GetValue(Nothing), """")
```

```
        If SplitArray(0).Trim.Length > 0 Then
            Return SplitArray(0).Replace("%1", "")
        Else
            Return SplitArray(1).Replace("%1", "")
        End If
    Catch
        Return ""
    End Try
End Function
```

And here's how you might call it in your application:

```
Dim strPath As String = GetAssociatedProgram(TextBox1.Text)
System.Diagnostics.Process.Start(strPath)
```

Retrieving a Drive Serial Number

Download supporting files at www.apress.com.
The files for this tip are in the "Ch7–Get Drive Serial" folder.

The serial number of a drive sounds like a relatively unimportant factor and certainly not worthy of an entry in this book. But it can actually prove highly useful.

Many developers, for example, check which drive Windows is installed on and then send the serial number of the drive (alongside other unique system information) to their online validation service to "activate" the product. If they spot a particular user installing their product on a number of machines with different serial numbers, they suspect piracy and refuse to "activate" the product any further.

So, you see, retrieving a volume serial number can be very handy indeed.

To begin, you'll need to set a reference to the System.Management DLL. Click on Project ➤ Add Reference, find and highlight System.Management, click on Select, then hit OK.

Next, add the following function to your project:

```
Public Function GetDriveSerial(ByVal DriveLetter As String) As String
    ' Returns the serial number of the specified drive
    ' ie, GetDriveSerial("c:")
    Dim strSelectText As String = "Win32_logicaldisk='" & DriveLetter & "'"
    Dim objMO As New System.Management.ManagementObject(strSelectText)
    objMO.Get()
    Return CType(objMO.Properties("VolumeSerialNumber").Value, String)
End Function
```

And this is our GetDriveSerial function. It works by creating an instance of the ManagementObject, then using an SQL-like string to retrieve details about the specified disk. We then pick out and return the "VolumeSerialNumber" property.

Here's how we might call this function in code:

```
Label1.Text = GetDriveSerial("C:")
```

The .NET Replacement for App.Path

A lot of confusion surrounds how to find out the startup path of your application —the .NET equivalent of the App.Path property we had in Visual Basic 6. I've personally written my own elongated routines, when in fact the solution is incredibly simple.

If you want to find out the application path of your Windows application, just reference the StartupPath property of the Application object, as so:

```
Dim strPath As String = Application.StartupPath
```

Note that the returned path doesn't include a trailing slash.

If you're developing a class library or similar project, however, you might stumble upon a slight problem. You see, not all projects support the Application object. In these cases, you can use the System.Reflection class to analyze the executing assembly and return its location. A little like this:

```
Dim strPath As String = System.Reflection.Assembly.GetExecutingAssembly().Location
```

A bit more in depth, but still pretty darn simple.

INI Files Will Never Die: How to in .NET

 Download supporting files at www.apress.com.
The files for this tip are in the "Ch7—INI Files" folder.

Microsoft has been trying to get developers to move away from INI files for quite some time, pithily suggesting using the registry instead... despite the fact that it's rarely a suitable replacement. Well, this "hint" persists with .NET, which proudly boasts absolutely no intrinsic support for INI files.

But, of course, there's always a workaround.

In previous versions of Visual Basic, you'd access your INI file through the API. Well, in VB .NET, we can simply do the same. Admittedly, Microsoft would prefer us to run "safe," "managed" code within the .NET Framework—it can then automatically handle resources for you and ensure a more error-free environment.

However, you can still access "unmanaged" code, such as functions within the Windows API and COM components, with great ease.

In fact, here I've developed a class to encapsulate the functionality of some of those older INI file API functions. The fact that they're wrapped up in a class also means that, should you ever implement another method of handling such settings, you can simply edit your code while the interfaces remain the same.

Anyway, enough talk—here's my class code:

```
Public Class IniFile
    ' API functions
    Private Declare Ansi Function GetPrivateProfileString _
        Lib "kernel32.dll" Alias "GetPrivateProfileStringA" _
        (ByVal lpApplicationName As String, _
        ByVal lpKeyName As String, ByVal lpDefault As String, _
        ByVal lpReturnedString As System.Text.StringBuilder, _
        ByVal nSize As Integer, ByVal lpFileName As String) _
        As Integer
    Private Declare Ansi Function WritePrivateProfileString _
        Lib "kernel32.dll" Alias "WritePrivateProfileStringA" _
        (ByVal lpApplicationName As String, _
        ByVal lpKeyName As String, ByVal lpString As String, _
        ByVal lpFileName As String) As Integer
    Private Declare Ansi Function GetPrivateProfileInt _
        Lib "kernel32.dll" Alias "GetPrivateProfileIntA" _
        (ByVal lpApplicationName As String, _
        ByVal lpKeyName As String, ByVal nDefault As Integer, _
        ByVal lpFileName As String) As Integer
    Private Declare Ansi Function FlushPrivateProfileString _
        Lib "kernel32.dll" Alias "WritePrivateProfileStringA" _
        (ByVal lpApplicationName As Integer, _
        ByVal lpKeyName As Integer, ByVal lpString As Integer, _
        ByVal lpFileName As String) As Integer

    Dim strFilename As String

    ' Constructor, accepting a filename
    Public Sub New(ByVal Filename As String)
        strFilename = Filename
    End Sub
```

```vb
' Read-only filename property
ReadOnly Property FileName() As String
    Get
        Return strFilename
    End Get
End Property

Public Function GetString(ByVal Section As String, _
    ByVal Key As String, ByVal [Default] As String) As String
    ' Returns a string from your INI file
    Dim intCharCount As Integer
    Dim objResult As New System.Text.StringBuilder(256)
    intCharCount = GetPrivateProfileString(Section, Key, _
        [Default], objResult, objResult.Capacity, strFilename)
    If intCharCount > 0 Then GetString = _
        Left(objResult.ToString, intCharCount)
End Function

Public Function GetInteger(ByVal Section As String, _
    ByVal Key As String, ByVal [Default] As Integer) As Integer
    ' Returns an integer from your INI file
    Return GetPrivateProfileInt(Section, Key, _
        [Default], strFilename)
End Function

Public Function GetBoolean(ByVal Section As String, _
    ByVal Key As String, ByVal [Default] As Boolean) As Boolean
    ' Returns a boolean from your INI file
    Return (GetPrivateProfileInt(Section, Key, _
        CInt([Default]), strFilename) = 1)
End Function

Public Sub WriteString(ByVal Section As String, _
    ByVal Key As String, ByVal Value As String)
    ' Writes a string to your INI file
    WritePrivateProfileString(Section, Key, Value, strFilename)
    Flush()
End Sub

Public Sub WriteInteger(ByVal Section As String, _
    ByVal Key As String, ByVal Value As Integer)
    ' Writes an integer to your INI file
    WriteString(Section, Key, CStr(Value))
```

```
        Flush()
    End Sub


    Public Sub WriteBoolean(ByVal Section As String, _
        ByVal Key As String, ByVal Value As Boolean)
        ' Writes a boolean to your INI file
        WriteString(Section, Key, CStr(CInt(Value)))
        Flush()
    End Sub


    Private Sub Flush()
        ' Stores all the cached changes to your INI file
        FlushPrivateProfileString(0, 0, 0, strFilename)
    End Sub


End Class
```

After you've added this class code to your application, here's how you may want to use it:

```
Dim objIniFile As New IniFile("c:\data.ini")
objIniFile.WriteString("Settings", "ClockTime", "12:59")
Dim strData As String = _
    objIniFile.GetString("Settings", "ClockTime", "(none)")
```

> **TOP TIP** *As I mentioned earlier, Microsoft doesn't really like people using INI files. It doesn't fit in with its* vision. *They would prefer developers use code like this only as a stop-gap measure while upgrading existing systems, then move onto an XML-based method of storing settings. Visit* www.gotdotnet.com/ userfiles/demeester/XMLINIFile.zip *for an INI file replacement, using XML. But, of course, it's completely up to you.*

Dates, Numbers, Strings

Not all techniques neatly fit under one header. This one covers a whole bundle of tricks, from the intelligent way to identify a date to an algorithm generating memorable passwords, from encryption in a mere twelve lines of code to random numbers... that actually work. And then some. Just read on!

Is That a Whole Number, or Not?

It's sometimes useful to check whether the user has entered a whole number, such as 5, or perhaps a decimal, such as 3.142.

No problem: the following little function will check for you. Simply pass in your number to IsWholeNumber. It checks whether the item passed is numeric, then verifies that it's a whole number. If so, it returns True; anything else and it passes back False.

Here's the code:

```
Public Function IsWholeNumber(ByVal Number As Object) As Boolean
    ' Returns true if the passed item is a whole number
    If IsNumeric(Number) Then
        If CInt(Number) = Number Then Return True
    End If
End Function
```

And, finally, here's how you might use it:

```
Dim blnIsWhole As Boolean
blnIsWhole = IsWholeNumber(5)
blnIsWhole = IsWholeNumber(3.142)
```

Checking for a Date the Intelligent .NET Way

Download supporting files at www.apress.com.
The files for this tip are in the "Ch7—IsDate" folder.

Back in good ol' Visual Basic 6, we had one function dedicated to letting us know whether something was a date or not. It was called, appropriately enough, IsDate. With .NET, however, that function has been reserved for the Microsoft.VisualBasic namespace—and, if you use that, you're deemed one of the "old crowd."

A much better way of checking for a date is to write an equivalent .NET function for the job. Or rather, just copy mine.

The following replacement function is also called IsDate, however is much smarter than its VB6 equivalent. For example, not only is "01/01/2004" interpreted as a date, but so are "Jan 1, 2004" and "28 February 1975"—which is something the old IsDate couldn't even imagine.

Ready? Here's the code you'll need. Just pass in a string and it'll return a Boolean result, depending on whether the passed item is in a recognized date format:

```
Public Function IsDate(ByVal DateIn As String) As Boolean
    Dim datDateTime As DateTime
    Dim blnIsDate As Boolean = True
    Try
        ' Attempt to parse date
        datDateTime = DateTime.Parse(DateIn)
    Catch e As FormatException
        ' Error parsing, return False
        blnIsDate = False
    End Try
    Return blnIsDate
End Function
```

And here's how you might call the function:

```
If IsDate("Jan 1, 2004") Then
    MessageBox.Show("This is a date!")
Else
    MessageBox.Show("This is NOT a date!")
End If
```

But what if you do get someone passing in something like "January 1, 2004" and want to translate it into a DateTime (Date equivalent) data type—ready for, say, storing in a database? Simply use the sixth line of code from our function to change your text into the required data type. Easy!

1st, 2nd, 3rd: Using Ordinal Numbers in Your App

Download supporting files at www.apress.com.
The files for this tip are in the "Ch7–Ordinal Numbers" folder.

As a human being, I like to read my dates properly. That means "December 1st 2002", rather than "December 1 2002". But computers don't have much of a clue when it comes to such quirks of the English language. They simply care for numbers—not ordinals, like "2nd" or "43rd".

Something like that requires intelligence. And that's exactly what the following neat function builds into your application. Pass it a number and it'll look up the appropriate suffix through a series of Select routines, and then return the ordinal value.

Here's the code:

```
Public Function GetOrdinal(ByVal Number As Integer) As String
    ' Accepts an integer, returns the ordinal suffix

    ' Handles special case three digit numbers ending
    ' with 11, 12 or 13 - ie, 111th, 112th, 113th, 211th, et al
    If CType(Number, String).Length > 2 Then
        Dim intEndNum As Integer = CType(CType(Number, String). _
            Substring(CType(Number, String).Length - 2, 2), Integer)
        If intEndNum >= 11 And intEndNum <= 13 Then
            Select Case intEndNum
                Case 11, 12, 13
                    Return "th"
            End Select
        End If
    End If


    If Number >= 21 Then
        ' Handles 21st, 22nd, 23rd, et al
        Select Case CType(Number.ToString.Substring( _
            Number.ToString.Length - 1, 1), Integer)
            Case 1
                Return "st"
            Case 2
                Return "nd"
            Case 3
                Return "rd"
            Case 0, 4 To 9
                Return "th"
        End Select
    Else
        ' Handles 1st to 20th
        Select Case Number
            Case 1
                Return "st"
            Case 2
                Return "nd"
            Case 3
```

```
                Return "rd"
            Case 4 To 20
                Return "th"
        End Select
    End If
End Function
```

Here's how you may use this GetOrdinal function in code. (See Figure 7-5 for my sample application.) Enjoy:

```
Dim strNumber As String
strNumber = "38" & GetOrdinal(38)
MessageBox.Show(strNumber)
```

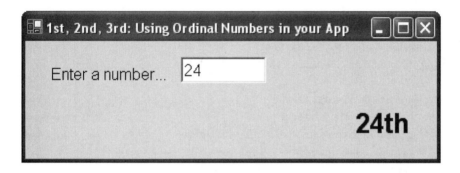

Figure 7-5. Enter a number and get its suffix with this sample application.

Random Numbers... That Work!

Download supporting files at www.apress.com.
The files for this tip are in the "Ch7–Random Numbers" folder.

After reading at least a dozen articles on how to generate random numbers, I'm sorry to say that technical writers are still getting it wrong.

Don't misunderstand me: generating random numbers is actually very easy. You simply create a new instance of the System.Random class, passing in a "seed" value. Then you use the object .Next method to return a fresh value. The problem is that most developers place the new instance of the Random class inside the function that generates the number itself.

This means that, if the function is run a number of times at speed, the "seed" (typically a value based on the number of "ticks" for the current date and time) given to the Random class may be the same each time. Now, the Random class is never *truly* random and simply runs a formula to "randomize" the next number. Because most developers are declaring a new instance of the class inside the function, it gets created afresh with every single call, follows its same formula with the same seed to generate a random number—and creates one exactly the same as the last! (Until, at least, the tick "seed" value alters.)

The trick is to declare the new Random class *outside* of the function that retrieves the next random number. This way you generate the seed only once and are getting the "randomizer" formula to cycle through its formula and ensure the next chosen number is truly random.

Here's my code. Note that you no longer have to declare new objects (such as objRandom, here) at the top of your class or module; you can do it just above the function, to aid clarity of code:

```
Dim objRandom As New System.Random( _
    CType(System.DateTime.Now.Ticks Mod System.Int32.MaxValue, Integer))

Public Function GetRandomNumber( _
    Optional ByVal Low As Integer = 1, _
    Optional ByVal High As Integer = 100) As Integer
    ' Returns a random number,
    ' between the optional Low and High parameters
    Return objRandom.Next(Low, High + 1)
End Function
```

And here's how you may use this function in code:

```
Dim intDiceRoll As Integer
intDiceRoll = GetRandomNumber(1, 6)
MessageBox.Show("You rolled a " & intDiceRoll.ToString)
```

Finding the Number of Days in a Month

If you knew how many complicated VB6 algorithms I've written to calculate the number of days in a month, you'd think me a crazed developer. I've written code that accepts a month and year, then formats the month so it's the start of the next month, then takes away one day, then retrieves the actual day part of the date... and so on, et cetera.

When I first visited .NET, I continued writing these complicated functions. Until, that is, I discovered some of the delights of System.DateTime.

This structure includes a shared DaysInMonth function. Just pass it the year and month and it'll return an integer containing the number of days in that month, useful for business applications and calendar-based programs.

Here's a little sample code demonstrating the function in use:

```
Dim shtDayCount As Short
shtDayCount = System.DateTime.DaysInMonth("2003", "2")
MessageBox.Show("There are " & shtDayCount.ToString & _
    " days in that month")
```

Easy when you know how, isn't it?

Adding and Subtracting Days, Months, Years

Many tips never made it to this book, simply because I deemed them "must knows" that any Visual Studio .NET programmer would easily grasp on their own, without some strange author regurgitating the obvious. The Replace function of the String class, for example.

That was almost the case with this tip, but, over the past three months, I've seen five different printed code snippets demonstrating how to add days, months, and years to a date. And they all looked extremely confusing.

The truth is, adding or subtracting days, months, and years is easy!

Like the String class, the DateTime class includes its own shared supporting methods and functions—including AddDays, AddMinutes, AddHours, AddYears, and AddMonths. Simply call them, passing in a number (positive or negative), and it'll change your variable value.

For example:

```
Dim MyDate As DateTime
MyDate = Now
MyDate.AddDays(7) ' Change date to one week from now
MessageBox.Show(MyDate)
```

Simple, isn't it?

Calculating the Next Working Day

Download supporting files at www.apress.com.
The files for this tip are in the "Ch7–Next Working Day" folder.

Sometimes you don't just want to add a certain number of days to a date, you want to take working days into account: five working days until delivery, or two working days in which the customer needs a response.

Difficult? Not at all. The following nifty AddWorkingDays function does it all for you. Simply pass in a date, alongside the number of working days you want to shift the date by. For example, pass in a 5 to get the fifth working day after your date, or "-1" to return the last working day.

Here's the code you'll need:

```
Public Function AddWorkingDays(ByVal DateIn As DateTime, _
    ByVal ShiftDate As Integer) As DateTime
    ' Adds the [ShiftDate] number of working days to DateIn
    Dim datDate As DateTime = DateIn.AddDays(ShiftDate)
    ' Loop around until we get the need non-weekend day
    While Weekday(datDate) = 1 Or Weekday(datDate) = 7
        datDate = datDate.AddDays(IIf(ShiftDate < 0, -1, 1))
    End While
    Return datDate
End Function
```

And here's how you might call it in your application:

```
Dim datNewDate As DateTime = AddWorkingDays(Today, -1)
MessageBox.Show("The last working day was " & datNewDate)
```

Easy Check for a Leap Year

Checking for a leap year used to be a sticky task. But, after reading the "Finding the Number of Days in a Month" snippet, you might think it's as simple as checking the number of days in February. You're wrong: it's even easier.

The System.DateTime class includes a neat little shared IsLeapYear function. It accepts a year and returns a True or False as appropriate. Here's a little sample code showing it in action:

```
Dim blnIsLeapYear As Boolean
blnIsLeapYear = System.DateTime.IsLeapYear( _
    DateTime.Now.Year)
MessageBox.Show("This " & _
    IIf(blnIsLeapYear, "is", "is not") & " a leap year")
```

This code takes the current year and passes it to the IsLeapYear function. It then displays a message, confirming whether this is a leap year or not. Easy!

Figuring Out Quarters

Download supporting files at www.apress.com.
The files for this tip are in the "Ch7—Quarters" folder.

Business applications often need to figure out quarters, which are the four three-month periods in any year, beginning at the start of January and going through to the end of March, then April to June, July to September, and finally, October to December.

Calculating the opening and closing quarter dates for a particular date is a common task for programmers. So, to save you from figuring out how to write that code, the following ready-to-run functions do it all for you:

```
Public Function FirstDayOfQuarter(ByVal DateIn As DateTime) As DateTime
    ' Calculate first day of DateIn quarter,
    ' with quarters starting at the beginning of Jan/Apr/Jul/Oct
    Dim intQuarterNum As Integer = (Month(DateIn) - 1) \ 3 + 1
    Return DateSerial(Year(DateIn), 3 * intQuarterNum - 2, 1)
End Function

Public Function LastDayOfQuarter(ByVal DateIn As DateTime) As DateTime
    ' Calculate last day of DateIn quarter,
    ' with quarters ending at the end of Mar/Jun/Sep/Dec
    Dim intQuarterNum As Integer = (Month(DateIn) - 1) \ 3 + 1
    Return DateSerial(Year(DateIn), 3 * intQuarterNum + 1, 0)
End Function
```

To use either of these functions, simply pass in the date you wish to retrieve the quarter for, and it'll return the appropriate beginning/end date as a DateTime data type (an exact equivalent of the Date data type).

And here's an example of how you might call these functions. (See Figure 7-6 for my sample application.)

```
Dim CurrentQuarterStart As DateTime = FirstDayOfQuarter(Now)
Dim CurrentQuarterEnd As DateTime = LastDayOfQuarter(Now)
MessageBox.Show("Current quarter start: " & CurrentQuarterStart & _
    Chr(10) & Chr(13) & "Current quarter end: " & CurrentQuarterEnd)
```

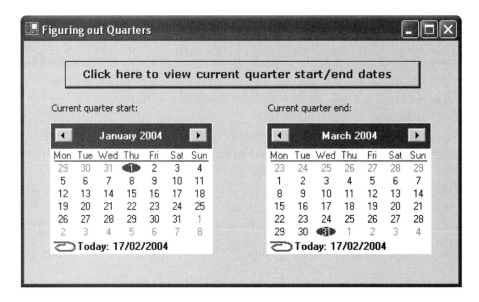

Figure 7-6. Using the MonthCalendar control to display the current quarter start and end dates

Calculating the Years Between Two Dates

 Download supporting files at www.apress.com.
The files for this tip are in the "Ch7–Years Between Dates" folder.

Business applications often find it useful to calculate the number of years between two particular dates, such as the date a customer first ordered and the present date, perhaps to see whether they apply for a "loyalty" discount or a free gift.

Don't scramble in the code window. Just use my next little snippet. Simply call YearsBetweenDates, passing in a start date and end date. It'll return an Integer containing the number of full years between the specified dates:

```
Public Function YearsBetweenDates(ByVal StartDate As DateTime, _
    ByVal EndDate As DateTime) As Integer
    ' Returns the number of years between the passed dates
    If Month(EndDate) < Month(StartDate) Or _
      (Month(EndDate) = Month(StartDate) And _
      (EndDate.Day) < (StartDate.Day)) Then
        Return Year(EndDate) - Year(StartDate) - 1
    Else
        Return Year(EndDate) - Year(StartDate)
    End If
End Function
```

Converting a String to "Proper Case"

 Download supporting files at www.apress.com.
The files for this tip are in the "Ch7–Proper Case" folder.

Initiating someone into the use of the StrConv function to generate "proper case" text was always exciting for me. This was built-in intelligence, and I used to use it to excite every new Visual Basic 6 programmer I taught.

You can still access the StrConv function to capitalize the first letter of every word and lowercase the rest, like this:

```
Dim strSentence As String = "MaRlenA on THE WAll"
strSentence = Microsoft.VisualBasic.StrConv(strSentence, _
    VbStrConv.ProperCase)
' Returns: Marlena On The Wall
```

However, this is using the Microsoft.VisualBasic namespace, which was included to help VB6 programmers shift to .NET. What we really need is a pure .NET Framework method of converting to title case. And that's just what I have here, in this nifty little function:

```
Public Function ProperCase(ByVal Text As String) As String
    ' Converts the passed chunk of text to "Proper Case"
    Dim objCulture As New System.Globalization. _
        CultureInfo("en-US")
    Return objCulture.TextInfo.ToTitleCase(Text.ToLower)
End Function
```

Here, we create a new CultureInfo class, passing in the culture code for America ("en-US", or "en-GB" for Great Britain—however, this really makes no difference to this snippet). We then use the TextInfo object within that class, passing a lowercased version of our text to the ToTitleCase function. We convert to lowercase first because fully capitalized words are not automatically converted to title case in this culture. We then return our result.

And that's it: a true .NET technique for implementing proper case. (See Figure 7-7 for my sample application.)

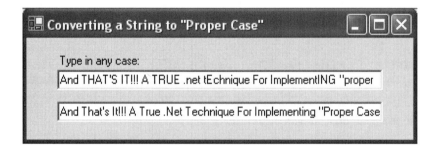

Figure 7-7. My sample "proper case" application

Storing Text Snippets on the Clipboard

We've all worked with the Windows clipboard before, whether to copy a picture from Adobe PhotoShop over to PowerPoint, or simply cut and paste a bundle of text in Microsoft Word.

And adding clipboard integration to your own application isn't as difficult as it sounds. You simply need to use the Clipboard object. To set data to the clipboard, simply pass it as a parameter to the SetDataObject method, as so:

```
Clipboard.SetDataObject(TextBox1.Text)
```

You can also retrieve data from the clipboard, using the GetDataObject.GetData function. Here, we're retrieving simple text from the clipboard, but you could use the GetDataObject.GetDataPresent function to find out what's on the clipboard, then retrieve and manipulate anything from sound files to bitmaps:

```
TextBox1.Text = Clipboard.GetDataObject.GetData(DataFormats.Text)
```

Generating Memorable Passwords, Automatically

Download supporting files at www.apress.com.
The files for this tip are in the "Ch7–Memorable Passwords" folder.

Generating automatic passwords for your users is a common programming scenario. However, due to the techniques typically employed, most autogenerated passwords end up looking like *YPSWW9441*—which, although highly secure, also end up completely unmemorable.

The following function generates a password using alternating friendly consonants and vowels, making for much more memorable passwords. Asking the function to generate a five-character password, for example, may result in *BONES* or *LAMOT*.

To use this function, call GeneratePassword, passing in the length of your desired password. The final password will be returned as a string:

```
Public Function GeneratePassword(ByVal Length As Integer) As String
    ' Creates a memorable password of the specified Length
    Dim blnOnVowel As Boolean
    Dim strTempLetter As String
    Dim strPassword As String
    Dim intCount As Integer
    For intCount = 1 To Length
        If blnOnVowel = False Then
            ' Choose a nice consonant - no C, X, Z, or Q
            strTempLetter = CType(Choose(CType(GetRandomNumber(1, 17), Double), _
                "B", "D", "F", "G", "H", "J", "K", "L", "M", _
                "N", "P", "R", "S", "T", "V", "W", "Y"), String)
            ' Append it to the password string
            strPassword += strTempLetter
            ' Swich to vowel mode
            blnOnVowel = True
        Else
            ' Choose a vowel
            strTempLetter = CType(Choose(CType(GetRandomNumber(1, 5), Double), _
                "A", "E", "I", "O", "U"), String)
            ' Append it to the password string
            strPassword += strTempLetter
```

```
            ' Switch back again, ready for next loop round
            blnOnVowel = False
        End If
    Next
    Return strPassword
End Function


Dim objRandom As New System.Random(CType((System.DateTime.Now.Ticks _
    Mod System.Int32.MaxValue), Integer))
Public Function GetRandomNumber(Optional ByVal Low As Integer = 1, _
    Optional ByVal High As Integer = 100) As Integer
    ' Returns a random number,
    ' between the optional Low and High parameters
    Return objRandom.Next(Low, High + 1)
End Function
```

You could use the GeneratePassword function as so (see Figure 7-8 for my sample application):

```
Dim MyPassword As String
MyPassword = GeneratePassword(5)
MessageBox.Show(MyPassword)
```

Figure 7-8. Generating a memorable five-character password in just one click

Encryption in Just Twelve Lines of Code!

Download supporting files at www.apress.com.
The files for this tip are in the "Ch7–Simple Encryption" folder.

At times, you may want to very simply encrypt a small piece of text to store in the registry, a database, or file, but you don't want the overhead or complexity of a government-standard encryption technique.

A much simpler encryption method is required, and the following function provides just that. It's called Crypt: pass it your plain text and it'll encrypt it; pass it your encrypted text and it'll decrypt it. It's simple and all in fewer than fifteen lines of code:

```
Public Function SimpleCrypt(ByVal Text As String) As String
    ' Encrypts/decrypts the passed string using a
    ' simple ASCII value-swapping algorithm
    Dim strTempChar As String, i As Integer
    For i = 1 To Len(Text)
        If Asc(Mid$(Text, i, 1)) < 128 Then
            strTempChar = CType(Asc(Mid$(Text, i, 1)) + 128, String)
        ElseIf Asc(Mid$(Text, i, 1)) > 128 Then
            strTempChar = CType(Asc(Mid$(Text, i, 1)) - 128, String)
        End If
        Mid$(Text, i, 1) = Chr(CType(strTempChar, Integer))
    Next i
    Return Text
End Function
```

It's not recommended for highly confidential information (as anyone with this script could also decrypt your data), but it's nonetheless highly useful. Here's how you might use this function (see my sample application in Figure 7-9):

```
Dim MyText As String
' Encrypt
MyText = "Karl Moore"
MyText = Crypt(MyText)
MessageBox.Show(MyText)
' Decrypt
MyText = Crypt(MyText)
MessageBox.Show(MyText)
```

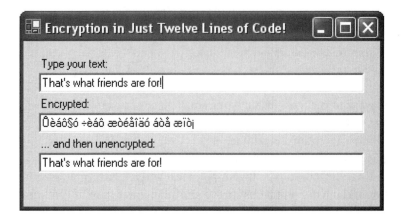

Figure 7-9. An example that uses our simple Crypt *function to both encrypt and decrypt at once*

Implementing Powerful MD5 Encryption

Download supporting files at www.apress.com.
The files for this tip are in the "Ch7–MD5" folder.

So, simple encryption just isn't good enough for you, huh? Well, you may as well rocket straight to the top and check out the power of MD5 (Message Digest 5) encryption, a powerful data security algorithm used by many large organizations throughout the globe.

Pass data to the MD5 algorithm and it'll return a small "fingerprint" of the data. If the data changes, no matter how small the alteration, the fingerprint changes. This is one-way encryption: the fingerprint can't be turned back into the original data. You can only compare the fingerprint with the source data and see if they match.

For example, you may store password fingerprints ("message digests") in a database password field. When the user logs on, you simply compare his or her typed password with the fingerprint using MD5: if they match, you grant the user access.

It's all ultra-secure: you aren't storing the actual password anywhere, only the fingerprint.

Sound powerful? The .NET Framework includes cryptography classes directly supporting the MD5 standard, and I've created two functions to perform its two most common operations.

The first, GetMD5Hash, accepts your data as a simple string. It then calculates and passes back the MD5 fingerprint—the "message digest", the "hash"—as an array of bytes ready for you to perhaps store in your database. Don't forget, this is one-way. Once something is encrypted, you can't decrypt it.

The second, CheckMD5Hash, accepts an array of bytes (your hash) and a string, such as the byte array from your database password field and the password that your user has entered. The string is then converted into a hash itself and the individual bytes compared, bit by bit. If it all matches, you've got a winner—and a True is returned.

Here's the code:

```
Public Function GetMD5Hash(ByVal Text As String) As Byte()
    ' Generates an MD5 hash for the specified Text
    On Error Resume Next
    Dim objAscii As New System.Text.ASCIIEncoding()
    Dim bytHash As Byte() = _
        New System.Security.Cryptography.MD5CryptoServiceProvider(). _
        ComputeHash(objAscii.GetBytes(Text))
    Return bytHash
End Function


Public Function CheckMD5Hash(ByVal OriginalHash As Byte(), _
    ByVal Text As String) As Boolean
    ' Checks an MD5 hash against the specified Text
    ' Returns True if we have a match
    On Error Resume Next
    Dim objAscii As New System.Text.ASCIIEncoding()
    Dim intCount As Integer, blnMismatch As Boolean
    Dim bytHashToCompare As Byte() = GetMD5Hash(Text)
    If OriginalHash.Length <> bytHashToCompare.Length Then
        Return False
    Else
        For intCount = 0 To OriginalHash.Length - 1
            If OriginalHash(intCount) <> bytHashToCompare(intCount) Then
                Return False
            End If
        Next
        Return True
    End If
End Function
```

Here's a simple example using the two preceding functions. The first line generates an MD5 hash, and the second checks it against our password:

```
Dim bytHash() As Byte = GetMD5Hash("password")
Dim blnMatch As Boolean = CheckMD5Hash(bytHash, "password")
```

Remember that this is highly powerful, currently unbreakable encryption. And all in just a few lines of cool .NET code. Exciting stuff.

Converting a String into the Color Type

It's often useful to be able to convert from a string into an actual type, and vice versa—a technique that may seem especially difficult when it comes to colors. Imagine, for example, that your program allows users to customize their application colors. You need a method of storing the settings, probably as strings in the registry. Maybe your program actually prompts the user to type in a color. They may request green, or aqua, or just plain old gray, but you need a method of converting this value into an actual Color type.

Thankfully, the .NET Framework team figured you might want to do that, and include a neat ColorConverter class to help you.

Here's an example designed for a Windows application. The first chunk takes the string "Green" and changes it into a Color type, finally setting it as the BackColor of your form ("Me"). The second takes a Color type and displays a matching color string:

```
' Instantiate ColorConverter class
Dim objCConv As New System.Drawing.ColorConverter()

' Retrieve a Color object from a string
Dim objColor As System.Drawing.Color = _
    CType(objCConv.ConvertFromString("Green"), Color)
 Me.BackColor = objColor

' Retrieve a string from a Color object
Dim strColor As String = _
    objCConv.ConvertToString(Me.BackColor)
MessageBox.Show(strColor)
```

That's it! Don't forget: Windows applications also have access to the Color-Dialog control, which allows the user to select a color and returns a Color type. You may wish to integrate this into applications that use such color conversion code. Good luck!

Binding a Combo Box to Enumeration Values

 Download supporting files at www.apress.com.
The files for this tip are in the "Ch7–Enum Binding" folder.

By their very nature, enumerations lend themselves easily to being displayed in list controls, such as the combo box. You want to take their text entries and display them to the user, with the related values being stored alongside each item.

This was impossible in previous versions of Visual Basic, but it's easily done with .NET.

Firstly, let's look at a Web example. Here, we have a custom function that accepts a System.Type object, along with the actual list control you want populated. It then clears the box and adds all items from the enumeration, along with their related item values. You can then use and reference the items (and values) in the box as you would normally.

Here's the code:

```
Public Sub AddEnumToList(ByVal GetSystemType As System.Type, _
    ByVal List As System.Web.UI.WebControls.ListControl)
    ' Populates the specified list with the
    ' names and values of the passed system type
    Dim strNames As String(), arrValues As System.Array
    Dim intCount As Integer
    strNames = [Enum].GetNames(GetSystemType)
    arrValues = [Enum].GetValues(GetSystemType)
    List.Items.Clear()
    For intCount = LBound(strNames) To UBound(strNames)
        List.Items.Add(New _
            System.Web.UI.WebControls.ListItem(strNames(intCount), _
            arrValues.GetValue(intCount)))
    Next
End Sub
```

And here's an example of how you could use this function. Note the use of GetType surrounding the name of your enumeration:

```
AddEnumToList(GetType(NameOfEnum), DropDownList1)
```

With Windows forms, it works a little differently. The provided list controls do not inherently support individual item values, unless you're performing a more complex binding operation; therefore, the simplest method is to list the text items from the enumeration, then figure out the related values later (if required at all).

So, to get the list of items, set the DataSource equal to a string array containing the items from your enumeration. You can obtain this through the System.Enum.GetNames function. Here's a code sample demonstrating how to do this:

```
ComboBox1.DataSource = System.Enum.GetNames(GetType(NameOfEnum))
```

This takes the individual text items from your enumeration and adds them to your list-based control in the order of their related values, from lowest to highest (and not in the order in which you declared them). Then, when you need to figure out the underlying value of the selected item, you'll need to run code a little like this:

```
Dim strNames As Array = _
    System.Enum.GetValues(GetType(NameOfEnum))
Dim strValue As String = _
    strNames(ComboBox1.SelectedIndex)
```

And that's how to bind a list control to an enumeration. It sounds difficult, but once you know how....

Graphics and Fonts

The visual side of your applications can be very exciting, and the following bundle of drawing code snippets will help you really take advantage of some of the new graphic capabilities in your VB .NET. Use my ready-to-run code snippets to do everything from converting file image formats to writing your own screensavers, designing your own arty icons to adding gradient backdrops in code. Read on, Rembrandt!

Designing Your Own Arty Icons

You can create your own icons in VB .NET by selecting Project ➤ Add New Item from the menu, then choosing Icon File and clicking on Open. From here, use any of the dozen drawing tools to create your perfect ICO file. (See Figure 7-10.)

To change a Windows form to use this icon, click on the ellipsis next to its Icon property in the Properties window. Then navigate to your project folder and select the ICO file you just created.

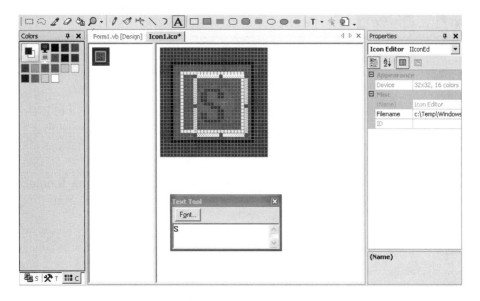

Figure 7-10. Strangely, I didn't pass art....

The Basics of Working with Fonts

You can list all the currently installed TrueType and OpenType fonts on your system by cycling through the font families in the System.Drawing.FontFamily.Families namespace.

For example:

```
Dim MyFontFamily As FontFamily
For Each MyFontFamily In System.Drawing.FontFamily.Families
    ComboBox1.Items.Add(MyFontFamily.Name)
Next
```

You can set the font for a particular control in code by creating a new Font object, then setting it to the control Font property. For example:

```
Dim MyFont As Font
MyFont = New Font("Verdana", 8)
TextBox1.Font = MyFont
```

Crafty Conversion Between Graphic Formats

 Download supporting files at www.apress.com.
The files for this tip are in the "Ch7–Convert Image Format" folder.

Need a function to convert between bitmap, GIF, EMF, JPEG, PNG, WMF, and ICO image formats, among others? Don't buy a third-party control: this conversion is exactly what my next crafty little snippet does. And all in a mere dozen lines of code.

Just call ConvertImage, passing in the filename of your current file, the desired format of your new file (using the enumeration), and your new filename. And that's it:

```
Public Sub ConvertImage(ByVal Filename As String, _
    ByVal DesiredFormat As System.Drawing.Imaging.ImageFormat, _
    ByVal NewFilename As String)
    ' Takes a filename and saves the file in a new format
    Try
        Dim imgFile As System.Drawing.Image = _
            System.Drawing.Image.FromFile(Filename)
        imgFile.Save(NewFilename, DesiredFormat)
    Catch ex As Exception
        Throw ex
    End Try
End Sub
```

Here's an example of using this to convert a GIF image into a Windows bitmap:

```
ConvertImage("c:\img1.gif", _
    System.Drawing.Imaging.ImageFormat.Bmp, "c:\img2.bmp")
```

Rotating and Flipping Is Easy!

 Download supporting files at www.apress.com.
The files for this tip are in the "Ch7—Rotate Image" folder.

Back in the golden olden days of programming, rotating and flipping an image either meant performing complicated bit-by-bit image swaps or getting out your wallet to plunk down for a third-party control.

With the .NET Framework, the System.Drawing namespace makes it much easier. As we saw in the last tip, the Image class provides functionality that will bowl over graphic developers of old.

This book isn't about graphics, however, and so it isn't my intention to focus on them. But rotating and flipping images is a relatively common business requirement, especially with the number of letters scanned into modern applications and faxes received through the Internet, so this little tip is designed to demonstrate just how easy it can be.

Firstly, load your image into your application—either directly into an Image object or into the PictureBox control, as so:

```
PicBox.Image = System.Drawing.Image.FromFile("c:\sample.gif")
PicBox.SizeMode = PictureBoxSizeMode.StretchImage
```

Then, behind your rotate buttons, add functions similar to the following:

```
Dim objImage As Image = PicBox.Image
objImage.RotateFlip(RotateFlipType.Rotate90FlipNone)
PicBox.Image = objImage
```

Here, we extract the graphic from behind our PictureBox control as an Image object. We then run the .RotateFlip method, passing in one of many possible enumeration arguments: here, we're using Rotate90FlipNone, meaning that it should rotate the image 90 degrees and not flip it. We could, however, have chosen RotateNoneFlipX for a horizontal flip. Or any of the other fourteen options.

Finally, we set the Image property of our PictureBox back to our Image object, and the control displays our newly rotated image. A complete doddle!

Drawing with Windows Forms

Download supporting files at www.apress.com.
The files for this tip are in the "Ch7–Drawing" folder.

This book deals primarily with the business world. We've talked about databases, setting up Web services, and utilizing powerful encryption algorithms. But we haven't discussed *drawing* in your application. So, in the interest of developing your all-round super programmer mindset, let this tip serve as a quick overview.

First off, you may have noticed that there's no Shape control with .NET. If you want to draw, you need to revert to code. Thankfully, it's not all sticky API code anymore. Microsoft has repackaged all that old drawing functionality, added a little more, and christened it GDI+ (the old system was known as the GDI, standing for *graphical device interface*).

How can you use it? Basic drawing is actually pretty simple. You need to know just three core pieces of information. First, when drawing, you need a digital "sheet of paper" to work with. This is an object based on the Graphics class, and, if you worked a lot with graphics in VB6, you're probably best imagining this as an encapsulated Windows device context.

When you have this area to work on, you need to know what tools to work with, and there are really only two possibilities here. There's our second item, the Pen class, which allows you to set up the style of line you want. And then there's our third item, the Brush class, which is designed for filling in areas and defining how that "fill" will look.

Once you have the items, you use methods of the Graphics object (our sheet of paper) to put the tools into work. All the Draw... methods take your pen style and draw something, and all the Fill... methods take your brush style and fill something. So, for example, I may call the FillRectangle function of my Graphics object, passing in a purple Brush object and various dimensions, and a purple rectangle would be drawn for me.

Let's look at a little sample code to help explain away this weird-sounding phenomenon. This commented snippet is intended to run behind a Windows form:

```
' Get Graphics object from our form, our "sheet of digital drawing paper"
Dim objGraphics As System.Drawing.Graphics = Me.CreateGraphics

' Create new Pen, color blue, width 10
Dim objPen As New Pen(Color.Blue, 10)
' Draw line using pen from
```

```
' 45 across, 45 down to 95 across, 95 down
objGraphics.DrawLine(objPen, 45, 45, 95, 95)

' Draw arc, this time using built-in green pen
' 8 across, 10 down to 30 across, 30 down
' with a 90 degree start angle and 180 degree sweep
objGraphics.DrawArc(Pens.Green, 8, 10, 30, 30, 90, 180)

' Create new Brush-based object, color purple
Dim objBrush As New SolidBrush(Color.Purple)
' Draw rectangle area using brush
' start at 100 across, 100 down,
' carry on for 50 across, 50 down
objGraphics.FillRectangle(objBrush, 100, 100, 50, 50)

' Draw ellipse, this time using built-in orange brush
objGraphics.FillEllipse(Brushes.Orange, 10, 10, 30, 30)
```

Understand what is happening here? We're just setting up our Pen- or Brush-inherited objects, then passing them along with parameters to methods of the Graphics object. (See Figure 7-11 for the result.)

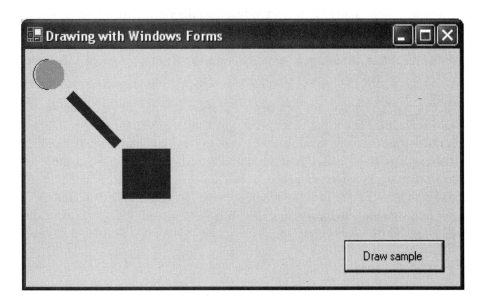

Figure 7-11. The colorful result of our lines of code

Speaking of the `Graphics` object, here's a reference list of the most popular drawing methods, alongside their core parameters (most of which have multiple overloaded implementations):

- `DrawArc`: Draws part of an ellipse. Parameters are `Pen` object, list of coordinates, and start/end angle values for the arc in degrees.

- `DrawBezier`: Draws a Bezier curve. Parameters are `Pen` object and list of control points from which the curve is generated.

- `DrawLine`: Draws a straight line. Parameters are `Pen` object and list of coordinates.

- `DrawString`: Draws text to your area. Parameters are text to add, `Font` object, `Brush`-inherited object, and coordinates.

- `FillEllipse`: Draws a filled ellipse (circle). Parameters are `Brush`-inherited object (such as the SolidBrush) and list of coordinates (or Rectangle object defining those points).

- `FillPie`: Draws a pie section. Parameters are `Brush`-inherited object, list of coordinates (or `Rectangle` object), and start/end angle values for the pie segment in degrees.

- `FillPolygon`: Draws a polygon (think a circle with eight sides). Parameters are `Brush`-inherited object, array of seven points, and fill mode. The seventh point automatically connects to the last to create the polygon.

- `FillRectangle`: Draws a rectangle. Parameters are `Brush`-inherited object and list of coordinates.

Of course, that's not all. You can create transparent brush fills, for example. You can also use the `GraphicsPath` and `Transform` classes, which form the real "plus" part of GDI+. You can even incorporate DirectX to give your graphics real spunk.

Look up "drawing" (and related subitems) in the help index for more information. Alternatively, check out `http://msdn.microsoft.com/vbasic/donkey.asp` for "Donkey .NET"—a rehash of a classic game, created in Visual Basic .NET and incorporating graphics to blow your socks off.

Add an Exciting Gradient Backdrop, in Code!

Download supporting files at www.apress.com.
The files for this tip are in the "Ch7–Gradient" folder.

Want to add a little more visual impact to your application? How about adding an appealing gradient backdrop to your forms and in just a few lines of code?

That's exactly what this next snippet of code does for you. It accepts top and bottom gradient colors as arguments, then defines the brush and area to paint and displays the effect. Here's the code you'll need:

```
Private Sub DrawFormGradient(ByVal TopColor As Color, ByVal_

        BottomColor As Color)
    ' Draws a gradient using the specified colors
    ' on the entire page
    Dim objBrush As New Drawing2D.LinearGradientBrush _
        (Me.DisplayRectangle, _
        TopColor, _
        BottomColor, _
        Drawing2D.LinearGradientMode.Vertical)
    Dim objGraphics As Graphics = Me.CreateGraphics()
    objGraphics.FillRectangle(objBrush, Me.DisplayRectangle)
    objBrush.Dispose()
    objGraphics.Dispose()
End Sub
```

Next, you need to call the code—typically in response to the Paint event of your Form, like this:

```
Private Sub Form1_Paint(ByVal sender As Object, _
    ByVal e As System.Windows.Forms.PaintEventArgs) Handles MyBase.Paint
    DrawFormGradient(Color.Blue, Color.AliceBlue)
End Sub
```

Here, we're running our function each time that our form is "painted" (that is, "drawn" on the computer screen). It then paints our gradient: a rich blue mixing into a lighter blue. (See Figure 7-12.) Of course, if that's too bold, you may opt for the more subtle White blending into PapayaWhip. Or the mysterious Black merging into DarkOrchid. Or the XP-styled White into CornflowerBlue. But the coloring is, of course, up to you.

Two quick tips: with a little editing, you can change the brush from painting Vertical to Horizontal, ForwardDiagonal, or BackwardDiagonal; and, in the interest of general usability, don't overuse gradients. It could be scary.

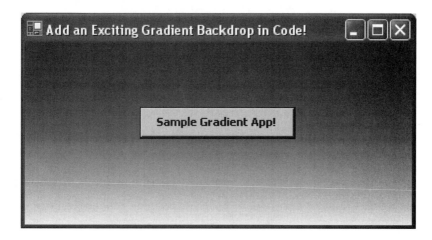

Figure 7-12. My blue to alice blue form. In black and white.

Starting Your Own Screensaver

Download supporting files at www.apress.com.
The files for this tip are in the "Ch7–Screensaver" folder.

Screensavers are often seen as a no-go area for VB .NET programmers. They're not even EXE files and surely fall more within the realm of graphic designers and game developers. *Incorrect.*

The simple fact is that a screensaver, with a .scr file extension, is nothing more than a renamed executable. It's a regular Windows application that has traditionally been developed to display images and look pretty, warding off the terrors of now nonexistent screen burnout.

If you view the Display options through the control panel, you'll see a list of existing screensavers. These are simply files with the .scr extension found in the Windows system directory (that is, c:\Windows\System32).

But how do these applications know to respond to do things such as display the settings box or launch the screensaver? By using parameters. (See "The Power of Command-Line Parameters" tip in Chapter 2 to find out how to read these.) Imagine you click on the Preview button—Windows launches the related SCR file, along with the parameter "/p". The application then needs to look at this value and "preview" display the screensaver.

Other standard parameters are available as well: "/s" informs the screensaver that it needs to display its settings box, and "/a" tells you to display a "change password" dialog box. Then there's the big one: the "/s" parameter indicates that you should run your full screensaver, perhaps displaying graphics in code and exiting when the user moves his or her mouse.

Seem simple enough? Matters like this are almost always best demonstrated through example—and, thankfully, Microsoft has made that task a little easier for me. Surf over to http://msdn.microsoft.com/vbasic/downloads/samples/ and click the screensaver sample link, or access it directly at http://msdn.microsoft.com/library/en-us/dnvssamp/html/vbcs_CreateaScreensaverwithGDI.asp. (The files are also available at www.apress.com, alongside the source for this entire book.)

It doesn't demonstrate the more-advanced features, such as password support or utilizing preview mode, but it does provide a solid grounding on the basics. I've personally written articles on some of the more-advanced features; you may want to check out Developer.com at www.developer.com to dig these up, or you can download existing .NET screensaver code by performing a quick search at www.googlegroups.com.

And that's it: a screensaver is just an EXE file renamed with an .scr extension and placed in the Windows system directory. It accepts parameters and responds accordingly.

Your task is to merge this knowledge together with a little nifty graphics code to create your own screensaver: perhaps a logo-based application that scrolls company news across the screen, or a saver that displays family photographs, selectable through the settings screen. Good luck!

Using the Registry and Event Log

Want to store your settings in the registry? Or are you looking for a ready-to-run function for writing to the Event log? Then sit back and begin reading: this is the section for you!

How to Read and Write the Registry

The registry is a great place to store your application settings. It's used by almost every Windows application, and you can view its entire contents by selecting Start ➤ Run and launching regedit.exe.

To manipulate the registry in your code, you need to use objects inside the Microsoft.Win32 namespace. To simplify this process, the following functions encapsulate all the required code for you, allowing you to read from or write to the registry in just a line of code.

The first function is called ReadFromRegistry. It accepts a location and name of the key to retrieve, returning a string value:

```
Public Function ReadFromRegistry(ByVal Location As String, _
    ByVal Name As String) As String
    ' Returns a value from the registry
    Dim MyKey As Microsoft.Win32.RegistryKey
    MyKey = Microsoft.Win32.Registry.CurrentUser.OpenSubKey(Location)
    ReadFromRegistry = CType(MyKey.GetValue(Name), String)
    MyKey.Close()
End Function
```

The second block of code is a method called WriteToRegistry. It accepts a location, key name, and the actual string to store with the key:

```
Public Sub WriteToRegistry(ByVal Location As String, _
    ByVal Name As String, ByVal Data As String)
    ' Writes a value to the registry
    Dim MyKey As Microsoft.Win32.RegistryKey
    MyKey = Microsoft.Win32.Registry.CurrentUser.CreateSubKey(Location)
    MyKey.SetValue(Name, Data)
    MyKey.Close()
End Sub
```

You could use the preceding functions as follows:

```
WriteToRegistry("Software\White Cliff\MyApp", "Username", "John")
MessageBox.Show(ReadFromRegistry("Software\White Cliff\MyApp", _
    "Username"))
```

Note that my sample functions save and retrieve data specific to the current user in the CurrentUser (HKEY_CURRENT_USER) portion of the registry. If you wish to store global data, accessible by whomever is logged in, simply change this to use the LocalMachine class.

You can also store other types of data in the registry. For more information, look up "Registry class, about Registry class" in the help index, or check out the Microsoft MSDN feature at http://msdn.microsoft.com/library/en-us/ dv_vstechart/html/vbtchaccessingregistrywithvisualbasicnet.asp.

Putting Messages in the Event Log

 Download supporting files at www.apress.com.
The files for this tip are in the "Ch7–Event Log" folder.

The event log is a haven for system administrators. All the great programs use it to record details of how everything went: the batch update completed successfully, the midnight virus update failed, peak usage on Monday occurred at 13:37 P.M.

Now, you too can plug into and place your entry in the log. Here's my own little function to show you how:

```
Public Function WriteToEventLog(ByVal Entry As String, _
    Optional ByVal AppName As String = "VB.NET Application", _
    Optional ByVal EventType As _
    EventLogEntryType = EventLogEntryType.Information, _
    Optional ByVal LogName As String = "Application") As Boolean
    ' Writes an entry to the Event Log
    Dim objEventLog As New EventLog()
    Try
        ' Register app as an Event Source
        If Not objEventLog.SourceExists(AppName) Then
            objEventLog.CreateEventSource(AppName, LogName)
        End If
        objEventLog.Source = AppName
        ' Send entry
        objEventLog.WriteEntry(Entry, EventType)
        Return True
    Catch Ex As Exception
        Return False
    End Try
End Function
```

To use, simply call the WriteToEventLog function, passing in an empty string. You can also optionally specify the application name, event type, and the log to use (that is, "Application"). If you specify a nonexistent log, one will be created for you. The function returns a Boolean dependent on its success.

To finish us off, here are examples of WriteToEventLog in use (see Figure 7-13 to see what this does in the event log):

```
' Simple event log addition
WriteToEventLog("Application has failed to find STARTUP.INI")
' Slightly more complex sample
WriteToEventLog("Unable to parse request LOGON", _
    "Authenticator", EventLogEntryType.Error, "Special Log")
```

> **TOP TIP** *If you take time to explore the* EventLog *class, you'll find many interesting properties to take your work with the event log even further. Most importantly, you'll find* .Clear *and* .Delete *methods at your disposal, allowing you to perform actions even the Event Viewer doesn't support.*

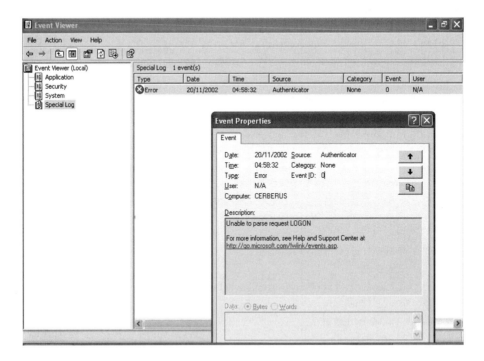

Figure 7-13. Our complex event log sample shown in the Event Viewer

Distributed Computing

It's a term that covers a whole bundle of technologies. So here's a section to match: a whole mound of secrets dedicated to the world of distributed computing. From the quick guide to using MSMQ, to the cheat's guide to XML, to the five steps to transactions with COM+, and more!

The Cheat's Guide to XML

They write entire books on it. They hold conferences dedicated to it. I know at least three cafés named after it. It's XML, it's eXtensible Markup Language, it's an excellent addition to your résumé

But just what is it, really? XML is a method of storing structured data in a pure text format. It uses a system of tags to embed its information, such as a list of customers and their orders. And, as an XML "document" is simply one chunk of text (no matter how in depth or complex the information it holds or the relationships among the individual chunks of information), it is still simply text, making XML an ideal cross-platform data storage mechanism.

> **TOP TIP** *You can learn more about the official XML specification by checking out documents from the World Wide Web Consortium at* www.w3.org/XML/.

To demonstrate this concept, here's a sample, relatively simple XML document:

```xml
<?xml version="1.0"?>
<articles>
    <article id="10">
    <site>VB World</site>
    <type>codesnippet</type>
    <title>The Cheat's Guide to XML</title>
    <shortname>xmlcheat</shortname>
    <description>Need to learn XML fast? .e.t.c. </description>
    <author>Karl Moore</author>
    <authorEmail>karl@karlmoore.com</authorEmail>
    <pages>
    <page number="1">
    <title>Introduction</title>
    <body>Yadda ... yadda ... yadda ...</body>
    </page>
```

```
<page number="2">
<title>Getting More Complicated</title>
<body>Etc ... etc ... etc ... </body>
</page>
</pages>
</article>

<article id="11">
<site>VB Square</site>
<type>review</type>
<title>Review of WebZinc .NET</title>
<shortname>webzinc</shortname>
... and so on ..
</article>
</articles>
```

Here, you can see we have a top-level <articles> tag, containing numerous <article> items. Each item contains an associated unique id attribute, plus numerous subelements that list details such as the site, author name, and a related <pages> segment, listing individual pages and the body text. See how it works? Articles, to article, to pages, to page. It's relational data, stored in a pure text format.

> **TOP TIP** *One simple way to demonstrate the relational style of XML document is to add an XML file (Project ➤ Add New Item) to your Visual Studio .NET project, type in something similar to the preceding XML, then click on Data. You'll be shown your data in grid format—ready for viewing, editing, or adding to!*

So, you pretty much understand what an XML document is: it looks a bit like HTML, stores relational data in tags, plus it's pure text so it can be used cross-platform. What can you use it for? Imagine it as the new, cooler, slightly younger brother of the comma-separated or tab-delimited file format. Anything they can do, XML can do better.

How can you integrate XML with your VB .NET applications? Well, there are five key techniques:

- Create a Web service to expose data from your application. (See Chapter 4, "The Lowdown on Web Services.")

- Read an XML document in code.

- Write an XML document in code.

- Use XML with your DataSets.

- Use XML with SQL Server.

The rest of this tip provides working examples of these last four techniques.

Reading an XML Document in Code

The XmlDocument class in the System.Xml namespace provides everything you need to parse XML data. To use, simply create a new instance of the class, use the .Load or .LoadXml method to get data into the object, then start parsing using the available methods and functions.

Such techniques are typically best demonstrated through sample code—so here's a snippet that uses a common method of cycling through various nodes in the XmlDocument object, retrieving key pieces of information. It's based on the sample XML document shown earlier, and, with a little cross-referencing, should be relatively easy to follow through:

```
' Create new XmlDocument object
Dim objDoc As New System.Xml.XmlDocument()
' Load actual XML
objDoc.Load("c:\filename.xml")
' Create placeholders for node list and individual nodes
Dim objNodeList As System.Xml.XmlNodeList
Dim objNode, objNodeChild As System.Xml.XmlNode
' Retrieve list of article elements
objNodeList = objDoc.GetElementsByTagName("article")
' Cycle through all article elements
For Each objNode In objNodeList
    ' Display article ID numbers
    MessageBox.Show(objNode.Attributes("id").InnerText)
    ' Cycle through all child node of article
    For Each objNodeChild In objNode
        ' Display article site names
        If objNodeChild.Name = "site" Then
            MessageBox.Show(objNodeChild.InnerText)
        End If
    Next
Next
```

After a little reviewing, you can see this is really pretty simple, and this recursive-style code can be easily ported to practically any situation. No matter whether you're handling an XML file created by another application or parsing an XML stream straight from the Net (for example, www.slashdog.org/slashdot.xml), the XmlDocument object can help you out.

> **TOP TIP** *When loading an XML document, you may want to check its structure, ensuring that it adheres to the expected . You do this through an XML schema. We don't cover this here, but you can learn more by looking up "XML, validating XML" in the help index.*

Writing an XML Document in Code

The XmlTextWriter class in the System.Xml namespace can be jolly useful when it comes to outputting XML. To use it, create a new instance of the class, passing a new filename or an appropriate stream in the constructor, plus a potential "encoding" option.

Next, start your document with the .WriteStartDocument method and continue using others, such as .WriteStartElement, .WriteAttributeString, WriteElementString, and .WriteEndElement to create the document. When you're finished, .WriteEndDocument to close all open tags, .Flush to save changes to the file, then .Close.

This is another beast best explained by example, so here goes:

```
' Create a new XmlTextWriter object
Dim objWriter As New System.Xml.XmlTextWriter( _
    "c:\mydocument.xml", System.Text.Encoding.UTF8)
With objWriter
    ' Set the formatting to use neat indentations
    .Formatting = Xml.Formatting.Indented
    ' Write document opening
    .WriteStartDocument()
    ' Begin core XML
    .WriteStartElement("articles")
    ' First article...
    .WriteStartElement("article")
    .WriteAttributeString("id", "10")
    .WriteElementString("site", "VB-World")
    .WriteElementString("type", "codesnippet")
    .WriteElementString("author", "Karl Moore")
```

```
            ' Write list of associated pages
            .WriteStartElement("pages")
            .WriteStartElement("page")
            .WriteAttributeString("number", "1")
            .WriteElementString("title", "My Title")
            .WriteElementString("body", "This is my body text")
            .WriteEndElement()
            .WriteStartElement("page")
            .WriteAttributeString("number", "2")
            .WriteElementString("title", "My Second Title")
            .WriteElementString("body", "This is my 2nd body text")
            ' Close open elements
            .WriteEndElement()
            .WriteEndElement()
            .WriteEndElement()
            .WriteEndElement()
            ' ... Add any further articles here ...
            ' Close document
            .WriteEndDocument()
            .Flush()
            .Close()
        End With
```

Simple enough? It's a very straightforward procedural method of creating an XML file that should suit all XML developers. (See Figure 7-14 for the results of this sample, displayed in Internet Explorer.)

But why not simply build your own XML string and write it straight to a file? Three reasons. First, there are situations in which extra XML tags need to be added to adhere to the official specification. For example, you may be storing HTML in one of your elements. HTML, of course, contains <tags> that may be misinterpreted as actual XML elements. As such, the XmlTextWriter follows the official specification and adds CDATA clauses to the statement, ensuring that any readers correctly identify this as text, not actually part of the document structure. So, firstly, it's a bit more intelligent than a quick file-write routine.

Second, it's very good at automatically handling developer cock-ups, which means, if you have any tag that you've forgotten to close correctly, the XmlTextWriter will automatically step in and fill the gap for you. How kind.

And third—well, it can save data in that pretty indented manner. Personally, I'd prefer not to attempt implementing this with just a regular string. Way too messy.

That's it: the XmlTextWriter. Simple, elegant, procedural. An understated class that could save you hours.

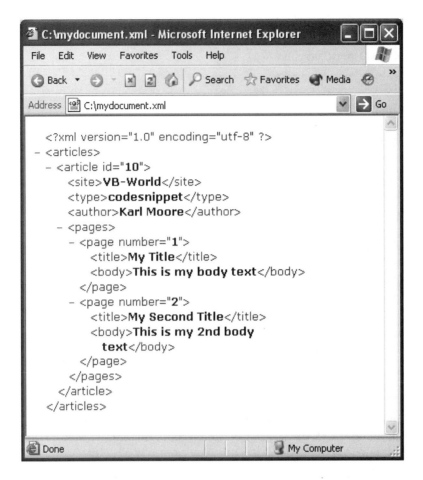

Figure 7-14. Our produced XML document, viewed in Internet Explorer

Using XML and DataSets

DataSets were covered back in Chapter 4 ("Working with Data"). They're basically multitable Recordsets with a few extra frills—and one of those frills is their ability to both accept and output XML with ease.

But how? You need to know about three key DataSet members.

First, there's .GetXml. This excellent function returns an XML representation of the data in your DataSet. It's simple to use and returns a string containing data from all the tables in your DataSet. For example:

```
<MyDataSet xmlns="http://www.karlmoore.com/MyDataSetSchema.xsd">
  <wc_vbwn_article_listing>
    <id>5</id>
    <tag>bettersplit</tag>
    <siteListingid>1</siteListingid>
    <type>3</type>
    <userLevel>3</userLevel>
    <title>VB: A Better Split Function</title>
    <description>When using the Split function ...</description>
    <authorCommunityListingid>3</authorCommunityListingid>
    <added>2002-10-20T13:38:00.0000000+01:00</added>
        <live>true</live>
  </wc_vbwn_article_listing>
  </MyDataSet>
```

The second useful member is the .WriteXml method, which accepts a stream or filename and essentially writes the results of .GetXml directly to it. It saves you writing a separate file-save routine and automatically applies all the fancy indenting, too.

Well, we've had two methods of getting XML out of the DataSet, so now here's our third handy DataSet member—the .ReadXml function, which loads XML into the DataSet. You can use this function with practically any XML source, but I'd recommend sticking to either a simple XML stream, or one that you've previously extracted from the DataSet or have an XSD schema for. It's not required; it's simply a recommendation from experience: complex XML structures aren't as easily manipulated through a DataSet.

> **TOP TIP** *If you're creating a DataSet and want to read straight from an XML file, you may want to first specify an XML schema definition (XSD) so you can catch any data errors. To do this, simply use the schema equivalents of the members we've covered here—*.GetXmlSchema, .WriteXmlSchema, *and* .ReadXmlSchema *—passing your XSD filename as appropriate. If you don't have an XML schema, you can create one manually in VS .NET (Project ➤ Add New Item ➤ XML Schema), or allow it to generate one for you by creating a typed DataSet. See the "Quick, Editable Grid" tips in Chapter 4 ("Working with Data") for a demonstration of generating this XSD "template." If you're completely confused and have no idea what an XML schema is, imagine it as a rulebook for the data in your XML document. Look up "XML Schema, about XML Schema" for more information.*

The Three Words to SQL Server XML Success

Three simple words: *For XML Auto*. Adding these to the end of your SQL statement will result in SQL Server 2000 (and above) returning an XML representation of your data, rather than your regular table of information.

For example, a statement such as SELECT username, password FROM users FOR XML AUTO may return something like this:

```
... <users username="KarlMoore" password="TEST123"/>
    <users username="SuzanneVega" password="MARLENA123"/> ...
```

How can you extract and use this data? My favorite method is simply extracting the XML from the first returned field using .ExecuteScalar, then slapping it straight into an XmlDocument object. After that, I can do what I like —save it, edit it, XSL it, whatever:

```
' Setup Command
Dim objCommand As New System.Data.SqlClient.SqlCommand( _
    "SELECT field1, field2, field3, field4 " & _
    "FROM table1 FOR XML AUTO", _
    MyConnection)
' Retrieve XML
Dim strXML As String = _
    objCommand.ExecuteScalar
' Load data into XmlDocument, adding root level <data> tags
Dim objDoc As New System.Xml.XmlDocument()
objDoc.LoadXml("<data>" & strXML & "</data>")
' … continue as appropriate …
```

The SqlCommand object actually provides its own method—.ExecuteXmlReader—specifically for handling XML data coming back from SQL Server. This function returns an XmlReader object, a sort of forward-only, read-only version of the XmlDocument. Here, I cycle through a few entries, then close the reader:

```
' Setup Command
Dim objCommand As New System.Data.SqlClient.SqlCommand( _
    "SELECT field1, field2, field3, field4 " & _
    "FROM table1 FOR XML AUTO", _
    SqlConnection1)
' Retrieve XMLReader object
Dim objReader As System.Xml.XmlReader = _
    objCommand.ExecuteXmlReader
```

```
' Loop round entries
Do While objReader.Read
    MessageBox.Show(objReader.GetAttribute("field3"))
Loop
' Close XMLReader, freeing up connection
objReader.Close
```

Personally, I don't like working with the XMLReader like this—it's relatively inflexible and ties up your connection until you close the object—but it has certain niche uses, so is listed here for completeness.

Quick XML Review

XML is an interesting topic. Although a lot of unwarranted industry hype surrounds what is still simply a chunk of HTML-like text, there's no denying that that chunk of text is still a great idea and one that won't be fading away anytime soon.

Here, in this rather elongated tip, we've covered the basics of working with XML. There's still much more you might want to learn, however. You may wish to take a further look at more-complex schemas and really understand how they can help you validate your XML, for example. (Look up "XML Schemas, ADO. NET datasets and" and "XML Schemas, creating" in the help index to assist in solidifying these concepts.)

Or you may wish to explore the whole bundle of extra classes in the System.Xml namespace we haven't covered here (the XmlValidatingReader class, for example) or check out the extra XML-related features of SQL Server (the XMLDATA parameter, for instance).

And that's not all. There's also the world of XSL (Extensible Style Sheet Language). You can imagine this almost like a "mail merge" document for your XML. It contains HTML and various XSLT (XSL Transformation) elements, and tells it how to process your XML: put this there, change that to this, cycle through these elements and display them here. It's practically a mini programming language on its own. Find out more for yourself by following a VS .NET walkthrough; look up "XSL, identity transformation" in the help index.

Not everyone will use XML, and fewer still will go all the way with schemas and XSL, so we're going to end this tip here. But remember: XML is a growing standard and beginning to infiltrate all areas of development. So, whether you think it concerns you or not, it might be worthwhile giving XML a peek. You might just surprise yourself.

Further reading: check out www.apress.com for the latest XML titles.

Six Steps to Basic Transactions with COM+

It took me a good few weeks to get my head around the world of transactions in .NET. I spent an absolute age trying to figure out what had happened to Microsoft Transaction Server (MTS).

If you're in the same boat, I'm sorry to inform you that MTS died some time ago. It was merged into a host of services christened COM+ ("We didn't communicate that very well," a Microsoft publicist told me) and is now incorporated in classes under the System.EnterpriseServices namespace. It's all done very differently from the days of yesteryear, too: transactional components in .NET require no complicated configuration nor manual registration. Transactions can be set up and performed entirely in code.

> **TOP TIP** *Many developers used MTS for the database connection pooling it offered. If that's all you're wanting, good news: in .NET, all the* SqlConnection *objects used on a machine are automatically pooled for you, regardless of whether you're using COM+ (the "new MTS"). Look up "connection pooling, ADO.NET connections" in the help index for more information.*

> **ANOTHER TOP TIP** *If you're looking to implement transactions and are only using* one *database on* one *machine, you probably don't need the power nor overhead of COM+ transactions. Check out the SQL Server transaction sample in the Essentials section of Chapter 4 for more information.*

But let's start at the beginning. What exactly is a transaction? A transaction is an operation that must be undertaken as a whole, or not at all. The age-old example of a bank still stands: if your application takes money out of one account to deposit in another, and your machine crashes halfway through, you really don't want to lose that money. You either need to do it all or nothing. If an error occurs during any part of that process, the whole thing needs to be undone.

That's what COM+ enables you to do: implement a stable, time-tested undo mechanism in your code, easily. It can automatically "roll back" your edits in any transaction-aware application, such as SQL Server or Microsoft Message Queue—even if the edits are made on different machines. On the other hand, if all goes well, all edits (no matter which machine they are made upon) are "committed."

How can you put all this into play? Well, you need to start with a class that inherits the "ServicedComponent" class, the base functionality of any transaction. You can then add attributes to your class and its methods, depending on how you want to implement your transaction. You can also work with a ContextUtil object, to commit or abort the transaction.

TOP TIP *Looking for a walkthrough guide to creating your first transaction? Surf to the MSDN article at* http://support.microsoft.com/ default.aspx?scid=kb;en-us;Q315707 *for a simple Northwind database sample project.*

Six core steps are involved in setting up an automatically registering COM+ transactional class. Simply open your project—Windows application, class library, or other—and follow this to-do list:

1. *Reference the* System.EnterpriseServices *DLL.* Click on Project ➤ Add Reference, select System.EnterpriseServices, then click on OK.

2. *Create your core transaction-aware class.* Click on Project ➤ Add New Item, and select Transactional Component. Enter a name, click on Open, and then alter the TransactionOption.Supported value to TransactionOption.Required. Alternatively, click on Project ➤ Add Class and use the following "neater" base for your work.

```
' Automatic transaction template
Imports System.EnterpriseServices
<Transaction(TransactionOption.Required)> _
    Public Class ClassName
    Inherits ServicedComponent

End Class
```

TOP TIP *Here, we have the* Transaction *attribute set with the value* TransactionOption.Required, *the most common setting. This means that, if you are already inside a transaction and call a member of this class, it runs its code and informs the parent transaction how the operation went (and, if it failed, will likely rollback the results of parent transactions, a sort of code domino effect). On the other hand, if you are not in a transaction, this option will create one for you. Other possible options here are* Disabled, NotSupported, RequriesNew, *and* Supported.

3. *Add your transaction-aware methods and functions.* If you want to take advantage of automatic committing, which 'saves' all changes if no error occurs, or performs a rollback if an exception does occur, then use code similar to the following:

```
<AutoComplete()> Public Sub MemberName()
    ' Do processing here, such as accessing
    ' a transaction-aware database.
    ' If exception occurs, transaction fails.
End Sub
```

4. *Use ContextUtil if you wish to control transactions manually.* Instead of relying on an exception to be caught, you may wish to control the whole transaction manually. You do this using the ContextUtil object, with code similar to the following:

```
Public Sub MemberName()
    ' Do processing here, maybe with error handling
    ' When you're satisfied all has worked, run...
    ContextUtil.SetComplete()
    ' If, however you have experienced problems or caught
    ' an exception, roll everything back by running...
    ContextUtil.SetAbort()
End Sub
```

5. *Generate a "strong name" for your application.* To take part in a transaction, COM+ requires your application to have a strong name. This is a random public/private key, merged with your application name, version number, and culture information (if available). To generate the strong name key pair, click on Programs ➤ Microsoft Visual Studio .NET ➤ Visual Studio .NET Tools ➤ Visual Studio .NET Command Prompt. From the DOS-style window, type "sn -k c:\mykeyname.snk" and press Return. You should get a "Key pair written" success message. Open the directory (in this case, the root of the c: drive) to check the file is there—this is your random public/private key pair file. Next, add the following line to AssemblyInfo.vb, telling the application which key pair to utilize for the strong name (for simplicity, we're using a hard coded reference to the path here; using a relative path appears to behave inconsistently between certain VS .NET builds):

```
<Assembly: AssemblyKeyFileAttribute("c:\mykeyname.snk")>
```

> **TOP TIP** *If you plan to use your transactional component outside of the .NET world, you'll need to do three things at this point: provide your assembly with a title in the AssemblyInfo.vb file (used for the COM+ Catalog), manually expose your .NET assembly to COM (see "exposing .NET Framework components to COM"), and register your component in the COM+ Catalog (see "automatic transactions, .NET Framework classes", step four).*

6. Start using your transactional component! If you've developed an internal class, simply call it directly from within your application. Or if you've created the class inside a Class Library project, compile your assembly and then reference from another application.

And that's all there is to implementing basic cross-machine transactions in your applications. Don't get me wrong: COM+ supports many, many more features, such as object and thread pooling, nested transactions, remoting, true MSMQ integration, special security mechanisms, and more. But these simple steps at least provide a handy reference to the base method of handling transactions across multiple machines, our method of ensuring it all happens together... or not at all.

For further reading, check out *Distributed .NET Programming in VB.NET* from Apress (ISBN 1-59059-068-6).

> **TOP TIP** *You can view your COM+ transactional components by clicking on Programs ➤ Administrative Tools ➤ Component Services, and then navigating down to Component Services ➤ Computers ➤ My Computer ➤ COM+ Applications. (See Figure 7-15.) Here, you should be able to view your automatically registered transactional component, plus see any transactions in progress. (Look out for those exciting animated icons!)*

ANOTHER TOP TIP *By simply running our application like this, our COM+ transactional component is automatically registered for us the first time it is used. This isn't a bad thing, but you should be aware of a few things about it. First, your transactional component is registered as a library component, meaning you can't view success/failure statistics via the Distributed Transaction Coordinator. (In Component Services, navigate to My Computer ➤ Distributed Transaction Coordinator). You can change this manually through your application properties (in Component Services, navigate to My Computer ➤ COM+ Applications, view properties for your app, select Activation tab)—or look up "COM+ services, registering serviced components" in the help index for more information. Second, if you change the type of your transaction component (that is, from RequiresNew to Supported), you'll need to reregister your assembly (see the preceding help topic), or alter the COM+ application properties. COM+ does not automatically comprehend that you've changed the transaction attribute. Third, due to a number of interoperability issues, Windows XP and 2000 machines will not show the animated Component Services icon when a library component is involved in a transaction. It's not a huge issue, but certainly one worry to cross off your list of debugging concerns.*

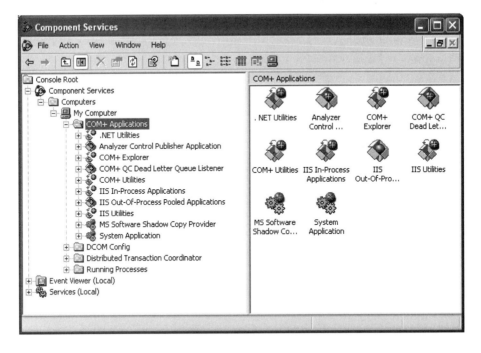

Figure 7-15. Viewing our transactional components in Component Services

Quick Guide to Using MSMQ

 Download supporting files at www.apress.com.
The files for this tip are in the "Ch7–MSMQ Sample" folder.

Microsoft Message Queue (MSMQ) is one of those widgets a lot of developers have heard about, but few really feel confident playing with. It's a tool for the big boys, or so many will have you believe, and not a technology that those working in companies turning over less than ten billion a year should be using.

This, as you may suspect, is balderdash.

But, just in case you haven't heard of MSMQ, let's start at the beginning. What exactly is it? MSMQ is a product now integrated into Windows 2000 and 2003. It allows your applications to send messages and for other applications to pick up those messages. The message may be sent to applications on the same computer, or on a different computer. The other computer doesn't even have to be online when the message is sent; it will be automatically delivered when a connection is made.

In other words, MSMQ is email for your code.

Here's how it works. To send a message, you set up a MessageQueue object, specifying a queue "path." (If you're playing along with the email analogy, imagine this as the mail address.) You check whether the queue path exists: if not, you create it. Next, you simply send your message. It'll then wait in your analogical Outbox and send itself to that queue when possible (say, immediately, or the next time you connect to the network).

So that's how you send a message. But how about receiving one?

To receive a message, your application needs to "tune in" to your queue path and turn up the volume. When your application notices that a message has been received, your MessageQueue object fires off an event for you to respond to. You may look at the message and confirm payment on a customer order, add a comment to the user profile, or update existing stock levels. Your message doesn't just have to be pure text either: you can "serialize" objects and send those as well.

Let's look at how we can implement MSMQ technology in our applications in six easy steps:

1. Check that Microsoft Message Queue is installed. It's likely you've already got MSMQ on your machine, but, just in case, open up the control panel and go to Add/Remove Programs. Click on the Add/Remove Windows Components button and ensure that Message Queuing is checked. If not, check it and follow through the wizard. If you're using Windows NT 4, download the option pack from www.microsoft.com/NTServer/nts/downloads/recommended/NT4OptPk/ and select to install Microsoft Message Queue Server 1.0.

2. Reference `System.Messaging.dll`. With your project open, click on Project ➤ Add Reference and select the System.Messaging.dll, then click on OK.

3. Add a `MessageQueue` object to your class. Drag and drop the `MessageQueue` item from the Components tab on the toolbox onto your form or class in Design mode.

4. Change the `Path` property. Alter the `Path` property to the queue you wish to use. This is a combination of the machine name and the queue ("mailbox") name. On my machine, for example, I'm using "`nemean\private$\testapp`" as my `Path` property. *Nemean* is the name of the other computer on the network, *testapp* is the name of my queue, and the *private$* bit in the middle indicates that this is a private queue. (Public queues are also available, and these work in exactly the same way, but are "published" throughout the network, unlike private queues. They also require that your administrator first set up a special MSMQ network. A sample queue `Path` for a public queue might be `nemean\testapp`.)

> **TOP TIP** *You can browse the existing queues, either on your local machines or machines on your network, by clicking on View ➤ Server Explorer, then navigating to a machine and viewing the Message Queues node. (See Figure 7-16.)*

5. In your client application, add the code to send your message. The following chunk of sample code demonstrates checking for the existing of a queue, creating it if it isn't available, and then sending a message. The message is split into two parts: the body and a "label" (the equivalent of an email subject line), as shown here:

```
' Check for existence of queue
If MessageQueue1.Exists(MessageQueue1.Path) = False Then
    MessageQueue1.Create(MessageQueue1.Path)
End If

' Send message - body and "label"
MessageQueue1.Send( _
    "ConfirmOrderTotal: $69.95", _
    "Customer:952")
```

6. In your server application, add code to "receive" your message. First, you'll need to tune in by running the `.BeginReceive` function of your `MessageQueue` object. You may do this when your application starts, say, in response to the form `Load` event:

```
' Run this at the beginning to
' "listen" for new messages
MessageQueue1.BeginReceive()
```

When a message drops in, the `ReceiveCompleted` event of the `MessageQueue` object kicks in, passing with it a "handle" to the message. You then use this to receive the whole message, process it, then once again begin "listening" for any new messages. Here's sample code to do just that, to be used in response to the `ReceiveCompleted` event:

```
' Receive message
Dim objMsg As System.Messaging.Message = _
    MessageQueue1.EndReceive(e.AsyncResult)

' Process the message -
' here, we're simply showing it to the user
MessageBox.Show(objMsg.Label & " - " & objMsg.Body)

' Begin "listening" again
MessageQueue1.BeginReceive()
```

That's it: this is literally all you need to do to send and receive messages in your application. These, of course, are just the facts. To bring them to life in the real world, you need to add imagination. Which applications would benefit from being able to communicate through messages? How can this technology help those with laptops, those who are often on the road and offline for most of the day? Where in your company is there a need to perhaps serialize and queue up `Customer`, `Order`, or `Stock` objects, waiting to be processed? And that is where you come in.

For further reading, check out `www.apress.com` for the latest MSMQ titles.

TOP TIP *There's more to be discovered in the world of MSMQ. To learn more about serializing objects so they can be sent through MSMQ, look up "serializing messages" in the help index. To "peek" at messages without actually removing the message from the original queue, look up "peeking at messages" in the help index. To find out about receiving a delivery acknowledgment for a message you sent, look up "message queues, acknowledging delivery to" in the help index.*

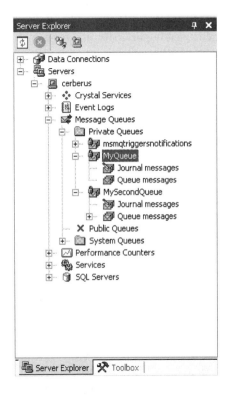

Figure 7-16. Viewing available queues through the Server Explorer

Which to Choose: Web Services vs. Remoting

Web services and remoting are both methods of getting computers to communicate and share data with each other. Both techniques can work through IIS, both can pass data through firewalls, both can use HTTP for communication, and both can use SOAP-compliant data formatting. But, ever since Microsoft dropped the curtains on the .NET Framework, developers have been asking, "Erm, so what's the difference between the two?"

It's a good question—and one that few Microsoft support engineers enjoy answering. However, there *is* a difference, and this tip will reveal all.

Web services are part of ASP.NET and hosted in IIS. With Web services, you can expose stateless functions to the world, which are typically called through HTTP and a SOAP XML-based response automatically returned.

Remoting is a technology that allows .NET applications to talk to each other, instantiating classes running on another machine. Remoting is more flexible than Web services, but it doesn't necessarily conform to any open standard. It can be thought of as the most flexible replacement for DCOM and requires a program running on the target machine as the "server."

Yes, there's some overlap between the two technologies, but the decision over which to choose is relatively simple.

Do you need to expose your data to the outside world using open standards? Do you need to utilize caching easily? Are your clients working on a non-.NET platform? Do you need any of the special IIS features, such as security and logging? Are you unable to run a remoting "server" program on the target machine? If you answered yes to any of these questions, then you need to use Web services. Check out Chapter 5 for more information. Sample Web services include an online telephone directory or a product query service.

Do you need to use stateful objects in your development work? Do you require the use of properties and events? Do you need to use the raw binary TCP socket for faster communication? Do you need a custom "server" host for your program? Are 100% of your clients going to be .NET applications? Would you prefer not to use IIS, but rather peer-to-peer communication? If you answered yes to any of these questions, then you need to use .NET remoting. Try looking up "remoting communication" in the help index to learn more. Sample uses for .NET remoting include a proprietary instant messaging application or the excellent Terrarium project (www.gotdotnet.com/terrarium/).

If, however, you're somewhat indifferent to all of these questions, go for Web services. They're easier to get started with and, seasoned with a few custom hacks, can be expanded upon to do most things.

So there we have it: Web services are easy, they're for open standards, they're for SOAP and IIS. Remoting is for .NET-to-.NET applications, it's for complex objects, it's for speed and customization. They are different, but they do overlap. That's just the way it is.

For further reading, check out *Distributed .NET Programming in VB.NET* from Apress (ISBN 1-59059-068-6).

Visual Studio Tips

Figure out how to really use your Visual Studio development environment to the max with this ace collection of secrets. From your quick guide to upgrading, COM and the API, to the tricks behind the VS .NET Command window, from a little-known place you can store often-used code to how you can tell if you're running in the IDE—and much more.

Writing a Developer TODO: List

The Task window in VB .NET is a great way of keeping track of tasks that are related to your project. For example, if you have code issues or compile errors, VB .NET will automatically list them here.

You can also add your own comments to the Task list, with the TODO keyword. To use this feature, simply add a comment to your code that starts with the TODO keyword. It will automatically be added to your existing Task list. For example:

```
' TODO: Rewrite function so works with .DOC files
```

To view the Task list, select View ➤ Other Windows ➤ Task List from the menu, or press Ctrl+Alt+K. The Task list often filters its contents, so it displays only certain information. To view everything, right-click on your list and select All Tasks ➤ All. (See Figure 7-17.)

> **TOP TIP** *Fed up with the* TODO *keyword? Users of Visual Studio .NET 2003 (Everett) have automatic support for the "HACK" prefix, which works in the exact same way as* TODO *yet attracts much more kudos. You can edit the Task list keywords yourself by editing the values in Tools ➤ Options ➤ Environment ➤ Task List.*

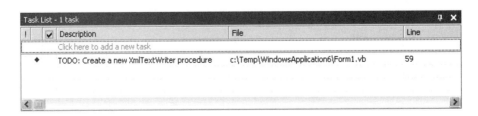

Figure 7-17. If only all TODO lists were this short....

Storing Often-Used Code in the Toolbox

There's an easy way to store often-used code and templates in VS .NET. Simply drag and drop your code straight onto one of the toolbox tabs, such as the General tab. (See Figure 7-18.) When you need to use it again, simply drag and drop back into your code window. And, best of all, these snippets persist from project to project, saving even more development time.

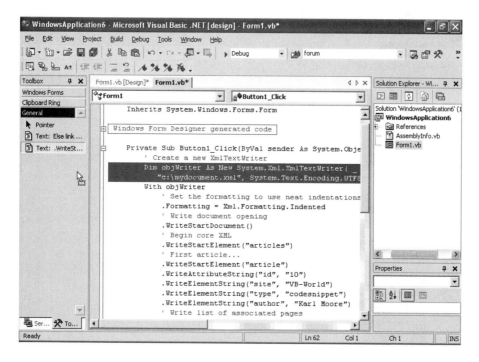

Figure 7-18. Adding code to the toolbox

Organizing Your Project with Folders

Overwhelmed with the number of files that now make up your application? Starting to loose track of which VB files do what? Well, there's a simple method of keeping track. Use folders!

Right-click on your project in the Solution Explorer and select Add ➤ New Folder. Then simply drag and drop your existing code files into the new folders. For example, you may have one folder called "User Interface" to store your forms, or a folder called "Database Code" to store your data access classes.

Don't worry: there's no extra configuration required, and your entire project compiles as normal with no extra effort. It simply allows you to organize your project the way it should be.

A simple tip, but one that can turn chaos into control within minutes. (See Figure 7-19.)

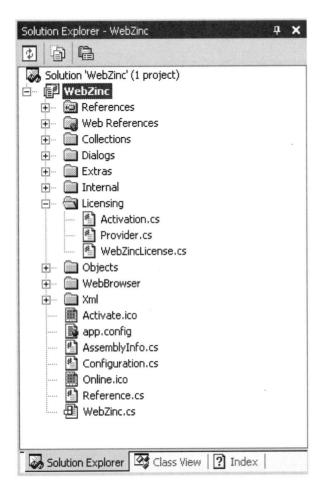

Figure 7-19. One of my company C# projects, really taking advantage of folders

Figuring out the Command Window

The Command window in Visual Studio .NET allows you to both perform command operations as well as evaluate statements (see Figure 7-20), depending on its mode. To open the Command window, select View ➤ Other Windows ➤ Command Window from the menu, or press Ctrl+Alt+A.

The Command mode allows you to access common Visual Studio .NET commands. To enter this mode, type ">cmd" into the window and press the Enter key. After this, you can access the various menu commands by typing them directly into this window (for example, Window.CloseAllDocuments to close all current documents). Type "alias" for a full list of alias shortcuts (for example, CloseAll).

The more-useful Immediate mode is used for evaluating and executing statements while your code is paused at runtime. To enter this mode, type "immed" into the window and press Enter. After this, you can use the window to run commands, set variables, or read values (for example, MyVariable = "Etc" or ? MyVariable). Visual Studio .NET 2003 users also get the popup properties/methods list, allowing them to browse an object.

Press the F1 key while inside the Command window for more information on the commands available.

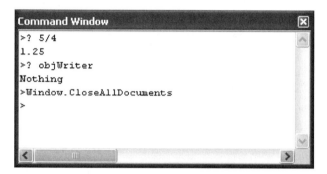

Figure 7-20. A sample command window in use

Discovering Whether You're Running in the IDE

Previous versions of Visual Basic made it easy to figure out whether you were running your application through the IDE (Integrated Development Environment). It simply allowed you to check which "mode" your application was in. VB .NET, however, isn't quite as easy going.

The most common method of figuring out whether the application is running in the .NET IDE is to check the System.Diagnostics.Debugger.IsAttached property to determine whether if a debugger is attached to the currently executing code. If so, you can safely assume your code is running from within the IDE.

If you're designing your own controls, you might also run into the situation where your code is running in design mode—while you want it to execute only during "full" runtime. In this situation, simply check the DesignMode property of your component (that is, from inside your control: Me.DesignMode). If it returns True, you're running in the IDE—so cut your code short.

Simple solutions to common questions, and definitely worth remembering.

Saving Time by Recording Macros

If you have a repetitive task that you often perform in the Visual Studio .NET development environment, you might want to consider creating it as a macro and running it when you require that functionality once more.

For example, you might create a macro to print all the open documents, add customized revision markers, change project properties to standardize your development, or insert common routines.

You can get highly in-depth with macros, writing code to perform almost any task. However, the simplest method is to simply record your activities and have Visual Studio .NET write the code for you. You can do this by selecting Tools ➤ Macros ➤ Record TemporaryMacro. To play it back, select Run TemporaryMacro from the same menu, or press Ctrl+Shift+P.

For more information on recording macros, look up "macros, recording" in the help index. For more information on macros in general, look up "macros, Visual Studio .NET" in the help index.

Using the VS .NET Command Prompt

As you work through the Visual Studio .NET documentation, you'll start to realize just how many tools require you to run them from the command line for full control.

However, setting the proper directory and locating the exact EXE file required via the command prompt can prove troublesome. Thankfully, Visual Studio .NET comes with a feature that automatically sets up a command prompt with all the correct environment variables ready for you to use.

To access this, select Start ➤ Programs ➤ Microsoft Visual Studio .NET ➤ Visual Studio .NET Tools ➤ Visual Studio .NET Command Prompt. (See Figure 7-21.) Task complete!

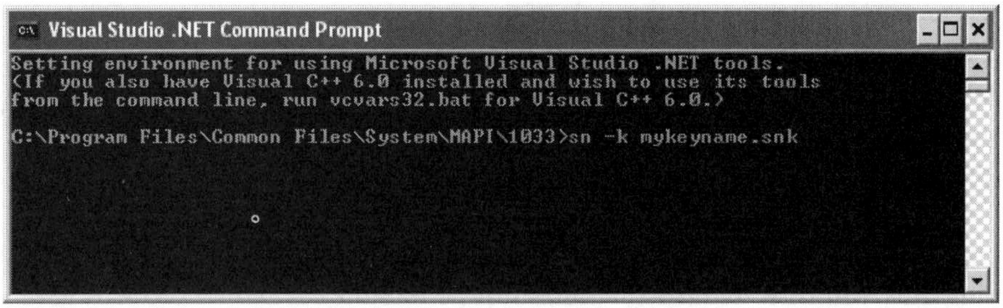

Figure 7-21. The command prompt, ready for use

The Old School: Upgrading, COM, and the API

Most books like to dedicate a good couple of chapters to moving from the old school of Visual Basic 6 programming. This one is different, of course. In the interest of saving your time and cutting all those excess pages, I'm going to chop it all down to just three simple paragraphs—one dedicated to each of the main topics: upgrading, COM, and the API.

First, upgrading. Yes, you can do it; simply open your existing Visual Basic 6 project in VS .NET, and an upgrade wizard will pop up and do its darned hardest to move your code to .NET. Most of the time it simply alters your functions so they use those in the rather uncool `Microsoft.VisualBasic` namespace, implemented in the .NET Framework to allow VB6 people to upgrade without feeling lost. On the whole, I'd recommend only fresh development work be undertaken in .NET: simple "ports" like this never really work or are done for all the wrong reasons.

Second, COM. Frankly, it's just too big to die. If you want to use a COM DLL/EXE in your application (for automating Word, say), click on Project, Add Reference, and select your item through the COM tab, then click OK. If you want to use a COM control, right-click on the toolbox, select Customize Toolbox, check a COM component, and click on OK. Note that you may experience a slight performance knock due to .NET having to interoperate with the world of COM, but on the whole things should work pretty much the same as they did before. Also, if you want COM-supporting languages to see your .NET widgets, that's possible too. Look up "exposing .NET Framework components to COM" in the help index for more information.

Finally, the Windows API. Although it's still available on Windows machines, Microsoft is trying to drag everyone into the .NET Framework, which allows you to write "managed" code, with resources monitored and allocated for you automatically. It also fits in with the long-term Microsoft vision of a "sort of" platform-independent programming language (that is, one based on a framework, not Windows). You can, however, still call the API directly with ease (as demonstrated in the "INI Files Will Never Die: How to in .NET" tip earlier in this chapter). You can read more about this by looking up "Windows API, calling" in the help index. Still, if possible, I'd recommend that you figure out a .NET alternative to the API; either search the newsgroups at `www.googlegroups.com` or check out the .NET section of `www.allapi.net`, a Web site listing API functions and their related .NET equivalents. (Although the site has unfortunately stopped updating its pages, it still serves as a highly useful reference.)

CHAPTER 8

Unveiled: The Hidden .NET Language

THERE'S A HIDDEN LANGUAGE somewhere in the world of .NET. It's a language that few know about, yet thousands could benefit from. It's a language so potentially complex it can take hours to understand just one line of code.

It's the language of *regular expressions*.

So, what is a regular expression? Microsoft rather blandly defines it as a "concise and flexible notation for finding and replacing patterns of text." That's like saying Big Ben is an interesting clock. You see, expressions are *so much more* than that. They're a highly cool method of taking a specially written piece of text, an expression—similar to the way you'd use the "*.doc" expression when searching for Word documents—then using it to manipulate your text in a special way.

For example, you may want to find all matches for a particular expression in a piece of text (such as finding all the U.S. telephone numbers in a document). You may wish to check whether a piece of text adheres to a particular expression (such as checking that a credit card number is of the correct format). You may wish to replace certain text using your expression (such as removing expletives from forum posts), or reorganize the text using your expression (such as changing an American-styled date into a British one).

It's powerful—and can save you hours of development time.

I'll give you an example. Previously, I've written function upon function, each dozens of lines long, to perform the complex task of searching a chunk of HTML for links and extracting as appropriate. It was in-depth. It took me at least two days and was buggy as hell.

If I would've known about regular expressions, however, I could've implemented a little code to use the expression a.*href\s*=\s*(?:""(?<1>[^""]*)""|(?<1>\S+)). It looks confusing. It *is* confusing. But it also does the bug-free job of my line-upon-line of my weird `Mid`, `InStr`, and `Like` code.

How It Works

Everything you need to make regular expressions work hides under the `System.Text.RegularExpressions` namespace. The main class behind this namespace is `Regex`, which hosts a handful of functions for manipulating text using your expression.

So, how do you write your expression in the first place? Dozens of books, thousands of Web sites, and millions of magazine articles all offer to teach you this very skill. You see, regular expressions are nothing new: they've been around forever. They have only just been made intrinsically available to the Visual Basic developer, however, through the .NET Framework.

Anyone can learn how to write a regular expression. Looking up "regular expressions, overview" in the help index will give you a pretty good lowdown, but that's not what this book is about. This book is about providing you with instant solutions to everyday programming problems.

In other words, I'm going to show you the exact regular expressions you need to deal with 95% of the situations you'll come across. I'll show you expressions I've created to search for links in HTML, expressions to check for a correct U.S. or U.K. telephone numbers, expressions to validate the major credit cards, expressions that can enforce secure passwords, and expressions that ensure data is correct and can be used with the `RegularExpressionValidator` control.

I'll drop in tips on how to personalize the expressions. I'll provide commented sample code to demonstrate how to use these regular expressions in Visual Basic .NET. I'll show you what will create a "match" and what won't. The hard work has been done—and all you need to do is take advantage of it. Ready?

> **TOP TIP** *If you're looking for a solid tutorial on regular expressions, check out Dan Appleman's* Regular Expressions with .NET *e-book on Amazon.com. It's instantly downloadable and priced at approximately $14. There's also a new, free software package available to help you design and edit your regular expressions. It's called "RegexDesigner .NET" and is available for download at* `www.sellsbrothers.com/products/`.

Your Regex Library

Are you ready to explore your own exclusive library of ready-to-run regular expressions, sample code and all? Here's a listing of the exciting tips we'll be covering in this chapter:

- Exactly-One-Digit Checker

- Real Number Matcher

- Alphanumerical Matcher: No Spaces or Dots

- 24-Hour Clock Time Check

- Identifying Valid Dates

- File Path and Extension Check

- Checking for Repeated Words

- Getting Capitalized Words

- Matching Numbers from a String

- Who Are You?—Name Checker

- Naughty-Word Filter Expression

- True Email Address Validation

- Validating a Web Site Address

- Internet URL Matcher: FTP, HTTP, HTTPS

- Checking for a Valid Domain

- IP Address Checker

- Extracting Links and Images from HTML

- Checking HTML Color Codes

- Credit Card Validation

- Password Format Enforcing Expression

- Defining Your Own HTML: Custom Tags, with Expressions

- ISBN Checker

- Is That a GUID?

- U.S. ZIP Code Checker

- U.S. Social Security Number Checker

- U.S. Phone Number Checker

- U.S. State Checker

- U.K. Postal Code Matcher

- U.K. National Insurance Number Check

- U.K. Telephone Number Validator

- Converting American and British Dates

- French, German, and Japanese Expressions

- The Simple Cure for "Loose" Expressions

Enough talk. A little less conversation, a little more action....

Exactly-One-Digit Checker

Starting off simply, we're going to look at two regular expressions that will match exactly one digit—firstly, any digit between zero and nine, and, secondly, one digit between a certain range. We'll be using the `System.Text.RegularExpressions.Regex.IsMatch` shared function to compare a value with our expression. If a match occurs, a `True` is returned.

One-Digit Regular Expression

Expression: `^\d$`
Sample matches: 0, 5, 3
Sample nonmatches: K, 492, Jazz
Sample VB .NET code:
```
Dim blnMatch As Boolean, strValue As String = "5"
blnMatch = System.Text.RegularExpressions.Regex.IsMatch( _
    strValue, "^\d$")
```

One Digit in Range Regular Expression

Expression: ^[5-8]$ (the 5 and 8 boundaries can be altered to any single digit)
Sample matches: 5, 6, 8
Sample nonmatches: 3, 9, K
Sample VB .NET code:

```
Dim blnMatch As Boolean, strValue As String = "10"
blnMatch = System.Text.RegularExpressions.Regex.IsMatch( _
    strValue, "^[5-8]$")
```

Real Number Matcher

It's often useful to check for a *real* number, without having to resort to the less-flexible and now-defunct IsNumeric function. This regular expression does just that and allows for an optional positive or negative sign, too.

Real Number Regular Expression

Expression: ^[-+]?\d+(\.\d+)?$
Sample matches: 18, +3.142, -0.20
Sample nonmatches: 540-70, .70, 250x
Sample VB .NET code:

```
Dim blnMatch As Boolean, strValue As String = "-0.20"
blnMatch = System.Text.RegularExpressions.Regex.IsMatch( _
    strValue, "^[-+]?\d+(\.\d+)?$")
```

Alphanumerical Matcher: No Spaces or Dots

It's occasionally useful to check whether a string consists of purely alphabetical and numeric characters—and not the likes of spaces, dots, backslashes, or other weird whatnots. This expression is best used to ensure a user has chosen an acceptable username and password during signup.

Alphanumerical Regular Expression

Expression: `^[a-zA-Z0-9]+$`
Sample matches: karlmoore, 10b, green63
Sample nonmatches: 3.142, United Kingdom, $48
Sample VB .NET code:
```
Dim blnMatch As Boolean, strValue As String = "karl.moore"
blnMatch = System.Text.RegularExpressions.Regex.IsMatch( _
    strValue, "^[a-zA-Z0-9]+$")
```

24-Hour Clock Time Check

This next regular expression can be a real gem. It checks for a valid time in the HH:MM 24-hour clock format.

24-Hour HH:MM Regular Expression

Expression: `^([0-1][0-9]|[2][0-3]):([0-5][0-9])$`
Sample matches: 12:00, 19:34, 02:57
Sample nonmatches: 02:57am, 12:18 PM, 24:00
Sample VB .NET code:
```
Dim blnMatch As Boolean, strValue As String = "17:57"
blnMatch = System.Text.RegularExpressions.Regex.IsMatch( _
    strValue, "^([0-1][0-9]|[2][0-3]):([0-5][0-9])$")
```

Identifying Valid Dates

It's often useful to identify valid dates, but, with `IsDate` now relegated to the "uncool" `Microsoft.VisualBasic` namespace, developers are looking for another method of checking.

This little expression checks that the format of a value matches the format XX/XX/YYYY, where "XX" can be either one or two digits and "YYYY" is always exactly four digits. It's not foolproof, as the sample matches show, but it's useful as a stopgap check. (See "Checking for a Date the Intelligent .NET Way" in Chapter 7 for a more sound method of checking for a valid date.)

XX/XX/YYYY Date Checker Regular Expression

Expression: ^\d{1,2}(\/|-)\d{1,2}(\/|-)\d{4}$
Sample matches: 1/1/2004, 20/05/1975, 99/99/9999
Sample nonmatches: 1/1/04, 001/01/2004, 08-08-2004
Sample VB .NET code:

```
Dim blnMatch As Boolean, strValue As String = "05/02/2004"
blnMatch = System.Text.RegularExpressions.Regex.IsMatch( _
    strValue, "^\d{1,2}(\/|-)\d{1,2}(\/|-)\d{4}$")
```

File Path and Extension Check

Imagine that the user types in a filename. You may not want to use the typed file just yet (perhaps it doesn't exist), but check that its path format is correct and that the file extension is appropriate. The following expression does just that, and even handles network locations.

File Path Regular Expression

Expression: ^([a-zA-Z]\:|\\)\\([^\\]+\\)*[^\/:*?"<>|]+\.DOC(1)?$ *(alter the DOC here to your "valid" file extension, use "IgnoreCase")*
Sample matches: c:\data.doc, e:\whitecliff\staff\km\file.DOC, \\network\km\file.doc
Sample nonmatches: c:\, c:\myreport.txt, sitrep.doc
Sample VB .NET code:

```
Dim blnMatch As Boolean, strValue As String = "c:\files\report.doc"
blnMatch = System.Text.RegularExpressions.Regex.IsMatch( _
    strValue, "^([a-zA-Z]\:|\\)\\([^\\]+\\)*[^\/:*?""<>|]+\.doc(1)?$", _
    System.Text.RegularExpressions.RegexOptions.IgnoreCase)
```

Checking for Repeated Words

Code for handling regular expressions is pretty standard. In fact, there are three core techniques: using .IsMatch as we have so far; using .Replace as we will shortly; and, retrieving a list of matches from a chunk of text and then cycling through the results. That's the format adopted by the following regular expression, which checks for repeated words in a string—especially useful for error checking. This expression works using back references and word boundaries and is generally a little more complex than the ones we've seen so far.

Repeated-Words Regular Expression

Expression: \b(\w+)\s+\1\b (*use "IgnoreCase"*)
Sample matches: apple apple, and the the views were amazing, Truly truly
Sample nonmatches: karl, an occurrence, didn't didn't (*apostrophe, hyphens and most other nonalphabetic characters split words*)
Sample VB .NET code:

```
    ' Setup class references
Dim objRegEx As System.Text.RegularExpressions.Regex
Dim objMatch As System.Text.RegularExpressions.Match
' Create regular expression
objRegEx = New System.Text.RegularExpressions.Regex( _
    "\b(\w+)\s+\1\b", _
    System.Text.RegularExpressions.RegexOptions.IgnoreCase _
    Or System.Text.RegularExpressions.RegexOptions.Compiled)
' Match our text with the expression
objMatch = objRegEx.Match("Why didn't they they ask Evans?")
' Loop through matches and display captured portion in MessageBox
While objMatch.Success
    Dim strMatch As String
    strMatch = objMatch.Groups(1).ToString
    MessageBox.Show(strMatch)
    objMatch = objMatch.NextMatch()
End While
```

Getting Capitalized Words

This next expression is relatively simple and could have a number of different uses, like identifying "proper" nouns such as names and places, or picking out keywords for summarizing a document. It matches with words that begin with a capitalized letter and have the rest of the word in lowercase. Watch out, however: this expression uses word boundaries, defining words as an alphabetic string separated by nonalphabetic characters. So this means that *didn't* is classed as two separate words (*Didn* and *t*). Worth keeping in mind.

Capitalized-Word Regular Expression

Expression: (\b[^\Wa-z0-9_][^\WA-Z0-9_]*\b)
Sample matches: Amazing, Peter, Bonbon
Sample nonmatches: james, VB .NET, BizArre
Sample VB .NET code:

```
    ' Setup class references
Dim objRegEx As System.Text.RegularExpressions.Regex
Dim objMatch As System.Text.RegularExpressions.Match
' Create regular expression
objRegEx = New System.Text.RegularExpressions.Regex( _
    "(\b[^\Wa-z0-9_][^\WA-Z0-9_]*\b)", _
    System.Text.RegularExpressions.RegexOptions.Compiled)
' Match our text with the expression
objMatch = objRegEx.Match("VB.NET Secrets is A ReAl amazin' Read!")
' Loop through matches and display matching value in MessageBox
While objMatch.Success
    Dim strMatch As String
    strMatch = objMatch.Value
    MessageBox.Show(strMatch)
    objMatch = objMatch.NextMatch()
End While
```

Matching Numbers from a String

Being able to pick out the numbers from a string is a highly useful type of artificial intelligence. You may wish to automatically parse appropriate account numbers from an email message and suggest them to your customer service advisor, for example. This expression enables you to pass it a string and return individual matches on all the sets of numerical data contained therein. The expression is actually similar to the "Real Number Matcher" tip earlier, but, instead of just checking whether one string matches, our code searches and returns all matches in a string.

Matching-Numbers Regular Expression

Expression: (\d+\.?\d*|\.\d+)
Sample matches: 75, 0.01, 812.15
Sample nonmatches: one, eight pounds, £-.
Sample VB .NET code:

```
' Setup class references
Dim objRegEx As System.Text.RegularExpressions.Regex
Dim objMatch As System.Text.RegularExpressions.Match
' Create regular expression
objRegEx = New System.Text.RegularExpressions.Regex( _
    "(\d+\.?\d*|\.\d+)", _
    System.Text.RegularExpressions.RegexOptions.Compiled)
' Match our text with the expression
objMatch = objRegEx.Match("John is 50. Acct #32315. Owes $34.21.")
' Loop through matches and display matching value in MessageBox
While objMatch.Success
    Dim strMatch As String
    strMatch = objMatch.Value
    MessageBox.Show(strMatch)
    objMatch = objMatch.NextMatch()
End While
```

Who Are You?—Name Checker

I like this one. It's cool. It's intelligent. It's a name checker: simply pass in the first and/or last name of a person in any case, and it'll match on a "valid" name. It's not perfect, but it'll filter out many incorrect name formats, such as those containing invalid characters or numerical data. It's great for quickly removing invalid entries in your mailing list or deleting spam from your inbox.

Valid-Name Regular Expression

Expression: ^[a-zA-Z]+(([\'\,\.\-][a-zA-Z])?[a-zA-Z]*)*$
Sample matches: K. Moore, Mike O'Brien, Elizabeth Du-Banter
Sample nonmatches: Karl01, Mike_brien, john--doe
Sample VB .NET code:

```
Dim blnMatch As Boolean, strValue As String = "Visual Basic .NET"
blnMatch = System.Text.RegularExpressions.Regex.IsMatch( _
    strValue, "^[a-zA-Z]+(([\'\,\.\- ][a-zA-Z ])?[a-zA-Z]*)*$")
```

Naughty-Word Filter Expression

If you're running a site where users are allowed to make unmoderated posts, you may need to screen offensive language. Well, this regular expression can help filter even the naughtiest of swear words. It matches a whole word and will replace it with the phrase of your choice. You simply need to replace the sample words with your own, separating each entry with the pipe character (|).

Profanity Filter Regular Expression

Expression: (\bdamn\b)|(\bhell\b) (*change to use your own words. Use "IgnoreCase" where appropriate*)
Sample matches: damn, to hell with that, you are a Hell's Angel
Sample nonmatches: be damned, hello squire, hellish bean
Sample VB .NET code:

```
Dim objRegEx As New System.Text.RegularExpressions.Regex( _
    "(\bdamn\b)|(\bhell\b)", _
    System.Text.RegularExpressions.RegexOptions.IgnoreCase)
Dim strValue As String = "Oh hell, fiend, damn you!"
Dim strResult As String = _
    objRegEx.Replace(strValue, "#@%$!!")
```

True Email Address Validation

You'll find many email address regular expressions winging around the Web these days, but they never really take into account the variety of addresses that are available, and usually cater only to mainstream users with AOL accounts. Those with email addresses based on an IP address, or using little-known country codes, often get ignored. The following regular expression, however, adheres to the email address naming specification and should match on all valid addresses.

Real Email Regular Expression

Expression: ^([a-zA-Z0-9_\-\.]+)@((\[[0-9]{1,3}\.[0-9]{1,3}\.[0-9]{1,3}\.)|(([a-zA-Z0-9\-]+\.)+))([a-zA-Z]{2,4}|[0-9]{1,3})(\]?)$
Sample matches: karl@karlmoore.com, foo12@bar6.edu, a.lan@bury.tv
Sample nonmatches: karl, @karlmoore.com, john@johnsplace

Sample VB .NET code:
```
Dim blnMatch As Boolean, strValue As String = "karl@karlmoore.com"
blnMatch = System.Text.RegularExpressions.Regex.IsMatch(strValue, _
    "^([a-zA-Z0-9_\-\.]+)@((\[[0-9]{1,3}\.[0-9]{1,3}\.[0-9]{1,3}\.)" & _
    "|(([a-zA-Z0-9\-]+\.)+))([a-zA-Z]{2,4}|[0-9]{1,3})(\]?)$")
```

Validating a Web Site Address

Looking to ensure that your user has entered a correctly formatted Web site address, including the HTTP? This is the regular expression for you.

Web Site Address Regular Expression

Expression: `^(http://([\w-]+\.)+[\w-]+(/[\w- ./?%&=]*)?)$`
Sample matches: `http://www.karlmoore.com, http://mtv.com/`
Sample nonmatches: `www.yahoo.com, cnn.com`
Sample VB .NET code:
```
Dim blnMatch As Boolean, strValue As String = "http://www.bbc.co.uk/"
blnMatch = System.Text.RegularExpressions.Regex.IsMatch(strValue, _
    "^http://([\w-]+\.)+[\w-]+(/[\w- ./?%&=]*)?")
```

Internet URL Matcher: FTP, HTTP, HTTPS

Most supposed "URL" regular expressions don't match against the likes of ftp:// and https://. But not this one—it will match against all ftp://, http://, and https:// URLs. Here, I'm also using three sets of code to demonstrate the expression: first, a simple match; second, cycling through a document and extracting all matching URLs; and, third, "hyperlinking" all matches using the .Replace function and *$0* "match goes here" statement setup.

FTP/HTTP/HTTPS URL Regular Expression

Expression: `(http|ftp|https):\/\/[\w]+(.[\w]+)([\w\-`
`\.,@?^=%&amp;:/~\+#]*[\w\-\@?^=%&amp;/~\+#])?`
Sample matches: `https://www.karlmoore.com, ftp://ftp.download.com/`
Sample nonmatches: `www.yahoo.com, cnn.com, HTTP://www.km.com/`

Sample VB .NET code #1:

```
Dim blnMatch As Boolean, strValue As String = "ftp://files.mysite.com/"
blnMatch = System.Text.RegularExpressions.Regex.IsMatch(strValue, _
    "^((http|ftp|https):\/\/[\w]+(.[\w]+)" & _
    "([\w\-\.,@?^=%&amp;::/~\+#]*[\w\-\@?^=%&amp;/~\+#])?)$")
```

> **TOP TIP** *You may notice that the expression used here is slightly different from the one listed previously. That's because we're "tightening" it to ensure that our string exactly matches and doesn't contain any excess. You'll find a full explanation later in this chapter, with "The Cure for 'Loose' Expressions" tip.*

Sample VB .NET code #2:

```
' Setup class references
Dim objRegEx As System.Text.RegularExpressions.Regex
Dim objMatch As System.Text.RegularExpressions.Match
' Create regular expression
objRegEx = New System.Text.RegularExpressions.Regex( _
    "(http|ftp|https):\/\/[\w]+(.[\w]+)([\w\-\.,@?^=" & _
    "%&amp;::/~\+#]*[\w\-\@?^=%&amp;/~\+#])?", _
    System.Text.RegularExpressions.RegexOptions.Compiled)
' Match our text with the expression
objMatch = objRegEx.Match("<html> http://www.samplesite.com/ " & _
    "etc etc ftp://samplesite.com/ </html>")
' Loop through matches and display matching value in MessageBox
While objMatch.Success
    Dim strMatch As String
    strMatch = objMatch.Value
    MessageBox.Show(strMatch)
    objMatch = objMatch.NextMatch()
End While
```

Sample VB .NET code #3:

```
' Setup objRegEx, passing in expression ("pattern")
Dim objRegEx As New System.Text.RegularExpressions.Regex( _
    "(http|ftp|https):\/\/[\w]+(.[\w]+)([\w\-\.,@?^=" & _
    "%&amp;::/~\+#]*[\w\-\@?^=%&amp;/~\+#])?")
' Our actual value
Dim strValue As String = "<html> http://www.samplesite.tv/ " & _
    "etc etc ftp://www.samplesite.com/ </html>"
' Finding matches and replacing with "HREF" and actual match
Dim strResult As String = _
    objRegEx.Replace(strValue, "<a href=""$0"">$0</a>")
```

Checking for a Valid Domain

Whether you're running your own domain sales service or are making regular automated updates to the DNS zone files, being able to check that a domain adheres to a valid format is an important feat—and it's one that this next regular expression will help you overcome.

Note that this expression will allow something like "www.karlmoore.com", as it could theoretically be a valid sub-domain. If you don't want this to occur, you may wish to check whether the first three characters are "www."—and if so, strip them out.

Domain-Format Regular Expression

Expression: `^[a-zA-Z0-9]+([a-zA-Z0-9\-\.]+)?\.(com|org|net|mil|edu|info)$`
(add more domain suffixes in the same format, as required)
Sample matches: karlmoore.com, secure.whitecliff.net, my-valid-domain.edu
Sample nonmatches: karlmoore!.com, kmcom, test.co.uk, 127.0.0.1
Sample VB .NET code:

```
Dim blnMatch As Boolean, strValue As String = "example.com"
blnMatch = System.Text.RegularExpressions.Regex.IsMatch( _
   strValue, "^[a-zA-Z0-9]+([a-zA-Z0-9\-\.]+)?\.(com|org|net|mil|edu|info)$", _
      System.Text.RegularExpressions.RegexOptions.IgnoreCase)
```

IP Address Checker

It's not the most common requirement in the world, but validating the format of an IP address can be awfully difficult if you're doing it in code. With a regular expression however, it's easy, as this next number demonstrates.

IP Address Regular Expression

Expression: `^(25[0-5]|2[0-4][0-9]|[0-1]{1}[0-9]{2}|[1-9]{1}[0-9]{1}|`
`[1-9])\.(25[0-5]|2[0-4][0-9]|[0-1]{1}[0-9]{2}|[1-9]{1}[0-9]{1}|`
`[1-9]|0)\.(25[0-5]|2[0-4][0-9]|[0-1]{1}[0-9]{2}|[1-9]{1}[0-9]{1}|`
`[1-9]|0)\.(25[0-5]|2[0-4][0-9]|[0-1]{1}[0-9]{2}|[1-9]{1}[0-9]{1}|[0-9])$`
Sample matches: 127.0.0.1, 255.255.255.0, 168.87.32.1
Sample nonmatches: 256.0.0.1, 123.abc.etc.1, 0.255.255.255

Sample VB .NET code:

```
Dim blnMatch As Boolean, strValue As String = "123.456.789.101"
blnMatch = System.Text.RegularExpressions.Regex.IsMatch(strValue, _
  "^(25[0-5]|2[0-4][0-9]|[0-1]{1}[0-9]{2}|[1-9]{1}[0-9]{1}|[1-9])\." & _
  "(25[0-5]|2[0-4][0-9]|[0-1]{1}[0-9]{2}|[1-9]{1}[0-9]{1}|[1-9]|0)\." & _
  "(25[0-5]|2[0-4][0-9]|[0-1]{1}[0-9]{2}|[1-9]{1}[0-9]{1}|[1-9]|0)\." & _
  "(25[0-5]|2[0-4][0-9]|[0-1]{1}[0-9]{2}|[1-9]{1}[0-9]{1}|[0-9])$")
```

Extracting Links and Images from HTML

If you're looking to extract all the links or images from an HTML string, you're in luck. I've got just the tip for you. Simply flick back to Chapter 7, "More .NET Secrets" and check out the regular-expression-based "Tricks of Parsing a Web Page for Links and Images" tip in the Internet section.

Checking HTML Color Codes

This is another one of those expressions that, although you probably won't use it all too often, when you do, it's a lifesaver. This baby checks for valid HTML hexadecimal color codes. Whether they're the three-digit types (one of the 216 Web-safe colors) or in full six-digit form, hash (#) or no hash, this expression will check their validity. It's useful if you're putting together your own graphics or HTML application, or are allowing users to customize colors on your site.

HTML Color Code Regular Expression

Expression: ^#?([a-f]|[A-F]|[0-9]){3}(([a-f]|[A-F]|[0-9]){3})?$
Sample matches: 00FF00, #0000FF, #039
Sample nonmatches: orange, 0x000000, #000FF
Sample VB .NET code:

```
Dim blnMatch As Boolean, strValue As String = "#0000FF"
blnMatch = System.Text.RegularExpressions.Regex.IsMatch(strValue, _
    "^#?([a-f]|[A-F]|[0-9]){3}(([a-f]|[A-F]|[0-9]){3})?$")
```

Credit Card Validation

Imagine that you're designing an offline orders system. Your sales people want to be able to record credit card details for debiting later. Wouldn't it be nice to at least check the basic format of the card number to ensure greater accuracy? This expression does just that, matching on all major credit cards, including VISA (length of 16 characters, prefix of 4), MasterCard (length of 16, prefix between 51 and 55), Discover (length of 16, prefix 6011), and American Express (length of 15, prefix 34 or 37). You can even insert optional hyphens between each set of digits.

Credit Card Regular Expression

Expression: ^((?:4\d{3})|(?:5[1-5]\d{2})|(?:6011)|(?:3[68]\d{2})|(?:30[012345]\d))[-]?(\d{4})[-]?(\d{4})[-]?(\d{4}|3[4,7]\d{13})$

Sample matches: 6011-1234-5678-1234 *(Discover)*, 5401 2345 6789 1011 *(MasterCard)*

Sample nonmatches: 3401-123-456-789, 3411-5555-3333-111

Sample VB .NET code:

```
Dim blnMatch As Boolean, strValue As String = "5420206023965209"
blnMatch = System.Text.RegularExpressions.Regex.IsMatch(strValue, _
    "^((?:4\d{3})|(?:5[1-5]\d{2})|(?:6011)|" & _
    "(?:3[68]\d{2})|(?:30[012345]\d))[ -]?(\d{4})" & _
    "[ -]?(\d{4})[ -]?(\d{4}|3[4,7]\d{13})$")
```

Password Format Enforcing Expression

Numerous password-related regular expressions are available on the Internet. This is one of my personally created favorites, however. It checks that the first letter of the password is a letter, that the password is between 4 and 15 characters in length, and that only letters, numbers, and the underscore character are used. Anything else, and it's no match.

Password Format Regular Expression

Expression: `^[a-zA-Z]\w{3,14}$`
Sample matches: abcd, SuPeR, password24
Sample nonmatches: oh boy, 12km, longinvalidpassword
Sample VB .NET code:

```
Dim blnMatch As Boolean, strValue As String = "MyInvalidPassword"
blnMatch = System.Text.RegularExpressions.Regex.IsMatch(strValue, _
    "^[a-zA-Z]\w{3,14}$")
```

Defining Your Own HTML: Custom Tags, with Expressions

I run an online forum and know how tricky it can be allowing users to post HTML. They can send the whole page design haywire; they insert little scripts to make windows pop up; they turn my scrollbar a funny color. In short, those few naughty users screw things up—and that's why I and numerous other Webmasters enjoy implementing a little pseudo-HTML.

How? They design a number of their own tags and get users to type them directly—such as *[url]http://www.yahoo.com/[/url]*. When the pages are served up these tags are processed, using regular expressions, and regular HTML is put in their place. You can use buttons to automatically insert the tags through JavaScript (see how you compose a post at my own www.vbforums.com for an example), and can even embed one tag inside another.

This tip shares a number of the most commonly requested tags, encapsulated in one chunk of commented sample code. After you've figured out the general structure of these custom tags, you'll find it easy to customize them to your exact requirements.

> **TOP TIP** *If you want to strip any HTML initially entered by the user, check out the "Converting HTML to Text, Easily" tip in the Internet section of Chapter 7 ("More .NET Secrets").*

Custom Tag Regular Expressions

Sample VB .NET Code:

```
' Turns [url]http://www.cnn.com/ /[/url]

' into <a target="_blank" href=
' "http://www.cnn.com/">http://www.cnn.com/</a>
 strResult = System.Text.RegularExpressions.Regex.Replace(YourData, _
    "\[url[^>]*?=\s*?[""'']?([^'"" >]+?)[ '""]?\]([^\""]*?)\[/url\]", _
    "<a target=""_blank"" href=""$1"">$2</a>", _
    System.Text.RegularExpressions.RegexOptions.IgnoreCase)


' Turns [url=http://www.cnn.com/]CNN[/url]
' into <a target="_blank" href="http://www.cnn.com/">CNN</a>
 strResult = System.Text.RegularExpressions.Regex.Replace(YourData, _
    "\[URL\]([^\""]*?)\[/URL\]", _
    "<a target=""_blank"" href=""$1"" target=""_new"">$1</a>", _
    System.Text.RegularExpressions.RegexOptions.IgnoreCase)


' Turns [email]myname@domain.com[/email]
' into <a href="mailto:myname@domain.com">myname@domain.com</a>
 strResult = System.Text.RegularExpressions.Regex.Replace(YourData, _
    "\[email\]([^\""]*?)\[/email\]", _
    "<a href=""mailto:$1"">$1</a>", _
    System.Text.RegularExpressions.RegexOptions.IgnoreCase)


' Turns [email=myname@domain.com]Click here to email me[/email]
' into <a href="mailto:myname@domain.com">Click here to email me</a>
 strResult = System.Text.RegularExpressions.Regex.Replace(YourData, _
    "\[email[^>]*?=\s*?[""'']?([^'"" >]+?)[ '""]?\]([^\""]*?)\[/email\]", _
    "<a href=""mailto:$1"">$2</a>", _
    System.Text.RegularExpressions.RegexOptions.IgnoreCase)


' [b]some text[/b] produces bold text
 strResult = System.Text.RegularExpressions.Regex.Replace(YourData, _
    "\[b\]([^\""]*?)\[/b\]", "<b>$1</b>", _
    System.Text.RegularExpressions.RegexOptions.IgnoreCase)


' [u]some text[/u] produces underlined text
 strResult = System.Text.RegularExpressions.Regex.Replace(YourData, _
    "\[u\]([^\""]*?)\[/u\]", "<u>$1</u>", _
    System.Text.RegularExpressions.RegexOptions.IgnoreCase)
```

```
' [i]some text[/i] produces italicised text
strResult = System.Text.RegularExpressions.Regex.Replace(YourData, _
   "\[i\]([^\""]*?)\[/i\]", "<i>$1</i>", _
   System.Text.RegularExpressions.RegexOptions.IgnoreCase)


' [color=blue]some text[/color] produces blue text
strResult = System.Text.RegularExpressions.Regex.Replace(YourData, _
   "\[color[^>]*?=\s*[""']?([^'"" >]+?)[ '""]?\]([^\""]*)\[/color\]", _
   "<font color=""$1"">$2</font>", _
   System.Text.RegularExpressions.RegexOptions.IgnoreCase)


' [size=4]some text[/size] produces size 4 text
strResult = System.Text.RegularExpressions.Regex.Replace(YourData, _
   "\[size[^>]*?=\s*[""']?([^'"" >]+?)[ '""]?\]([^\""]*)\[/size\]", _
   "<font size=""$1"">$2</font>", _
   System.Text.RegularExpressions.RegexOptions.IgnoreCase)


' [font=courier]some text[/font] produces Courier font text
strResult = System.Text.RegularExpressions.Regex.Replace(YourData, _
   "\[font[^>]*?=\s*[""']?([^'"" >]+?)[ '""]?\]([^\""]*)\[/font\]", _
   "<font face=""$1"">$2</font>", _
   System.Text.RegularExpressions.RegexOptions.IgnoreCase)


' Turns [img]http://www.karlmoore.com/km/images/km_splash.gif[/img]
' into <img src=" http://www.karlmoore.com/km/images/km_splash.gif">
strResult = System.Text.RegularExpressions.Regex.Replace(YourData, _
   "\[img\]([^\""]*?)\[/img\]", "<img src=""$1"">", _
   System.Text.RegularExpressions.RegexOptions.IgnoreCase)
' Turns [quote]Do or do not, there is no try.[/quote]
' into <blockquote><p><hr>My block quite.<hr></p></blockquote>
strResult = System.Text.RegularExpressions.Regex.Replace(YourData, _
   "\[quote\]([^\""]*?)\[/quote\]", _
   "<blockquote><p><hr>$1<hr></p></blockquote>", _
   System.Text.RegularExpressions.RegexOptions.IgnoreCase)
```

ISBN Checker

Practically every book you'll find in your local library has an International Standard Book Number (ISBN), and they all adhere to one simple format: they're ten digits and optionally end with an "X". And that's exactly what this next regular expression checks for. This expression is useful for error checking your media library database or for those running the next Amazon.com.

ISBN Regular Expression

Expression: ^\d{9}[\d|X]$
Sample matches: 1234567890, 159059021X, 123456789X
Sample nonmatches: 159059021-X, IsbnNumber, X1234568X
Sample VB .NET code:
```
Dim blnMatch As Boolean, strValue As String = "159059021X"
blnMatch = System.Text.RegularExpressions.Regex.IsMatch(strValue, _
    "^\d{9}[\d|X]$")
```

Is That a GUID?

Globally unique identifiers (GUIDs) are alphanumeric characters grouped together in strings of 8-4-4-4-12 in length. This regular expression checks as to the general format of a GUID. If it contains either letters or numbers in this sequence, along with dashes, it matches.

GUID Regular Expression

Expression: ^[A-Z0-9]{8}-[A-Z0-9]{4}-[A-Z0-9]{4}-[A-Z0-9]{4}-[A-Z0-9]{12}$
(use "IgnoreCase")
Sample matches: 87374201-1CB6-46A2-AEAB-C0F2F8ABA75D
Sample nonmatches: 873742011CB646A2AEABC0F2F8ABA75D
Sample VB .NET code:
```
Dim strValue As String = New System.Guid().NewGuid.ToString
Dim blnMatch As Boolean
blnMatch = System.Text.RegularExpressions.Regex.IsMatch(strValue, _
    "^[A-Z0-9]{8}-[A-Z0-9]{4}-[A-Z0-9]{4}-[A-Z0-9]{4}-[A-Z0-9]{12}$", _
    System.Text.RegularExpressions.RegexOptions.IgnoreCase)
```

U.S. ZIP Code Checker

ZIP codes in the United States come in two different formats: the older five-digit type (90210), and the newer and more complex nine-digit version, the ZIP+4, divided by a dash into parts of five then four (60126-8722). This regular expression checks for both, and returns a match if valid.

U.S. ZIP Code Regular Expression

Expression: ^(^\d{5}(-\d{4})?)$

Sample matches: 90210, 60126-8722, 10101

Sample nonmatches: 9O21O (*letter O rather than zero*), 60126-87234, UsZip-Code

Sample VB .NET code:

```
Dim blnMatch As Boolean, strValue As String = "90210"
blnMatch = System.Text.RegularExpressions.Regex.IsMatch(strValue, _
    "^(^\d{5}(-\d{4})?)$")
```

U.S. Social Security Number Checker

Social security numbers in the United States always follow a definite pattern. Nine digits in total, dotted with hyphens as so: NNN-NN-NNNN. The following expression returns a match if compared with a set of characters that exactly match this format.

U.S. Social Security Regular Expression

Expression: ^\d{3}-\d{2}-\d{4}$

Sample matches: 123-45-6789, 101-56-5032, 103-49-1232

Sample nonmatches: 123456789, 123-456-789, Social_Security

Sample VB .NET code:

```
Dim blnMatch As Boolean, strValue As String = "123-45-6789"
blnMatch = System.Text.RegularExpressions.Regex.IsMatch(strValue, _
    "\d{3}-\d{2}-\d{4}$")
```

U.S. Phone Number Checker

U.S. telephone numbers can be entered in a variety of different formats. This neat little expression enforces a little standardization, matching against only the following national and statewide formats: NNN-NNN-NNNN and NNN-NNNN.

U.S. Phone Regular Expression

Expression: ^(?:\d{3}-)?\d{3}-\d{4}$
Sample matches: 555-555-5555, 555-5555, 123-456-7890
Sample nonmatches: 1231231234, 123 456 7890, 001.123.4567
Sample VB .NET code:

```
Dim blnMatch As Boolean, strValue As String = "(123) - 123-1234"
blnMatch = System.Text.RegularExpressions.Regex.IsMatch(strValue, _
    "^(?:\d{3}-)?\d{3}-\d{4}$")
```

U.S. State Checker

Two-character state abbreviations are common input fields on data entry forms. But it's a nightmare validating whether the user has entered a correct value. Wouldn't it be useful to encompass all that logic into one handy regular expression? Here it is. This matches on any valid two-character state abbreviation, from Washington (WA) to California (CA).

U.S. State Regular Expression

Expression: ^A[KLRZ]$|^C[AOT]$|^D[CE]$|^FL$|^GA$|^HI$|^I[ADLN]$|
^K[SY]$|^LA$|^M[ADEINOST]$|^N[BCDHJMVY]$|^O[HKR]$|^PA$|^RI$|^S[CD]$|^T[NX]
$|^UT$|^V[AT]$|^W[AIVY]$
Sample matches: MI, AK, OH
Sample nonmatches: OD, Michigan, S.C.
Sample VB .NET code:

```
Dim blnMatch As Boolean, strValue As String = "CA"
blnMatch = System.Text.RegularExpressions.Regex.IsMatch( _
  strValue, "^A[KLRZ]$|^C[AOT]$|^D[CE]$|^FL$|^GA$|^HI$|^I[ADLN]$|" & _
    "^K[SY]$|^LA$|^M[ADEINOST]$|^N[BCDHJMVY]$|^O[HKR]$|" & _
    "^PA$|^RI$|^S[CD]$|^T[NX]$|^UT$|^V[AT]$|^W[AIVY]$")
```

U.K. Postal Code Matcher

Americans attempting to validate U.K. postal codes must feel slightly dazed.
There's no simple five-digit solution here. The United Kingdom has at least six
different types of postal code that are quite normal and recognizable to the inhab-
itants of England, Wales, and Scotland. These are LN NLL, LLN NLL, LNN NLL,
LLNN NLL, LLNL NLL, and LNL NLL, where L represents a letter and N depicts a
number. And this cute little expression matches the lot.

U.K. Postal Code Regular Expression

Expression: ^[a-zA-Z]{1,2}[0-9][0-9A-Za-z]{0,1} {0,1}[0-9][A-Za-z]{2}$
Sample matches: DN14 8PX, W1C 7PQ, n1 8af
Sample nonmatches: M18-4NQ, S663 9AY, 90210
Sample VB .NET code:

```
Dim blnMatch As Boolean, strValue As String = "DN14 8PX"
blnMatch = System.Text.RegularExpressions.Regex.IsMatch(strValue, _
    "^[a-zA-Z]{1,2}[0-9][0-9A-Za-z]{0,1} {0,1}[0-9][A-Za-z]{2}$")
```

U.K. National Insurance Number Check

The U.K. National Insurance number is the equivalent of the U.S. Social Security
number. It does, however, have a slightly different format: LLNNNNNNL. The following expression checks for this exact combination of letters and numbers and
returns a match as appropriate.

U.K. National Insurance Number Regular Expression

Expression: ^[A-Za-z]{2}[0-9]{6}[A-Za-z]{1}$
Sample matches: WC723814X, PF482301X, AI393150D
Sample nonmatches: 12345678X, P4F82301X, WC7238144X
Sample VB .NET code:

```
Dim blnMatch As Boolean, strValue As String = "KM123456Y"
blnMatch = System.Text.RegularExpressions.Regex.IsMatch(strValue, _
    "^[A-Za-z]{2}[0-9]{6}[A-Za-z]{1}$")
```

U.K. Telephone Number Validator

A U.K. landline or mobile telephone number can come in any of three core formats: NNN NNNN NNNN, NNNN NNN NNN, or NNNNN NNN NNN. This neat expression checks for each of these formats, allowing for optional spaces.

U.K. Telephone Number Regular Expression

Expression: (0\d{2} ?\d{4} ?\d{4}$)|(0\d{3} ?\d{3} ?\d{3}$)|(0\d{4} ?\d{3} ?\d{3}$)
Sample matches: 020 1234 1234, 01405 123 123, 01142 212 123
Sample nonmatches: 020-1234-1234, +44 20 1234 1234, 12345678
Sample VB .NET code:

```
Dim blnMatch As Boolean, strValue As String = "020 1234 1234"
blnMatch = System.Text.RegularExpressions.Regex.IsMatch(strValue, _
    "(0\d{2} ?\d{4} ?\d{4}$)|(0\d{3} ?\d{3} ?\d{3}$)|" & _
    "(0\d{4} ?\d{3} ?\d{3}$)")
```

Converting American and British Dates

The Americans and British get along very well together. Their date formats, however, don't. An American would write 10/1/2004 for October 1st, 2004, whereas a Brit would interpret it as the 10th of January 2004. That's where the following regular expression could come in handy: it takes a date and, using the Replace function, "groups," and back references, it switches the day and month parts around, therefore converting between the two formats.

American/British Date Regular Expression

Expression: \b(?<part1>\d{1,2})/(?<part2>\d{1,2})/(?<year>\d{2,4})\b
Sample matches: 5/12/02 *(becomes 12/5/02)*, 20/05/2003 *(becomes 05/20/2003)*, 31/12/2005 *(becomes 12/31/2005)*
Sample nonmatches: 5-12-02, 31/12/'03, December 31, 2003
Sample VB .NET code:

```
Dim strValue As String = "31/12/2002"
Dim strNewValue As String = _
    System.Text.RegularExpressions.Regex.Replace(strValue, _
    "\b(?<part1>\d{1,2})/(?<part2>\d{1,2})/(?<year>\d{2,4})\b", _
    "${part2}/${part1}/${year}")
```

French, German, and Japanese Expressions

This next lot of regular expressions, I just can't claim credit for. They come directly from the sample expressions suggested by the ASP.NET RegularExpressionVal-idator control. (See the "Five Steps to Regular Expressions" tip in Chapter 3 for more information.) They're listed here for reference only, minus example code:

- French phone number: (0(\d|\d))?\d\d \d\d(\d \d| \d\d)\d\d

- French postal code: \d{5}

- German phone number: ((\(0\d\d\) |(\(0\d{3}\))?\d)?\d\d \d\d \d\d|\(0\d{4}\) \d \d\d-\d\d?)

- German postal code: (D-)?\d{5}

- Japanese phone number: (0\d{1,4}-|\(0\d{1,4}\) ?)?\d{1,4}-\d{4}

- Japanese postal code: \d{3}(-(\d{4}|\d{2}))?

The Simple Cure for "Loose" Expressions

If you're writing code using regular expressions you've extracted from books or found on the Internet, you may need to do just a little work before sticking them into your application.

Imagine, for example, that you decided to use the Microsoft regular expression for validating a French postal code—*\d{5}*—asking for five simple digits. You'd expect to get IsMatch returning True on something like "12345". But you wouldn't think it'd match on "ABC12345XYZ" now, would you?

Well, it does.

Why? Because the expression is too loose. So long as it finds at least one match in the string, it'll give your code the official nod. The fact that your database may end up full of completely corrupt data is of no consequence.

> **TOP TIP** *If the* IsMatch *function returns a* True, *you can find out which part is matching through the* Match *function. If multiple parts match, you can cycle through them all using the* Matches *collection.*

The trick is to *tighten up* your expression. But how? Follow my simple rule: just add ^(to the beginning of your expression and)$ to the end. This will result in IsMatch returning a True only when there is an exact match, and no excess.

So, with the slightly amended *^(\d{5})$*, something like "12345" will match, but "ABC12345XYZ" won't. Just the way you want it.

Watch out, however: you want to use tightening with only the IsMatch function. If you want to cycle through a list of matches (think the second code sample of the "Internet URL Matcher: FTP, HTTP, HTTPS" tip), don't tighten your expression. Here, you want it to be loose and search the whole text for matching patterns. Also, although we've demonstrated that the regular expressions behind the RegularExpressionValidator control are loose, the actual control checks for exact matches, so don't be put off using it.

In all of the examples given in this chapter, I've automatically tightened or loosened depending on the situation. Now you know the ^(and)$ technique, you can take it one step further, customizing these and other expressions to exactly meet your requirements.

Good luck!

CHAPTER 9

The Quick C# Translation Guide

C# IS THE NEW all-singing, all-dancing .NET language. It's fresh, it's the result of mixing C and the .NET Framework, it's the one language every self-respecting author is writing books about these days (*ahem*). It comes with the biggest stamp of Microsoft approval and, rumor has it, is in fact Bill Gates' love child.

But the truth is, C#—pronounced *C sharp*—is practically identical to VB .NET.

After all, it's based on the .NET Framework, just like VB .NET. It uses all the same base classes and compiles down to the same intermediate language. It accesses databases, writes to the registry, and displays forms in exactly the same way.

There are a couple of little-used, hoity-toity differences, but nothing the experienced Visual Basic programmer would want to switch languages for. Indeed, there are quite a number of reasons why one wouldn't want to move to C#. However, realistically, both of the .NET languages are virtually identical when it comes to capability.

Capability, *yes*, but not syntax. C# will almost certainly look alien to you, especially if you've never dabbled in the likes of C or Java.

Still, who cares? You program in Visual Basic .NET and shouldn't need to worry about C#. *True...* however, with the plethora of new C#-based content hitting the market—from books to Web sites to videos—who's betting you'll soon find a chunk of code you need to translate across to VB .NET. That is, of course, if you haven't already.

Or maybe one of your in-house programmers is writing C# code as part of your project. The two languages will easily work together—but, when debugging, will you be able to glance through that code and understand what's going on?

That's when you need a quick translation guide—to be specific, *this* quick translation guide. In this final chapter, I'll be showing you common statements in C#, explain what's happening, and provide the VB .NET equivalent. You'll also learn how to cheat at the translation process, plus find out where you can learn more about the language.

It's like one of those Berlitz Spanish guides. It won't teach you to speak the language. But, with a bit of flicking through the pages, you'll soon be able to figure out just what's being said.

Anyway, watch out C#. The VB guys are coming.

Translating C# to VB .NET

Before diving straight into our C# listings, let's look at a chunk of sample code to get a feel for how the language looks.

Here, we have a standard C# snippet that does something pretty simple. It's a function called readTextFromFile that takes a filename as an argument and returns a string containing the text from that file:

```
public string readTextFromFile(string filename)
{
        // reads data from a text file
        try
        {
                string strText;
                System.IO.StreamReader objReader =
                        System.IO.File.OpenText(filename);
                strText = objReader.ReadToEnd();
                objReader.Close();
                return strText;
        }
        catch
        {
                return "";
        }
}
```

And here is the corresponding code in Visual Basic .NET:

```
Public Function ReadTextFromFile(ByVal Filename As String) As String
    ' Reads data from a text file
    Try
        Dim strText As String
        Dim objReader As System.IO.StreamReader = _
            System.IO.File.OpenText(Filename)
        strText = objReader.ReadToEnd
        objReader.Close()
        Return strText
    Catch
        Return ""
    End Try
End Function
```

You probably feel more at home with the VB .NET version; however, you can easily spot the common elements. The comments. The declaring of a variable. The Try-Catch blocks. Arguments into the procedure. It's all there, just organized in a slightly different way.

The following 22 pointers highlight the key differences in the C# language. When you're converting a code snippet you don't understand, one of these sections should demonstrate the VB .NET equivalent. Just look up the heading that's most relevant, then use the instructions or table within the section to translate the C# code into VB .NET.

Ready? Let's go!

Translation Listing

Here's a quick reference list of the 22 points we'll be covering in this brief translation guide:

1. Comments: // welcome to C#

2. Remove the End-of-Line Semicolon;

3. Data Types: int, bool, float, DateTime

4. Functions: public bool writeEventLog(string entry)

5. Methods: public void activateAlarm()

6. Variables: string strText;

7. String Contents: \n and @

8. Objects: myObject = new myClass();

9. Scope: public, private, internal, static

10. Arguments: ref and out keywords

11. Arithmetic: x++;

12. If-Then: if (x > y) { ... } else {...}

13. Comparison: == and != and & and |

14. Select Case: switch {x} {...}

15. Loops: for (x=1; x<=10; x+=1) {...}

16. Errors: try {...} catch {...} finally {...}

17. The Mystery of this

18. Events: obj.event += new class.delegate(handler);

19. Classes: Properties

20. Classes: Constructors and Finalizers

21. Class Interfaces: myInterface myObject2 = (myInterface)myObject1;

22. Class Inheritance Keywords: base, virtual, abstract, sealed

1. Comments: // welcome to C#

You can easily spot comments in C#. They come in three different formats—regular comments, multiline comments, and XML comments—but they always begin with at least one forward slash. In VB .NET, these are declared using an apostrophe character at the start of each new comment line.

Here are examples of regular and multiline comments in C#:

```
// accepts an order number and returns courier
/* this is a comment that spans
    multiple lines */
```

And here's how they'd look in VB .NET:

```
' this is a regular comment
' this is a comment that spans
' multiple lines
```

C# also supports XML comments. VB .NET, however, doesn't, so you'll need to convert these to regular comments.

2. Remove the End-of-Line Semicolon;

Every statement in C# ends with a semicolon, which allows code to span multiple lines without the need for a continuation character—simply a semicolon when the end of the statement is eventually reached. In VB .NET, we remove the semicolon, plus use a continuation character (the underscore) if our code spans multiple lines.

Here's a C# example:

```
System.IO.StreamReader objReader =
    System.IO.File.OpenText(filename);
```

And here's how it'd look in VB .NET:

```
Dim objReader As System.IO.StreamReader = _
   ,System.IO.File.OpenText(Filename)
```

3. Data Types: int, bool, float, DateTime

On first glance, it would seem C# uses different data types to VB .NET. This, however, is not the case: both languages support the same data types (they have to, in order to adhere to the Common Language Runtime specification, the heart of the .NET Framework). However, they do call them different things.

For example, a bool in C# is a Boolean in VB .NET. To help you translate, here's a table demonstrating the differing data types:

C# DATA TYPE	VB .NET EQUIVALENT
int	Integer
float	Single
DateTime	Date/DateTime
bool	Boolean
null	Nothing

4. Functions: public bool writeEventLog(string entry)

Functions in C# are not *explicitly* referred to as functions, but are rather just procedures with return data types. They can be easily converted to VB .NET by adding a keyword or two and changing the positioning of the data types.

Here's an example function declaration in C#. You can see that the curly brackets define the boundaries of the procedure:

```
public bool isUserOnline(int id)
{
        // code goes here
}
```

And here's the equivalent code in VB .NET. You can see I've added the Function keyword, altered the arguments, and edited and repositioned the data types:

```
Public Function IsUserOnline(ByVal id As Integer) As Boolean
    ' code goes here
End Function
```

5. Methods: public void activateAlarm()

C# doesn't have methods as VB .NET developers would know them. Rather, it has procedures with "void" return types, meaning they return nothing. To translate into VB .NET, once again you need to add a few keywords and reposition the VB .NET equivalent data types.

Here's a C# example of a skeletal subroutine. The void keyword represents its return data type:

```
public void signout()
{
    // code goes here
}
```

And here's how you'd write that in VB .NET:

```
Public Sub Signout()
    ' code goes here
End Sub
```

6. Variables: string strText;

Declaring variables in C# is done in reverse VB .NET style. In VB .NET, we "Dim (your variable name) As (your data type)". In C#, you forget the Dim and As and simply declare your data type first followed by the variable name.

Here are a couple of examples demonstrating C# variable declarations:

```
bool blnAvailable;
int intUserid = 5;
string strText, strData;
```

And here's how you'd write something like that in VB .NET:

```
Dim blnAvailable As Boolean
Dim intUserid As Integer = 5
Dim strText, strData As String
```

7. *String Contents: \n and @*

If you see any suspicious-looking strings in C# code, be warned: you may be looking at an *escape character*. These begin with a backslash and are interpreted as special characters, such as a tab or line feed. VB .NET does not support escape characters, so you'll need to replace these with the character equivalent.

The most common C# character literal is \n, which represents a new line in a string. To translate this across to VB .NET, you'll need to replace it with the vbNewLine constant, or character codes 10 and 13. You may also see double forward slashes, such as "c:\\data.txt". These are interpreted as a single slash and can be written as such in VB .NET.

If you see a backslash followed by any other character, look up "escape characters" in the help index and use the relevant character or constant in your ported VB .NET code.

Watch out, though: if you see the @ character before the string, it's being interpreted *literally*. That means something like this in C#:

```
x=@"This is not \n a new line";
```

... is interpreted literally as "\n" and not a new line. Just be careful when translating across.

8. *Objects: myObject = new myClass();*

Declaring objects in C# is pretty similar to the way in which you handle variables, except with the occasional new keyword thrown in for good taste. Once again, translating to VB .NET is simply a case of switching the data types and their positioning.

Here are a couple of C# examples. The first creates a placeholder for an object, then sets it to a new instance of a class. The second declares and creates a new instance in one line:

```
// first example
myClass myObject1;
myObject1 = new myClass();
// second example
myClass myObject2 = new myClass();
```

And here's how this C# code would port across to VB .NET. However, as `MyClass` is a reserved word in VB, I've changed the name of the class to `MyClassItem` for demonstration purposes:

```
' First example
Dim MyObject1 As MyClassItem
MyObject1 = New MyClassItem()
' Second example
Dim MyObject2 As New MyClassItem()
```

9. Scope: public, private, internal, static

Scope in C# works in pretty much the same way as in Visual Basic. You may see `public` and `private` keywords preceding the actual declaration. There are, however, a couple of extras you might find in C# code: `internal` and `static`.

The `internal` keyword is the equivalent of `Friend` in VB .NET. It allows that particular variable or object to be used from anywhere within its assembly. Programs using the assembly cannot access it. To convert to VB .NET, simply replace `internal` with `Friend`.

The `static` keyword in C# has two possible equivalents in VB .NET. If it's used to declare a variable inside a chunk of code, stick with the `Static` keyword in VB: such static variables retain their values even after the termination of the procedure in which they are used. If, however, it's used to declare the scope for a procedure itself or a public variable, replace with the `Shared` keyword: this makes the procedure available without requiring a new instance of its class. In brief: replace `static` with `Shared` if it's used to declare a procedure or external variable; otherwise, keep it as is.

10. Arguments: ref and out keywords

In Visual Basic 6, the default method of passing arguments was by reference. In VB .NET, it's by value, using the `ByVal` keyword. C# is exactly the same, passing arguments by value as its default setting, but it doesn't use a keyword to explicitly declare this.

So, if you look at an argument and it has no extra keywords, the value is being passed by value.

If your argument utilizes the `ref` keyword, however, it's being passed by reference. Simply replace `ref` with the VB .NET equivalent keyword, `ByRef`.

There's a third possibility: the C# keyword `out`, which has no direct VB .NET equivalent. This is used for passing "uninitialized" variables, where the actual value is ignored and the variables' only real use is for passing data back out of the procedure. This has no real relevance in VB because uninitialized variables can be passed in regardless. Therefore, replace out with the VB .NET keyword, ByRef.

11. Arithmetic: x++;

When it comes to arithmetic, C# and VB .NET are very similar. However, three specific operands are particular to C# that can confuse the developer when porting to Visual Basic.

Here's a list of the differences, alongside equivalent VB .NET code:

C# CODE	VB .NET EQUIVALENT
x++;	x+=1
x--;	x-=1
x = x % 100	x = x Mod 100

12. If-Then: if (x > y) { ... } else {...}

In both C# and VB .NET, the If-Then flow is relatively similar. The main difference, however, is that C# uses those {curly brackets} to define the boundaries of code that runs if a particular condition is met.

Here's a sample If statement in C#. Note the lack of a Then keyword, plus the surrounding brackets around the statement to evaluate:

```
if (blnOnline)
{
        // do something
}
else
{
        // do something else
}
```

Now, the exact equivalent in VB .NET:

```
If blnOnline Then
    ' Do something
Else
    ' Do something else
End If
```

We can clearly see that, to convert this C# statement over to VB .NET, we just remove the brackets and add a couple of extra keywords. Nothing too drastic there.

13. Comparison: == and != and & and |

When using logical If statements, you often compare two particular values. However, C# and VB .NET have different ways of doing this. Equal-to, Not-equal-to, And, and Or are all operands that the two languages represent in vastly different ways. Here's how:

C# CODE	VB .NET EQUIVALENT
if (x == y) {...}	If x = y Then ...
if (x != y) {...}	If x <> y Then ...
if (foo & bar) {...}	If foo And bar Then ...
if (foo && bar) {...}	If foo AndAlso bar Then ...
if (b1|b2) {...}	If b1 Or b2 Then ...
if (b1||b2) {...}	If b1 OrElse b2 Then ...
if (!b1) {...}	If Not b1 Then ...
~ (as bitwise operator)	Not

14. Select Case: switch {x} {...}

The switch statement is C#'s equivalent of a Select Case. The problem is, the statement is so messy that most C# developers tend to opt for a nested If-Then equivalent. But, just in case you encounter it, let's look at an example:

```
switch (variable)
{
        case "x":
        case "y":
                // code 1
                goto case "z";
        case "z":
                // code 2
                break;
        default:
                // code 3
                break;
}
```

And now here's how that code may look in VB .NET:

```
Select Case variable
    Case "x", "y"
        ' Code 1
        ' "goto case" not supported - see tip
    Case "z"
        ' Code 2
    Case Else
        ' Code 3
End Select
```

From this comparison, it's not only easy to see how to transport the C# version over to VB .NET. It's also quite apparent why the keyword-extrapolated C# switch statement is little seen in the developer world.

> **TOP TIP** *Watch out! There is a very small difference between the C# and VB .NET code here. The* goto case *statement in C# doesn't have a VB .NET equivalent. It's used to tell C# to skip to another case and evaluate it, whereas VB .NET simply exits the* Select Case *statement after it's found a match and run the relevant code. It's probable that this won't affect you in the slightest, but, if your code needs to continue evaluating every case statement, convert it into one big* If-Then-ElseIf *statement in VB .NET.*

15. Loops: for (x=1; x<=10; x+=1) {...}

Loops in C# look very different to loops in VB .NET. In fact, you can look at a C# loop and suddenly thank goodness you're on the Visual Basic side of the fence. A C# loop is almost like a manual VB loop, where you increment the loop number in code, set the increment yourself, specify the starting point, and so on.

Let's look at a C# sample. The top line in particular needs explanation. The arguments after the for statement are *(initializer; looping condition; iterator)*. Here, the initializer is an integer variable called x, which is initially set to 1. The condition is that it should loop while x is less than or equal to 10. The iterator states that x should increase by 1 with each loop round:

```
for (int x=1; x <= 10; x++)
{
        // code goes here
        break;    // exits the loop
        // code goes here
        continue; // skips to end of loop
        // code goes here
}
```

Now let's look at the exact same loop, but this time implemented in VB .NET:

```
Dim x As Integer
For x = 1 To 10
    ' code goes here
    Exit For ' exits the loop
    ' code goes here
    GoTo EndOfLoop ' skips to end of loop
    ' code goes here
EndOfLoop:
Next
```

If the iterator in the C# example would have increased the "x" counter by more than one, we would've needed to add the Step keyword to the end of our VB .NET For loop.

There are more than just For loops in the programming world, however. You also have While, Do, and For Each loops. Let's look at a quick conversion table for these slightly-less-complex loop types:

C# CODE	VB .NET EQUIVALENT
while (*condition*) {	While *condition*
...	...
}	End While
do {	Do
...	...
} while (*condition*);	Loop While/Until *condition*
foreach (datatype varname in collection) {	For Each varname In collection
...	...
}	Next

16. Errors: try {...} catch {...} finally {...}

The `Try...Catch...Finally` method of handling errors in VB .NET applies equally in C#. However, as ever, there's a slight syntax difference: C# defines the error handling blocks through curly brackets, rather than the VB .NET method of writing code under each statement then finishing with an `End Try` command.

Here's a sample chunk of C# `Try...Catch...Finally` error handling code:

```csharp
try
{
        // code
}
catch (System.Exception e)
{
        // code
        string strErrorMsg = e.Message;
}
finally
{
        // code
}
```

Now, here's how that code would look in VB .NET. As you can see, it's practically the same:

```vbnet
Try
    ' code
Catch e As System.Exception
    ' code
    Dim strErrorMsg As String = e.Message
Finally
    ' code
End Try
```

So, when dealing with `Try...Catch...Finally` blocks, simply remove the curly brackets and add an `End Try`. Sorted!

17. The Mystery of this

You'll see the this keyword used frequently in C# code. It's often misinterpreted, but is quite simply the equivalent of the VB .NET Me keyword. It refers to the base object: if you're behind a form, it refers to your form; if you're writing code for a class, it refers to the class. Simply replace this with Me.

18. Events: obj.event += new class.delegate(handler);

Surprise, surprise: events in C# are handled differently than in VB .NET. In C# you create an event by setting up a delegate (an event signature object), then declare an item of that delegate type. VB .NET can use delegate objects, too, as the following conversion table shows, but developers typically opt for the more common (and simpler) method of using the Event keyword.

I won't be explaining the intricacies of delegates here—look up "delegates, events and" in the help index if you want to learn more—but I've created the following table containing common C# event code, the VB .NET equivalent, and a description as to what each line is doing.

So, take that chunk of C# code, rearrange each line a little, slot in the appropriate keywords, and you're rolling.

DESCRIPTION:	Set up a delegate
C# CODE:	`public delegate void myDelegate();`
VB .NET EQUIVALENT:	`Public Delegate Sub MyDelegate()`

DESCRIPTION:	Declare event based on delegate
C# CODE:	`public myDelegate myEvent;`
VB .NET EQUIVALENT:	`Public Event MyEvent() As MyDelegate`

DESCRIPTION:	Call an event
C# CODE:	`myEvent();`
VB .NET EQUIVALENT:	`RaiseEvent MyEvent()`

DESCRIPTION:	Add procedure to run when event fires
C# CODE:	`myObject.myEvent += new myEventClass.myDelegate (myProcedureToRunForThisEvent);`
VB .NET EQUIVALENT:	`AddHandler MyObject.MyEvent, AddressOf myProcedureToRunForThisEvent`

19. Classes: Properties

Properties in C# look slightly different to VB .NET. They use the {block format} you're probably getting used to by now, plus the Set portion doesn't explicitly pass in a value argument. Converting to VB .NET simply involves a little editing.

Here's a sample C# property:

```
private string strName;
public string customerName
{
        get
    {
                return strName;
    }
        set
    {
                strName=value;
        }
}
```

And now, the equivalent in VB .NET. As you can see, the conversion is easy:

```
Private strName As String
Public Property CustomerName() As String
    Get
        Return strName
    End Get
    Set(ByVal Value As String)
        strName = Value
    End Set
End Property
```

20. *Classes: Constructors and Finalizers*

The code used for declaring namespaces and classes in C# ports easily across
to VB .NET. Simply remove the curly brackets and add the End Class statement.
Leave VS .NET to sort out the casing for you—and you're up and running!

However, you'll never see a New or Finalize procedure in your C# class—
methods we'd use in VB .NET as constructors and finalizers. Why? Because, yup,
they're different in C#.

Here's a sample class in C#, containing just a constructor and a finalizer. As
you can see, the constructor is an "almost procedure" bearing the name of the
class. The finalizer is similar, although with a proceeding ~ squiggle. (If you
remember, ~ represents Not, meaning that this is the opposite of the constructor):

```
public class sampleClass
{
        public sampleClass()
   {
                // constructor code
        }
        ~sampleClass()
        {
                // finalizer code
        }
}
```

Here, we have the equivalent code in VB .NET. As you can see, we simply
replace the C# constructor and finalizer with the VB .NET New and Finalize
equivalent. We also add one simple line of code to finalize the base class
(MyBase.Finalize), code that is automatically generated behind the C# scenes
yet needs to be manually added in VB .NET:

```
Public Class SampleClass
    Public Sub New()
        ' Constructor code
    End Sub
    Protected Overrides Sub Finalize()
        MyBase.Finalize()
        ' Finalizer code
    End Sub
End Class
```

21. Class Interfaces: myInterface myObject2 = (myInterface)myObject1;

If the code you are reading uses interfaces, you'll need to do some sharp editing to make it work in Visual Basic. Of course, VB .NET uses the Implements keyword to inherit an interface. C#, however, is a little less explicit, simply listing the class to inherit the interface from after the main class definition. The way in which it implements polymorphism is also a little puzzling—no CType here, thank you very much.

Here's a table that demonstrates possible C# class interface code, alongside a description and the VB .NET equivalent. Simply replace one with the other.

DESCRIPTION:	Create an interface
C# CODE:	```public interface myInterface{```
	``` public void myMethod();```
	```}```
VB .NET EQUIVALENT:	```Public Interface MyInterface```
	``` Public Sub Method```
	```End Interface```
DESCRIPTION:	Implement an interface
C# CODE:	```public class sampleClass :```
	``` myInterface```
VB .NET EQUIVALENT:	```Public Class SampleClass```
	``` Implements MyInterface```
DESCRIPTION:	Implementing multiple interfaces
C# CODE:	```public class sampleClass :```
	``` myInterface1, myInterface2```
VB .NET EQUIVALENT:	```Public Class Sample Class```
	``` Implements MyInterface1```
	``` Implements MyInterface1```
DESCRIPTION:	Sample implementation
C# CODE:	```void myInterface1.myMethod()```
	```void myInterface2.myMethod()```
VB .NET EQUIVALENT:	```Sub ProcedureName1() Implements MyInterface1.MyMethod```
	```Sub ProcedureName2() Implements MyInterface2.MyMethod```
DESCRIPTION:	Converting to an interface type
C# CODE:	```myInterface myObject2 = (myInterface)myObject1;```
VB .NET EQUIVALENT:	```MyObject2 = CType(MyObject1, MyInterface)```
DESCRIPTION:	Calling an implemented method
C# CODE:	```((myInterface)myObject2).myMethod();```
VB .NET EQUIVALENT:	```MyObject2.MyMethod()```

22. *Class Inheritance Keywords:* base, virtual, abstract, sealed

It's one of those controversial developer topics: inheritance, the ability for your class to inherit the interface and functionality of another. This allows you to build a common "base" class that other classes can build upon (that is, a Person class may be the base for both Employee and Client classes). There are frills you can take advantage of, as well: for example, you can "override" one of the members of the base class if you need some special functionality.

Inheritance is new to this release of Visual Basic and is the final key to turning VB into a fully object-oriented programming (OOP) language. However, whole books are dedicated to the topic of inheritance, its technical background, and why you should (and shouldn't) use it. But this isn't one of them. If you need more information, get hunting at one of the popular online bookstores or look up "inheritance, overview" in the help index for a quick review.

However, if you're just looking to convert your C# code over to Visual Basic, you're in luck. It's simply a matter of switching a couple of keywords. Here's the list; just replace one with the other and, hey presto!

C# CODE	VB .NET EQUIVALENT
base	MyBase
virtual	Overridable
override	Overrides
abstract	MustInherit
sealed	NotInheritable
public class childClass:	Public Class ChildClass
baseClass	Inherits BaseClass
public childClass():	Public Sub New()
base()	MyBase.New()

Cheating at the Conversion

So, you've figured out the essentials of reading C# code. But, when you've got to translate a whole bundle across to VB .NET, or are reading exceptionally long, difficult chunks, it just might be worthwhile being resourceful.

In other words, *cheat.*

Try surfing down to `www.kamalpatel.net`, where you'll find the excellent C# to VB .NET Web service. Simply copy and paste your block of C# code into the box at `www.kamalpatel.net/ConvertCSharp2VB.aspx`, then click the Generate button. Within seconds you'll be shown the VB .NET equivalent. You can even download the full source, so you can convert C# code offline, too.

ASP.NET trainer Dan Wahlin also has his own version available, which will even port entire folders of C# code over to VB .NET. You can check his contribution out at `www.aspalliance.com/aldotnet/examples/translate.aspx`.

Excellent stuff. Happy cheating!

Where to Go from Here

You're looking to learn more about C#? Here are details of my favorite C#-related sources: from books to Web sites, videos to more Web sites. Go wild!

- *The .NET Languages: A Quick Translation Guide* (Brian Bischof, $29.95, Apress, 1-893115-48-8): This is one excellent book, and it's obvious that Bischof put a lot of work into compiling it. This book is basically a longer version of this chapter, with full-featured examples showing how to translate between VB6, VB .NET, and C#. I tend to learn "hands on"—however this is one of the few programming books I've actually spent time reading. Top stuff.

- *C# and the .NET Platform* (Andrew Troelsen, $59.95, Apress, 1-893115-59-3): This is one big book that will teach you pretty much everything. With masses of real-world code samples, this book will teach even those new to the world of programming how to get running with the C# language. Hefty, yes. Textbook style, yes. But a solid introduction in more ways than one.

- *Professional C#* (Simon Robinson et al., $59.99, Wrox, 1-861004-99-0): Written by a whopping nine authors, this is another big book with plenty to offer. It dives into the real nitty gritty early on and takes no prisoners. It's best used as a technical reference guide for those already using the language.

- **AppDev Courses** (www.appdev.com): If you learn visually, you might be interested in the range of video courses offered by AppDev. The courses are available on CD-ROM and video; I've seen them myself and admit to being suitably impressed. Another C# video provider is Keystone Learning Systems at www.keystonelearning.com.

- **Visual C# .NET Homepage** (http://msdn.microsoft.com/vcsharp/): Microsoft's home for Bill's favorite language. Enough said.

- **GotDotNet.com** (www.gotdotnet.com/team/csharp/): Microsoft-supported community site with a friendly feel and a focus on learning from the ground up. Also, check out the Microsoft ASP.NET site at www.asp.net.

- **C# Corner** (www.c-sharpcorner.com): Dodgy Web address and curious design, but nonetheless a healthy resource with plenty of categorized C# features and code snippets.

- **Master C#** (www.mastercsharp.com): This personal site from Saurabh Nandu is packed with tons of useful, techie code. Not for the beginner, but definitely one to bookmark.

- **VB Forums** (www.vbforums.com): Once my own little baby, this site is now part of Internet.com and boasts a fantastic C# forum. Ask your questions and get your answers.

And that's all for C#. Yes, it may look confusing at first—but once you venture in, you'll realize it's really not all that difficult. Just keep curious, keep open-minded and keep the caffeine flowing.

Enjoy!

Appendix

I: Installing VS.NET

So, you've decided Visual Basic .NET is the programming language for you and need to slap it on your machine?

First off, you need to buy it. And that means making our first decision. You see, Visual Studio .NET comes in four separate flavors: Professional, Enterprise Developer, Enterprise Architect, and Academic.

If you're the penny-pinching type, the Professional version of Visual Studio .NET is the cheapest of the range and is bundled with Visual Basic .NET, Visual C++ .NET, and Visual C# .NET. It allows you to do everything we cover in this book, including build and run Windows applications, Web applications, and Web services.

If you're feeling a little more affluent, however, Enterprise Developer is most probably your best bet. It includes all the features of the Professional version, plus comes with Visual SourceSafe and developer editions of .NET server products such as SQL Server and Windows 2000/2003.

The third option, Enterprise Architect, features all the above, plus a few system modeling features used by manager folk. And, finally, the Academic version is similar to the Professional version plus includes a number of extra wizards specific to the academic community and a particularly attractive price tag too—but it's available only to student types. D'oh!

In reality, it doesn't really matter which version you pick—even the basic product contains everything you need to get started. My best bet for most programmers? Go for Enterprise Developer: it contains everything you need, without going overboard. (It'll still take a bite out of your wallet, however.)

So, you've reviewed the options and chosen an appropriate version of Visual Studio .NET. Now, can your machine handle it?

To run the software, you'll need at least a PC with a Pentium II-class processor capable of 450MHz or higher. It's also recommended that you have 500MB of disk space available on your system drive, along with a potential 3GB handy for the actual installation.

In terms of operating system and RAM, Visual Studio .NET will install on Windows 2003 Server (with 160MB of RAM), Windows 2000 Server (with 192MB of RAM), Windows 2000 Professional (with 96MB of RAM), Windows XP Professional (with 160MB of RAM), and Windows NT 4.0 Workstation (64MB of RAM).

Of course, the rule of thumb here is more is better. And less? Oh, that's just disastrous.

A quick word of advice here: you won't want to install Visual Studio .NET on an NT 4.0 machine. Why? Windows NT doesn't support ASP.NET, one of the biggest areas of .NET, and it also doesn't allow for COM+ or multiprocessor garbage collection. The rest of this installation guide presumes you *didn't* choose NT 4.0.

So, your machine is capable of running your version of Visual Studio .NET? Next, you need to ensure that you have the right software already on the machine. What does this mean? First off, you need to set up Internet Information Services (IIS) on your computer if you don't already have it. This allows your machine to act as a Web server and create the Web applications we cover in Chapter 3 and 5. You can check whether this is already installed by seeing whether the Internet Services Manager program exists on your computer (Programs ➤ Administrative Tools ➤ Internet Services Manager).

To set up IIS on Windows 2000/2003/XP, open the control panel, select the Add/Remove Programs applet, and choose Add/Remove Windows Components. In the Windows Components wizard, select Internet Information Services (IIS) from the Components list and click on Next to begin the installation.

> **TOP TIP** *If you install IIS after setting up Visual Studio .NET, you'll need to take a few extra steps. Lookup the " Uh-oh: Installing IIS After Visual Studio .NET" tip in Chapter 3 for more information.*

Next up, if you plan to compile code related to Microsoft Messaging Queue (MSMQ, see the "Quick Guide to Using MSMQ" in Chapter 7), you'll need to install Message Queuing Services. To do this, follow the same procedure as installing Internet Information Services, except this time selecting the Message Queuing Services option.

So, you've purchased your version of Visual Studio .NET, found a machine capable of running it, and installed all the necessary software prerequisites? Great stuff. Now you're ready to rumble.

First off, make sure that you're logged in with administrative permissions. Why? Some features such as the debugger create their own system accounts and require such privileges to set them up. Note, however, that after the installation your VS.NET user doesn't necessarily need administrative privileges to run the application.

Right then: it's time for the actual installation. Take your Setup CD-ROM or DVD and insert it into your computer. The setup should automatically start; if not, open the drive via My Computer and double-click on the Setup.exe file.

You'll be guided through the entire installation process. This typically involves entering your serial number, selecting an installation directory, copying files, and configuring your machine. The whole process will last at least an hour, so get that kettle boiling.

> **TOP TIP** *If you experience problems during the Visual Studio .NET setup, refer to Readme.htm in the root directory of your installation disk. It often provides useful information on known issues or last-minute workarounds.*

After the installation has finished, you'll want to perform just a couple of actions to fine-tune your copy of Visual Studio .NET.

First off, launch it. To do this, select Start ➤ Programs ➤ Microsoft Visual Studio .NET ➤ Microsoft Visual Studio .NET. In later revisions of the program, you may be prompted with a screen asking you to register online or via telephone using a special key. You can skip this initially, but the program will run only a set number of times before you're forced to spill the beans to Microsoft.

In Visual Studio .NET, let's first set up your preferences. On the Start page, click on the My Profile link down the left-hand side. From the Profile dropdown list, select Visual Basic Developer. This will set Visual Basic as the default language, plus apply a set of typical keyboard shortcuts, as taught in this book and used in VB6.

Next up, you might consider checking for any updates, such as service releases or, more likely, bug fixes. To do this, select Help ➤ Check for Updates from the menu. You'll need an Internet connection to download the latest files.

And that's it! You've successfully installed Visual Studio .NET on your development machine.

One quick note for when you start creating projects in Visual Studio .NET: the Option Strict setting is turned off by default. You can set this value either in code or by right-clicking on your project in the Solution Explorer, selecting Properties, and choosing the Build item.

This value dictates that all object types must be explicitly declared, and any non-exact matches will prevent your application from compiling. For example, with Option Strict turned on, you could not create a string and set an Integer value to it. Instead, you would have to physically convert this value. (Look up "type conversion" in the help index for more information.) With Option Strict turned off, Visual Basic handles all this automatically for you.

This Option Strict addition was added to help build enterprise projects that are more bug free, although it can prove inflexible and hinder learning Visual Basic. All samples in this book are based on this default setting of Option Strict turned off.

II: Default Project Files

When you create a new VB project in Visual Studio .NET, you'll notice numerous files and references added by default, creating a starting point for your application.

Translating these additions back to the real world can often be a confusing task. Therefore, the following sections detail the most-common project types and related template settings.

Windows Application

When creating a Windows application, the following visible items are automatically added to your project:

- *AssemblyInfo.vb*: Used to describe your assembly plus contains versioning information. Edit this file to alter such data.

- *Form1.vb*: Standard Windows form, ready for you to manipulate.

- *Default references to*:

  - *System*: The mother of the .NET Framework base classes. Includes commonly used value and reference data types, plus defines events and event handlers, interfaces, attributes, and processing exceptions.

  - *System.Data*: Contains classes to handle ADO.NET data access.

  - *System.Drawing*: Contains classes to handle GDI+ graphics functionality.

  - *System.Windows.Forms*: Contains classes for creating Windows-based form applications.

  - *System.Xml*: Contains classes that provide standards-based support for processing XML.

- *Default namespace imports (Project, Imports)*:

  - Microsoft.VisualBasic

  - System

  - System.Collections

  - System.Data

  - System.Diagnostics

  - System.Drawing

  - System.Windows.Forms

Class Library

When creating a class library, the following visible items are automatically added to your project:

- *AssemblyInfo.vb*: Used to describe your assembly, plus contains versioning information. Edit this file to alter such data.

- *Class1.vb*: Standard class template, ready for you to manipulate.

- *Default references to*:

  - *System*: The mother of the .NET Framework base classes. Includes commonly used value and reference data types, plus defines events and event handlers, interfaces, attributes and processing exceptions.

  - *System.Data*: Contains classes to handle ADO.NET data access.

  - *System.Xml*: Contains classes that provide standards-based support for processing XML.

- *Default namespace imports (Project, Imports)*:

  - Microsoft.VisualBasic

  - System

  - System.Collections

  - System.Data

  - System.Diagnostics

Web Application

When creating a Web Application, the following visible items are automatically added to your project:

- *AssemblyInfo.vb*: Used to describe your assembly, plus contains versioning information. Edit this file to alter such data.

- *Global.asax*: Contains template code for responding to application-level events raised by ASP.NET, such as Application_Start.

- *Styles.css*: Empty CSS file, used to set page styles.

- *Web.config*: Contains your ASP.NET application settings, such as authentication and session settings.

- *<ProjectName>.vsdisco*: XML-based file used by ASP.NET when dynamically discovering Web services on the server, only required if you add a Web Service to your application.

- *WebForm1.aspx*: Blank Web Form, ready for you to manipulate.

- *WebForm1.aspx.vb*: Underneath WebForm1.aspx in the Solution Explorer hierarchy (click on Show All Files to open directly), this file contains a class file for the default WebForm1.aspx page, containing system generated and user code.

- *Default References to*:

  - *System*: The mother of the .NET Framework base classes. Includes commonly used value and reference data types, plus defines events and event handlers, interfaces, attributes, and processing exceptions.

  - *System.Data*: Contains classes to handle ADO.NET data access.

  - *System.Drawing*: Contains classes to handle GDI+ graphics functionality.

  - *System.Web*: Contains classes for browser/server communication.

  - *System.Xml*: Contains classes that provide standards-based support for processing XML.

- *Default namespace imports (Project, Imports)*:

  - Microsoft.VisualBasic

  - System

  - System.Collections

  - System.Configuration

  - System.Data

  - System.Drawing

  - System.Web

  - System.Web.UI

  - System.Web.UI.HtmlControls

  - System.Web.UI.WebControls

Web Service

When creating a Web service, the following visible items are automatically added to your project:

- *AssemblyInfo.vb*: Used to describe your assembly, plus contains versioning information. Edit this file to alter such data.

- *Global.asax*: Contains template code for responding to application-level events raised by ASP.NET, such as Application_Start.

- *Web.config*: Contains your ASP.NET application settings, such as authentication and session settings.

- *<ProjectName>.vsdisco*: XML-based file used by ASP.NET when dynamically discovering Web services on the server."

- *Service1.asmx*: The actual Web service file, which references the underlying assembly (your code compiled into a DLL).

- *Service1.asmx.vb*: Underneath service1.asmx in the Solution Explorer hierarchy (click on "Show All Files" to open directly), this file contains a class file for the default Web service page, holding system-generated and user code.

- *Default References to:*

  - *System*: The mother of the .NET Framework base classes. Includes commonly used value and reference data types, plus defines events and event handlers, interfaces, attributes and processing exceptions.

  - *System.Data*: Contains classes to handle ADO.NET data access.

  - *System.Web.Services*: Contains classes enabling you to build and consume XML Web services.

  - *System.Web*: Contains classes for browser/server communication.

  - *System.Xml*: Contains classes that provide standards-based support for processing XML.

- *Default namespace imports (Project, Imports)*:

  - Microsoft.VisualBasic

  - System

  - System.Collections

  - System.Configuration

  - System.Data

  - System.Drawing

  - System.Web

  - System.Web.UI

  - System.Web.UI.HtmlControls

  - System.Web.UI.WebControls

III: Windows Form Controls

When working with Windows Forms, you have 46 default Toolbox controls available for use. The following, alphabetically sorted list provides a simple description of each to help you choose which is best for the task at hand.

All items noted as components have no form-visible interface, and their actions must be manipulated in code. Here goes *<breathe in>*:

1. *Button:* Standard button the user can click to perform actions.

2. *CheckBox:* Allows the user to check an On or Off option.

3. *CheckedListBox:* Displays a list of items with a checkbox next to each.

4. *ColorDialog:* Component, allows the user to select a color from a dialog box.

5. *ComboBox:* Displays a list of options in a drop-down box.

6. *ContextMenu:* Component, allows you to create a pop-up menu.

7. *CrystalReportViewer:* Executes and displays a Crystal Report document.

8. *DataGrid:* Displays tabular data from a DataSet, plus allows for updates.

9. *DateTimePicker:* Allows the user to select a single date from a list of dates or times.

10. *DomainUpDown:* Displays strings that a user can browse through and select from.

11. *ErrorProvider:* Component, highlights errors in a user-friendly manner.

12. *FontDialog:* Component, allows the user to select a font via a dialog box.

13. *GroupBox:* Acts as a visible container for other controls.

14. *HelpProvider:* Component, associates an HTML help file with a Windows application.

15. *HScrollBar* and *VScrollBar:* Horizontal and vertical scroll bars, to allow for programmatic scrolling through a list of items.

16. *ImageList:* Component, stores images for use on other controls, such as the ToolBar and TreeView.

17. *Label:* Displays read-only text.

18. *LinkLabel:* Displays a Web-style link with a click event.

19. *ListBox:* Allows the user to select one or more items from a list.

20. *ListView:* Displays a list of items with icons, Windows Explorer-style.

21. *MainMenu:* Displays application menus.

22. *MonthCalendar:* Allows the user to select a date or range of dates from a month-by-month calendar.

23. *NotifyIcon:* Allows you to add icons to the system taskbar.

24. *NumericUpDown:* Displays a predetermined set of numbers that the user can browse through and select from.

25. *OpenFileDialog:* Component, allows users to select files to open via a standard dialog box.

26. *PageSetupDialog:* Component, displays a dialog box allowing the user to change page setup details for printing.

27. *Panel:* Provides grouping of controls, such as RadioButton controls.

28. *PictureBox:* Displays graphics in BMP, GIF, JPEG, WMF, and ICO format.

29. *PrintDialog:* Component, allows user to select a printer, the number of pages to print, and other settings via a standard dialog box.

30. *PrintDocument:* Component, allows user to set properties that describe what to print and then to actually print it.

31. *PrintPreviewControl*: Allows you to display a PrintDocument as it will appear when printed, without any user interface extras.

32. *PrintPreviewDialog*: Component, displays a PrintDocument in a dialog box, as it will appear when printed, alongside options to print, zoom, and move between pages.

33. *ProgressBar:* Indicates the progress of an operation graphically.

34. *RadioButton*: Allows the user to select an option from two or more exclusive buttons.

35. *RichTextBox*: Allows users to enter, display, and manipulate text with formatting.

36. *SaveFileDialog*: Component, allows the user to specify a save filename via a standard dialog box.

37. *Splitter*: Allows the user to resize a docked control, typically used for splitting forms into two components.

38. *StatusBar*: Displays status information, typically at the bottom of a form.

39. *TabControl*: Displays multiple tabbed pages, each containing their own controls.

40. *TextBox*: Allows editable, multiline input from the user.

41. *Timer*: Component, raises an event to run your code at specified intervals.

42. *ToolBar*: Displays menus and picture buttons that activate commands.

43. *ToolTip*: Component, displays text when the user hovers the mouse over controls.

44. *TrackBar*: Displays a bar for the user to position, perhaps for setting a numeric value or navigating through a large amount of information.

45. *TreeView*: Displays a hierarchy of items that can be expanded and collapsed, Windows Explorer-style.

<breathe out>

You can add extra controls by right-clicking on the Toolbox, selecting "Customize Toolbox", and using the popup dialog to choose the COM and .NET controls you wish to add.

IV: VB.NET Data Types

The following table lists the data types that are available in VB.NET, listed alongside their Common Language Runtime (CLR) base type.

VB DATA TYPE NAME	CAN HOLD	SIZE IN MEMORY	CORRESPONDING CLR TYPE
Boolean	True or False	2 bytes	System.Boolean
Byte	0 to 255	1 byte	System.Byte
Char	One single character	2 bytes	System.Char
Date	January 1, 0001 00:00:00 through to December 31, 9999 11:59:59 PM	8 bytes	System.DateTime
Decimal	0 through to +/- 79,228,162,514,264,337, 593,543,950,335 with no decimal point; 0 through +/-7.9228162514264337593543950335 (with 28 places to the right of the decimal point)	16 bytes	System.Decimal
Double (double-precision floating-point)	-1.79769313486231570E+308 through to -4.94065645841246544E-324 fornegative values; 4.94065645841246544E-324 through to 1.79769313486231570E+308 for positive values	8 bytes	System.Double
Integer	-2,147,483,648 through to 2,147,483,647	4 bytes	System.Int32
Long (long integer)	-9,223,372,036,854,775,808 through to 9,223,372,036,854,775,807	8 bytes	System.Int64
Object	Any type can be stored in an Object variable	4 bytes	System.Object (class)
Short	-32,768 through to 32,767	2 bytes	System.Int16
Single (single-precision floating-point)	-3.4028235E+38 through to -1.401298E-45for negative values; 1.401298E-45 through 3.4028235E+38 for positive values	4 bytes	System.Single
String	0 to approximately 2 billion Unicode characters	Depends on platform	System.String (class)
User-Defined Types	Each member of the structure is determined by its data type	Depends on platform	System.ValueType (inherits from)

In the .NET world, you officially have two different "types": value types and reference types. Value types simply contain core values and are stored on the application stack. Sample value types include Boolean, Integer, and Date.

Reference types are stored on the runtime heap, pointing to a particular object in memory. All objects derived from classes are reference types, including the String type, all arrays, forms, and so on.

In the many applications, this behind-the-scenes difference will have no or little impact on our programming. With powerful, highly requested applications, however, take the following two details into account:

- All reference types are handled by the .NET Framework garbage collection process. This means that unused objects are marked for deletion and destroyed, say, every few minutes. At busy times, this can result in a lot of objects just consuming memory, waiting to be destroyed. So, where possible, use the more efficient value types.

- Strings are more efficiently concatenated using the StringBuilder class. Using the simple & concatenation command can result in wasted memory strings that require garbage collection.

V: VB.NET Naming Conventions

It's good programming practice to use standard prefixes with your controls and variables. This ensures your code remains clear and understandable. The following list provides an overview of popular conventions:

ITEM	PREFIX	EXAMPLE
Form	frm	frmMain
Class	cls / C	clsOrder
Module	mod	modGeneric
Label	lbl	lblUsername
LinkLabel	lnk	lnkVisitSite
Button	btn	btnOK
TextBox	txt	txtPassword
CheckBox	chk	chkRemember
RadioButton	rad	radMale
GroupBox	grp	grpOptions
PictureBox	pic	picAuthor
DataGrid	grd	grdOrders

ITEM	PREFIX	EXAMPLE
ListBox	lst	lstSubscribed
CheckedListBox	clst	clstExtras
ComboBox	cbo	cboRoomNumber
TreeView	tvw	tvwFolders
ListView	lvw	lvwFiles
TabControl	tab	tabSettings
DateTimePicker	dtp	dtpAppointment
Timer	tmr	tmrCheck
Splitter	spl	splGeneral
ProgressBar	pbar	pbarTimeLeft
RichTextBox	rtf	rtfDocument
ImageList	imgl	imglToolbar
ToolBar	tlb	tlbMain
MenuItem	mnu	mnuFileExit
String	str	strAnalysis
Date	dat	datLastVisit
Boolean	bln	blnFlag
Short	sht	shtCurrent
Decimal	dec	decRate
Long	lng	lngSystemID
Integer	int	intCount
Byte	byt	bytAge
Char	chr	chrFirst
Single	sgl	sglRemaining
Double	dbl	dblTotalBalance
Structure (User-Defined Type)	udt	udtCustomer
Object	obj	objRandom
DataSet	ds	dsmembers
DataRow	dr	drEntry
OleDbConnection or SqlConnection	conn	connLuxor
OleDbCommand or SqlCommand	cmd	cmdDelete
OleDbDataAdapter or SqlDataAdapter	da	daUserList
OleDbDataReader or SqlDataReader	rdr	rdrItems
Crystal Report	rpt	rptSales

It is also common practice to prefix module-level variable declarations with "m" and global declarations with "g"—although, as ever, this is not enforced and simply serves as a suggestion to help assist your development.

You can also find a full list of recommended code styling guidelines for your Visual Basic program, by looking up "naming conventions, Visual Basic" in the help index.

Index

Symbols and Numbers

+= operator, example of, 17

; (semicolon) in C#, meaning of, 338–339

"404, Page Not Found" error, troubleshooting, 112–113

A

ACT (Application Center Test), 119–120

ADO.NET
explanation of, 127
and working with databases in code, 128

ADO.NET objects, resource for, 130

alert warnings, raising in ASP.NET, 74

alphanumerical matcher in Regex library, example of, 313–314

Amazon.com, querying for Web services, 190–193

American and British dates, converting with Regex, 332

Anchor property, use of, 28

animated GIFs, displaying without browser control, 32–33

application instances, checking for, 44–45

Application object, using with ASP.NET applications, 66

application updates, downloading, 62

applications. *See also* ASP.NET applications; developer secrets for ASP.NET; Web applications; Windows applications
building for .NET Compact Framework, 216–218
creating from PDAs, 215–220
deploying on .NET Compact Framework, 218–220
printing from, 51–54

App.Path property, .NET replacement for, 248

arrays, changes in, 15

ASIN (Amazon standard identification number), explanation of, 190–191

ASP.NET
accessing Code window with, 11
changing text properties in, 11
creating Web sites with, 9–12
displaying Properties window in, 10
explanation of, 3
sending mail in, 87–88
Server.Transfer versus Response.Direct in, 113–114
testing Web applications in, 12

ASP.NET applications. *See also* applications; developer secrets for ASP.NET; Web applications; Windows applications
Application object used with, 66
compiling, 68
cookies used wit, 67
debugging, 68
deploying, 123
development essentials of, 64–68
encoding and decoding strings in, 68
maintaining state of Web forms in, 65
Session object used with, 65
system requirements for, 64
using query strings with, 67–68

ASP.NET Forms authentication, setting up, 100–102

ASP.NET Forums, using code from, 105

ASP.NET hosts, storing files on, 122–123

ASP.NET Mobile Controls, advisory about, 210

ASP.NET Web service project, features of, 4

assemblies
explanation of, 21
location of, 25
renaming, 24

asynchronous access, performing with Web services, 197–198

authentication in ASP.NET, explanation of, 100–103

B

Babel Fish, features of, 185–186

bitmaps, converting GIF images to, 272

British and American dates, converting with Regex, 332

BufferOutput property, example of, 90

ByVal keyword, use of, 17

369

C

c:\inetpub\wwwroot\ directory
  alternatives in ASP.NET, 107–108
C#
  arguments in, 342–343
  arithmetic in, 343
  class inheritance keywords in, 352–353
  class interfaces in, 351–352
  classes in, 349–353
  comparison operands in, 344
  constructors and finalizers in, 350
  data types in, 339
  event handling in, 348
  functions in, 339
  If-Then statements in, 343–344
  loops in, 345–346
  methods in, 340
  objects in, 341–342
  overview of, 335
  properties in, 349
  resources for, 353–354
  scope in, 342
  semicolon (;) used in, 338–339
  spotting comments in, 338
  string contents in, 341
  switch statements in, 344–345
  this keyword in, 348
  translating to Visual Basic .NET,
    336–353
  Try...Catch...Finally method in, 347
  variables in, 340
C# to VB .NET Web service, address for,
  353
CAB files, creating for use with .NET
  Compact Framework, 219–220
caching
  ASP.NET applications, 108–109
  controlling in client browser in HTML,
    115
capitalized words, getting with Regex,
  316–317
CGI scripts, posting streams of data to,
  232–234
client caching, preventing with meta tags
  in ASP.NET, 115
Clipboard, storing text snippets on, 262
code
  downloading live from Web servers,
    61–62
  protecting with obfuscation, 59–60
  storing in toolbox, 303
code regions, collapsing, 7
code techniques for ASP.NET
  adding real-time HTML to pages,
    89–90
  ASP.NET Forums, 105

authentication in five steps, 100–102
changing page titles in code, 85
creating images dynamically, 96–97
creating user-friendly URLs, 88–89
filling out email fields automatically,
  85–86
Forms authentication without
  Web.config, 102
integrating with PayPal's instant
  payment notification, 106
sending mail, 87
storing settings, 104
storing uploaded files in databases,
  92–94
thumbnail generation on the fly, 98–99
uploading files, 90–92
working with uploaded images, 95–96
color types, converting strings into, 268
columns
  displaying in DataGrids, 142
  suppressing display in Windows
    forms, 140
COM+ transactions
  six steps to, 292–296
  viewing, 295
combo boxes
  adding autocomplete to, 34–36
  binding to enumeration values,
    269–270
command-line parameters, using, 37
Command method, executing SQL
  statements with, 128
command prompt, using in Visual Studio
  .NET, 306
Command window, figuring out in Visual
  Studio, 304–305
CompareValidator control in ASP.NET,
  use of, 71–72
"connection closed" errors,
  troubleshooting, 198
Connection objects, using with
  databases, 130
connection string creators, making,
  132–133
console applications, creating, 206–208
ContextMenu controls
  adding for use with system tray, 34
  description of, 362
ContextUtil object, using with COM+
  transactions, 294
controls, snapping cursors to, 39
cookies, using with ASP.NET applications,
  67
credit cards, validating with Regex, 324
CSS (cascading style sheets), learning, 84

currency, formatting in Web grids, 149–151

cursors, snapping to controls, 39

custom tag regular expressions in Regex, example of, 326–327

D

data paging with Web grids, 168–169

data types
  in C# and Visual Basic .NET, 339
  in Visual Basic .NET, 365–366

DataAdapters
  using with Access databases, 129
  using with databases, 130
  viewing data coming back from, 141

database information, exposing with Web services, 181–183

databases. *See also* developer secrets for databases
  accessing, 126
  essentials of, 126–130

DataGrids
  adding dropdown boxes to, 162
  clicking anywhere and selecting with, 156–157
  color-coding with, 151–152
  versus DataSets, 146
  displaying selected columns in, 142
  example of, 140
  exporting to Excel, 171–173
  formatting data in, 150
  personalizing, 163–165
  sorting with, 169–171
  in Windows forms, 362

DataLists versus DataGrids, 168

DataSets
  coding for use with Web services, 181–183
  versus DataGrids, 146
  returning from Excel spreadsheets, 173–175
  using XML with, 288–289

DataSets versus Recordsets, 136

dates
  calculating years between, 260–261
  checking for, 252
  formatting in Web grids, 149–151

days, adding and subtracting, 257

days in months, finding number of, 256–257

debugging in ASP.NET, 109–110

developer secrets for ASP.NET, 89–90. *See also* applications; ASP.NET; Web applications; Windows applications

ASP.NET Forums, 105

authentication in five steps, 100–102

c:\inetpub\wwwroot\ directory alternatives, 107–108

caching applications to increase speed, 108–109

changing page titles in code, 85

checking uptime in .NET, 117–118

creating default Enter buttons, 77

creating images dynamically, 96–97

creating scrollable micro windows, 83

creating user-friendly URLs, 88–89

debugging in nine steps, 109–110

displaying Web warning messages, 73–77

filling out email fields automatically, 85

Forms authentication without Web.config, 102

hiding error code from clients, 111

integrating with PayPal's instant payment notification, 106

.IsClientConnected used for long processes, 114–115

learning CSS (cascading style sheets), 84

moving list items up and down, 81–82

moving Web servers, 121–122

Panel control usage, 79–80

preventing client caching with meta tags, 115

resizing in Web applications, 82

sending mail, 87

Server.Transfer versus Response.Direct in, 113–114

Session End event troubleshooting, 116

SmartNavigation property, 78

stopping users from right-clicking, 82

storing files with ASP.NET hosts, 122–123

storing settings, 104

storing uploaded files in databases, 92–94

stress testing Web applications, 119–121

subfolders in Web applications, 106

thumbnail generation on the fly, 98–99

uploading files, 90–92

uploading files larger than 4MB, 115

user controls, 78–79

user interface, 71–84

validation-controls five-step checklist, 71–73

working with uploaded images, 95–96

developer secrets for databases. *See also* databases
    cheating with SQL, 134–135
    checking SQL Server availability, 137–138
    clicking anywhere and selecting with Web grids, 156–157
    color-coding Web grids, 151–152
    confirming Web deletes, 153–154
    creating editable Web grids, 141–147
    creating editable Windows grids, 138–140
    data paging with Web grids, 168–169
    exporting Web grids to Excel, 171–173
    finding last identity number added, 133–134
    formatting Web-grid data, 149–151
    generating GUIDs quickly, 131–132
    getting Microsoft to write your code, 175–176
    making connection string creators, 132–133
    personalizing Web data binding, 163–165
    returning DataSets from Excel spreadsheets, 173–175
    returning multiple tables into DataSets, 136–137
    selecting Web-form grid items with Hotmail, 154–156
    sorting with Web grids, 169–171
    using dropdown boxes in Web grids, 158–166
    using HTML in Web grids, 147–148
    using hyperlinks in Web grids, 148–149
developer secrets for .NET
    adding and subtracting days, months, and years, 257
    adding gradient backdrops, 277–278
    adding Web shortcuts to Favorites menu, 234–235
    binding combo boxes to enumeration values, 269–270
    calculating next working day, 258
    calculating years between dates, 260–261
    checking for dates, 252–253
    checking for identical files, 239–240
    checking for leap years, 258–259
    checking for whole numbers, 252
    COM+ transactions, 292–296
    converting between graphic formats, 272
    converting HTML to text, 231–232
    converting strings into color types, 268
    converting strings to proper case, 261–262

creating Web browsers, 225–226
dates, numbers, and strings, 251–270
designing icons, 270–271
determining availability of Internet connections, 236–237
distributed computing, 283–301
drawing with Windows forms, 274–276
encryption in twelve lines of code, 265–266
figuring out quarter dates, 259–260
finding number of days in months, 256–257
functions for reading and writing files, 237–238
generating passwords, 263–264
graphics and fonts, 270–279
implementing MD5 encryption, 266–268
manipulating files, 238–239
manipulating files and folders, 237–251
MSMQ (Microsoft Message Queue) guide, 297–300
.NET replacement for App.Path property, 248
parsing Web pages for links and images, 229–231
posting data to Web, 232–234
putting messages in event logs, 281–282
retrieving drive serial numbers, 247–248
retrieving IP addresses, 235–236
retrieving paths to default programs, 246–247
retrieving special folder paths, 245
rotating and flipping images, 273
snatching HTML from Web pages, 227
snatching HTML with timeouts, 227–229
starting screensavers, 278–279
storing text snippets on Clipboard, 262
temporary-file management, 241
translating bytes to strings, 244–245
using INI files, 248–251
using ordinal numbers in applications, 253–255
using random numbers, 255–256
using registry and event logs, 279–282
Visual Studio tips, 302–307
watching directories for changes, 243–244
Web services versus remoting, 300–301
working with directories, 242
working with fonts, 271

working with the Internet, 225–237
XML cheat's guide, 283–291
developer secrets for Web services. *See also* Web services
adding Google to search programs, 187–189
caching to improve performance, 185
changing URLs without recompiling, 199
exposing database information quickly and easily, 181–183
finding best Web services, 199–200
performing asynchronous access, 197–198
performing online language translations, 185–186
preparing to publicize Web services, 184–185
querying Amazon.com, 190–193
troubleshooting "connection closed" errors, 198
using TerraServer Web service, 193–196
developer secrets for Windows forms applications. *See also* forms; Windows forms
adding autocomplete to combo boxes, 34–36
browsing performance counters, 57–58
capturing screens, 40–41
changing tab order, 33
checking for previous instances, 44–45
converting RTF to HTML, 45–48
creating navigation bars, 41–42
creating number-only text box, 32
creating ultra-thin clients, 60–62
customizing MonthCalendar control, 31
determining user clicks in dialog boxes, 50–51
displaying animated GIFs without browser control, 32–33
drag and drop from Windows Explorer, 48–50
examining current environment, 57
highlighting errors with ErrorProvider control, 29–30
learning LinkLabel control, 30
making forms transparent, 27
printing from applications, 51–54
protecting code with obfuscation, 59–60
replacing ToolTips, 27
resetting forms, 37–38
resizing Windows forms, 28

snapping cursors to buttons, 39
splitting panels, 28–29
using command-line parameters, 37
using .PrintForm method, 54–56
visual inheritance facts, 56
Windows XP themes, 42–44
working with system tray, 33
developer TODO lists, writing in Visual Studio, 302
Device properties for MIT, list of, 212–213
DeviceSpecific component of Mobile Web applications, purpose of, 211
dialog-box display, passing response to code responsible for, 50–51
directories
watching for changes, 243–244
working with, 242
distributed computing, explanation of, 1
Distributed Transaction Coordinator, accessing, 296
div tags, using with scrollable micro windows, 83
Dock property, use of, 28
domains, checking validity with Regex, 322
DOS-style console applications, creating, 206–208
Dotfuscator, Web address for, 60
drag and drop from Windows Explorer, 48–50
drive serial numbers, retrieving, 247–248
dropdown boxes, using in Web grids, 158–166

E
email address validation in Regex, example of, 319–320
email fields, filling out automatically in ASP.NET, 85
encryption, example of, 265–268
Enter buttons, creating default enter button with ASP.NET, 77
enumeration values, binding combo boxes to, 269–270
error code, hiding from clients in ASP.NET, 111
error handling in Visual Basic .NET, 23–24, explanation of, 18–19
ErrorProvider controls
highlighting errors with, 29–30
in Windows forms, 363
event logs, putting messages in, 281–282
Excel
exporting Web grids to, 171–173
troubleshooting blank pages in, 172

Excel spreadsheets, returning DataSets from, 173–175
exception handling, example of, 18–19
expressions, tightening up using Regex, 333–334

F

FAQs (frequently asked questions), Windows DataGrid newsgroup, 140. *See also* resources; Web sites
Favorites menu, adding Web shortcuts to, 234–235
File class, example of, 238–239
file extensions, matching programs to, 246–247
files. *See also* temporary files
   checking identical status of, 239–240
   functions for reading and writing to, 237–238
   moving, deleting, and attributes, 238–239
   path and extension check in Regex, example of, 315
   storing in databases after uploading, 92–94
   uploading when larger than 4MB using ASP.NET, 115
   uploading with ASP.NET, 90–92
FileSystemWatcher components, adding to Windows services, 203
Fill* and Draw* methods used with Graphics objects, explanations of, 276
folder paths, retrieving, 245
folders, organizing projects with, 303–304
fonts, working with, 271
For XML Auto, adding to SQL statements, 290
foreign key values, retrieving when using dropdown boxes in Web grids, 163–165
forms. *See also* developer secrets for Windows forms applications; Windows forms
   displaying in Windows applications, 23
   making transparent, 27
   maximizing on startup, 23
   moving between in MIT, 214
   resetting, 37–38
Forms authentication in ASP.NET, setting up, 100–102
FTP/HTTP/HTTPS URL regular expression, example of, 320–321

G

GDI+, using, 274–276
GIF images, converting to Windows bitmaps, 272
Global.asax events, troubleshooting, 116
Google, using with Web services, 187–189
gradient backdrops, adding to applications, 277–278
graphic formats, converting between, 272
Graphics objects, methods used with, 276
grids, binding table data to, 126
GUID regular expression, example of, 328
GUIDs (globally unique identifiers), generating quickly, 131–132

H

Hotmail, selecting Web-form grid items Hotmail-style, 154–156
HTML color codes, checking with Regex, 323
HTML (HyperText Markup Language)
   converting from RTF to, 45–48
   converting to text, 231–232
   defining with custom tags and expressions using Regex, 325–327
   extracting links and images from using Regex, 323
   displaying with panels, 80
   snatching from Web pages, 227
   snatching with timeouts, 227–229
   using in Web grids, 147–148
hyperlinks, using in Web grids, 148–149

I

icons, designing, 270–271
IDE (Integrated Development Environment), determining running in, 305
IIS (Internet Information Services)
   installing after Visual Studio .NET, 123
   setting up on Windows 2000 or Windows XP, 356
images
   creating dynamically with ASP.NET, 96–97
   rotating and flipping, 273
   using after uploading with ASP.NET, 95–96
   converting between formats, 272
images and links, parsing Web pages for, 229–231
INI files, using in .NET, 248–251
infinite loop. *See* loop, infiniteInternet connection, determining availability of, 236–237

Internet URL matcher for FTP, HTTP, and HTTPS in Regex, examples of, 320–321
IP addresses
    checking with Regex, 322–323
    retrieving, 235–236
ISBN checker in Regex, example of, 328

L
languages, translating between through Web services, 185–186
leap years, checking for, 258–259
links and images
    extracting from HTML using Regex, 323
    parsing Web pages for, 229–231
list items, moving up and down in ASP.NET, 81–82
loop, infinite. See infinite loop

M
macros, recording to save time in Visual Studio .NET, 306
mailto: tags, example of, 86
MD5 (Message Digest 5) encryption, implementing, 266–268
MDI applications, creating, 23
menus, adding to Windows applications, 22
messages
    putting in event logs, 281–282
    sending and receiving with MSMQ, 297–300
micro windows, scrolling with ASP.NET, 83
MIT (Mobile Internet Toolkit), creating applications with, 208–215
Mobile-aware code, writing, 212–214
mobile devices, advisory about, 213
mobile pages, adding to projects, 214
Mobile Web applications
    creating, 208–215
    designing, 210–211
    testing, 214–215
months
    adding and subtracting, 257
    finding number of days in, 256–257
MSDE (Microsoft Desktop Engine), downloading, 128
MSMQ (Microsoft Message Queue), guide to, 297–300
MTS (Microsoft Transaction Server), fate of, 292

N
name checker in Regex, example of, 318
named ranges, in Excel, accessing with OLE DB code, 174
namespaces
    changing for Web services, 185
    shortcut for typing of, 14
navigation bars, creating, 41–42
.NET application updater component, Web address for, 62
.NET Compact Framework
    building applications for, 216–218
    deploying applications of, 218–220
    overview of, 215–216
.NET Framework
    installing in RAM for .NET Compact Framework, 218–219
    understanding, 13–14
Nokia Mobile Internet Toolkit, Web address for, 214
NT 4.0 machines, advisory about installing Visual Studio .NET on, 356
number-only text boxes, creating, 32
numbers, matching from strings using Regex, 317–318

O
obfuscation, protecting code with, 59–60
ordinal numbers, using in applications, 253–255

P
page titles in ASP.NET, changing in code, 85
paging
    advisory about editing with, 168
    explanation of, 168
Panel controls
    in ASP.NET, 79–80
    in Windows forms, 363
panels, splitting, 28–29
password format enforcing expression in Regex, example of, 324–325
passwords, generating, 263–264
PayPal's instant payment notification, using ASP.NET to integrate with, 106
PDAs (personal digital assistants), creating applications for, 215–220
percentages, formatting in Web grids, 149–151
performance counters, browsing, 57–59
phone number checker in Regex, example of, 330

Pocket PC 2002 emulators, testing CAB deployment on, 220.PrintForm method, using, 54–56
printing from applications, 51–54
profanity filter expression in Regex, example of, 319
programs, opening in default applications, 246–247
projects
    creating with Visual Studio .NET, 3–4
    organizing with folders, 303–304

Q

quarter dates, figuring out, 259–260
query strings, using with ASP.NET applications, 67–68

R

random numbers, generating, 255–256
real number matcher in Regex library, example of, 313
Recordsets versus DataSets, 136
reflection, explanation of, 61
Regex library contents, 323
    alphanumerical matcher without spaces or dots, 313–314
    checking for repeated words, 315–316
    checking for valid domains, 322
    checking HTML color codes, 323
    converting American and British dates, 332
    credit card validation, 323
    cure for "loose" expressions, 333–334
    defining HTML with custom tags and expressions, 325–327
    email address validation, 319
    exactly-one-digit checker, 312–313
    French, German, and Japanese expressions, 333
    getting capitalized words, 316–317
    GUIDs (globally unique identifiers), 328
    identifying valid dates, 314–315
    Internet URL matcher for FTP, HTTP, and HTTPS, 320–321
    IP address checker, 322–323
    ISBN checker, 328
    matching numbers from strings, 317–318
    name checker, 318
    password format enforcing expression, 324–325
    real number matcher, 313
    rile path and extension check, 315

U.K. National Insurance number, 331
U.K. postal code matcher, 331
U.K. telephone number validator, 332
U.S. phone number checker, 330
U.S. social security number checker, 329
U.S. state checker, 330
U.S. zip code checker, 329
validating Web site address, 320
word filter expression, 319
registry, reading and writing, 280–281
regular expressions
    dynamics of, 310
    explanation of, 309
RegularExpressionValidator control in ASP.NET, use of, 71–72
remoting versus Web services, 300–301
RequiredFieldValidator control in ASP.NET, use of, 71–72
resources. *See also* FAQs (frequently asked questions); Web sites
    C#, 353–354
    for COM+ transactions, 295
    MSMQ (Microsoft Message Queue), 299
    for PDA applications, 220
    regular expressions, 310
    Visual Basic .NET, 353–354
    Web services versus remoting, 301
right-clicking, stopping on Web pages, 82
RTF, converting to HTML, 45–48

S

screen capturing, 40–41
screensavers, starting, 278–279
serial numbers of drives, retrieving, 247–248
Server Explorer
    opening to create editable Windows grids, 138
    opening to edit Web grids, 141
    viewing services with, 205
server paths, determining for Web applications, 68
Server.Transfer versus Response.Direct in ASP.NET, 113–114
Session End event, troubleshooting with ASP.NET, 116
Session object, using with ASP.NET applications, 65–66
settings, storing in ASP.NET, 104
smart device applications
    creating, 220
    purpose of, 5

SmartNavigation property, using with ASP.NET, 78
social security number checker in Regex, example of, 329
sorting with Web grids, 169–171
Splitter controls in Windows forms, description of, 364
SQL Server CE, running on handhelds, 220
SQL Server Centric .NET Code Generator, benefits of, 175–176
SQL Server, checking availability of, 137–138
SQL Server connection strings, generating, 133
SQL Server XML retrieval, instructions for, 290–291
SQL statements
    adding For XML Auto to, 290
    examples of, 127, 128
    simplifying creation of, 135
SQL (Structured Query Language), cheating with, 134–135
strings
    converting into color types, 268
    declaring in Visual Basic .NET, 14–15
    encoding and decoding in ASP.NET applications, 68
    matching numbers from using Regex, 317–318
system tray, working with, 33–34

T
tab order, changing, 33
table information, binding to grids, 126
tables
    dragging and dropping, 159
    returning into DataSets, 136
temporary files, managing, 241. *See also* files
Terrarium project, Web address for, 301
TerraServer Web service, viewing the world with, 193–196
text, converting HTML to, 231–232
text files, functions for reading and writing to, 237–238
text snippets, storing on Clipboard, 262
thin-client, creating, 60–62
thumbnails, generating on the fly with ASP.NET, 98–99

timeouts, snatching Web pages with, 227–229
TODO lists, writing in Visual Studio, 302Toolbox

controls for Windows forms, 362–364
storing often-used code in, 303
ToolTips, 364
    naming for system tray, 34
    replacing, 27
transactions
    managing with COM+, 292–296
    using with databases, 130

U
U.K. National Insurance number in Regex, example of, 331
U.K. postal code matcher in Regex, example of, 331
U.K. telephone number validator in Regex, example of, 332
URLs (uniform resource locators)
    changing for Web services without recompiling, 199
    creating user-friendly URLs with ASP.NET, 88–89
U.S. phone number checker in Regex, example of, 330
U.S. social security number checker in Regex, example of, 329
U.S. state checker in Regex, example of, 330
U.S. ZIP code checker in Regex, example of, 329
user controls, manipulating with ASP.NET, 78–79

V
valid dates, identifying with Regex, 314–315
validation-controls five-step checklist in ASP.NET, 71–84
VB .NET. *See* Visual Basic .NET
Visual Basic language
    array alterations in, 15
    changes in, 13–19
    integer upgrades in, 14
    replacement of Set statement in, 18
    replacement of Variable and Currency data types in, 15
    string upgrades in, 14–15
Visual Basic .NET, 19
    arguments in, 342–343
    arithmetic in, 343
    arrays in, 15
    block-level scoping in, 17
    ByVal keyword as default in, 17
    class inheritance keywords in, 352–353
    class interfaces in, 351–352

Visual Basic .NET *(continued)*
  classes, 349–353
  comparison operands in, 344
  constructors and finalizers in, 350
  creating Web applications with, 64
  data types in, 339, 365–366
  declaring properties with, 16
  declaring strings in, 14–15
  and default properties, 18
  error handling in, 18–19
  event handling in, 348
  functions in, 339
  generating GUIDs in, 132
  If-Then statements in, 343–344
  loops in, 345–346
  Me keyword in, 348
  methods in, 340
  naming conventions in, 366–368
  Object type in, 15
  objects in, 341–342
  operators in, 15–16
  properties in, 349
  resources for, 353–354
  scope in, 342
  Select Case statements in, 344–345
  shared keyword in, 13
  string contents in, 341
  translating C# to, 336–353
  Try...Catch...Finally method in, 347
  user-defined types in, 17
  variables in, 340
visual inheritance facts, overview of, 56
Visual Studio .NET
  adding XML files to, 284
  advisory about creating projects in, 357
  browsing hidden samples distributed with, 220
  creating Web applications with, 64
  creating Windows applications in, 22
  default project files in, 358–362
  explanation of, 2
  exploring, 3–9
  installing, 355–358
  installing IIS after, 123
  launching, 3, 357
  setting up preferences in, 357
  system requirements for, 355
  using ACT from, 120
Visual Studio .NET tips
  discovering whether running in IDE, 305
  figuring out Command window in, 304–305
  organizing projects with folders, 303–304

saving time by recording macros, 306
storing often-used code in toolbox, 303
upgrading, COM, and Windows API, 307
using command prompt, 306
writing a developer TODO list, 302
VS .NET. *See* Visual Studio .NET

W
Web applications. *See also* applications; ASP.NET applications; developer secrets for ASP.NET; Windows applications
  changing default icon for, 26
  checking setup of virtual folders for, 110
  creating, 9–12
  creating in Visual Studio .NET, 64
  creating with Visual Basic .NET, 64
  debugging with ASP.NET, 68
  determining server paths for, 68
  Dotfuscator, 60
  printing from, 51–54
  resizing with ASP.NET, 82
  result of creating in Visual Studio .NET, 358
  stress testing in ASP.NET, 119–121
  subfolders in, 106
  testing in ASP.NET, 12
Web browser, creating your own, 225–226
Web control libraries, features of, 4
Web data binding, speeding up and personalizing, 163–165
Web grids
  clicking anywhere and selecting with, 156–157
  color-coding, 151–152
  confirming deletes, 153-154
  editing, 141–147
  exporting to Excel, 171–173
  formatting data in, 149–151
  selecting multiple items Hotmail-style, 154-156
  sorting with, 169–171
  using dropdown boxes in, 158–166
  using HTML in, 147–148
  using hyperlinks in, 148–149
Web pages
  canceling right-clicks on, 82
  parsing for links and images, 229–231
  snatching HTML from, 227
Web, posting data to, 232–234
Web servers
  downloading code from live, 61–62
  moving with ASP.NET, 121–122

Web services. *See also* developer secrets for Web services
  accessing, 180
  adding method descriptions for, 184
  adding service descriptions for, 184
  C# to VB .NET, 353
  compiling, 182
  components of, 178
  creating application projects for, 179
  versus DCOM, 178
  discovering for use in Visual Studio .NET applications, 179–180
  essentials of, 178–180
  examples of, 178
  finding, 199–200
  managing requests with, 178
  overview of, 177–178
  preparing for publicizing of, 184–185
  versus remoting, 300–301
  renaming ASMX files for, 184
  renaming classes of, 184
  result of creating in Visual Studio .NET, 361–362
  viewing, 179
Web shortcuts, adding to Favorites menu, 234–235
Web site addresses, validating with Regex, 320
Web sites. *See also* FAQs (frequently asked questions); resources
  Amazon.com resources page, 192
  authentication parts of, 103
  creating with ASP.NET, 9–12
  Donkey.NET, 276
  essentials of, 64–68
  formatting data in DataGrids, 150
  INI file replacement, 251
  Microsoft guide, 25
  MIT (Mobile Internet Toolkit), 210
  .NET Framework, 218
  Nokia Mobile Internet Toolkit, 214
  registry, 281
  regular expressions, 310
  screensaver sample link, 279
  security guidelines, 58
  SQL Server Centric .NET Code Generator, 176
  Terrarium project, 301
  transactions, 293
  XMethods, 199–200
  XML specification, 283
  XtraNavBar Suite, 41
Web warning messages, displaying in ASP.NET, 73–77
Web.config file
  adding personal settings to, 104

altering for Forms authentication, 103
  checking for syntax errors in, 109
  checking if Debug attribute is set to True, 110
whole numbers, checking for, 252
Windows 2000, setting up IIS on, 356
Windows applications. *See also* applications; ASP.NET applications; developer secrets for ASP.NET; Web applications
  adding menus to, 22
  arranging child windows in, 23
  benefits of, 21
  changing copyright and versioning information for, 24
  changing startup objects for, 24
  compiling, 24–25
  creating, 5
  creating in Visual Studio .NET, 22
  displaying forms in, 23
  essentials of, 22–25, 22–26
  renaming, 24
  result of creating in Visual Studio .NET, 358
  running, 8
  running in debug mode, 24
Windows Explorer, dragging and dropping from, 48–50
Windows forms. *See also* developer secrets for Windows forms applications; forms
  adding controls to Toolbox in, 364
  binding data to controls on, 126–127
  drawing with, 274–276
  resizing, 28
  suppressing column display in, 140
  toolbox controls for, 362–364
Windows grids, editing, 138–140
Windows service projects, building services with, 4
Windows services
  creating, 202–206
  installing, 203–206
  overriding events in, 203
  running code during installation of, 204
Windows XP, setting up IIS on, 356
Windows XP themes, seven steps to taking advantage of, 42–44
word capitalizations, getting with Regex, 316–317
word filter expression in Regex, example of, 319
word repetition, checking with Regex, 315–316
working day, calculating, 258

X

XML cheats guide, 283–291
XML documents
  checking structure of, 286
  example of, 283–284
  reading in code, 285–286
  writing in code, 286–288
XML (eXtensible Markup Language)
  review of, 291
  using with DataSets, 288–289

Y

years, adding and subtracting, 257
years between dates, calculating, 260–261

Z

ZIP code checker in Regex, example of, 329